MW00388126

SPANISH AS
A HERITAGE LANGUAGE
IN THE UNITED STATES

GEORGETOWN STUDIES IN SPANISH LINGUISTICS SERIES
JOHN M. LIPSKI, *Series Editor*

Sociolingüística y pragmática del español
Carmen Silva-Corvalan

Sonido y sentido: Teoría y práctica de la pronunciación del español contemporáneo con audio CD
Jorge M. Guitart

Varieties of Spanish in the United States
John M. Lipski

Spanish Phonology: A Syllabic Perspective
Sonia Colina

El español en contacto con otras lenguas
Carol A. Klee y Andrew Lynch

SPANISH AS A HERITAGE LANGUAGE IN THE UNITED STATES
THE STATE OF THE FIELD

SARA M. BEAUDRIE AND MARTA FAIRCLOUGH, EDITORS

Georgetown University Press
Washington, DC

© 2012 Georgetown University Press. All rights reserved. No part of this book may be reproduced or utilized in any form or by any means, electronic or mechanical, including photocopying and recording, or by any information storage and retrieval system, without permission in writing from the publisher.

Library of Congress Cataloging-in-Publication Data

Spanish as a heritage language in the United States : the state of the field / edited by Sara M. Beaudrie and Marta Fairclough.
    p.   cm.
Includes bibliographical references and index.
ISBN 978-1-58901-938-6 (pbk. : alk. paper)
1. Spanish language—Study and teaching—United States.   2. Spanish language—Acquisition.   3. Education, Bilingual—United States.   4. Hispanic Americans—Languages.   I. Beaudrie, Sara M.   II. Fairclough, Marta Ana.
PC4068.U5S63 2012
468′.0071073—dc23
2012007818

♾ This book is printed on acid-free paper meeting the requirements of the American National Standard for Permanence in Paper for Printed Library Materials.

15   14   13   12   9   8   7   6   5   4   3   2   First printing

To my husband, Alan, for his patience and loving
support throughout these years
SARA M. BEAUDRIE

To my amazing daughters, Nevena, Sabrina, and Tabatha
MARTA FAIRCLOUGH

Contents

List of Illustrations   ix

List of Abbreviations   xi

Introduction: Spanish as a Heritage Language in the United States   1
Sara M. Beaudrie and Marta Fairclough

PART I: AN OVERVIEW OF THE FIELD

1   Spanish Heritage Language Maintenance: Its Legacy and
Its Future   21
Susana V. Rivera-Mills

2   Investigating Language Ideologies in Spanish as a Heritage
Language   43
Jennifer Leeman

3   Policy and Planning Research for Spanish as a Heritage Language:
From Language Rights to Linguistic Resource   61
Glenn Martínez

4   Key Concepts for Theorizing Spanish as a Heritage Language   79
Andrew Lynch

PART II: LINGUISTIC PERSPECTIVES

5   The Grammatical Competence of Spanish Heritage Speakers   101
Silvina Montrul

6   Pragmatics and Discourse: Doing Things with Words in Spanish
as a Heritage Language   121
Derrin Pinto

7   Code-Switching: From Theoretical to Pedagogical Considerations   139
    Ana M. Carvalho

PART III: LEARNERS' PERSPECTIVES

8   SHL Learners' Attitudes and Motivations: Reconciling
    Opposing Forces   161
    Cynthia M. Ducar

9   Identity and Heritage Learners: Moving beyond Essentializations   179
    Kim Potowski

PART IV: PEDAGOGICAL PERSPECTIVES

10 Research on University-Based Spanish Heritage Language
    Programs in the United States: The Current State of Affairs   203
    Sara M. Beaudrie

11 Meeting the Needs of Heritage Language Learners: Approaches,
    Strategies, and Research   223
    Maria M. Carreira

12 Advanced Biliteracy Development in Spanish as a Heritage
    Language   241
    M. Cecilia Colombi and Joseph Harrington

13 Language Assessment: Key Theoretical Considerations in the
    Academic Placement of Spanish Heritage Language Learners   259
    Marta Fairclough

Afterword: Future Directions for the Field of Spanish as a
Heritage Language   279
    Guadalupe Valdés

Contributors   291

Index   295

Illustrations

FIGURES

I.1   Distribution of the Hispanic/Latino Population as a Percentage
       of the Overall Population, 1980   3

I.2   Distribution of the Hispanic/Latino Population as a Percentage
       of the Overall Population, 2006   4

9.1   Model of Influences on Ethnic Identity   184

TABLES

I.1   States with the Largest Hispanic Populations   5

I.2   Dimensions in Heritage Language Learner Profiles   8

9.1   Individual and Collective Identity Types   181

10.1   Number of US Universities Offering SHL Programs   208

10.2   Number of SHL Course Offerings Compared with the Size of
       the Hispanic Student Population   209

10.3   Number of SHL Courses Offered at Universities in Various
       US Regions   211

13.1   Types of Language Tests   261

Abbreviations

CS   code-switching

HL   heritage language

L1   first (native) language

L2   second language

SHL   Spanish as a heritage language, or Spanish heritage language

SLA   second-language acquisition

Introduction

SPANISH AS A HERITAGE LANGUAGE IN THE UNITED STATES

Sara M. Beaudrie, University of Arizona
Marta Fairclough, University of Houston

THE TREMENDOUS GROWTH in the field of Spanish as a heritage language (SHL) at the turn of the twenty-first century is evident in the recent explosion of journal articles, books, master's theses and doctoral dissertations, conferences, and organizations (e.g., Colombi and Alarcón 1997; Webb and Miller 2000; Roca and Colombi 2003). Most of the relevant research, however, has been published in professional journals or volumes of selected conference proceedings. Because of the prominence of Spanish in the United States, it has outpaced other heritage languages in research and has reached a key point where expert synthesis and direction in each of the subfields of research is warranted. The present book is the first single volume to summarize our understanding of the main issues related to SHL in the United States. The content and scope are unique in that this work brings together leading experts to provide a panoramic view of current research trends in the field. This chapter provides current data on Hispanics and the Spanish language in the United States, definitions of Spanish as a heritage language and heritage language learners, and an overview of the content of this volume.

HISPANICS IN THE UNITED STATES

The history of Spanish in what is currently the United States began in 1513, when the Spanish Crown started conquering and settling the American South. This area experienced successive Spanish, Mexican, and American domination (for a historical overview with a linguistic focus, see Balestra, Martínez, and

Moyna 2008), and its Spanish-speaking population grew over the years from several thousands to millions, while other geographic regions of the country began experiencing Hispanic migration for the first time. The present-day numeric and geographic expansion appears clearly illustrated in figures I.1 and I.2. Whereas in 1980 Hispanics accounted for 6.4 percent of the overall population (14.6 million), in 2006 those figures reached 44.3 million Hispanics, or 14.8 percent of the total US population of 299 million.

In 2010 the US Census reported that the Hispanic/Latino population in the United States reached 50.5 million, not counting approximately 4 million residents of Puerto Rico. Hispanics constituted 16.3 percent of the country's total population, making them the nation's largest minority. Although Latinos continue to be concentrated in certain US states (see table I.1), the Hispanic presence seems to be ubiquitous, no longer only in major urban areas of such traditional population centers as New York, Texas, California, and Florida, but also in small towns all over the United States. By 2050, the number of Hispanics in the United States is projected to reach 132.8 million, about 30 percent of the nation's population.

The Pew Hispanic Center (2009) reports that in 2009 about 60 percent of the Hispanic population was born in the United States and that 70 percent speak Spanish at home. Although United States–resident Latinos come from all over the world, the majority (65.5 percent) are of Mexican origin, an additional 9.1 percent are Puerto Rican, and 3.6 percent and 3.5 percent are of Salvadoran and Cuban origin, respectively, with the remaining 18 percent distributed among the other Spanish-speaking countries. Census estimates also indicate that worldwide as of 2009, only Mexico (with 111 million people) had a larger Latino population than the United States.

SPANISH AS A HERITAGE LANGUAGE
IN THE UNITED STATES

The growth and increasing importance of Spanish in all US regions is being reflected in changes throughout government, media, business, and education (for an overview, see Potowski and Carreira 2010). As US Hispanics have gained economic power and political influence, attention directed to research in and teaching of the Spanish language has grown correspondingly.

The study of US Spanish and of Spanish/English contact phenomena has been ongoing for several decades, beginning with ethnographic studies and evolving to sociolinguistic research predominantly based on the generational model of minority language variation and change. Meanwhile, innovations occurred within the educational arena between the 1970s and 1990s, including transitional bilingual education programs for young children, ESL programs for Spanish

Figure I.1   Distribution of the Hispanic/Latino Population as a Percentage of the Overall Population, 1980

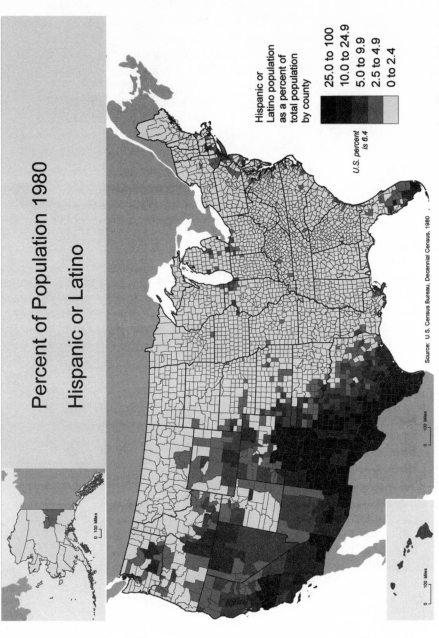

Percent of Population 1980

Hispanic or Latino

Hispanic or
Latino population
as a percent of
total population
by county

25.0 to 100
10.0 to 24.9
5.0 to 9.9
2.5 to 4.9
0 to 2.4

*U.S. percent
is 6.4*

Source: U.S. Census Bureau, Decennial Census, 1980

0   100 Miles

0   100 Miles

0   100 Miles

Source: U.S. Census Bureau Hispanic population data, 1980–2006.

Figure I.2 Distribution of the Hispanic/Latino Population as a Percentage of the Overall Population, 2006

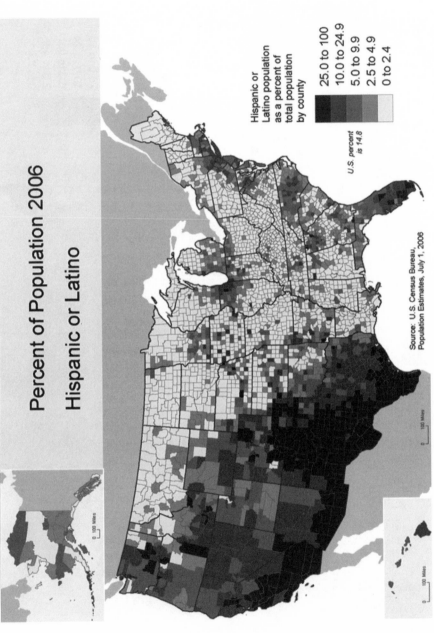

Percent of Population 2006

Hispanic or Latino

Hispanic or
Latino population
as a percent of
total population
by county

25.0 to 100
10.0 to 24.9
5.0 to 9.9
2.5 to 4.9
0 to 2.4

U.S. percent
is 14.8

Source: U.S. Census Bureau,
Population Estimates, July 1, 2006

Source: U.S. Census Bureau Hispanic population data, 1980–2006.

Table I.1   States with the Largest Hispanic Populations

State	Population
California	13,683,187
Texas	9,151,255
Florida	3,987,190
New York	3,274,572
Arizona	2,031,990

Source: Pew Hispanic Center (2009).

speakers with limited or no English ability, and Spanish courses for Spanish-English bilinguals (Valdés 1997).

It was in the 1990s that the field of heritage languages began gaining strength, as various disciplines and subdisciplines fed into the well-established field of Spanish in the United States. The result was rapid consolidation of *Spanish as a heritage language* into an area of study that draws from political, psychological, linguistic, pedagogical, and other disciplines, and has as one of its main objectives Spanish language maintenance. The crucial importance of heritage language (HL) education for language maintenance situates Spanish teaching in a central position within the SHL field.

Current US federal and state education policies have substantially weakened or eliminated numerous SHL programs at both the primary and secondary levels (Wright 2007). At the postsecondary level, however, many language departments across the country have initiated or increased the number of course offerings specifically designed for SHL learners. This tremendous growth is a response to the growing interest among Hispanic students in developing their Spanish proficiency and the sheer increase in the size of Hispanic student enrollment, which has expanded almost fourfold in the past three decades (NCES 2007).

HERITAGE LANGUAGES AND
HERITAGE LANGUAGE LEARNERS

The term *heritage languages* has gained increasing currency in the United States educational research circles, especially since the 1990s, and is used to refer to minority languages (i.e., languages other than English). The term originated in Canada, where it has been in use since the 1970s (Cummins 2005). In Australia and the United Kingdom, the term *community languages* is more common (Wiley 2005). Although *heritage languages* has been widely adopted by US academics, it has attracted some criticism. For many, the term evokes the past rather than the present or future (Wiley 2001; García 2005). For García (2005, 602), "the use of the term *heritage languages* in the United States signals a losing of ground for language minorities that was gained during the civil rights era." On the other hand, however, *heritage language* is a more "neutral and inclusive term" that lacks the stigma attached to other terms such as *minority, indigenous, immigrant,* or *ethnic* (Hornberger 2005, 102). In fact, the label implies that HL populations inherit a cultural and linguistic patrimony and, in this sense, has more positive than negative connotations. Such an attitude has also opened doors to increased teaching and learning of nonmajority languages. As García explains (2005, 602; referencing Cummins 2005): "The use of the term *heritage languages in education* . . . provides a way to 'crack' today's homogeneous monolingual schooling of very different children in the United States, providing a space for the use of languages other than English in educating children." It is in this context that the term *heritage languages* is used throughout this book. This choice acknowledges that the majority of scholars and educators have embraced the HL label as an alternative that both avoids stigmatizing terminology and simultaneously promotes language learning and, in some cases, also reverses language shift (Wiley 2001).

The single label *heritage languages* encompasses a wide range of languages with different histories in the United States. Fishman (2001) categorizes them as indigenous, colonial, or immigrant languages. Cummins (2005) also proposes a fourth category: refugee. Spanish has historically crossed all these categories. As Bale (2010) explains, Spanish was first introduced in the United States as a colonial language, making it indigenous to those territories annexed by the United States in the nineteenth century. It is also the largest immigrant language in the country.

Defining *heritage language speakers* (or *learners*) has been notably more difficult, as evidenced in the variety of suggested definitions (see, e.g., Beaudrie and Ducar 2005; Draper and Hicks 2000; Fishman 2001; Valdés 2001; Van Deusen-Scholl 2003). Understandably, because they "attempt to apply a single label to a complex situation (Wiley 2001, 29), these terms mean different things to different people and thus we currently lack definitions upon which all agree." Determining who is included under this term, however, has crucial implications for issues of identity as well as inclusion and exclusion (Wiley 2001). Most definitions proposed to date have centered around two distinct elements: a personal or familiar connection to a particular group (Fishman 2001) or a certain degree of proficiency in the language (Valdés 1997). Valdés's definition is the most widely used for research and educational purposes, because proficiency in the language is viewed as a required element in those contexts. According to this definition, a heritage language learner is an individual "who is raised in a home where a non-English language is spoken. The student may speak or merely understand the heritage language and be, to some degree, bilingual in English and the heritage language" (Valdes 2000, 1). Due to the language proficiency requirement, this definition has often been criticized as too narrow.

In the present book, we prefer to adopt Fishman's (2001) broad and inclusive definition, because it can encompass the diverse research topics our contributors address. Thus, we define a *heritage language learner* (or *speaker*) as an individual who has a personal or familial connection to a nonmajority language (Fishman 2001). This definition foregrounds two crucial elements that differentiate this population: their connection to the language and the status of the language relative to the dominant language.

Adopting a broad definition of HL learners has important implications for both research and practice. First, it encompasses such a diverse range of cultural profiles that the specific population of interest needs to be clearly and amply characterized in each individual context. Second, the term in and of itself does not imply either low or high proficiency in the language. Third, typical comparison groups, such as native speakers or bilingual speakers, can be problematic so they should be avoided or the rationale for comparison thoroughly explained and justified. For example, many HL learners consider themselves native speakers, especially if the HL is their first language or if they acquire it as young children. The same holds true for comparisons of fluent bilinguals with HL learners because, of course, many HL speakers consider themselves fluent bilinguals.

In sum, the SHL population within the United States possess similar characteristics due to their cultural and linguistic connection to a nonmajority language, whether they speak the language, understand it, or simply see it as part of their family history. This broad definition encompasses a heterogeneous population with multiple individual circumstances that need to be thoroughly profiled for both educational and research purposes. The more specifically a learner's profile is described, the easier it will be to make comparisons across contexts. Furthermore, a detailed delineation of each student's profile makes it unnecessary to adopt multiple definitions of HL learners to accommodate specific contexts. The existence of multiple definitions has merely contributed to confusion and hindered research (Bale 2010). It has also helped exclude certain segments of the HL population who may identify with the heritage language and feel a strong motivation to connect to their roots by learning the language and trying to participate in the HL community.

The different dimensions that need to be considered when profiling or grouping this diverse population are illustrated in table I.2 and are conceived as different points in a continua that exemplify possible degrees of diversity on the various dimensions. In later chapters these dimensions will be discussed as they pertain to Spanish in the United States (see also Alarcón 2010; Beaudrie 2009; Carreira and Kagan 2011; Valdés 1997).

OVERVIEW OF THIS BOOK

This volume contributes to the field of SHL generally and to the field of HL education within applied linguistics more narrowly. It is primarily intended to

Table I.2   Dimensions in Heritage Language (HL) Learner Profiles

	LANGUAGE ACQUISITION DIMENSION	
Birth	Age of English acquisition	Puberty
Birth	Age of HL acquisition	Childhood
English first	Order of English/HL acquisition	HL first
	HISTORICAL DIMENSION	
First generation	Generational status	United
generation		States–born
	EDUCATIONAL DIMENSION	
Incipient	Literacy level in English	Advanced
Incipient	Literacy level in HL	Advanced
Minimal	Amount of schooling in HL and English	Extensive
	LINGUISTIC DIMENSION	
Unbalanced	Amount of contact with Spanish/English	Balanced
Vernacular	HL variety	Standard
Minimal	HL proficiency	Fluent
	AFFECTIVE DIMENSION	
Low	Motivation towards HL maintenance and use	High
Negative	Linguistic attitudes	Positive
Low	Linguistic self-confidence	High
	CULTURAL DIMENSION	
Weak	Ethnolinguistic identity	Strong
Low	Competence in heritage culture	High

serve as a reference tool for SHL researchers and as a foundational text for gradu-ate students in SHL pedagogy and research courses, as well as for educators who teach SHL courses and want to be informed of research trends and outcomes in the field. This book may also be integrated into applied linguistics courses and undergraduate methodology courses for future teachers of Spanish. The book would also be of interest to researchers of other heritage languages worldwide. Given the interdisciplinary nature of the HL field, certain chapters will also appeal to scholars in the fields of bilingualism, sociolinguistics, linguistics, sec-ond language acquisition, literacy, and language assessment.

The contributors to this volume take an interdisciplinary perspective on SHL research and recognize the central position of SHL education within the field. Each chapter summarizes an area of major growth in scholarship, outlines the current state of knowledge, and offers a research agenda for the future by addressing the following questions:

1. What are the main issues addressed in the research in the particular topic?
2. What can be learned from early studies?
3. Based on recent research, what is the current understanding of the main issues?
4. What should a research agenda in the subfield look like?

The book is organized around four main parts with chapters that address a range of topics:

- a sociohistorical summary of Spanish maintenance and change in the United States (chapter 1);
- the politics of linguistic ideologies and language policy and planning (chapters 2 and 3);
- theoretical concepts that frame the field and controversies about how they are defined (chapter 4);
- linguistic aspects of Spanish, including variationist linguistic, formal linguistic, and psycholinguistic studies at levels ranging from specific linguistic units to extended discourse, pragmatics, and code-switching (chapters 5–7);
- psychological aspects of language, such as HL students' motivation to learn Spanish, individual and societal attitudes, and issues of identity (chapters 8–9); and
- SHL pedagogy, which is largely derived from theories and research in language arts and foreign language instruction; topics include data on the number and distribution of SHL programs, (bi)literacy, instructional models and practices, and assessment issues (chapters 10–13).

Part I

Part I offers an overview of the field of SHL from historical (chapter 1), sociopolitical (chapters 2 and 3), and theoretical (chapter 4) perspectives. These chapters place the contents of the volume within a broad context and provide a complete understanding of the teaching of Spanish as a heritage language from numerous angles.

In chapter 1 Susana Rivera-Mills covers more than 120 years of research on language maintenance and shift related to SHL in the United States, with a comprehensive bibliography. The author covers three main topics: First, she presents a historical account of the research surrounding SHL maintenance, beginning in the late nineteenth century when interest centered on the Spanish of Mexican

American communities in the US Southwest. Next, she reviews the current state of research in this area and its relationship to SHL education. Although historically most studies have concentrated on the major US Hispanic groups (Mexican, Puerto Rican, and Cuban), recently the lens has widened to other communities, including United States–born Hispanics. Meanwhile, the focus has shifted from intergenerational studies of language shift based on Fishman's model to studies addressing sociolinguistic and sociopolitical issues. This new interdisciplinary research has had important implications for the areas of language policy and HL education. Finally, Rivera-Mills describes the lack of dialogue between researchers and educators in Spanish language maintenance and SHL education as one of the main limitations of current research and advocates for incorporating research findings into the reality of the HL classroom.

In chapter 2 Jennifer Leeman analyzes the values and belief systems that define language ideologies, documenting how those ideologies are interconnected with other social phenomena and are clearly reflected in educational settings, specifically in the teaching of SHL. After presenting Kroskrity's (2004) five-level theoretical model of language ideology and its application to Spanish, she turns to *standard language ideology*, the most heavily researched language ideology within the SHL field. It views the standard variety of Spanish as superior to vernacular dialects and as crucial to academic and socioeconomic success. Next, Leeman critically examines specific areas within SHL education that reproduce dominant ideologies, beginning with educational policies and educational contexts, then moving on to classroom implications, ranging from curricula and materials to teaching practices and professionals. For the future, Leeman suggests expanding the research agenda to other types of language ideologies beyond the standard language, exploring ideologies in educational settings through ethnographic studies, and moving beyond the SHL classroom to the broader context both inside and outside the academic world.

In chapter 3 Glenn Martínez begins by illustrating language policy through two real events: a custody hearing that denies a mother the right to speak Spanish to her daughter and an article in a popular magazine poking fun at Spanish speakers' reactions to negative perceptions about their language. Martínez then reviews the history and evolving definitions of language policy and planning, beginning with Kloss's promotion-oriented and tolerance-oriented policies of the 1970s. To this model, Wiley (2004) added the three categories of expediency-oriented, restriction-oriented, and repression-oriented, in order to account for the consequences of policies that shape and inform language interventions (Ruiz 2010). Ruiz's seminal 80s paper defines and contrasts three orientations that have dominated US language policymaking: language as problem, language as right, and language as resource. Martínez illustrates how these three orientations have manifested themselves sequentially in SHL instruction: the HL was initially viewed as a problem, then as a right during the civil rights and Vietnam War eras, and finally as a resource beginning in the 1990s with the professionalization of SHL education and launching of several national initiatives. Future research should treat Spanish as a resource and SHL education should focus on Spanish as a career skill. The chapter concludes by strongly encouraging SHL teachers and researchers to actively shape public opinion through their professional endeavors.

In chapter 4 Andrew Lynch offers a critical overview of significant theoretical and ideological issues for the SHL field. It begins with a historic account of the concept of diglossia, as proposed by Ferguson in the late 1950s, as adapted by Fishman in the 1970s, and as connected to Spanish/English bilingualism in the United States. Lynch then focuses on several key concepts integrally associated with diglossia that seem to have guided the conceptualization and evolution of the SHL field, particularly the notions of register and standard language as they relate to the construct of language proficiency. He also emphasizes the power of social agency, which he believes should guide future theories of SHL, and questions the validity of the intergenerational language transmission model that sociolinguistic studies of US Spanish have relied on for decades. The author concludes that SHL currently lacks a guiding theory, that new models of language and bilingualism are needed, and that the main focus of SHL should shift to identity and affective issues.

Part II

Part II presents research on linguistic aspects of Spanish, ranging from grammar (chapter 5) to pragmatics and oral discourse (chapter 6) and code-switching (chapter 7). In chapter 5 Silvina Montrul begins by outlining the two main orientations to describing HL knowledge, either as a range from minimal to advanced language proficiency or as a function of generation of immigration (first, second, third, etc.). Montrul describes SHL speakers as a linguistically heterogeneous group whose speech in adulthood is often characterized by incomplete acquisition or language attrition. Historically, grammatical variation among SHL speakers has been studied within a sociolinguistic framework using cross-generational studies. Montrul reviews important research from this perspective, then focuses on studies conducted in specific regions of the United States: Los Angeles (Silva-Corvalán 1994), Houston (Lipski 1993), and New York (Otheguy, Zentella, and Livert 2007). The second section of the chapter examines more recent research on the grammatical competence of SHL speakers from formal linguistic and psycholinguistic perspectives. This research analyzes language knowledge and processing rather than merely patterns of language use. Research from both sociolinguistic and psycholinguistic perspectives concurs however that the performance of SHL speakers differs significantly from that of native speakers. Montrul then turns to the very limited classroom-based research on the differences between HL and L2 learners of Spanish. In addition to increasing classroom-based studies, future SHL research should try to integrate sociolinguistic and formal approaches and also study bilingual children, both cross-sectionally and longitudinally.

In chapter 6 Derrin Pinto reviews features of the oral discourse of SHL speakers. Although the systematic study of pragmatics and discourse analysis is relatively new, Pinto predicts that interest in these areas will continue to grow. After defining and briefly describing the phenomena of speech acts, social deixis (pronoun usage), discourse markers, discourse strategies, and oral academic discourse, Pinto describes specific studies of these phenomena in various US Spanish/English bilingual communities and in the Spanish language classroom. Regarding research limitations, Pinto highlights methodological issues such as baselines for data comparison; qualitative versus quantitative approaches; and the historic focus on speech production and neglect of the receptive/interpretive side of language. Areas in need of further research are dialectal variation, (im)politeness, a wider range of speech acts, interactions between HL and L2 Spanish learners, other types of deixis, and the effects of teaching pragmatics/discourse strategies to SHL learners in the classroom. The chapter ends with pedagogical suggestions for the SHL classroom.

In chapter 7 Ana Carvalho describes code-switching among US Spanish speakers, beginning with a historical overview of code-switching research, from the first seminal works to current studies in sociolinguistics, conversational analysis, psycholinguistics, and syntax. Then the author discusses the "myth" about code-switching in relation to bilingual linguistic competence and argues that although the phenomenon presents covert prestige based on solidarity among speakers, it is usually perceived negatively, as a sign of language deficiency. The next section of the chapter describes the syntactic constraints present in code-switching as well as its social and discursive functions. Carvalho insists upon the importance of understanding this phenomenon, typical of language-contact situations. Since code-switching is usually part of the linguistic repertoire of HL learners, educators involved in HL pedagogy need to be aware of the rules that govern it and its importance as a practice in the bilingual community.

Part III

Part III focuses on learner perspectives in terms of motivation and attitudes (chapter 8) and identity (chapter 9). Although research specific to SHL is still in its infancy, it is expanding rapidly, and there is a healthy body of research in related fields to draw on. Both chapters thus approach the key issues surrounding these topics from a broad perspective that extends beyond SHL.

In chapter 8 Cynthia Ducar provides a comprehensive overview of research on attitudes and motivation in the SHL context, while simultaneously integrating research on second language and HL acquisition. After defining key terms, she documents a robust positive correlation between motivation and second language achievement. The almost complete dominance of Gardner's (1985) socioeducational model of second language learning has understandably crossed over to research in the HL and SHL contexts. Moving beyond methodological aspects, Ducar discusses significant differences between the HL learning and second language acquisition contexts, particularly with regard to identity formation, social milieu, self-confidence, and anxiety. Important motivators for HL learners are both integrative (such as establishing cultural connections through language) and instrumental (e.g., broadening one's career opportunities). Research on the attitudes of SHL students suggests that they have positive attitudes toward Spanish but often undervalue the variety of Spanish they speak, which leads to linguistic insecurities. Ducar argues for the need to move away from a quantitative, sociopsychological approach and toward a multimethod sociocultural approach when studying SHL students' language, attitudes, and motivations. Also crucial for future research is to acknowledge the importance of the sociocultural context in motivating HL students to learn Spanish.

In chapter 9 Kim Potowski explores identity, using the stories of three fictional victims of identity theft from a Citibank commercial to illustrate the powerful role that language plays in the identification and construction of many aspects of identity, not only linguistic, but also ethnic, racial, national, migrant, gender, and socioeconomic. She moves on to document how individual identity has historically been essentialized as simply membership in groups based on, for example, social class, religion, or educational background. Identity is in reality a multifaceted, complex construct that goes beyond such universals. After laying out basic tenets of modern approaches to the study of identity (namely, *performativity, ambivalence, hybridity*, and *communities of practice*) and describing connections among identity, language, and ethnicity, Potowski reviews identity research specific to SHL speakers and bilingual Latinos in the United States. Throughout her review, she raises central issues such as the key role of identity in HL development, as well as how US Latinos' Spanish and English proficiency and variety of spoken Spanish influence their identity. She also highlights the importance of identity in the HL classroom and the fundamental role the SHL instructor plays in validating students' sense of cultural identity and making positive connections between their variety of Spanish and their sense of ethnolinguistic identity. The chapter concludes with directions for future research and implications for the HL classroom.

Part IV

Finally, part IV covers important aspects of SHL pedagogy: language curricula and programs, instructional approaches, biliteracy development, and language assessment. Although interest in these areas has grown in recent years, much research remains to be done in identifying and evaluating effective approaches and strategies in order to ensure quality education for all SHL learners.

In chapter 10 Sara Beaudrie reviews the history of SHL education in the United States, highlighting the progress that the field has made since its inception in the 1970s. She documents SHL program offerings in US postsecondary institutions both in the Southwest and nationwide. There has been a near doubling of SHL program offerings at universities with at least 5 percent Hispanic enrollment, although most programs still offer only one or two SHL courses. SHL courses are now available in twenty-six US states and the District of Columbia. For most US states, Beaudrie also found a direct positive correlation between SHL course availability and the size of the Hispanic student population at particular universities. Surveys of SHL students' perspectives on whether their language learning needs are being met reveal that the foreign-language classroom is not the ideal environment for them and that discrepancies exist between what SHL programs offer and what the students expect. Finally, Beaudrie concludes by stressing the need for more qualitative and quantitative research in order to identify effective teaching, curricular, and programmatic practices for SHL learners; for a stronger focus on students' feedback in order to identify program strengths and weaknesses and make sound programmatic and curricular decisions; and for a stronger emphasis on program evaluation and teacher development issues in order to strengthen instruction.

In chapter 11 Maria Carreira addresses instructional approaches, strategies, and research, beginning with a historical overview of the approaches to SHL instruction that have prevailed in US classrooms since the 1970s: the normative approach in the early years and the comprehensive approach since the 1980s. The author advocates for a critical approach that teaches SHL students about the functions, distribution, and evaluation of dialects while raising their awareness of language, power, and social inclusion and addressing their sociolinguistic needs. Recent research on grammatical competence—particularly the correlation between age of acquisition and level of HL competence attained—has important implications for instruction. Classroom research also suggests that HL learners benefit from explicit instruction, including negative evidence. Because SHL learners have diverse language profiles and learning needs, Carreira advocates for differentiated instruction, and offers concrete classroom activities and strategies to implement this approach. Professional development is one of the most pressing needs in the SHL field, and there have been several recent proposals to strengthen this area. The chapter concludes with directions for future research and a call to increase the availability of SHL courses as a top priority or, if not possible, to develop guidelines, methods, and materials for use in mixed classes in order to meet the needs of SHL learners.

In chapter 12 Cecilia Colombi and Joseph Harrington summarize research on advanced biliteracy development in the SHL population. After discussing the status of nonmajority languages in the United States and the resulting lack of opportunities to develop advanced academic literacy in these languages, the authors explain the unique linguistic and educational needs and challenges facing

SHL learners. Two contemporary theories about literacy and biliteracy development are presented: the autonomous model and the ideological model. Moving to biliteracy development, the authors review common definitions of biliteracy as well as Hornberger's continua model, a multidimensional framework that analyzes factors that can promote or inhibit biliteracy development. Finally, the authors explain the systemic functional grammar model, a linguistic perspective on literacy and biliteracy that has proven to be very useful in identifying particular lexicogrammatical and discourse-semantic indices of language development over time. Because language can never be isolated from its social context, biliteracy development is understood as the simultaneous expansion of individuals' meaning-making potential and evolution of their membership in a particular social group, in this case the public sphere at the professional level.

Finally, in chapter 13 Marta Fairclough raises important issues in language assessment, namely, the purposes of testing, types of assessments, proficiency models, test qualities, and developments in test design due to advances in technology. The existing research on language testing in the field of HL education in the United States is summarized next. Whereas research on second language assessment has grown exponentially in the last few decades, research in HL assessment has been scant. The rapidly increasing number of SHL programs has led to a corresponding need for and interest in developing appropriate placement assessments. The author devotes a whole section to reviewing studies on placement. Finally, by combining what the language assessment field has to offer with what has been accomplished in SHL assessment, Fairclough proposes directions for future research.

The volume ends with an afterword by Guadalupe Valdés, whose contributions to the field over the years have inspired many of us. She concludes by offering her expert opinion on future directions for the SHL field.

As editors of this volume we tried to carefully select authors for each chapter and organize and review its contents to make this compilation a significant contribution to the SHL research field. We started this project with three main goals in mind: (1) to offer the reader an overview of how much has already been accomplished in this growing and fascinating area of research; (2) to show how through "dialogue" with other research fields and subfields, research in SHL has been invigorated, growing stronger and more sophisticated; and (3) to point out some future challenges and suggest research agendas that will continue to strengthen research studies on SHL. We foresee that in the decades to come studies on Spanish as a heritage language in the United States will increase exponentially and the field will become one of the foremost areas of language research at the national and international levels. We have no doubt that the exceptional work of the contributors to this volume will facilitate such endeavors.

REFERENCES

Alarcón, Irma. 2010. "Advanced Heritage Learners of Spanish: A Sociolinguistic Profile for Pedagogical Purposes." *Foreign Language Annals* 43 (2): 269–88.

Bale, Jeffrey. 2010. "International Comparative Perspectives on Heritage Language Education Policy Research." *Annual Review of Applied Linguistics* 30:42–65.

Balestra, Alejandra, Glenn Martínez, and María Irene Moyna. 2008. "Recovering the US Hispanic Linguistic Heritage: Part I." In *Recovering the US Hispanic Linguistic Heritage: Sociohistorical Approaches to Spanish in the United States*, edited by Alejandra Balestra, Glenn Martínez, and María Irene Moyna. Houston: Arte Público Press.

Beaudrie, Sara. 2009. "Spanish Receptive Bilinguals: Understanding the Cultural and Linguistic Profile of Learners from Three Different Generations." *Spanish in Context* 6 (1): 85–104.

Beaudrie, Sara, and Cynthia Ducar. 2005. "Beginning-Level University Heritage Language Programs: Creating a Space for All Heritage Language Learners." *Heritage Language Journal* 3 (1). Available at www.heritagelanguages.org.

Carreira, Maria, and Olga Kagan. 2011. "The Results of the National Heritage Language Survey: Implications for Teaching, Curriculum Design, and Professional Development." *Foreign Language Annals* 44 (1): 40–64.

Colombi, M. Cecilia, and Francisco X. Alarcón, eds. 1997. *La enseñanza del español a hispanohablantes: Praxis y teoría*. Boston: Houghton Mifflin.

Cummins, Jim. 2005. "A Proposal for Action: Strategies for Recognizing Heritage Language Competence as a Learning Resource within the Mainstream Classroom." *Modern Language Journal* 89:585–92.

Draper, Jamie B., and June H. Hicks. 2000. "Where We've Been: What We've Learned." In *Teaching Heritage Language Learners: Voices from the Classroom*, edited by John Webb and Barbara Miller. New York: American Council on the Teaching of Foreign Languages.

Fishman, Joshua. 2001. "300-Plus Years of Heritage Language Education in the United States." In *Heritage Languages in America: Preserving a National Resource*, edited by Joy Peyton, Donald Ranard, and Scott McGinnis. McHenry, IL: Center for Applied Linguistics and Delta Systems.

García, Ofelia. 2005. "Positioning Heritage Languages in the United States." *Modern Language Journal* 89:601–5.

Gardner, Robert. 1985. *Social Psychology and Second Language Learning: The Role of Attitudes and Motivation*. London: Edward Arnold.

Hornberger, Nancy, ed. 2005. "Heritage/Community Language Education: US and Australian Perspectives." *International Journal of Bilingual Education and Bilingualism* (Special Issue), 8:2–3.

Kroskrity, Paul. 2004. "Language Ideologies." In *A Companion to Linguistic Anthropology*, edited by Alessandro Duranti. Malden, MA: Blackwell.

Lipski, John. 1993. "Creoloid Phenomena in the Spanish of Transitional Bilinguals." In *Spanish in the United States*, edited by Ana Roca and John Lipski. Berlin: Mouton.

NCES (National Center for Education Statistics). 2007. *Status and Trends in the Education of Racial and Ethnic Minorities*. NCES Report 2007039. Washington, DC: US Government Printing Office.

Otheguy, Ricardo, Ana Celia Zentella, and David Livert. 2007. "Language and Dialect Contact in Spanish in New York: Toward the Formation of a Speech Community." *Language* 83:770–802.

Pew Hispanic Center. 2009. "Statistical Portrait of Hispanics in the United States, 2009: Table 1—Population, by Race and Ethnicity, 2000 and 2009." http://pewhispanic.org/files/factsheets/hispanics2009/Table%201.pdf.

Potowski, Kim, and María Carreira. 2010. "Spanish in the United States." In *Language Diversity in the USA*, edited by Kim Potowski. Cambridge: Cambridge University Press.

Roca, Ana, and M. Cecilia Colombi. 1988. "Orientations in Language Planning." In *Language Diversity: Problem or Resource?* edited by Sandra McKay and Sau-ling Cynthia Wong. Boston: Heinle and Heinle.

———, eds. 2003. *Mi lengua: Spanish as a Heritage Language in the United States: Insights from Research and Practice*. Washington, D.C.: Georgetown University Press.

Ruiz, Richard. 2010. "Reorienting Language as Resource." In *International Perspectives on Bilingual Education*, edited by John Petrovic. Charlotte: Information Age.

Silva-Corvalán, Carmen. 1994. *Language Contact and Change: Spanish in Los Angeles*. Oxford: Oxford University Press.

US Census Bureau. 2006. "Hispanics in the United States." www.census.gov/population/ www/socdemo/hispanic/hispanic_pop_presentation.html.

———. 2009. "Facts for Features." www.census.gov/newsroom/releases/archives/facts_ for_features_special_editions/cb09-ff17.html.

———. 2010. "American FactFinder." http://factfinder2.census.gov/faces/nav/jsf/pages/ index.xhtml.

Valdés, Guadalupe. 1997. "The Teaching of Spanish to Bilingual Spanish-Speaking Students: Outstanding Issues and Unanswered Questions." In *La enseñanza del español a hispanohablantes: Praxis y teoría*, edited by M. Cecilia Colombi and Francisco X. Alarcón. Boston: Houghton Mifflin.

———. 2000. "Introduction." In *Spanish for Native Speakers, Volume I*. AATSP Professional Development Series Handbook for Teachers K–16. New York: Harcourt College.

———. 2001. "Heritage Language Students: Profiles and Possibilities." In *Heritage Languages in America: Preserving a National Resource*, edited by Joy Peyton, Donald Ranard, and Scott McGinnis. McHenry, IL: Center for Applied Linguistics and Delta Systems.

Van Deusen-Scholl, Nelleke. 2003. Toward a Definition of Heritage Language: Sociopolitical Pedagogical Considerations. *Journal of Language, Identity, and Education* 2 (3): 211–30.

Webb, John, and Barbara Miller. 2000. *Teaching Heritage Language Learners: Voices from the Classroom*. New York: American Council on the Teaching of Foreign languages.

Wiley, Terrence. 2001. "On Defining Heritage Languages and their Speakers." In *Heritage Languages in America: Preserving a National Resource*, edited by Joy Peyton, Donald Ranard, and Scott McGinnis. McHenry, IL: Center for Applied Linguistics and Delta Systems.

———. 2004. "Language Planning, Language Policy and the English-Only Movement." In *Language in the USA: Themes for the Twenty-First Century*, edited by Edward Finnegan and John Rickford. Cambridge: Cambridge University Press.

———. 2005. "The Reemergence of Heritage and Community Language Policy in the US National Spotlight." *Modern Language Journal* 89 (4): 594–601.

Wright, Wayne. 2007. "Heritage Language Programs in the Era of English-Only and No Child Left Behind." *Heritage Language Journal* 5. Available at www.heritage languages.org.

PART I

An Overview of the Field

Spanish Heritage Language Maintenance

ITS LEGACY AND ITS FUTURE

Susana V. Rivera-Mills, Oregon State University

THERE IS LITTLE DOUBT that the number of Latinos in the United States is on the rise, and with them the Spanish language. In research released in 2010 by the economist José Luis García Delgado, the Spanish language is second, behind English, in the number of US speakers. Delgado states that, in the United States, Spanish is rapidly becoming "a cultural product very much valued by second and third generations of Hispanics, well educated, and wishing to remain faithful to their roots and the language" (García Delgado 2010, 178). And this phenomenon is not exclusive to the United States; with 350 million total speakers, Spanish is the third most widely spoken language in the world, behind Mandarin and Hindi. Even English, with 340 million native speakers in the world, takes a back seat to Spanish.

In the United States, college students are learning Spanish in large numbers, major book companies are publishing Spanish language editions, and corporate America is increasingly selling itself through Spanish language advertisements and Spanish programming, such as CNN en Español, CBS Telenoticias, Univisión, and Telemundo for both US and Latin American Spanish-speaking audiences. In addition, immigration and a relatively high birthrate continue to lead to increasing numbers of Spanish speakers in all US regions. If we were to stop with these burgeoning numbers, it would seem that all is well with Spanish in the United States; however, the case is not that simple.

The Spanish language has had a long and important journey, encompassing more than four centuries of US history. It is true that in this twenty-first century the number of Latinos and Spanish speakers continues to increase each year.

However, the number of Latinos that do not speak their heritage language also continues to increase (for a detailed review of the status of Spanish, see Veltman 1988, 1990). The complexity of this tension between Spanish heritage language maintenance and shift/loss to English forms the core of this chapter, which thus focuses on three general topics: a historical account of the research surrounding Spanish heritage language maintenance and the shift to English; the current state of this area of research in relation to education and the role it plays in the maintenance of Spanish as a heritage language; and a look at the future of this research, including innovative educational models that both promote Spanish heritage language maintenance and also can help us to better understand the variables in the process of language maintenance and shift.

HISTORICAL OVERVIEW

Studies of the various issues regarding Spanish language maintenance and shift have been present since the late nineteenth century in the form of either newspaper columns and popular magazine articles (Bourke 1896) or academic dissertations and formal scholarship (Espinosa 1909; Gray 1912). Much of this initial research focused on the maintenance of Spanish as a native language (Baker 1953), the issues that pertain to linguistic changes (e.g., phonology, morphology, lexicon) (Espinosa 1909, 1911–13), and the displacement of Spanish (Espinosa 1917) by the influence of English as the dominant language.

Aurelio Espinosa laid a solid foundation for research on Southwest Spanish (e.g., Espinosa 1909, 1911, 1911–13, 1914–15). His groundbreaking work not only documented varieties of what is now US Spanish but also established new research paradigms in the field of linguistics. Equally important, through his research, he established the value of studying Southwest Spanish. At the time, this variety of Spanish was considered to be corrupt, deficient, a language of the poor and uneducated, and not worthy of serious scientific study (Bills and Vigil 2008; Lipski 2008; Morrill 1918). However, this view soon changed and other scholars were motivated to build on Espinosa's solid foundation.

Since Espinosa's initial studies, the topic of Spanish language use in the southwestern region of the United States has expanded to include issues surrounding Spanish language maintenance and the shift to English well beyond this region's geographical borders. In addition, this research has promoted the recognition of a new emerging identity in the Spanish of the United States. No longer was the focus of study solely on linguistic variations or the maintenance of Spanish as a native language; additional dimensions were introduced in the 1960s and continued into the 1970s as more scholars focused on Chicano Spanish (Aguirre 1978; Braddy 1965; Sánchez 1972), the Spanish of the Southwest (Bowen and Ornstein 1976; Christian and Christian 1966; May 1966), and Spanish heritage/native speakers (AATSP 1970; US Office of Education 1972; Valdés and García-Moya 1976).

In the 1960s the Chicano Movement brought about awareness that the Spanish language was an important element of community identity and social activism. Following Espinosa's pathbreaking view that Southwest Spanish was worthy of academic research, Eduardo Hernández-Chávez, Andrew Cohen, and Anthony Beltramo (1975) published *El Lenguaje de los Chicanos: Regional and Social Characteristics Used by Mexican Americans*, an important work that motivated new interest in the study of Spanish as it exists in its social contexts in the United States' Southwest and beyond. This work served as a foundation for future notable studies, such as Peñalosa's (1980) *Chicano Sociolinguistics* and Sánchez's (1983) *Chicano Discourse*. By the late 1970s, following the significant social changes brought about by the Chicano Movement and the reclaiming of a Chicano identity and language, research on Spanish in the United States exploded, which provided opportunities for scholarship that would further develop the study of Spanish heritage language maintenance and shift.

Research now shifted to more refined and complex theoretical frameworks in order to better measure the process of language shift and to include additional social variables, such as identity (Le Page and Tabouret-Keller 1985), linguistic attitudes (Hurtado and Gurin 1987; López 1978; Silverstein 1979), and diachronic analyses of intergenerational language shift (Ortíz 1975). The need to understand how to best measure the process whereby a language is maintained or lost motivated scholars to propose research methodologies and theoretical frameworks for this subarea of linguistic study (Fishman 1964, 1966; Labov 1970, 1972; Milroy 1980). Currently, it is agreed that the maintenance of a language is manifested in its historical stability. To be maintained, a language must be transmitted from one generation to the next. If there is no transmission from parents to children and grandchildren, the product is language loss (Bills 2010). The measurement of maintenance or loss is based on the proportion of Spanish speakers within an ethnic group. This proportion is referred to as "language loyalty," or as the "intergenerational transmission" of the language, which can be classified as maintenance. These types of measurements take into account variables such as mother tongue, use of language, language proficiency, and language attitudes. The variable of proficiency also includes proficiency in English because it seems that loss begins with bilingualism among the immigrant generation and then quickly moves to English monolingualism in subsequent generations. Such measures have been affirmed in studies by Bills and his colleagues (Bills, Hudson, and Hernández-Chávez 2000; Bills, Hernández-Chávez, and Hudson 1995), and by Pearson and McGee (1993, 99), who studied middle-school students in Miami and concluded that "even for first-generation immigrants, many of whom did not learn the language until they were 7 or 8, 90% report using at least one-half English with their siblings by the time they are in

their early teens." The majority of research examining intergenerational transmission of the native language shows that after two or three generations, there is
a loss of Spanish (Bills 2005; Chávez 1988; González and Wherritt 1990; Hidalgo
1993; Rivera-Mills 2000b). The typical situation is for immigrants to become
bilingual by the second generation and monolingual English speakers by the
third generation (Hudson-Edwards and Bills 1982; Solé 1990).

The majority of researchers who have focused on this three-generation model
have based their theoretical framework on studies initiated by Joshua Fishman
(1964, 1965, 1966), who established a solid foundation for understanding the
dynamics of language contact between English and other languages in the United
States. His intergenerational model (Fishman 1964) proposes a specific pattern
for immigrant groups that has as its product monolingualism by the third generation. According to this basic pattern, the first generation learns English and
achieves a functional level of bilingualism, the second generation reaches a high
degree of bilingualism, and the third generation is monolingual in English. In
addition, Fishman proposes an extensive process for measuring this language
shift by introducing the principal variables that affect it, including habitual language use in specific domains, the degree of bilingualism, and language attitudes
(Fishman 1964, 1966). Other researchers (Grosjean 1982; Romaine 1995) have
used and confirmed this model, particularly among European immigrant families. Grosjean (1982) found the same intergenerational pattern, explaining that
the first generation of an immigrant family undergoes a cultural and linguistic
experience that favors a shift to the dominant language. Unless the first generation lives in isolated linguistic areas where contact with the dominant language
is limited, the dominant language begins to erode the native language due to
basic communicative needs. This motivation leads to bilingualism in the second
generation (assuming the native language is spoken in the home) and to a third
generation that becomes monolingual in the dominant language. Research established in the twentieth century confirmed this three-generational loss to English,
which was expedited by harsh punishments in public schools for many Spanish
speakers who spoke Spanish in public. Many Spanish-speaking children who
entered public school systems experienced corporal punishment for speaking
their home language at school (Hernández-Chávez 1989). Rivera-Mills and Villa
(2010, 12) report on a student who attended school in the early 1960s as saying:
"Un día me metieron una buena paliza por estar hablando mi lengua propia.
Me metieron una zurra tan grande que no podía andar, ni caminar bien" (One
day they gave me a good beating for speaking my own language. They gave me
such a whipping that I could barely walk).

Research on Spanish in the United States focused on the Southwest region
because this is where the majority of Spanish speakers lived and continue to live.
Yet as the Latino population grew and expanded throughout the United States,
so did the research and, with it, the various foci. Perhaps the first notable change

occurred in studies that no longer focused only on the Mexican American community but also on other Spanish-speaking communities with diverse backgrounds. Though Fishman had already embarked on studies of Puerto Rican communities in El Barrio in New York, little had been done to expand on his initial studies. However, it did not take long for others to follow in his footsteps. Ana Celia Zentella's research done among children of El Bloque, a neighborhood in New York, added valuable knowledge to scholars' understanding of the Puerto Rican community in the United States. Her study looks at linguistic competence as she provides a historical perspective on nearly four generations that shows a clear linguistic shift from Spanish to English. She documents the shift from Spanish/English bilingualism to English monolingualism, pointing to a clear loss of Spanish. In her article about Puerto Ricans in the United States, she compares data for 1980 and 1993 to show a historical perspective confirming the language loss that was occurring in this community (Zentella 1985, 1997).

In comparison with studies of Mexican American and Puerto Rican speech communities, fewer studies have looked at the maintenance of Spanish among Cubans in the United States. However, an early contribution was a study carried out by Carlos Solé (1979), which surveyed 268 high school students ages fifteen to eighteen years from Miami and concluded that this sample showed signs of the beginning of a shift from Spanish to English. Furthermore, he concluded in subsequent studies (Solé 1980, 1982) that "language shift seems to have already begun among young Cuban-Americans in spite of the recency of the Cuban arrival and settlement" (Solé 1982, 264). In another study Castellanos (1990) looks at the bilingualism of 214 Cubans from Miami. She examines various linguistic contexts and in all of them finds a significant discrepancy in the language use between the two generations that she distinguishes. The second generation had practically abandoned the exclusive use of Spanish with other members of their family, and particularly with their children. Castellanos (1990, 57) states: "We have provided abundant evidence of a progressive intergenerational displacement from Spanish to English in Dade County."

Summarizing the general situation of Cubans in the United States, García and Otheguy (1988) state that the second generation shows the same pattern of language preference toward English as that of second-generation Mexicans and Puerto Ricans. They conclude that second-generation Cubans, "even those living in Dade County and West New York, are for the most part English-dominant" (García and Otheguy 1988, 180).

All these studies, and others, provide strong documentation of the loss of Spanish among those of Spanish-speaking heritage (Bills, Hudson, and Hernández-Chávez 2000; Lope Blanch 1990; Silva-Corvalán 1994). Bills, Hudson, and Hernández-Chávez (2000, 24–25) confirm that Hispanics in the Southwest show sharp differences in their use of Spanish. This finding was especially true among those born in the United States who were further removed from the Spanish-dominant generation.

The value of research conducted in the early to middle twentieth century cannot be disputed. Scholars established a solid foundation of descriptive, analytical, and theoretical studies that clearly placed the sociolinguistic study of Spanish in the United States on a par with any other subfield of the social sciences. Current research has built upon this foundation and has thus expanded research on and knowledge of what continues to be a complex and dynamic field of study. It is to this research that we now turn.

TRANSITIONAL STUDIES

Several studies are worth noting as transitional studies (late 1980s to early 2000) that maintained the theoretical approach of previous research yet continued to expand the research of communities outside the traditional Southwest and brought scholarship into the twenty-first century. The work of Lourdes Torres, one prime example of such studies, contributed to the linguistic research on Puerto Ricans in the late 1990s in Brentwood, a suburb of New York on Long Island. The results of her survey also document language loss. As stated by Torres (1997, 117), "Compared to their parents and even young people of different Latino nationalities, Puerto Rican young people in Brentwood are using Spanish less, with fewer speakers, and under restricted contexts." Her findings agree with the conclusions reached by other researchers, such as García, Morin, and Rivera (2001), who study the *vaivén lingüístico* (shifting language) of the Puerto Rican community. García and her colleagues state that Spanish is in the heart though not always in the mouth of Puerto Ricans, and they affirm that a "shift to English is proceeding at the normal historical pace of three generations" (García, Morin, and Rivera 2001, 64).

Other studies also expanded to include mixed or heterogeneous communities of Spanish speakers along with social variables such as language attitudes, solidarity, communicative need, and intraethnic tensions (Galindo 1995, 1996; Hidalgo 1984, 1986, 1988; Mejías and Anderson 1988; Mills 2005; Rivera-Mills 2000a, 2002). At the time, the geographic area that was studied most frequently was northwestern Indiana. Attinasi's (1985) work examined language attitudes in a community of Puerto Ricans and Mexicans, comparing them with previous studies of Puerto Ricans in New York. His conclusions confirm those of previous studies showing a gradual shift to English. He states that "although most want to see Spanish continue, the pattern of usage seems to indicate less Spanish, and even less of the bilingual usage that would retain Spanish as a component in the speech repertoires of Hispanics" (Attinasi 1985, 45). Additional studies of this same area by Mendieta (1994, 1997) and by Mendieta and Molina (2000) expand on previous research methodology by including an analysis of census data indicating a low level of loyalty among Spanish speakers in both Gary and East Chicago, which again points to a gradual decline of Spanish language use in the home (Mendieta 1994, 74).

However, not all studies agree on a definite, intergenerational shift from Spanish to English among all speech communities. The case of Cuban Americans in Miami is one of much debate among scholars. Resnick's (1988) work sets a context by identifying the ways in which Spanish is used in Miami: (1) as an immigrant language, (2) as the mother tongue of the members of a large Cuban American community and their children, and (3) as the public language of work and government (Resnick 1988, 89). In the 1990s Boswell (1993, 1994, 1995) clearly set a context for language use by relating it to racial and ethnic segregation patterns, and the economic impact that such segregation brings to a community.

Though early studies by Solé (1979, 1982) and García and Otheguy (1988) pointed to a lack of stability in the bilingualism of Miami, more recent work by Roca (1991) and Lynch (2000) argues against this position in favor of a more stable bilingualism among the members of the second and third generations of Cuban Americans. Lynch (2000, 272) states: "Miami's mainstream has become English-Spanish bilingual. . . . A complete shift to English at the expense of bilingualism appears not to be a requirement for achieving the American dream in South Florida." This statement confirms Roca's (1991) earlier claims suggesting that current data support the sustained use of Spanish in Miami. There is little doubt that Miami represents a unique urban setting for a speech community. Future research will determine the vitality of Spanish among successive generations of Cuban Americans and other Hispanic groups.

These transitional studies contributed valuable information about groups beyond the Southwest. They provided detailed profiles of Cuban and Puerto Rican communities that enriched the sociolinguistic research of the time (Boswell 1994; Coles 1993; Lynch 2000; Resnick 1988; Roca 1991). At the same time, these studies and others began to expand the sociolinguistic framework by applying it to issues in education and language acquisition (Pedraza 1985; Potowski 2004a, 2004b).

OVERVIEW OF CURRENT RESEARCH

By far, the three major groups of Hispanics in the United States—Mexican, Puerto Rican, and Cuban—have been the focus of most current research. However, since the beginning of the twenty-first century, other recent immigrant communities have also begun to receive the attention of scholars. In particular, Central American communities have been added to the research literature as they too have become part of the United States' dynamic Latino population (Lipski 1986, 2000; Rivera-Mills 2000b). Rivera-Mills's (2000b) study of Fortuna, California, exemplifies this recent research into heterogeneous communities. Her sample included Mexicans, Salvadorans, South Americans, and United States–born participants. This study, once again, confirms an expedited shift toward English, which she attributes to the lack of solidarity in the community, the isolation from other Spanish-speaking groups, and the need to communicate in the dominant language. García and Otheguy (1988, 490) also describe a speech community with a heterogeneous profile. Their study examines two communities that include Puerto Rican, Cuban, Dominican, South American, and Central American participants, most of whom are recent immigrants. Its data show language use by three generations, with the inevitable loss of Spanish by the third generation. It is also noted that those who had lived in the United States for longer periods exhibited a more significant shift toward English. Lipski (1986) also contributed significantly to this research when studying communities of Salvadorans and Mexicans, and the tensions found between these two groups due to differing background and Spanish language varieties. In addition, his recent book on Spanish varieties in the United States presents a detailed overview of the major varieties spoken in the United States (Lipski 2008).

All these studies, whether of homogeneous or heterogeneous communities, continue to point to a gradual shift from Spanish to English by the third generation. Several recent studies have included census data analyses and observations extending into the fourth and fifth generations in an effort to see if the Spanish language can resist the three-generational path to English monolingualism. Though these studies remain few in number, they represent an important future direction for the field of heritage language maintenance. Mora, Villa, and Dávila (2005, 2006), using census data and a cohort of children at two different points in time (five to seven years old in 1980; and fifteen to seventeen years old in 1990), point to an increased use of Spanish in the geographical region studied. Mills (2005), in an Arizona study, shows a resilient use of Spanish into the fourth generation. Finally, Jenkins (2010a), using census data, points to an extensive use of Spanish beyond the traditional Southwest into the majority of US regions west of the Mississippi.

However, this recent research does not contradict previous findings regarding the maintenance of Spanish. Instead, it reflects another key phenomenon: the ongoing immigration of native Spanish speakers, who in turn strengthen the use of Spanish in the United States. This influx of native Spanish speakers allows patterns of a shift toward English to slow down so that no longer do we see the drastic loss in three generations, but the resiliency of Spanish well into the fourth generation and beyond (Anderson-Mejías 2005; Mora, Villa, and Dávila 2005; Rivera-Mills 2007). This phenomenon is particularly important in areas where there is a high density and loyalty of Spanish speakers (Jenkins 2010b; McCullough and Jenkins 2005).

In particular, the last ten years of research in this area have focused more on sociolinguistic and sociopolitical issues, such as the connection of language and identity (García 2007; Plaza 2009; Potowski and Matts 2008), language varieties and perceived prestige (Alfaraz 2002; Dumitrescu 2010; Villa 2009), language ideology (Leeman 2004, 2010), language politics (Cashman 2010; Train 2010), and language policy (Lacorte and Leeman 2009; Leeman 2004; Leeman, Rabin, and Román-Mendoza 2011). These interdisciplinary additions to the traditional variables of language maintenance and shift have created a robust body of research that encompasses the humanities, social sciences, and even natural sciences, and thus has far-reaching implications for important areas of language education and policy.

In keeping with this new profile for Spanish language influence and resiliency, academic courses for Spanish for heritage speakers have come to play a prominent role. As the field of Spanish language maintenance and shift in the United States has developed, it has been paralleled by a strong current of research on what was first called Spanish for native speakers but later came to be appropriately termed Spanish for heritage speakers. The other chapters in this book chronicle the history of this field and clearly demonstrate the complex issues involved in the identification of heritage speakers, the assessment of language competence in this group, placement, diversity of backgrounds, and teaching approaches that differ significantly from methodologies that pertain to Spanish as a second language. With the increase of heritage speakers in the Spanish classroom, there is a growing awareness that the traditional curriculum for Spanish as a second language is not sufficient for heritage speakers' needs. As a result, more universities are offering Spanish courses and programs that are specifically designed to meet the heritage student's needs. The number of courses offered and the types of programs available vary greatly from university to university, as do the teaching methodologies used. Despite the large body of research available on the issues of both language maintenance and shift, and of Spanish for heritage speakers, certain limitations of this research have left gaps that still need to be addressed.

LIMITATIONS OF CURRENT RESEARCH

Perhaps one of the most significant limitations of current research is that developments in the study of Spanish for heritage speakers have generally remained separate from research on issues of Spanish language maintenance and shift. Though some scholars have begun to see the area of language learning and maintenance as closely connected to social, ideological, and political dimensions (Achugar and Pessoa 2009; Sayer 2008), much remains to be done for educators to integrate sociolinguistic issues into heritage speakers' classroom as part of curriculum planning, teacher training, and material design. Some exceptional current research that is leading the way in this area has been done by Alarcón (2010), Beaudrie (2009), Beaudrie and Ducar (2005), García (2009, 2010), Garcia and Bartlett (2007), Leeman (2005, 2006–7, 2010), Lynch (2008), and Roca and Colombi (2003). These scholars have provided new perspectives for current sociolinguistic knowledge and research that lead us into transdisciplinary frameworks for this field of study. However, there is still a need to integrate these

findings into teacher training programs, material design, and curriculum planning, particularly in the public school setting. In addition, many of these findings
need to be integrated into heritage classroom discussions and pedagogies that
can help heritage students become more aware of their own Spanish variety in
the context of other US varieties (Martínez 2003a).

Research on Spanish language maintenance and shift has largely operated
within a framework that assumes language shift rather than supports language
maintenance efforts. Fishman's model demonstrating a three-generational language shift has formed the foundation for the majority of these studies. Definitions of the term "generation" have always been constructed starting from an
immigrant's perspective and thus have never included the long-standing nonimmigrant population of Mexican Americans who have always resided in the
Southwest region of the United States. In addition, the groups on which these
researchers have based their theories of language shift have been fairly homogenous and included a clear sequence of an immigrant generation that arrived
during a restricted period, such as the European origin migrations during the
early decades of the twentieth century (Fishman 1964). This was then followed
by subsequent generations that showed a tendency toward endogamy, creating a
fairly homogenous group with respect to its ethnic origin and language use patterns (Villa and Rivera-Mills 2010). The homogeneity of such groups lends itself
to a clear pattern of intergenerational language loss over a three-generation
period (Fishman 1964, 1966, 1971; Grosjean 1982; Romaine 1995). Though this
may be applicable to such homogeneous populations, with respect to the current
Hispanic population of the United States, as Bills, Hudson, and Hernández-
Chávez (2000, 15) state, "this is an oversimplified account of the actual state of
affairs." As more and more Spanish-speaking immigrants arrive in the United
States, it is necessary to take a closer look at what some scholars have referred to
as cyclical bilingualism (Silva-Corvalán 1994) and to study the factors that may
be contributing to the revival of Spanish in some speech communities.

Today, the situation of Spanish in the United States presents certain realities
that call for a reworking of the classic intergenerational model of language shift.
To begin with, Spanish is not a strictly immigrant language when compared
with other non-English, nonindigenous languages. It shares, in common with
indigenous languages, the fact that it was spoken in what is now the United
States before the arrival of English speakers. Furthermore, the Spanish-speaking
population of the United States is highly heterogeneous. The families of some
Spanish speakers have resided in the United States for centuries, whereas others
have just arrived from their country of origin. Census data indicate that although
in the Southwest the majority of this population is of Mexican origin, there are
also speakers from Central and South America and the Caribbean. Many of these
groups are regarded more as migrants rather than immigrants. Additionally, the
census shows that the majority of Latinos were born in the United States, not in

other countries. As a result, it becomes difficult to analyze patterns of language maintenance and shift using a traditional language shift framework.

To fully understand the complexity of identifying a generational language shift, one must also consider interlinguistic unions (e.g., interracial marriages in which one spouse speaks English and the other speaks Spanish) and the effect that these may be having in expediting or slowing the shift process. Lee and Edmonston (2005, 24) report that "as the number of Hispanic couples has surged, the percentage that include a non-Hispanic spouse has been fairly stable at between 23 percent and 25 percent."

To offer an alternative option to the traditional framework of language shift, Villa and Rivera-Mills (2010) propose a model that takes into consideration the many issues outlined above, including the notion of a reacquisition generation— that is, one that takes into account the experience of the heritage speaker who seeks to develop or reacquire Spanish in formal courses. This new model has yet to be widely tested in various speech communities and should be particularly used among heritage speakers when studying language shift as it relates to the reacquisition of Spanish. It is this reacquisition of Spanish by heritage speakers that has yet to be considered in the research literature in terms of its effect on the shift process and, even more important, the effect that it may have on the dynamics of a Spanish speech community.

Related to this topic, an additional limitation of research includes the question of expanding the concept of a speech community (Santa Ana and Parodi 1998). Linguistic attitudes have much to do with this concept. The sense of being a member of a speech community can encourage the use of its historic ethnic language, and the loss of identity when a community produces language loss.

As has been demonstrated by the various studies discussed in this chapter, Spanish is spoken in many different speech communities. It is difficult to define exactly what is meant by "speech community," but many researchers agree that such a community is a group of individuals who share the same linguistic attitudes and speaking norms with respect to a linguistic repertoire. Romaine (2004) and Wenger (1998) define a bilingual community as communities of practice where individuals interact and communicate regularly, sharing a repertoire of communal resources while engaging in various activities (for further exploration of the community of practice, see Cashman 2003; Martínez 2003b). For example, Hidalgo (1987) shows, based on a series of linguistic judgments, that participants from Mexico City and a group of Mexican Americans from California represent distinct speech communities despite sharing the same national/linguistic origin. It is the linguistic, habitual sharing and interaction that form the basic role that a small community plays in the maintenance of a minority language (Fishman 2001). Such a small community of great significance is the family—there is no doubt that patterns of language use in the home play a definite role in mother tongue retentiveness. This is why Fishman states in his book *Reversing Language*

Shift that "the priorities at various points in the [reversing language shift] struggle must vary, but they must, nevertheless, derive from a single, integrated theory
of language-in-society processes that places intergenerational mother tongue
transmission at the very center and that makes sure to defend that center before
setting out to conquer societal processes that are more distant, dubious, and
tenuous vis-à-vis such transmission" (Fishman 2001, 6).

The solidarity of a community as small as the family can cancel the effects of
the external forces of assimilation and encourage a type of covert prestige. In her
study of Dominicans in New York, Toribio (2000) found that Spanish carried
covert prestige as a symbol of national or group identity; it served as a unifying
and separatist function in this community.

However, emphasizing a small speech community can only provide a limited
perspective on what is needed to maintain and even revitalize a language, especially Spanish in the United States. So it is also important to create larger speech
communities. The Spanish speaker, besides participating in small communities,
also needs to be engaged with large-scale communities, and he or she must self-
identify as a member of these communities on various levels. Ofelia Garcia
expands on this concept: "Post–civil rights US Spanish . . . can only be strengthened by cultivating its US ethnic character with the culture, history, and literature of the Spanish-speaking world and by promoting it for the enrichment of
US Latinos. The protection of US Spanish in the face of the inevitable spread of
English, will . . . come by expanding it . . . within Latinos and their children"
(García 1993, 81).

In this sphere, education can play a strong role by creating additional speech
communities and expanding the active language domains for Spanish heritage
speakers. Further research is needed on how education can play a role in the
expansion of speech communities and domains for Spanish. Though many
scholars have studied the relationship between education and identity (Ardila
2005; Baugh 2000; Bayley and Schecter 2005; Bernal-Enríquez and Hernández-
Chávez 2003), much remains to be done in order to be able to propose educational models that not only keep the Spanish language alive but also extend its
reach and development among Spanish speakers without limiting Spanish heritage language practice to a prescriptive standard. Instead, the concept of speech
community needs to be broadened to include all US Spanish varieties, including
the ever-debated representations of "Spanglish" (Fairclough 2003). The tendency
for higher education to favor groups with greater socioeconomic status continues
to have a negative effect on Spanish speakers. It is through education that social
and cultural capital are acquired, and this process thus separates the members of
disadvantaged groups with fewer opportunities from those who have access to
education. In addition, educational systems continue to be the vehicle for linguistic and cultural assimilation into the dominant language and culture, still to
the detriment of heritage language maintenance efforts.

Despite these realities, efforts are emerging in the application of academic models that have found innovative ways to establish connections and partnerships with underserved communities. Among these innovative models are learning communities, service learning, and community-based learning, which represent current pedagogies of engagement (Leeman 2005). These approaches to developing communities in academia are being piloted throughout the United States and integrated into existing programs for Spanish heritage speakers (Rivera-Mills and Trujillo 2010). The effect that these pedagogies may have in aiding the maintenance of Spanish in heritage speakers or in strengthening Spanish speech communities remains to be researched.

In both the academic and nonacademic communities, additional social and political factors need to be considered further, including intraethnic discrimination and racism. As the Spanish-speaking population continues to grow in number and diversity, the phenomenon of Spanish varieties coming into contact within heterogeneous communities begins to play an important role in the politics and dynamics of various language spheres (Otheguy, Zentella, and Livert 2007; Potowski and Matts 2008). This reality affects existing language ideologies in relation to prestige varieties of Spanish and notions of "correct" versus "incorrect" Spanish. In addition, lines are drawn between recent arrivals and more established residents within a community. Hutchison (1988, 10), studying a Hispanic community in Chicago, observes that "the factors used . . . to categorize ethnic populations (language and culture) may form the very basis for stratification between subgroups within that population." This stratification is not due exclusively to external forces but to internal racism (classism, ethnicism).

Negative comments directed to various parts of the Latino mosaic of the United States are present in many Latino communities. The way that certain groups speak (Alfaraz 2002; Amastae and Elías-Olivares 1978; Galindo 1995, 1996), their accent (Lippi-Green 1997; Ryan and Carranza 1975; Ryan, Carranza, and Moffie 1977), and their lexical choices (Ardila 2005; Hidalgo 1988; Richardson 1999; Roca and Colombi 2003) are often criticized by various groups. Linguistic differences, prescriptive views, and those who hold fast to some abstract concept of a prestigious language standard are just a few of the obstacles for Spanish maintenance among heritage speakers. In what is now the United States, Spanish has been in contact with English, and with other varieties of Spanish, for more than two centuries, and its speech communities have changed considerably in recent decades. Stable, contact-tempered varieties of Spanish have emerged and are playing an increasing role in the maintenance and spread of Spanish in the United States. These realities cannot be ignored and need further research as they relate to interethnic and intraethnic attitudes within speech communities and, in turn, play a central role in the maintenance of the heritage Spanish language.

Related to these limiting attitudes, similar types of political actions by Latinos are seen as divisive when they strongly support English-only policies, anti-immigrant policies, antibilingual education proposals, and conservative/traditional educational policies that limit access and opportunities for heritage speakers of Spanish. Research studies of these varying dimensions of ideology, politics, and attitudes are needed in order to more fully explain the internal and external forces at play in the process of language loss. Success in future research will depend largely on scholars' willingness to further include transdisciplinary and collaborative projects in their fields of study.

CONCLUSION

Scholars need to recognize, along with researchers like Crawford (1996, 2008) and Fishman (2001), that they must not only consider the causes of language loss but also look at models for how to revitalize Spanish within the various speech communities. In the words of Zentella (2002, 330), "Spanish-speaking communities that recognize and respect the differences among themselves but are united in their defense of bilingualism should be in the forefront of the opening of . . . linguistic and cultural frontiers."

Being aware of the linguistic attitudes and ideologies that are prevalent in both the local and larger communities can help educators discern what participation structures and approaches to language and culture can better foster the heritage identity. This awareness of social, attitudinal, political, and economic factors can translate into pedagogical interventions that provide access and opportunities despite the issues of language and power at play. The development of a critical language awareness can help students and teachers understand how their discursive patterns and linguistic choices can either collude with or contest dominant language ideologies (Heller and Martin-Jones 2001). Achugar and Pessoa (2009, 220) state that "in this particular setting, this would mean: How can Anglo students become more proficient in the others' language? How can Spanish speakers expand their linguistic repertoire? And how can all participants question the values attached to particular language varieties?" In sum, if we are to truly revitalize Spanish among heritage speakers, it must be a systematic effort by both members of the Spanish-speaking community and those who are not members but share similar ideologies.

The complexity of the political, linguistic, social, economic, and educational issues involved in the maintenance of Spanish among heritage speakers offers a wealth of opportunities for research and, specifically, research that can provide outcomes that affect policies at all levels. Despite the impressive body of past research, scholars have just begun to understand the process of language maintenance and shift in the Spanish language in the United States. And just when researchers think that they have developed the right model or framework to explain this process, the demographics of the nation's Hispanic population will change so dramatically that additional work will need to be done on similar topics with a different approach. It is here that we stand today—at the edge of yet another significant period of Latino population growth that calls us to action, to research, and to affect change.

REFERENCES

AATSP (American Association of Teachers of Spanish and Portuguese). 1970. *Teaching Spanish in School and College to Native Speakers of Spanish.* Wichita: AATSP.

Achugar, Mariana, and Silvia Pessoa. 2009. "Power and Place: Language Attitudes towards Spanish in a Bilingual Academic Community in Southwest Texas." *Spanish in Context* 6 (2): 199–223.

Aguirre, Adalberto. 1978. *An Experimental Sociolinguistic Analysis of Chicano Bilingualism.* San Francisco: R&E Research Associates.

Alarcón, Irma. 2010. "Advanced Heritage Learners of Spanish: A Sociolinguistic Profile for Pedagogical Purposes." *Foreign Language Annals* 43 (2): 269–88.

Alfaraz, Gabriela G. 2002. "Miami Cuban Perceptions of Varieties of Spanish." In *Handbook of Perceptual Dialectology*, edited by Dennis Preston and Daniel Long. Philadelphia: John Benjamins.

Amastae, Jon, and Lucia Elías-Olivares. 1978. *Attitudes towards Varieties of Spanish. Aspects of Bilingualism*, edited by Michel Paradis. Fourth LACUS Forum. Columbia, SC: Hornbeam Press.

Anderson-Mejías, Pamela L. 2005. "Generation and Spanish Language Use in the Lower Rio Grande Valley of Texas." *Southwest Journal of Linguistics* 24:1–12.

Ardila, Alfredo. 2005. "Spanglish: An Anglicized Spanish Dialect." *Hispanic Journal of Behavioral Sciences* 27 (1): 60–81.

Attinasi, John. 1985. "Hispanic Attitudes in Northwest Indiana and New York." In *Spanish Language: Use and Public Life in the US*, edited by Lucía Elías-Olivares, Elizabeth Leone, Rene Cisneros, and John Gutiérrez. Berlin: Mouton de Gruyter.

Baker, Pauline. 1953. *Español para los hispanos.* Dallas: B. Upshaw. Subsequent printings by National Textbook Company, Skokie, IL.

Baugh, John. 2000. *Beyond Ebonics: Linguistic Pride and Racial Prejudice.* Oxford: Oxford University Press.

Bayley, Robert, and Sandra Schecter. 2005. "Family Decisions about Schooling and Spanish Maintenance: Mexicanos in California and Texas." In *Building on Strength: Language and Literacy in Latino Families and Communities*, edited by Ana Celia Zentella. New York: Teachers College Press.

Beaudrie, Sara. 2009. "Teaching Spanish Heritage Learners and the Nativeness Issue." *ADFL Bulletin* 41 (1): 94–112.

Beaudrie, Sara, and Cynthia Ducar. 2005. "Beginning-Level University Heritage Programs: Creating a Space for All Heritage Language Learners." *Heritage Language Journal* 3 (1): 1–26.

Bernal-Enríquez, Ysaura, and Eduardo Hernández-Chávez. 2003. "La enseñanza del español en Nuevo México: ¿Revitalización o erradicación de la variedad chicana?" In *Mi lengua: Spanish as a Heritage Language in the United States*, edited by Ana Roca and Cecilia Colombi. Washington, DC: Georgetown University Press.

Bills, Garland D. 2005. "Las comunidades lingüísticas y el mantenimiento del español en Estados Unidos." In *Contactos y contextos lingüísticos: El español en los Estados Unidos y en contacto con otras lenguas,* edited by Luís Ortíz López and Manel Lacorte. Madrid: Iberoamericana/Vervuert.

———. 2010. "Introduction. Whither Southwest Spanish? Issues in the Assessment of Maintenance or Loss." In *Spanish of the US Southwest: A Language in Transition,* edited by Susana V. Rivera-Mills and Daniel J. Villa. Madrid: Iberoamericana/Vervuert.

Bills, Garland, Eduardo Hernández-Chávez, and Alan Hudson. 1995. "The Geography of Language Shift: Distance from the Mexican Border and Spanish Language Claiming in the Southwestern US." *International Journal of the Sociology of Language* 114:9–27.

Bills, Garland, Alan Hudson, and Eduardo Hernández-Chávez. 2000. "Spanish Home Language Use and English Proficiency as Differential Measures of Language Maintenance and Shift." *Southwest Journal of Linguistics* 19 (1): 11–27.

Bills, Garland D., and Neddy A. Vigil. 2008. *The Spanish Language of New Mexico and Southern Colorado.* Albuquerque: University of New Mexico Press.

Boswell, Thomas D. 1993. "Racial and Ethnic Segregation Patterns in Metropolitan Miami, Florida, 1980–1990." *Southeastern Geographer* 33:82–109.

———. 1994. *The Cubanization and Hispanicization of Metropolitan Miami.* Miami: Cuban American National Council.

———. 1995. *Hispanic National Groups in Metropolitan Miami.* Miami: Cuban American National Council.

Bourke, John G. 1896. *Notes on the Language and Folk-Usage of the Rio Grande Valley.* Reprinted in 2009 by General Books LLC.

Bowen, J. Donald, and Jacob Ornstein. 1976. *Studies in Southwest Spanish.* Rowley, MA: Newbury House.

Braddy, Haldeen. 1965. "The Pachucos and Their Argot." *Southern Folklore Quarterly* 24:255–71.

Cashman, Holly R. 2003. "Red social y bilingüismo (inglés/español) en Detroit, Michigan." *Revista Internacional de Lingüística Iberoamericana* 2:59–78.

———. 2010. "Research, Responsibility and Repression: Anti-Bilingualism in Arizona." In *Spanish of the US Southwest: A Language in Transition,* edited by Susana V. Rivera-Mills and Daniel J. Villa. Madrid: Iberoamericana/Vervuert.

Castellanos, Isabel. 1990. "The Use of English and Spanish among Cubans in Miami." *Cuban Studies* 20:49–66.

Chávez, Eliverio. 1988. "Sex Differences in Language Shift." *Southwest Journal of Linguistics* 8:3–14.

Christian, Jane, and Chester Christian Jr. 1966. "Spanish Language and Culture in the Southwest." In *Language Loyalty in the United States,* edited by Joshua Fishman. The Hague: Mouton.

Coles, Felice Ann. 1993. "Language Maintenance Institutions of the Isleño Dialect of Spanish." In *Spanish in the United States: Linguistic contact and diversity,* edited by Ana Roca and John M. Lipski. Berlin: Mouton de Gruyter.

Crawford, James. 1996. "Seven Hypotheses on Language Loss: Causes and Cures." In *Stabilizing Indigenous Languages,* edited by Gina Cantoni. Flagstaff: Northern Arizona University.

———. 2008. "Heritage Languages in America: Tapping a 'Hidden' Resource." In *Advocating for English Learners: Selected Essays,* edited by James Crawford. Bristol, UK: Multilingual Matters.

Dumitrescu, Domnita. 2010. "Spanglish: An Ongoing Controversy." In *Building Communities and Making Connections*, edited by Susana V. Rivera-Mills and Juan Antonio Trujillo. Newcastle upon Tyne, UK: Cambridge Scholars.

Espinosa, Aurelio M. 1909. "Studies in New Mexican Spanish. Part I: Phonology." *Revue de Dialectologie Romane* 1:157–239.

———. 1911. *The Spanish Language in New Mexico and Southern Colorado*. Santa Fe: New Mexican Print Company.

———. 1911–13. "Studies in New Mexican Spanish. Part II: Morphology." *Revue de Dialectologie Romane* 3:251–86; 4:241–56; 5:142–72.

———. 1914–15. "Studies in New Mexican Spanish, Part III: The English Elements." *Revue de Dialectologie Romane* 6:241–317.

———. 1917. "Speech Mixture in New Mexico: The Influence of the English Language on New Mexican Spanish." In *The Pacific Ocean in History*, edited by H. Stevens and H. Bolton. New York: Macmillan.

Fairclough, Marta. 2003. "El (denominado) Spanglish en los Estados Unidos." *Revista Internacional de Lingüística Iberoamericana* 1 (2): 185–204.

Fishman, Joshua A. 1964. "Language Maintenance and Language Shift as Fields of Inquiry." *Linguistics* 9:32–70.

———. 1965. "Who Speaks What Language to Whom and When?" *Linguistics* 2:67–88.

———. 1966. *Language Loyalty in the United States*. The Hague: Mouton.

———, ed. 1971. *Advances in the Sociology of Language*, vol. 1. The Hague: Mouton de Gruyter.

———. 2001. *Reversing Language Shift*. Bristol, UK: Multicultural Matters.

Galindo, Letticia. 1995. "Language Attitudes toward Spanish and English Varieties: A Chicano Perspective." *Hispanic Journal of Behavioral Sciences* 17 (1): 77–99.

———. 1996. "Language Use and Language Attitudes: A Study of Border Women." *Bilingual Review/La Revista Bilingüe* 21 (1): 5–17.

García, Ofelia. 1993. "From Goya Portraits to Goya Beans: Elite Traditions and Popular Streams in US Spanish Language Policy." *Southwest Journal of Linguistics* 12:69–86.

———. 2007. "Lenguas e identidades en mundos hispanohablantesz: Desde una posición plurilingüe y minoritaria." In *Lingüística aplicada del español*, edited by Manel Lacorte. Madrid: Arco.

———. 2009. "Racializing the Language Practices of US Latinos: Impact on their Education." In *How the United States Racializes Latinos: White Hegemony and Its Consequences*, edited by José Cobas, Joe Feagin, and Jorge Duany. Boulder, CO: Paradigm.

———. 2010. "Latino Language Practices and Literacy Education in the US." In *Ethnolinguistic Diversity and Education: Language, Literacy and Culture*, edited by Marcia Farr, Lisya Selone, and Juyoung Song. New York: Routledge.

García, Ofelia, and Lesley Bartlett. 2007. "A Speech Community Model of Bilingual Education: Educating Latino Newcomers in the US." *International Journal of Bilingual Education and Bilingualism* 10:1–25.

García, Ofelia, and Ricardo Otheguy. 1988. "The Language Situation of Cuban Americans." In *Language Diversity: Problem or Resource?*, edited by Sandra McKay and Sauling Wong. New York: Harper & Row.

García, Ofelia, J. L. Morín, and K. Rivera. 2001. "How Threatened Is the Spanish of New York Puerto Ricans?" In *Can Threatened Languages Be Saved? Reversing Language Shift*, edited by Joshua Fishman. New York: Multilingual Matters.

García Delgado, José L. 2010. *El sector energético ante un nuevo escenario.* Madrid: Civitas Ediciones.

González, Nora, and Irene Wherritt. 1990. "Spanish Language Use in West Liberty, Iowa." In *Spanish in the United States: Sociolinguistic Issues,* edited by John Bergen. Washington, DC: Georgetown University Press.

Gray, Edward. 1912. "The Spanish Language in New Mexico: A National Resource." *University of New Mexico Bulletin Sociological Series* 1 (2): 37–52.

Grosjean, Francois. 1982. *Life with Two Languages: An Introduction to Bilingualism.* Cambridge, MA: Harvard University Press.

Heller, Monica, and Marilyn Martin-Jones. 2001. *Voices of Authority: Education and Linguistic Difference.* Westport, CT: Ablex.

Hernández-Chávez, Eduardo. 1989. "The Role of Suppressive Language Policies in Language Shift and Language Loss." *Estudios Fronterizos* 8:123–35.

Hernández-Chávez, Eduardo, Andrew Cohen, and Anthony Beltramo, eds. 1975. *El lenguaje de los Chicanos: Regional and Social Characteristics Used by Mexican Americans.* Arlington, VA: Center for Applied Linguistics.

Hidalgo, Margarita. 1984. "Attitudes and Behavior toward English in Juarez, Mexico." *Anthropological Linguistics* 26 (4): 163–97.

———. 1986. "Language Contact, Language Loyalty, and Language Prejudice on the Mexican Border." *Language and Society* 15:193–220.

———. 1987. "Español mexicano y español chicano: problemas y propuestas fundamentales." *Language Problems and Language Planning* 11 (2): 166–93.

———. 1988. "Perceptions of Spanish/English Code-Switching in Juarez, Mexico." In *Research Issues and Problems in United States Spanish I,* edited by Dennis Bixler-Marquez, Jacob Ornstein, and George Green. Edinburg: University of Texas–Pan American.

———. 1993. "The Dialectics of Spanish Language Loyalty and Maintenance on the US–Mexico Border: A Two-Generation Study." In *Spanish in the United States: Linguistic Contact and Diversity,* edited by Ana Roca and John Lipski. New York: Mouton de Gruyter.

Hudson-Edwards, Alan, and Garland D. Bills. 1982. "Intergenerational Language Shift in an Albuquerque Barrio." In *Spanish in the United States: Sociolinguistic Aspects,* edited by Jon Amastae and Lucía Elías-Olivares. Cambridge: Cambridge University Press.

Hurtado, Aída, and Patricia Gurin. 1987. "Ethnic Identity and Bilingual Attitudes." *Hispanic Journal of Behavioral Sciences* 9 (1): 1–18.

Hutchison, Ray. 1988. "A Critique of Race, Ethnicity and Social Class in Recent Leisure-Recreation Research." *Journal of Leisure Research* 20 (1): 10–30.

Jenkins, Devin L. 2010a. "Más allá del Mississippi: Demographic Change and Scholarly Shift in the Spanish-Speaking Southwest." Presidential address, Thirty-Ninth LASSO Conference, New Mexico State University, Las Cruces.

———. 2010b. "The State(s) of Spanish in the Southwest: A Comparative Study of Language Maintenance and Socioeconomic Variables." In *Spanish of the US Southwest: A Language in Transition,* edited by Susana V. Rivera-Mills and Daniel J. Villa. Madrid: Iberoamericana/Vervuert.

Labov, William. 1970. "The Study of Language in Its Social Context." *Studium Generale* 23: 30-87.

———. 1972. *Sociolinguistic Patterns*. Philadelphia: University of Pennsylvania Press.

Lacorte, Manel, and Jennifer Leeman, eds. 2009. *Español en Estados Unidos y en otros contextos de contacto: Sociolingüística, ideología y pedagogía/Spanish in the United States and Other Contact Environments: Sociolinguistics, Ideology and Pedagogy*. Madrid: Iberoamericana.

Lee, Sharon M., and Barry Edmonston. 2005. "New Marriages, New Families: US Racial and Hispanic Intermarriage." *Population Bulletin* 60:3–36.

Leeman, Jennifer. 2004. "Racializing Language: A History of Linguistic Ideologies in the US Census." *Journal of Language and Politics* 3 (3): 507–34.

———. 2005. "Engaging Critical Pedagogy: Spanish for Native Speakers." *Foreign Language Annals* 38 (1): 35–45.

———. 2006–7. "The Value of Spanish: Shifting Ideologies in US Language Teaching." *ADFL Bulletin* 38 (1–2): 32–39.

———. 2010. "Introduction. The Sociopolitics of Heritage Language Education." In *Spanish of the US Southwest: A Language in Transition*, edited by Susana V. Rivera-Mills and Daniel J. Villa. Madrid: Iberoamericana.

Leeman, Jennifer, Lisa Rabin, and Esperanza Román-Mendoza. 2011. "Identity and Activism in Heritage Language Education." *Modern Language Journal* 95 (4): 481–95.

Le Page, Robert B., and Andree Tabouret-Keller. 1985. *Acts of Identity: Creole-Based Approaches to Language and Ethnicity*. New York: Cambridge University Press.

Lippi-Green, Rosina. 1997. *English with an Accent: Language, Ideology, and Discrimination in the United States*. London: Routledge.

Lipski, John M. 1986. "Central American Spanish in the United States: El Salvador." *Aztlán* 17:91–124.

———. 2000. "The Linguistic Situation of Central Americans." In *New Immigrants in the United States*, edited by Sandra McKay and Sau-ling Wong. Cambridge: Cambridge University Press.

———. 2008. *Varieties of Spanish in the United States*. Washington, DC: Georgetown University Press.

Lope Blanch, Juan M. 1990. *El español hablado en el suroeste de los Estados Unidos: Materiales para su estudio*. Mexico City: Universidad Nacional Autónoma de México.

López, David E. 1978. "Chicano Language Loyalty in an Urban Setting." *Sociology and Social Research* 62:267–78.

Lynch, Andrew. 2000. "Spanish-Speaking Miami in Sociolinguistic Perspective: Bilingualism, Recontact, and Language Maintenance among the Cuban-Origin Population." In *Research on Spanish in the United States: Linguistic Issues and Challenges*, edited by Ana Roca. Somerville, MA: Cascadilla Press.

———. 2008. "The Linguistic Similarities of Spanish Heritage and Second Language Learners." *Foreign Language Annals* 41:252–81.

Martínez, Glenn. 2003a. "Classroom-Based Dialect Awareness in Heritage Language Instruction: A Critical Applied Linguistic Approach." *Heritage Language Journal* 1. Available at www.heritagelanguages.org.

———. 2003b. "Perceptions of Dialect in a Changing Society: Folk Linguistics along the Texas–Mexico Border." *Journal of Sociolinguistics* 7:38–49.

May, Darlene. 1966. "Notas sobre el tex-mex." *Boletín del Instituto Caro y Cuervo* 70:17–19.

McCullough, Robert E., and Devin L. Jenkins. 2005. "Out with the Old, In with the New? Recent Trends in Spanish Language Use in Colorado." *Southwest Journal of Linguistics* 24:91–110.

Mejías, Hugo, and Pamela Anderson. 1988. "Attitudes toward Spanish Use on the South Texas Border." *Hispania* 71 (2): 400–407.

Mendieta, Eva. 1994. "Índices de mantenimiento del español en el noroeste de Indiana." *Southwest Journal of Linguistics* 13 (1–2): 71–83.

———. 1997. "Actitudes y creencias en la comunidad hispana del noroeste de Indiana." *Hispanic Linguistics* 9 (2): 257–300.

Mendieta, Eva, and Isabel Molina. 2000. "Caracterización léxica del español hablado en el noroeste de Indiana." *Southwest Journal of Linguistics* 19 (2): 63–72.

Mills, Susana V. 2005. "Acculturation and Communicative Need in the Process of Language Shift: The Case of an Arizona Community." *Southwest Journal of Linguistics* 24:111–25.

Milroy, Lesley. 1980. *Language and Social Networks*. Oxford: Basil Blackwell.

Mora, Marie T., Daniel J. Villa, and Alberto Dávila. 2005. "Language Maintenance among the Children of Immigrants: A Comparison of Border States with Other Regions of the US." *Southwest Journal of Linguistics* 24:127–44.

———. 2006. "Language Shift and Maintenance among the Children of Immigrants in the US: Evidence in the Census for Spanish Speakers and Other Language Minorities." *Spanish in Context* 3:239–54.

Morrill, D. B. 1918. "The Spanish Language Problem." *New Mexico Journal of Education* 14:6–7.

Ortíz, Leroy. 1975. "A Sociolinguistic Study of Language Maintenance in the Northern New Mexico Community of Arroyo Seco." Ph.D. diss., University of New Mexico, Albuquerque.

Otheguy, Ricardo, Ana Celia Zentella, and David Livert. 2007. "Language and Dialect Contact in Spanish in New York: Toward the Formation of a Speech Community." *Language* 83 (4): 770–802.

Pearson, Barbara, and Arlene McGee. 1993. "Language Choice in Hispanic-Background Junior High School Students in Miami." In *Spanish in the US: Linguistic Contact and Diversity*, edited by Ana Roca and John Lipski. Berlin: Mouton de Gruyter.

Pedraza, Pedro, Jr. 1985. "Language Maintenance among New York Puerto Ricans." In *Spanish Language Use and Public Life in the United States*, edited by Lucia Elías-Olivares, Elizabeth A. Leone, René Cisneros, and John R. Gutiérrez. Berlin: Mouton de Gruyter.

Peñalosa, Fernando. 1980. *Chicano Sociolinguistics*. Rowley, MA: Newbury House.

Plaza, Dwaine. 2009. "Transnational Identity Maintenance via the Internet: A Content Analysis of Websites Constructed by Second Generation Caribbean-Origin Students in Post-Secondary Institutions." *Journal of the Sociology of Self-Knowledge* 7 (4): 37–52.

Potowski, Kim. 2004a. "Spanish Language Shift in Chicago." *Southwest Journal of Linguistics* 23:87–116.

———. 2004b. "Student Spanish Use and Investment in a Dual Immersion Classroom: Implications for Second Language Acquisition and Heritage Language Maintenance." *Modern Language Journal* 88:75–101.

Potowski, Kim, and Janine Matts. 2008. "MexiRicans: Interethnic Language and Identity." *Journal of Language, Identity, and Education* 7:137–60.

Resnick, Melvyn C. 1988. "Beyond the Ethnic Community: Spanish Language Roles and Maintenance in Miami." *International Journal of the Sociology of Language* 69:89–104.

Richardson, Chad. 1999. *Batos, bolillos, pochos and pelados: Class and Culture on the Southwest Texas Border*. Austin: University of Texas Press.

Rivera-Mills, Susana V. 2000a. "Intraethnic Attitudes among Hispanics in a Northern California Community." In *Research on Spanish in the United States: Linguistic Issues and Challenges*, edited by Ana Roca. Somerville, MA: Cascadilla Press.

———. 2000b. *New Perspectives on Current Sociolinguistic Knowledge with Regard to Language Use, Proficiency, and Attitudes among Hispanics in the US: The Case of a Rural Northern California Community*. Lewiston, NY: Mellen Press.

———. 2002. "Acculturation and Communicative Need: Language Shift in an Ethnically Diverse Hispanic Community." *Southwest Journal of Linguistics* 19 (2): 211–24.

———. 2007. "The Fourth Generation: Turning Point for Language Shift or Mere Coincidence." Paper presented at Twenty-First Conference on Spanish in the United States and Sixth Conference on Spanish in Contact with Other Languages, Arlington, VA.

Rivera-Mills, Susana V., and Juan Antonio Trujillo. 2010. *Building Communities and Making Connections*. Newcastle upon Tyne, UK: Cambridge Scholars.

Rivera-Mills, Susana V., and Daniel J. Villa. 2010. "Introduction. Spanish of the US Southwest: A Language in Transition." In *Spanish of the US Southwest: A Language in Transition*, edited by Susana V. Rivera-Mills and Daniel J. Villa. Madrid: Iberoamericana.

Roca, Ana. 1991. "Language Maintenance and Language Shift in the Cuban American Community of Miami: The 1990s and Beyond." In *Language Planning: Festschrift in Honor of Joshua A. Fishman on the Occasion of his 65th Birthday, Vol. III*, edited by David F. Marshall. Amsterdam: John Benjamins.

Roca, Ana, and M. Cecilia Colombi, eds. 2003. *Mi lengua: Spanish as a Heritage Language in the United States*. Washington, DC: Georgetown University Press.

Romaine, Suzanne. 1995. *Bilingualism*, 2nd ed. Oxford: Blackwell.

———. 2004. "The Bilingual and Multilingual Community." In *The Handbook of Bilingualism*, edited by Tej Bhatia and William Ritchie. Cambridge: Blackwell.

Ryan, Ellen B., and Miguel Carranza. 1975. "Evaluative Reactions toward Speakers of Standard English and Mexican-American Accented English." *Journal of Personality and Social Psychology* 31:855–63.

Ryan, Ellen B., Miguel Carranza, and Robert Moffie. 1977. "Reactions toward Varying Degrees of Accentedness in Speech of Spanish-English Bilinguals." *Language and Speech* 20:267–73.

Sánchez, Rosaura. 1972. "Nuestra circunstancia lingüística." *El Grito* 6:45–74.

———. 1983. *Chicano Discourse*. Rowley, MA: Newbury House.

Santa Ana, Otto, and Claudia Parodi. 1998. "Modeling the Speech Community: Configuration and Variable Types in the Mexican Spanish Setting." *Language in Society* 27:23–51.

Sayer, Peter. 2008. "Demystifying Language Mixing: Spanglish in School." *Journal of Latinos and Education* 7 (2): 94–112.

Silva-Corvalán, Carmen. 1994. *Language Contact and Change: Spanish in Los Angeles*. New York: Oxford University Press.

Silverstein, Michael 1979. "Language Structure and Linguistic Ideology." In *The Elements: A Parasession on Linguistic Units and Levels*, edited by Paul R. Clyne, William Hanks, and Carol Hofbauer. Chicago: Chicago Linguistic Society.

Solé, Carlos A. 1979. "Selección idiomática entre la nueva generación de cubano-americanos." *Bilingual Review/Revista Bilingüe* 6:1–10.

———. 1980. "Language Usage Patterns among a Young Generation of Cuban-Americans." In *Festschrift for Jacob Ornstein*, edited by Edward Blansitt and Richard Teschner. Rowley, MA: Newbury House.

———. 1982. "Language Loyalty and Language Attitudes among Cuban Americans." *Bilingual Education for Hispanic Students in the United States*, edited by Joshua Fishman and George Keller. New York: Teachers College Press.

Solé, Yolanda. 1990. "Bilingualism: Stable or Transitional? The Case of Spanish in the United States." *International Journal of the Society of Language* 84:35–80.

Toribio, Almeida Jacqueline. 2000. "¡Spanglish?! Bite Your Tongue!: Spanish–English Code-Switching among Latinos." In *Reflexiones 1999*, edited by Richard Flores. Austin: Center for Mexican American Studies.

Torres, Lourdes. 1997. *Puerto Rican Discourse: A Sociolinguistic Study of a New York Suburb*. Mahwah, NJ: Lawrence Erlbaum Associates.

Train, Robert W. 2010. "Reducing Spanish on the Margins of Empire: A Historical Perspective on Ideologies and Ecologies of Language Education in Sonoma County, California." In *Spanish of the US Southwest: A Language in Transition*, edited by Susana V. Rivera-Mills and Daniel J. Villa. Madrid: Iberoamericana.

US Office of Education. 1972. *Teaching Spanish in School and College to Native Speakers of Spanish*. Washington, DC: US Government Printing Office.

Valdés, Guadalupe, and Rodolfo García-Moya. 1976. *Teaching Spanish to the Spanish Speaking: Theory and Practice*. San Antonio: Trinity University.

Veltman, Calvin J. 1988. *The Future of the Spanish Language in the United States*. New York: Hispanic Policy Development Project.

———. 1990. "The Status of the Spanish Language in the United States at the Beginning of the 21st Century." *International Migration Review* 24:108–23.

Villa, Daniel J. 2009. "General versus Standard Spanish: Establishing Empirical Norms for the Study of US Spanish." In *Spanish in the United States and Other Contact Environments*, edited by Manel Lacorte and Jennifer Leeman. Madrid: Iberoamericana.

Villa, Daniel, and Susana V. Rivera-Mills. 2010. "An Integrated Multi-Generational Model for Language Maintenance and Shift: The Case of Spanish in the Southwest." *Spanish in Context* 6 (1): 26–42.

Wenger, Ettiene. 1998. *Communities of Practice: Learning, Meaning, and Identity*. Cambridge: Cambridge University Press.

Zentella, Ana Celia. 1985. "The Fate of Spanish in the US: The Puerto Rican Experience." In *The Language of Inequality*, edited by Joan Manes and Nessa Wolfson. The Hague: Mouton.

———. 1997. "Latino Youth at Home, in Their Communities, and in School: The Language Link—Latino Communities: Resources for Educational Change." *Special Issue of Education and Urban Society* 30 (1): 22–30.

———. 2002. "Latin@ Languages and Identities." In *Latinos: Remaking America*, edited by Marcelo Suárez-Orozco and Mariela Páez. Berkeley: University of California Press.

CHAPTER 2

Investigating Language Ideologies in Spanish as a Heritage Language

Jennifer Leeman, George Mason University

You are surrounded by true friends.

I N THE 1990S the study of language ideologies gained wide cun. within linguistic anthropology and sociolinguistics, and this theoretical framework is also proving valuable in the analysis of instruction in Spanish as a heritage language (SHL). Language ideologies consist of values and belief systems regarding language generally, specific languages or language varieties, or particular language practices and ways of using language (Kroskrity 2004; Woolard 1998). Examples of language ideologies include notions about the relative worth of different languages, what constitutes "correct" usage, how particular groups of people "should" speak in given situations, whether minority languages are compatible with citizenship, and whether one can "truly" belong to a given ethnic group without speaking the language associated with it. Although there are multiple understandings of exactly how to define language ideologies, there is wide agreement that they are rarely, if ever, exclusively about language. Instead, language ideologies mediate between language and broader social structures, and they are intertwined with ideologies about other social phenomena—such as gender, socioeconomic status, race, and nation—as well as with beliefs about the people who speak given languages or varieties or who engage in specific language practices.

Research on language ideologies has some overlap with studies of language attitudes. However, language attitude research has its roots in the field of psychology and thus tends to emphasize individual beliefs and to pay less attention to the politics of language. In contrast, the study of language ideologies, and of the language policies and actions that embody them, has emphasized the connection of ideologies to questions of power. This connection, as well as a focus on shared rather than individual beliefs about language, is apparent in Irvine's (1989, 255) definition of language ideologies as "the cultural system of ideas about social and linguistic relationships, together with their loading of moral and political interests." Thus, the study of language ideologies not only entails the examination of belief systems and their interaction with other social systems; it also explores how language ideologies emerge from and reinforce power relationships, as well as how certain ways of thinking about language simultaneously interact with other social structures. A key goal of research on language ideologies is to understand how seemingly commonsense and taken-for-granted notions about language are complicit in the reproduction of social hierarchies. For example, researchers have analyzed how monolingualist ideologies of language—which imagine monolingualism as a universal norm and link multilingualism to cognitive confusion, intergroup conflict, and a lack of national cohesiveness—contribute to the portrayal of bilingual speakers as intellectually compromised and of minority languages as inherently unpatriotic (Leeman 2004, in press; Schmidt 2002; Urciuoli 1996).

Because school is a key site where young people are socialized into hegemonic value systems, research on pedagogical policies, practices, and materials can shed light on how language ideologies are reproduced in SHL instruction. In particular, research on language ideologies in SHL can reveal and problematize implicit assumptions regarding the goals of language instruction, the value of Spanish, the kinds of people who speak Spanish, the relationship of Spanish to "authentic" Latino identity, and which kind of Spanish is "best," among other issues. In addition, research on language ideologies in SHL can also deepen our understanding of the relationship between educational contexts and language ideologies circulating in the broader society, such as those that privilege varieties of Spanish spoken by monolingual elites outside the United States and portray the language practices of bilinguals as deficient. Furthermore, by critically analyzing the language ideologies reflected and reinforced in SHL, this kind of research can challenge dominant hierarchies and suggest directions for a more socially responsive pedagogy.

LANGUAGE IDEOLOGIES AND SHL: THE THEORETICAL FRAMEWORK

In his synthesis of research on language ideologies, Kroskrity (2004) identifies five interrelated "levels of organization" or layers of meaning that characterize languages ideologies. This section defines these five levels and discusses their application to SHL. The first feature of language ideologies is that they are linked to the social, political, or economic interests of particular groups of people. Notions about which varieties of language are "standard," "correct," or aesthetically more pleasing are not neutral or arbitrary, and they serve to legitimate the accrual of disproportionate privilege, power, and material resources to speakers of preferred varieties while rationalizing the subordination of other language varieties and the people who speak them. So, too, the ideological linking of nation-states to single languages benefits those whose status and power are linked to national institutions. For example, when the Real Academia Española and the Instituto Cervantes represent Spanish as a unified language that allows for "diversity within unity" and they portray the development of "pan-Hispanic norms" as a consensual process among equals—such as in the Academia's *Diccionario pan-hispánico de dudas* (Pan-Hispanic dictionary of doubts)—it reflects the political and economic interests of the Spanish state as well as of the corporations and financial institutions that are seeking to maintain or increase their influence in Latin America (Del Valle 2009; Paffey and Mar-Molinero 2009).

The connection between language ideologies and specific interests is also apparent in SHL, and in Spanish teaching in the United States more broadly, where there is a historical tendency to view the literary and cultural production and the linguistic varieties associated with Spain as superior or more "legitimate" than those of the Americas. As Garcia (1993) and Villa (2002) have argued, this privileging of European Spanish has enhanced the cultural capital of Spaniards and (primarily Anglo) second-language (L2) speakers of this variety at the expense of Latin Americans and US Latinos, both inside and outside the academy.

Although researchers emphasize that language ideologies are culturally constructed, this should not be interpreted to mean that they are uniform within a society or a sociocultural group. Instead, ideologies are multiple and variable, which is the second level of organization identified by Kroskrity (2004). To some extent, this variation is a product of the multiplicity of groups with which speakers identify; conceptions of language can vary by gender, race, and class, as well as other social categories. In addition, not all members of a particular group take up dominant ideologies, and sometimes they actively resist them. Further, because dominant conceptions of language are situated in particular sociohistorical contexts, and because they are alternatively reinforced and resisted, language ideologies evolve over time. In SHL, this diachronic and synchronic variability is evident, for example, in perceptions of code-switching and the use of English loan words. Whereas many people, numerous language instructors among them, view codemixing as a sign of deficient linguistic knowledge or laziness, many others see it as a reflection of linguistic creativity and sophisticated bilingual abilities. The contextual variability of ideologies is also evident in the fact that in the United States, speaking varieties of Spanish that reveal the influence of English syntax or lexicon may open one up for disparagement or even assertions of "semilingualism," whereas outside the United States, the ability to sprinkle one's Spanish with Anglicisms is often associated with symbolic capital. Multiple conceptions of language sometimes coexist peacefully, whereas at other times competition and contestation lead to intense ideological debates and power struggles.

A third feature of language ideologies is that speakers' conscious awareness of them is variable within a given community and across ideologies. Individuals are not always cognizant of the language ideologies to which they subscribe; in some cases, ideologies are explicitly articulated and advocated for; in others, they emerge from, and are reflected in, practice and may not be available for conscious analysis. For example, in the early twentieth century the notion that French and German were inherently better suited for literary and intellectual production than other modern languages was explicitly stated as an argument for their being given priority in high school and postsecondary education (Leeman 2006–7). So, too, it is not uncommon to hear overt calls for the privileging of Peninsular Spanish over other varieties on the basis of Spain being the *madre patria*. In other cases, speakers may not be able to articulate the ideologies to which they subscribe, nor be aware of the underlying assumptions and values. For example, in their exhortations for immigrants to "learn English," and their belief that many newcomers "refuse" to do so, some opponents of language access policies tacitly participate in a dominant US ideology that constructs English acquisition as easy and rapid, and portrays any lack of English ability as a refusal to assimilate.

The degree to which individuals are aware of their own language ideologies is unrelated to the role of those ideological positions in promoting specific social or political interests, regardless of the individuals' explicit intentions. For example, people who subscribe to notions regarding the supposed purity and authority of European varieties of Spanish are not necessarily trying to promote Spanish economic interests in Latin America, privilege Spaniards and L2 speakers of Peninsular Spanish in language departments in the United States, or bolster Latin American racial hierarchies that subordinate people of indigenous or African descent. Moreover, they may not have any sense that their ideas about Spanish are in any way related to such issues. By the same token, even individuals who are negatively affected by particular conceptions of language may embrace the very ideologies that subordinate them. Indeed, speakers of contact varieties of Spanish are often vocal in their defense of language purity, just as speakers of stigmatized language varieties sometimes internalize dominant norms about the inadequacy of their own speech. Part of the power of language ideologies derives from the fact that they are naturalized and come to be understood as common sense, rather than a particular way of seeing the world. Once language ideologies and the interests they serve are rendered invisible, even people who are negatively affected by them often consent to their authority.

The fourth characteristic signaled by Kroskrity (2004) is that language ideologies mediate between social structures and forms of talk. The indexical relationships between linguistic phenomena and social systems, and in particular the linking of specific linguistic forms to specific sociocultural features, are shaped by ideologies. Irvine and Gal (2000) identify three ideological processes that are central to the assigning of social meaning to linguistic variation: iconization, fractal recursivity, and erasure. In iconization, "linguistic features that index social groups or activities appear to be iconic representations of them, as if a linguistic feature somehow depicted or displayed a social group's inherent nature or essence" (Irvine and Gall 2000, 37). This is evident, for example, in the traditional linguistic descriptions of Galician as archaic or conservative in comparison with Castilian Spanish, which is portrayed as innovative and progressive. As López (2007) shows, these representations are not objective descriptions but instead reflect and reproduce a larger ideological project to elevate Castile and naturalize both its political and linguistic dominance.

Fractal recursivity refers to the tendency of ideological features that differentiate among social groups or establish social hierarchies to be deployed at multiple levels or scales. Thus, the same features that distinguish between one group and another can also be used to discriminate within groups and subgroups recursively. For example, in her research in the Basque country, Echeverría (2003) found that the use of Basque (Euskerra) rather than Spanish was constructed as masculine and rural. At the same time, pronoun usage within Basque was ideologically linked to gender identities. Recursive distinctions are also apparent in the ideological construction of languages in the United States; all non-English languages are seen as suspect, but distinctions are made among different languages, with Spanish seen as particularly un-American and dangerous. Similarly, just as French has been constructed as better suited than Spanish for intellectual pursuits, European Spanish is favored over American varieties, and South American varieties are privileged compared with US varieties.

Finally, erasure is the process whereby information that is inconsistent with a particular ideological representation is rendered invisible. For example, the portrayal of the United States as a monolingual, English-speaking nation obscures its long history of multilingualism, just as the frequent referencing of "Spanish-speaking countries" and "Spanish-speaking world" in SHL and L2 Spanish textbooks discursively erases multilingualism in Latin America and Spain. Along the same lines, pedagogical guidelines such as the national *Standards for Foreign Language Learning* (2006) that frame university students of Spanish and local Latino communities as mutually exclusive categories constitute an erasure of heritage language speakers in the classroom (Leeman 2011).

The fifth level pointed to by Kroskrity (2004) is that ideologies of language play an important role in the performance of identity. It is now widely accepted that identity is not a single category that an individual "has." Instead, people construct and perform a constellation of different identities that change over time and according to context. Further, identity categories are not fixed a priori but are negotiated and constructed through practice and interaction with others. Thus, identity categories are socially constructed, and our identities emerge from some combination of the identities that we claim for ourselves and the identities that are ascribed to us by others. Language is an important means whereby individuals both perform and ascribe identities to others, and these identities, as well as the qualities they index, are tied up with ideologies of language.

Ideologies linking Latino identity to Spanish have been central to SHL instruction since its inception (Leeman, Rabin, and Román-Mendoza 2011b), with the construct of *heritage speaker* generally understood to reference not just linguistic knowledge or experience but also an ethnoracial identity linked to particular cultural knowledge or experience (for additional discussion of identity and SHL, see chapter 9 in this volume, by Potowski). The ideological coupling of Spanish and Latino identity is of course not limited to the SHL context, and it can be seen in the widespread essentialized conception of Latinidad, in which "Spanish-speaking" and "Latino" are used almost interchangeably, contributing to the racialization of Spanish and the portrayal of Latinos as unwilling to assimilate to (monolingual) Anglophone culture (Leeman, in press). In educational contexts, the notion that Latino identity requires proficiency in Spanish has been mostly commonly discussed with regard to the pressure felt by US Latinos, who are said to be caught in a double-bind: They are marginalized by Anglophones for their "impure" English or their association with Spanish; but they are also ostracized by Hispanophones for not speaking Spanish, or for speaking the "wrong kind" of Spanish.

Language ideologies have been shown to play a role in the language practices of minority groups (Guardado 2009), and one area of language use where ideologies may have a particular impact is in favoring either language maintenance or shift (see also chapter 1 in this volume, by Rivera-Mills). For example, the hegemonic construction of the United States as a monolingual, English-speaking nation and the portrayal of minority languages as both a personal liability and also a threat to national unity is apt to promote language shift by leading some bilingual parents—even parents with limited English competence—to converse with their children in English (see, e.g., Martínez-Roldán and Malavé 2004). So, too, ideologies and discursive practices that construct public space as white—such as speaking "mock Spanish," a covertly racist pseudo-Spanish (cf. Hill 2008)—and represent Spanish as the language of a racialized underclass—evident, for example, in Newt Gingrich's widely publicized characterization of Spanish as "the language of living in a ghetto"—may increase the likelihood that heritage speakers will give up their home language in favor of "the language of prosperity." In contrast, Bailey (2000) and Toribio (2000) suggest that among Dominicans in the United States, ideologies of race and language contribute to language maintenance, given that Spanish serves as a way to differentiate oneself from African Americans, regardless of similarities in phenotype, which underscores the fact that language ideologies and their implications are sociohistorically situated.

STANDARD LANGUAGE IDEOLOGY AND SHL

One of the most frequently researched language ideologies, particularly in the realm of SHL, is the standard language ideology. Although many laypeople and linguists alike use the term "standard language" to refer to language varieties perceived to be neutral, correct, uniform, and free of regionalisms, researchers working within the framework of language ideologies argue that given the inherent variability of language, such varieties do not actually exist (Milroy and Milroy 1999; Milroy 2007). Rather than actual varieties, "standard languages" are idealized abstractions sustained by the standard language ideology, or the bias toward modeling unchanging spoken language on written language, together with the conviction that the suppression of variation is both feasible and desirable (Lippi-Green 1994; Milroy 2007). Although "standard" varieties and the linguistic features associated with them typically are portrayed as inherently superior to "nonstandard" varieties and features, the elevation of particular varieties of language reflects the interests of powerful social groups and imbues their language practices with moral and intellectual authority and prestige.

The myth of the standard language circulates throughout societies and is buttressed both explicitly and implicitly by a wide variety of social and political institutions, such as in newspaper columns about "proper" or "correct" usage and in the entertainment industry's use of nonstandard features to index undesirable characteristics (Lippi-Green 1997). However, the educational system plays a central role in reproducing the standard language ideology; with their emphasis on inflexible grammar "rules" and "correct" usage, schools explicitly inculcate the notion that there is a single acceptable way to speak, and they mete out punishment to those who do not conform to the idealized norm. Students are routinely taught that nonstandard language is indicative of illogical or unintelligent thinking, as well as an obstacle to communication. In addition, the acquisition of the standard variety is portrayed as the key to academic and socioeconomic success, which downplays or ignores race-based and class-based discrimination and promotes adherence to linguistic authority (Macedo 1997).

Spanish is often described as a "pluricentric" language, meaning that there are multiple centers of linguistic prestige. Such descriptions usually posit a standard variety, sometimes referred to as the *norma culta* ("educated standard"), that is associated with the capital city of each country where Spanish is a national or official language. For example, Lope Blanch (2001) states that

> es evidente que en cada país hispanohablante existe una norma lingüística ejemplar, paradigmática, a la que los habitantes de cada nación tratan de aproximarse cuando de hablar bien se trata. Suele ella ser la norma culta de la ciudad capital: la madrileña para España, la bogotana para Colombia, la limeña para el Perú, etc.

> it is clear that in every Spanish-speaking country there is a paradigmatic, exemplar linguistic norm that the inhabitants of each nation try to approximate when their intention is to speak well. It is usually the educated norm of each capital city: the one from Madrid for Spain, the one from Bogotá for Colombia, the one from Lima for Peru, etc.

Although at first glance the recognition of the lack of a single universal standard appears to acknowledge the variation inherent in all language, the assertion that each nation has its own standard simultaneously negates geographic, social, and individual variation within nations, thus both reaffirming the standard language ideology and highlighting its link to constructions of nationalism. Further, the notion of the *norma culta* privileges the language of the educated elite, assumes a consensus among speakers regarding the superiority of this variety, and erases the sociopolitical implications of linguistic hierarchies.

Given the prominence of educational institutions in reproducing language ideologies and in socializing students into dominant values and producing consent, it is not surprising that much of the research on language ideologies in SHL pertains to the standard language ideology. The impetus for the creation of SHL programs emerged from the Chicano civil rights movement of the 1960s and 1970s and the sense that educational policy favoring monolingual English schooling denied Latinos their linguistic birthright. Nonetheless, even while seeking to elevate the status of Spanish relative to English, early SHL instruction did not challenge linguistic hierarchies *within* Spanish. Instruction was, and in many cases still is, oriented toward the acquisition of an idealized invariant prestige variety—alternately referred to as "standard Spanish," "academic Spanish," "*la norma culta*," or "universal Spanish"—and the suppression of "incorrect" forms. The standard language ideology is also reproduced via the treatment of linguistic variation in SHL educational materials and practices, which tends to acknowledge geographic variation while maintaining an overarching emphasis on uniformity. Further, as Carreira (2000) shows, the typical emphasis on lexical variation fails to highlight the systematic nature of intervarietal differences. Stressing the legitimacy of regional differences does little to validate the varieties and practices that are associated with marginalized social groups. Instead, linguistic practices common in multilingual contexts (e.g., code-switching and borrowing) and language varieties that do not conform to a *norma culta* are portrayed as nonstandard and, as such, incompatible with academic or professional pursuits. The weight of linguistic authority can be seen in the many textbooks' paired lists of structures and expressions labeled "se dice" ("one says") and "no se dice" ("one does not/should not say"), where the list of proscribed items consists solely of things that many SHL students do in fact say.

LANGUAGE IDEOLOGIES AND SHL:
POLICIES, PRACTICES, AND PRODUCTS

As was noted in previous sections, language ideologies are embodied in discourse and everyday practice, and they often become so naturalized that even people who are negatively affected by language ideologies come to accept them unquestioningly, which lends them even more power. Research on language ideologies

turns a critical eye to commonsense notions of language and seeks to problematize "speakers' . . . language and discourse as well as their positionality (in political economic systems) in shaping beliefs, proclamations, and evaluations of
linguistic forms and discursive practices" (Kroskrity 2004, 498).

Only recently have researchers and educators begun to explicitly examine SHL
within the framework of language ideologies. Therefore, this section's discussion
of language ideologies in SHL policies, sites, practices, and artifacts both provides
a synthesis of previous research and points the way forward by outlining the
domains for future research. Included in this discussion are studies that, though
not conducted within the theoretical framework of language ideologies, nonetheless have critically examined SHL educational policy, curricula, teaching materials, and pedagogical practices and have analyzed the portrayal of different
language varieties and language practices; the reproduction and naturalization
of linguistic hierarchies; and the relationship of classroom practices to broader
ideologies of cultural, racial, and national identities. Because heritage speakers of
Spanish often enroll in "traditional" Spanish courses, and because SHL courses
are now frequently housed in Spanish departments, studies of ideologies circulating more broadly in Spanish language education can also offer insights on language ideologies in SHL.

Educational Policy

Decisions about the kinds of knowledge and skills that should be included in
schools are inherently ideological, because they reflect implicit notions about,
for example, whether education is a right or a commodity, the "value" of different types of knowledge and experiences, and the societal role and goals of education—such as training the populace as a workforce, socializing children into
dominant culture and values, or preparing students for active engagement in a
democratic society.

The extremely limited options for L2 study at the K–12 level, and the fact that
language instruction is often among the first programs to be put on the chopping
block in hard economic times or in movements to "return to basics," is indicative of the relative lack of importance given to language education in the United
States, despite the surging popularity of discourses on globalization, diversity,
and preparing students for a globalized world. However, whereas L2 instruction
suffers from low status, chronic underfunding, and benign neglect, bilingual
education and SHL are often the targets of open opposition. This "differential
bilingualism" (Aparicio 2000)—or the simultaneous positive portrayal of L2
acquisition by Anglophones and negative construction of heritage speakers' cir-
cumstantial bilingualism—and the policies that embody it can contribute to feelings of shame and linguistic insecurity on the part of SHL students (Curtin
2007). Hostility toward SHL and Spanish language maintenance is tied up with

the ideological construction of the United States as a white, monolingual, English-speaking nation and the racialization of Spanish discussed above. Monolingual ideologies are also reflected in the tendency to frame L2 Spanish learning and learners as the norm and SHL as the exception, even in school districts where a majority of students come from Spanish-speaking homes (for further discussion of SHL policy, see chapter 3 in this volume, by Martínez).

Educational Contexts and Departments of Spanish

Although one might assume that Spanish departments would promote a more positive view of bilingualism, or that Spanish language educators might have a more critical analytical perspective on language, in fact Spanish departments are a key site for the reproduction of monolingualist and standard language ideologies. As Valdés and her colleagues (2003) documented in their ethnographic study of a university Spanish department, the symbolic elevation of monolingual Spanish and the concomitant subordination of the Spanish of US Latinos run through much departmental discourse—such as in discussions of undergraduate teaching and graduate coursework—and are also reflected in the relative status of faculty members. For instance, in interviews with Latina undergraduates at an elite liberal arts college, Urciuoli (2008, 268) found that many who enrolled in Spanish courses had experienced the portrayal of their home varieties as "regional" or "nonstandard," and although this portrayal was not universal, it was the "ideological default position." Urciuoli's study also highlighted the linguistic insecurity that some students experienced as a result of the tendency among Latino student organizations to construct Latino identity and authenticity as dependent on Spanish proficiency.

Course Goals and Teaching Practices

Course goals are the specific language-related learning outcomes that the curriculum and pedagogical practices are designed to foster. Curriculum design necessarily involves ideologies about what constitutes language (e.g., a collection of discrete grammar points vs. a sociocultural system of communication), what kind of Spanish is worth knowing, and the relative importance of linguistic, metalinguistic, and cultural knowledge, among other issues. In an early critique of the linguistic hierarchies embodied in SHL instruction, Valdés (1981) showed how many programs sought to eradicate the presumably substandard Spanish of bilingual and heritage speakers. Similarly, other early SHL research efforts, though focused primarily on the development of better pedagogical practices and teacher preparation, implicitly questioned the construction of SHL students' Spanish as inferior or illegitimate (for numerous examples, see Merino, Trueba, and Samaniego 1993; Valdés, Lozano, and García-Moya 1981).

In contrast with eradication-oriented approaches, Valdés (1981, 1997) and others advocated for SHL programs focusing on the expansion of students' linguistic repertoires to include prestige varieties and so-called academic registers, which was followed by the widespread adoption of pedagogical models based on the premise that only prestige varieties are "appropriate" for academic and professional settings. Researchers have critiqued the language ideologies underlying such appropriateness-based approaches, which on the surface appear to recognize the legitimacy of all varieties but are complicit in reproducing the standard language ideology and the privileged position of elite language varieties and practices (Fairclough 1992). In the case of SHL, an overriding emphasis on students' development of prestige varieties, "academic language," and formal writing conventions privileges these types of knowledge at the expense of others, presupposes that the goal of SHL students is to utilize Spanish in professional and academic domains, and can also inadvertently reproduce societal ideologies regarding Spanish and speakers of Spanish in the United States (Leeman 2005).

More and more schools and universities across the country are offering SHL courses (see chapter 10 in this volume, by Beaudrie), but for many SHL students, L2 Spanish courses are still the only option. Several recent ethnographic studies of university Spanish instruction have shown how L2 classroom discourses and practices sometimes reproduce negative stereotypes regarding Spanish and speakers of Spanish, present Spanish as a marketable asset, and reinforce monolingualist ideologies and practices (Pomerantz 2002, 2008). Classroom Spanish teaching practices were also found to reproduce broader language ideologies in Harklau's (2009) case study of two Latino high school students in the rural southeastern United States. Specifically, Harklau documented an elitist orientation to language and culture that marginalized the Latino students and relegated them to a position of inferiority relative to their white monolingual classmates.

Materials

Early examinations of textbooks in the field of language instruction tended to focus on the types of pedagogical approaches adopted, such as whether or not they included "communicative" activities. Such studies did not adopt a language ideologies approach to their analysis, nor did they explore the sociopolitical implications of different ways of conceptualizing language or language teaching, but nonetheless they revealed underlying notions about just what a language is, what students ought to learn, and how language learning takes place. In recent years, researchers have examined the readings included and the topics covered in Spanish textbooks in order to explore assumptions about "typical" students and their reasons for studying Spanish. For example, Herman's (2007) critical analysis of L2 Spanish textbooks revealed that students were imagined to be white, heterosexual, middle-class monolinguals who would likely encounter

Spanish in sightseeing trips outside the United States; other types of learners, speakers of Spanish, and uses for Spanish were erased in the textbook representation.

Teaching materials also reflect and reproduce ideologies about who speaks Spanish, both internationally and in the United States. Much like Spanish language media and advertising (cf. Dávila 2001), Spanish language textbooks tend to present a generic "Latin look" that fails to recognize the ethnoracial diversity of US Latinos and Latin Americans. Schwartz's (2006) analysis of "do-it-yourself" (self-study) Spanish textbooks also revealed an ideological construction and constriction of the possible identities for Spanish speakers and learners. Schwartz found discursive reflections of asymmetric power relations between speakers of English and Spanish, with Spanish portrayed as valuable to Anglos primarily for providing job-oriented directives to domestic employees.

As for SHL textbooks in particular, Leeman and Martínez (2007) examined titles and prefaces over a thirty-year period in order to explore changing discourses of multilingualism, cultural diversity, and Spanish in the United States in general, and with respect to SHL goals in particular. The analysis revealed an evolution in the construction of Spanish from a birthright rooted in the family and the ethnic community, to a globalized and commodified skill. Accompanying this evolution was a shift in the source of linguistic legitimacy and authority from the local community to an imagined global standard, with the objective of SHL reconfigured as the ability to communicate with monolingual speakers around the world, rather than with students' family or local community.

In a study focused on the representation and teaching of linguistic forms, Ducar (2009) analyzed SHL textbooks' treatment of language variation, particularly geographic variation. She found that even those textbooks that were specifically designed for a student population whose Spanish language heritage was overwhelmingly rooted in the Americas hewed to a pseudo-Castilian linguistic norm. For example, *vosotros*, a pronoun that occurs exclusively in Peninsular varieties of Spanish, was generally included and discussed, whereas *vos*, a pronoun common in parts of the Southern Cone and in widespread use in large swatches of Central and South America, was given scant if any mention at all.

Testing

Tests are used both inside and outside of the classroom—such as in placement, graduation and certification requirements, and other kinds of gate-keeping—and they have a unique ideological force in defining what constitutes language knowledge. Exams that emphasize isolated grammatical items, accent marks, and spelling conventions reward students who have had formal language instruction, and such tests devalue or erase the conversational, pragmatic, and cultural arenas where many SHL students excel. Despite testing procedures that favor L2 learners' experiences, when SHL students do not succeed, it is often taken as a sign that they are academically inferior or lazy. As Valdés (1994) has shown, proficiency exams imagine an educated monolingual Spanish speaker as the learning objective, and construct many bilingual practices as incorrect. So too, Advanced Placement and other exams that award college credit based on scores emphasize the language and cultural practices associated with monolingual elites outside the United States. Much L2 and heritage language acquisition research also relies on language tests, and this lends scientific legitimacy to the particular conceptions of linguistic knowledge reflected in those tests and buttresses the particular ideologies they embody, making this an area worthy of further analysis.

Hiring/Staffing

Particular understandings of what the "best" Spanish is and who speaks it are reflected in hiring practices for SHL and for Spanish as an L2, at both the K–12 and the postsecondary levels. On one hand, the negative experiences that many SHL students have during their schooling, together with the negative portrayal of their language varieties and practices, may discourage them from studying Spanish and thus contribute to the underrepresentation of US Latinos in teaching. On the other hand, the ideological elevation of an imagined monolingual standard and the notion that many US Latinos do not speak the "right" kind of Spanish buttress a linguistic hierarchy that places speakers educated in Spain and Latin America at the top, followed by L2 speakers of Spanish, and US bilinguals and SHL speakers on the lowest rung. Given the importance that many teaching credentialing processes give to the "officialized" language knowledge acquired in university settings, there is a tendency for teaching practices and the ideologies they embody to be self-reproducing.

FUTURE DIRECTIONS

Because the body of research on language ideologies and SHL teaching and learning is still relatively small, there remains a need for studies focusing specifically on language ideologies and SHL in all the areas outlined in the previous section. In addition, several current research foci should be broadened, and several other future directions are also worth mentioning.

One such expansion is in the types of language ideologies being investigated. As was discussed above, most (but not all) research on SHL language ideologies has explored the reproduction of the standard language ideology and the subordination of linguistic varieties and practices typical of the United States. In the future it will be of interest to expand our horizons regarding the kinds of language ideologies we investigate, as well as to explore how language ideologies intersect other ideologies and social categories. For example, researchers might conduct research on constructions of the value of different languages or of language learning in general, or they might explore how ideologies of gender are intertwined with the representation of different languages.

Whereas language ideological research examining SHL educational policies, approaches, and materials, and how they reproduce and reinforce dominant ideologies, has made important contributions, there is a clear need for ethnographic studies that explore how such ideologies are embodied in educational practice. Future research should look at what instructors actually do in the classroom, including how they use such artifacts, how they structure classes, how they discuss and respond to linguistic variation, and how they treat students. Such research should not focus exclusively on institutions and instructors; the scope must be expanded and shifted to include more consideration of learners themselves. Such studies should explore both the ideologies that students bring to class and how they engage with the ideologies they encounter—such as accepting and appropriating them, or alternatively, resisting and subverting them.

As was discussed above, research on SHL language ideologies has historically gone hand in hand with pedagogical innovation and reform, a trend that has come to fruition in recent proposals for approaches to SHL instruction designed to promote students' critical consciousness and agency (e.g., Leeman 2005; Martínez 2003), as well as in community service-learning programs where students take their developing critical awareness beyond the classroom walls by working on language-related community issues (e.g., Leeman, Rabin, and Román-Mendoza 2011a; Martínez 2010). More research is needed on the impact of such programs.

Another way in which SHL language ideologies research could productively be expanded is by looking beyond the immediate context of SHL instruction to the broader educational context in which it is embedded. It would be worthwhile to explore the impact of language ideologies circulating in upper level Spanish classes, in other departments, and throughout the university on SHL instruction. This research might include examinations of interactions between L2 and heritage speakers in culture, linguistics, and literature courses; analyses of the reasons that so many heritage speakers decide not to study Spanish; and considerations of language ideologies in courses in other departments.

Future research on language ideologies in SHL will shed light on the reproduction of language ideologies both inside and outside the academy and will also inform the development of pedagogically sound and socially responsible SHL and L2 Spanish language education.

ACKNOWLEDGMENT

I am grateful to Sara Beaudrie, Marta Fairclough, Glenn Martínez, Galey Modan, and the anonymous reviewers for their insightful comments and helpful suggestions.

REFERENCES

Aparicio, Frances. 2000. "Of Spanish Dispossessed." In *Language Ideologies: Critical Perspectives on the Official English Movement*, edited by Roseann Dueñas González and Idikó. Mahwah, NJ: Lawrence Erlbaum Associates.

Bailey, Benjamin. 2000. "Language and Negotiation of Racial/Ethnic Identity among Dominican Americans." *Language in Society* 29:555–62.

Carreira, Maria. 2000. "Validating and Promoting Spanish in the United States: Lessons from Linguistic Science." *Bilingual Research Journal* 24 (4): 423–42.

Curtin, Melissa. 2007. "Differential Bilingualism: Vergüenza and Pride in a Spanish Sociolinguistics Class." In *Seeking Identity: Language in Society*, edited by Nancy Mae Antrim. Newcastle, UK: Cambridge Scholars.

Dávila, Arlene. 2001. *Latinos, Inc.* Berkeley: University of California Press.

Del Valle, José. 2009. "Total Spanish: The Politics of a Pan-Hispanic Grammar." *PMLA* 124 (3): 880–86.

Ducar, Cynthia. 2009. "The Sound of Silence: Spanish Heritage Textbooks' Treatment of Language Variation." In *Español en Estados Unidos y otros contextos de contacto: Sociolingüística, ideología y pedagogía*, edited by Manel Lacorte and Jennifer Leeman. Madrid: Iberoamericana.

Echeverría, Begoña. 2003. "Language Ideologies and Practices in (En)gendering the Basque Nation." *Language in Society* 32 (3): 383–413.

Fairclough, Norman. 1992. "The Appropriacy of 'Appropriateness.'" In *Critical Language Awareness*, edited by Norman Fairclough. London: Longman.

García, Ofelia. 1993. "From Goya Portraits to Goya Beans: Elite Traditions and Popular Streams in US Spanish Language Policy." *Southwest Journal of Linguistics* 12 (1–2): 69–86.

Guardado, Martin. 2009. "Speaking Spanish like a Boy Scout: Language Socialization, Resistance, and Reproduction in a Heritage Language Scout Troop." *Canadian Modern Language Review* 66 (1): 101–29.

Harklau, Linda. 2009. "Heritage Speakers' Experiences in New Latino Diaspora Spanish Classrooms." *Critical Inquiry in Language Studies* 6 (4): 211–42.

Herman, Deborah. 2007. "It's a Small World After All: From Stereotypes to Invented Worlds in Secondary School Spanish Textbooks." *Critical Inquiry in Language Studies* 4 (2): 117–50.

Hill, Jane H. 2008. *The Everyday Language of White Racism*. Malden, MA: Wiley-Blackwell.

Irvine, Judith. 1989. "When Talk Isn't Cheap: Language and Political Economy." *American Ethnologist* 16 (2): 248–67.

Irvine, Judith, and Susan Gal. 2000. "Language Ideology and Linguistic Differentiation." In *Regimes of Language: Ideologies, Polities, and Identities*, edited by Paul Kroskrity. Santa Fe: School of American Research Press.

Kroskrity, Paul. 2004. "Language Ideologies." In *A Companion to Linguistic Anthropology*, edited by Alessandro Duranti. Malden, MA: Blackwell.

Leeman, Jennifer. 2004. "Racializing Language: A History of Linguistic Ideologies in the US Census." *Journal of Language and Politics* 3 (3): 507–34.

———. 2005. "Engaging Critical Pedagogy: Spanish for Native Speakers." *Foreign Language Annals* 38 (1): 35–45.

————. 2006–7. "The Value of Spanish: Shifting Ideologies in United States Language Teaching." *ADFL Bulletin* 38 (1–2): 32–39.

————. 2011. "Standards, Commodification, and Critical Service Learning in Minority Language Communities." *Modern Language Journal* (95) 4: 10–13.

————. In press. "Race, Language, and Latinos in the History of the US Census." In *A Political History of Spanish: The Making of a Language*, edited by José Del Valle. Cambridge: Cambridge University Press.

Leeman, Jennifer, and Glenn Martínez. 2007. "From Identity to Commodity: Ideologies of Spanish in Heritage Language Textbooks." *Critical Inquiry in Language Studies* 4 (1): 35–65.

Leeman, Jennifer, Lisa Rabin, and Esperanza Román-Mendoza. 2011a. "Critical Pedagogy beyond the Classroom Walls: Community Service-Learning and Spanish Heritage Language Education." *Heritage Language Journal* 8 (3): 1–21.

————. 2011b. "Identity and Activism in Heritage Language Education." *Modern Language Journal* 95 (4): 481–95.

Lippi-Green, Rosina. 1994. "Accent, Standard Language Ideology, and Discriminatory Pretext in the Courts." *Language in Society* 23 (2): 163–98.

————. 1997. *English with an Accent: Language, Ideology and Discrimination in the United States.* London: Routledge.

Lope Blanch, Juan M. 2001. "La norma lingüística hispánica." In *Congreso Internacional de la Lengua Española: El español en la Sociedad de la Información.* http://cvc .cervantes.es/obref/congresos/valladolid/ponencias/unidaddiversidad_ del_espanol/ 1_la norma_hispanica/lope_j.htm.

López, Luís. 2007. "The Origins of Spanish Revisited: Linguistic Science, Language Ideology and Nationalism in Contemporary Spain." *Bulletin of Spanish Studies* 84 (3): 287–313.

Macedo, Donaldo. 1997. "English Only: The Tongue-Tying of America." In *Latinos and Education: A Critical Reader*, edited by Antonia Darder, Rodolfo D. Torres, and Henry Gutiérrez, 269–80. New York: Routledge.

Martínez, Glenn. 2003. "Classroom-Based Dialect Awareness: A Critical Applied Linguistic Approach." *Heritage Language Journal* 1. Available at www.heritagelanguages.org.

————. 2010. "Medical Spanish for Heritage Learners: A Prescription to Improve the Health of Spanish-Speaking Communities." In *Building Communities and Making Connections*, edited by Susana Rivera-Mills and Juan Antonio Trujillo. Newcastle, UK: Cambridge Scholars.

Martínez-Roldán, Carmen, and Guillermo Malavé. 2004. "Language Ideologies Mediating Literacy and Identity in Bilingual Contexts." *Journal of Early Childhood Literacy* 4 (2): 155.

Merino, Barabara, Henry Trueba, and Fabian Samaniego, eds. 1993. *Language and Culture in Learning: Teaching Spanish to Native Speakers of Spanish.* Washington, DC: Falmer Press.

Milroy, James. 2007. "The Ideology of the Standard Language." In *Routledge Companion to Sociolinguistics*, edited by Carmen Llamas, Louise Mullany, and Peter Stockwell. London: Routledge.

Milroy, James, and Lesley Milroy. 1999. *Authority in Language*, 3rd ed. London: Routledge.

Paffey, Darren, and Clare Mar-Molinero. 2009. "Globalization, Linguistic Norms and Language Authorities: Spain and the Panhispanic Language Policy." In *Español en Estados Unidos y otros contextos de contacto: Sociolingüística, ideología y pedagogía*, edited by Manel Lacorte and Jennifer Leeman. Madrid: Iberoamericana.

Pomerantz, Anne. 2002. "Language Ideologies and the Production of Identities: Spanish as a Resource for Participation in a Multilingual Marketplace." *Multilingua* 21:275–302.

———. 2008. "'Tú necesitas preguntar en español': Negotiating Good Language Learner Identity in a Spanish Classroom." *Journal of Language, Identity and Education* 7 (3): 253–71.

Schmidt, Ronald, Sr. 2002. "Racialization and Language Policy: The Case of the USA." *Multilingua* 21:141–61.

Schwartz, Adam. 2006. "The Teaching and Culture of Household Spanish: Understanding Racist Reproduction in Domestic Discourse." *Critical Discourse Studies* 3 (2): 107–21.

Standards for Foreign Language Learning: Preparing for the 21st Century. 2006. 3rd rev. ed. Lawrence, KS: Allen Press.

Toribio, Almeida Jacqueline. 2000. "Nosotros somos dominicanos: Language and Self-Definition among Dominicans." In *Research on Spanish in the United States: Linguistic Issues and Challenges*, edited by Ana Roca. Somerville, MA: Cascadilla Press.

Urciuoli, Bonnie. 1996. *Exposing Prejudice: Puerto Rican Experiences of Language, Race, and Class.* Boulder, CO: Westview Press.

———. 2008. "Whose Spanish? The Tension between Linguistic Correctness and Cultural Identity." In *Bilingualism and Identity: Spanish at the Crossroads with Other Languages*, edited by Mercedes Niño-Murcia and Jason Rothman. Amsterdam: John Benjamins.

Valdés, Guadalupe. 1981. "Pedagogical Implications of Teaching Spanish to the Spanish-Speaking in the United States." In *Teaching Spanish to the Hispanic Bilingual*, edited by Guadalupe Valdés, Anthony Lozano, and Rodolfo García-Moya. New York: Teachers College Press.

———. 1994. *Bilingualism and Testing: A Special Case of Bias.* Norwood, NJ: Ablex.

———. 1997. "The Teaching of Spanish to Bilingual Spanish-Speaking Students: Outstanding Issues and Unanswered Questions." In *La enseñanza del español a hispanohablantes: Praxis y teoría*, edited by M. Cecilia Colombi and Francisco X. Alarcón. Boston: Houghton Mifflin.

Valdés, Guadalupe, Sonia V. González, Dania Lopez García, and Patricio Márquez. 2003. "Language Ideology: The Case of Spanish in Departments of Foreign Languages." *Anthropology and Education Quarterly* 7 (1): 3–26.

Valdés, Guadalupe, Anthony Lozano, and Rodolfo García-Moya, eds. 1981. *Teaching Spanish to the Hispanic Bilingual.* New York: Teachers College Press.

Villa, Daniel. 2002. "The Sanitizing of US Spanish in Academia." *Foreign Language Annals* 35:221–30.

Woolard, Katheryn. 1998. "Language Ideology as a Field of Inquiry." In *Language Ideologies: Practice and Theory*, edited by Bambi Schieffelin, Katheryn Woolard, and Paul Kroskrity. Oxford: Oxford University Press.

CHAPTER 3

Policy and Planning Research for Spanish as a Heritage Language

FROM LANGUAGE RIGHTS TO LINGUISTIC RESOURCE

Glenn Martínez, University of Texas–Pan American

O N A SIMMERING SUMMER DAY in the arid Texas Panhandle town of Amarillo, Marta Laureano walked into the courthouse to what she expected would be a routine child custody hearing. The outcome, however, turned out to be far from ordinary and within a day would make headlines in major newspapers from New York to Los Angeles. In the course of the hearing, state district judge Samuel Kiser learned that Laureano routinely spoke Spanish to her daughter. He ordered Laureano to speak only in English to her five-year-old and threatened to deny her custody of her daughter if she persisted in speaking Spanish to the girl: "If she starts first grade with the other children and cannot even speak the language that the teachers and the other children speak and she's a full-blood American citizen, you're abusing that child and you're relegating her to the position of housemaid. Now, get this straight. You start speaking English to this child because if she doesn't do good in school, then I can remove her because it's not in her best interest to be ignorant. The child will only hear English" (Verhovek 1995). The judge's ruling was swiftly criticized by numerous advocacy groups around the country and was characterized by the former Texas attorney general Dan Morales as "way off base" (Verhovek 1995).

Eight years after the uproar caused by Judge Kiser's ruling, Spanish made headlines again when the Australian comedian Barry Humphries, in the guise of the feisty Dame Edna, responded to the question of a torn romantic wondering about the value of learning Spanish in the February 2003 edition of *Vanity Fair*: "Forget Spanish, there's nothing in that language worth reading except *Don Quixote*, and a quick listen to the CD of *Man of La Mancha* will take care of that. There was a poet named Garcia Lorca, but I'd leave him on the intellectual back burner if I were you. As for everyone's speaking it, what twaddle! Who speaks it that you are really desperate to talk to? The help? Your leaf blower? Study French or German, where there are at least a few books worth reading, or, if you're American, try English" (cited by Emery 2003).

An immediate uproar ensued when the magazine hit newsstands in late January 2003. In a letter to the editor, Wendy Maldonado repudiated Dame Edna and asserted that "we are not just 'the help' and the 'leaf blowers.' We are architects and activists, journalists and doctors, governors and athletes, scientists and business people. . . . We speak Spanish, but we also speak fluent English, and many of us speak other languages as well" (cited by Emery 2003). She went on to demand a written apology from Dame Edna and the editors of *Vanity Fair* and called for a national boycott of the magazine until these demands were met. The visibly angry yet carefully crafted statement reverberated around the country, and it led major professional organizations such as the National Association of Hispanic Journalists and the National Council for La Raza to endorse Maldonado's call for a national boycott. Although the editors never apologized, they did release a statement saying that they regretted that the statements had caused offense but went on to point out that in this regard the fictional character Dame Edna is an "equal opportunity insulter" (Emery 2003).

These two events clearly illustrate an environment of hostility and subordination that has situated many Spanish heritage language communities in this country since the initial contacts of Anglo pioneers and Spanish settlers in the US Southwest in the nineteenth century (cf. Martínez 2008; García 1993). Marta Laureano's story illustrates how negative attitudes about Spanish can result in forceful interventions, sanctioned by the authority of the state, that silence Spanish-speaking voices and that erase the public representation of Spanish speakers in this country. The Dame Edna story, however, demonstrates how these deeply felt interventions ignite short fuses even when negative ideologies of Spanish are articulated for comedic effect. What these two stories tell us is that whereas ideologies of language (cf. Leeman, this volume) both shape and inform official interventions in language use, as in the case of Judge Kiser's ruling, official interventions also ignite language ideologies, as in Wendy Maldonado's response to Dame Edna's sordid advice. This interanimation provides an important framework for the review of language policy research in the field of Spanish as a heritage language (SHL).

DEVELOPMENT OF RESEARCH ON
LANGUAGE POLICY AND PLANNING

Language policy and language planning (LPLP) emerged as a field of research within applied linguistics during the early 1960s within the context of developing postcolonial nations (Fishman 1974). Within this framework, LPLP was closely related to concerns about national identity and economic development, and it was infused with perspectives from a variety of social science disciplines. In its early phases, LPLP research was characterized by a desire for regional unification, modernization, efficiency, and democratization. Language planning, within this early framework, was defined as the "organized pursuit of language problems, typically at the national level" (Fishman 1974, 79). Language itself was viewed as an ideologically neutral tool that could be designed and developed in order to serve these highly ideologically charged objectives (Ricento 2000; Ruiz 2010).

By the 1980s, however, LPLP expanded to consider interventions on language not only in developing nations, for the purpose of very immediate goals, but also in developed nations, for the purpose of maintaining long-standing social organizations (Ricento 2000). This expansion of LPLP research resulted in the formulation of a variety of competing, yet at the same time complementary, definitions. It also resulted in an increasing divergence between language planning and language policy. For example, Tollefson (1991, 16) defined language policy as "the institutionalization of language as a basis for distinctions among social groups. Language policy is one mechanism for locating language within social structure so that language determines who has access to political power and resources. Language policy is one mechanism by which dominant groups establish hegemony in language use."

This definition of language policy clearly locates language intervention in the hands of the few. The connection between language and power espoused in the definition, furthermore, characterizes language policy as a central activity in social organization and political control. The orientation toward language policy as the activity of the politically powerful is echoed in Shohamy's (2006, 22–23) more recent definition: "Language has become a tool for the manipulation of people and their behaviors, as it is used for political agendas in the battle over power, representation and voice. . . . Language turned from an open and free system to a tool for imposition, manipulation, and colonization, mostly by ideologues and politicians with the support of linguists and educationalists."

The notion of language policy as the sole domain of social elites, however, has been challenged in other definitions. Spolsky (2004), for example, characterizes language policy as the sum of language practices, language beliefs, and language management within speech communities. This definition provides new dimensions to language policy research that recognize the capacity for language intervention on the part of a broad range of stakeholders. Spolsky's definition, in part, reflects the accounting scheme that Cooper (1989) proposes for the study of language planning. According to Cooper, language planning analysis should be guided by the following underlying question: What actors attempt to influence what behaviors of which people for what ends under what conditions by what means through what decision-making process and with what effect? This scheme provides a useful conceptual distinction between language planning, which has to do primarily with actors, behaviors, people and ends, and language policy, which primarily concerns conditions, means, decision-making processes, and effects. At the same time, it also provides a degree of flexibility that allows for a multifaceted view of language planning in which competing actors propose competing policies through competing processes (cf. Kaplan and Baldauf 1997). The flexibility and partiality of language intervention efforts are essential to an understanding the environment in which SHL policy and planning research have been carried out.

LPLP research in the United States began in earnest with the appearance of Heinz Kloss's seminal work *The American Bilingual Tradition*, which was first published in 1977. In this book Kloss proposes two competing types of language policies in the United States: promotion-oriented policy and tolerance-oriented policy (Kloss 1998). In sum, Kloss argues that the American bilingual tradition can be characterized by a laissez-faire approach to languages, where tolerance-oriented policies have been the norm. Wiley (2004) has expanded on this inventory in order to take into account the often-unintended consequences of policy orientations. Within this framework US language policies fit into one of the following five categories: promotion-oriented, expediency-oriented, tolerance-oriented, restriction-oriented, and repression-oriented (Wiley 2004, 325–26). This expanded framework thus provides a space for policies that have elevated instruction in certain languages at certain times or that have restricted or repressed instruction in other languages at other times.

The difficulty in assessing America's bilingual tradition, however, seems to be less a product of appropriate theoretical frameworks and more a consequence of the tenuous balancing act of individual liberty and national interest in US policymaking. Spolsky, for example, wonders out loud if the United States has really had an official language policy or if it has instead relied exclusively on civil rights as the basis for language intervention and management (Spolsky 2004, 92–112). This question calls to mind the important heuristic approach outlined in Richard Ruiz's seminal paper "Orientations in Language Planning," originally published in the *NABE Journal* in 1984. In this paper, Ruiz argued that language planning and language policy in the United States must be evaluated in terms of the specific normative orientation toward language that it displays.

A language orientation, according to Ruiz (1988, 4), "refers to a complex of dispositions toward language and its role, and toward languages and their role in society." More recently, Ruiz has clarified what is meant by orientation. A language orientation is a normative framework that gives order to phenomena.

It is thus distinguishable from a particular conception or ideology of language. Although an ideology of language is a value or belief system regarding language (cf. chapter 2 in this volume, by Leeman), a normative orientation is an organizing frame that shapes and informs language interventions (Ruiz 2010).

Using this heuristic, Ruiz defines and contrasts three orientations that have dominated US language policymaking: language as problem, language as right, and language as resource. The language-as-problem orientation is the "orientation that language is a social problem to be identified operationally and resolved through treatments" (Ruiz 1984, 10). This orientation, according to Ruiz, often results in the social and cultural subordination of minority language communities. The language-as-right orientation is one that affirms the freedom to use a minority language and that protects from discrimination on the basis of this use (p. 11). This orientation, through its reliance on legal discourse, tends to create tensions and animosities between minority and majority language groups. The language as resource orientation, finally, "would tend to regard language minority communities as important sources for expertise. Not only could language-competent community members be used to train others; the whole community itself could afford multilingual opportunities to language students" (p. 17). The distinction between language as right and language as resource has recently been clarified by Ruiz. In proposing language as resource, Ruiz (2010, 165) does not mean to subordinate language rights. Instead, he views language as resource as a necessary precondition for language rights: "Unless one sees a language as a good thing in itself, it is impossible to affirm anyone's right to it. To say that one has a right to (be educated in) one's mother tongue—to say access to one's mother tongue is a linguistic human right—is to say, first, that the mother tongue is a good thing in itself."

POLICY AND PLANNING RESEARCH IN SPANISH AS A HERITAGE LANGUAGE

Ruiz's identification of language as problem, language as right, and language as resource has arguably been the most salient framework guiding SHL policy and planning in the United States. In this section I review how these orientations have shaped language policies and how they have directed outcomes in language planning.

Language as Problem

The earliest approaches to SHL instruction manifested a plainly language-as-problem orientation. SHL textbooks clearly portrayed the Spanish spoken by students as problematic, corrupt, and deriving from an ignorance of the language (cf. Leeman and Martínez 2007; and see chapter 2 in this volume, by Leeman).

Pauline Baker's 1966 textbook *Español para los hispanos* provides, perhaps, one of the clearest manifestations of this orientation (Baker 1966, i): "No creo equivocarme al decir que estamos presenciando una decadencia lamentable del español de los Estados Unidos. Entendemos grave error el considerarlo un mero dialecto del bello idioma, pero indudablemente acrecienta la tendencia de usar anglicismos, arcaísmos, provincialismos, etc., y es evidente un empobrecimiento de vocabulario."

Such pedagogical approaches recalled the violent and dehumanizing "No Spanish" language repression rules that existed in public schools throughout the Southwest during the twentieth century (MacGregor-Mendoza 2000). Notwithstanding the dominance of this orientation during the initial SHL instructional endeavors and its lingering presence in the infamous "Se dice/No se dice" lists in SHL textbooks, the language as problem orientation was clearly recognized and vehemently challenged by SHL educators and theorists.

Language as Right

The civil rights movement and the Vietnam War contributed to massive enrollments of Spanish-speaking students in higher education throughout the country (Leeman and Martínez 2007). The presence of large numbers of Spanish speakers in courses designed for second-language learners led to a new series of problems. As noted by Valdés (1981), the foreign language teaching profession was ill prepared to deal with the challenges of heritage learners in their classroom. In some cases, in fact, it was the students themselves who demanded specialized courses in Spanish for native speakers (Teschner 2000). Pioneering Spanish teachers quickly responded to these demands and began to develop pedagogies that were more consistent with the language backgrounds and sociolinguistic histories of these students.

In response to the language-as-problem approaches to SHL instruction discussed in the previous section, Guadalupe Valdés looked to the problems faced by her colleagues in English departments and made a bold new proposal for the development of a Spanish language arts curriculum for heritage learners. Valdés (1981, 19) envisioned a program designed for all Spanish speakers, a curriculum that would develop and enrich all language skills, and an overarching focus on developing wider communicative ability and enhanced self-image. The call for a Spanish language arts curriculum akin to the curriculum offered to English-speaking students throughout their entire educational career resounded loudly throughout the field and set an agenda for SHL that would last more than a decade. As this endeavor developed, it became clear that the underlying orientation was a language-as-right approach.

The development and implementation of a Spanish language arts curriculum was viewed by many as an important remedy for the public school system's continuous failure to actively participate in language maintenance and its some-times dogged refusal to affirm the cultural identity and contribution of Spanish-speaking students. Eduardo Hernández-Chávez (1993, 66) stated this succinctly: "Communication between different-language community members is weakened; the sense of a shared destiny is lost; intraethnic conflicts arise; historical knowl-edge fails to be passed on; and individuals suffer feelings of alienations from their shared historical ethnicity. These are some of the consequences, at least in part, of language loss. There are possibly others. Cultural alienation can have as its product poor educational performance, socioeconomic marginalization, and a host of other ills." In this commentary, Hernández-Chávez underscored that a negation of opportunities to maintain and develop the Spanish language is disenfranchising for many Chicanos and constitutes a violation of basic rights to community identity.

The language-as-right orientation was also infused in the Spanish language arts movement by literary scholars who saw Chicano literature as an essential ingredient of an integral program of Spanish language development. For exam-ple, Chabram Denersesian (1993, 140) argued that the inclusion of Chicano authors within accepted literary canons was a vehicle for the legitimization of the language of Spanish heritage learners. In her view, the inclusion of Chicano literary voices in a Spanish language arts programs provides a way of "contesting prevailing stereotypes which assume that Chicanos lack a rich literary history." Such stereotypes were, of course, a manifestation of the language-as-problem orientation.

Hidalgo (1997), furthermore, contended that language legitimization needed more than institutional support for the maintenance and recognition of literary traditions. Instead, Hidalgo proposed the need for corpus-planning activities in US Spanish varieties. In particular, she calls for lexicographic efforts that would result in dictionaries of spoken Spanish in the United States. She saw this effort as a way to bring legitimacy to the language spoken by Chicanos and also as a source of pride for students, who would see their own language codified and elevated to print form. At the same time, Hidalgo (1997, 119) called for public campaigns to elevate perceptions of Spanish in the community at large: "Para nuestros estudiantes y para el público en general, sería muy reconfortante saber que en los siglos de oro de las letras españolas, las imprentas de Venecia, Milán, Amberes, Bruselas, París y Lyon publicaban constantemente las obras de autores españoles. Una campaña en pro del español ayudaría a difundir la historia de la lengua española en los momentos históricos en que ésta alcanzó extraordinaria difusión. En Italia, en Francia y en Flandes eran muchos los que aprendían el español. Los clásicos franceses Corneille, Lesage y Moliere se inspiraron con avi-dez en fuentes españolas." Hidalgo's proposal, therefore, sought to rescue the untold or uncovered pedigree in Spanish within Western Civilization and to thus restore the language to its "rightful" status.

Language as Resource

By the late 1990s the professionalization of SHL had made important strides, and the message of a Spanish language arts curriculum had gained considerable traction both in language departments around the country and in professional organizations. In 1996 the American Council on the Teaching of Foreign Languages (ACTFL) reached an important milestone in its Goals 2000 initiative through the publication of the *Standards for Foreign Language Teaching*. The *Standards*, which were endorsed by forty-nine professional associations, for the first time reserved a clear and unambiguous place for heritage learners in language education. According to Valdés (2000a, 240), "the *Standards* were specifically written to take into consideration not only the needs of traditional foreign language learners but also the special strengths of home background or heritage learners." Furthermore, Draper and Hicks (2000, 28) specify the strategy by which the *Standards* carved out a space for heritage learners within language education: "The framework for communicative competence defined within the *Standards* provides a means for recognizing the skills that heritage learners bring to their studies (generally interpersonal communication skills) and a mechanism for focusing on the skills that need further work (general presentational skills). Furthermore, the inclusion of culture, connections, comparisons, and communities standards offers teachers options for expanding the curriculum for heritage languages beyond language itself to language use in real-world contexts."

The inclusion of heritage languages in the *Standards for Foreign Language Teaching* was a policy move that gave greater credence to the Spanish language arts proposals that had surfaced nearly twenty years earlier. A key difference in the earlier proposals and the codification of heritage languages in the standards, however, was an underlying orientation toward language as resource. Valdés (2000b, 15) herself makes this orientation patently clear in her introductory comments to the American Association of Teachers of Spanish and Portuguese's professional development handbook on Spanish for native speakers: "Heritage speakers bring with them many strengths and many abilities. In preparing to teach them, we must see these strengths, we must value them, and take joy in them. We must firmly resolve as a profession that we will not repeat the mistakes our country has made in the past. We must value heritage languages and heritage language speakers, and we must have a clear awareness about the fact that language maintenance efforts are as important a part of our profession as is the teaching of language to monolingual speakers of English."

The language-as-resource orientation that emerged in the late 1990s was further strengthened in the era after the terrorist attacks of September 11, 2001, and in the face of a glaring "language deficit" in the US intelligence community. The dire and immediate need for speakers of the so-called strategic languages such as Arabic and Farsi served to ratchet up discourses on the untapped national resource provided by heritage learners. The idea that these learners were uniquely positioned to develop advanced language skills in an abbreviated amount of time made them a particularly valuable resource for the nation at the time. The Alliance for the Advancement of Heritage Languages adopted the language-as-resource orientation as a central tenet of its mission. In its guiding principles, for example, it argues that the United States is in critical need of professionals with high-level language skills in a variety of areas. It also states that heritage learners have for too long been an untapped resource to meet these critical national needs (Ricento 2009). In a 2005 article originally published in the *Journal of Sociolinguistics*, Tom Ricento (2009, 128) launched an incisive critique of the discourse on language as resource within the heritage language movement. He contends that "if languages function in particular ways in particular communities, they are in fact resources and are recognized as such by those communities. They should not be viewed," he continues, "as resources by academics and language planners only when convenient to serve particular disciplinary or state interests, and otherwise ignored or suppressed, whether explicitly or covertly. This raises the important question of resources for whom? For what purpose or end?" This insightful question has proven to be the driving force of SHL policy and planning research in the last few years, and I next turn to a review of some of this work.

Spanish heritage learners have sometimes been viewed as a resource within language education itself. Quintana-Sarellana, Huebner, and Jensen (1997), for example, reported on a project in which Spanish heritage learners served as tutors and proficiency raters for Spanish second-language learners. Heritage learners received ACTFL Oral Proficiency Rating training and were given opportunities to develop language skills and cultural knowledge in preparation for their tutoring activities. Grant funding, furthermore, allowed the researchers to provide a stipend to heritage learners for their participation in the project. The results reported that both HL and SL students made considerable progress as a result of the project. They also showed that HL students obtained heightened self-esteem and improved academic performance in other classes. Notwithstanding the impressive gains made by this approach, there has not been a consistent effort to replicate it in large heritage language programs that coexist with second-language programs.

More recently, SHL has been viewed as a resource to bridge the Latino achievement gap more generally (cf. Gándara and Contreras 2009). Carreira (2007) notes that Latinos currently account for an unprecedented proportion of the national high school dropout rate. Further, she notes that the less assimilated and more Spanish dominant that Latino students are, the greater their likelihood to abandon school before graduation. In light of these dismal statistics, Carreira proposes a unique role for SHL teachers in the nation's public schools. She asserts that SHL teachers are in a position that will allow them to contribute in very valuable ways to Latino educational achievement. She cautions, however, that in order for teachers to fill this important role, they will need to move beyond the traditional roles assigned to language teachers. She argues that SHL teachers can contribute to Latino achievement in three ways. First, SHL teachers are in a position to use Spanish language instruction as a means to develop biliteracy and to improve higher-order skills that will be useful to students in all of their subjects. Second, she argues that SHL teachers can also improve educational achievement through the provision of content-based instruction. Finally, she notes the ability of SHL teachers to serve as a bridge for the incorporation of Latino parents into the school system. Spanish is certainly an area in which parents are subject matter experts and may easily assist their children while asserting their parental role. The opportunity to increase parental involvement should be seized by all SHL teachers through projects and other activities that directly involve parents and that create a comforting and reassuring space where they can interact with the school. Certainly, this new role for SHL will require policy changes, especially in the area of teacher preparation and credentialing. Spanish teachers will require new kinds of training and assessment in order to meet these important opportunities.

This is clearly evident from recent research from the South—a region where the Spanish-speaking population has grown exponentially during the past ten years. Colomer (2010), for example, conducted a study of Spanish instructors who served as dual-role interpreters in public schools in Georgia. On the basis of semistructured interviews with high school and middle school Spanish teachers, Colomer elucidates the challenges and frustrations faced by these teachers in attempting to assume the new role of cultural broker for non-English-speaking parents of Latino children. Noting the major differences between interpreter training and foreign language teacher training, she convincingly shows how being put in the situation of interpreter often demoralizes teachers. One of her interviewees, Felicity, reported: "Well, I don't know what the immunization record is in Spanish, first of all. And second of all, I don't know what it looks like. I can't describe it to this person—and I would just—if made me feel really stupid" (Colomer 2010, 497). This study reveals that new and different approaches to teacher training must be explored in order to respond appropriately to the changing demographics of schools. Policies including the introduction of interpreter training and language for the professions courses within language teacher training programs will be needed in order to appropriately capitalize on this significant resource.

Finally, SHL has recently been viewed as a resource for the professions that are progressively becoming more globally competitive. Workforce development in the United States, it is argued, must adjust to the international competition that has been spawned by globalization. Utilizing the linguistic resources of heritage learners has been seen as an expedient way to meet this workforce development challenge. For example, Carreira and Armengol (2001, 109) state that "one solution is to look to speakers of heritage languages and to consider the sophisticated expertise in language and knowledge of culture that they bring to the professional arena. Many have developed a level of language proficiency and depth of cultural understanding that would be difficult to replicate in even the most advanced second language learner." This chapter goes on to list in detail the language needs of a variety of professions, including journalism, entertainment, legal services, and health care.

A more recent study conducted by McGroarty and Urzúa (2009, 144) argued that "when the right conditions exist, bilingualism can be beneficial to all parties involved." The study set out to investigate the use of language in professional settings. It sheds light on the professional activities of three individuals working in managerial position in the United States. The individuals queried for this study were middle-class Mexicans who immigrated to the United States as adults. They were educated entirely in Mexico and learned English as a second-language in school in Mexico and perfected their bilingual skills upon arrival in the United States. The study demonstrated that bilingual skills are used by these managers for a variety of reasons. Sometimes they are used to provide technical support for maquila operations. At other times, they are used to place business telephone calls to clients abroad. Finally, the study showed that bilingual skills were often used in supervising the domestic Spanish-speaking workforce.

Although McGroarty and Urzúa present a compelling argument for the value of language in the workplace, they do not recognize the fact that the rewards of bilingualism are differentially distributed in the United States. The language skills and cultural knowledge of those educated abroad are often more highly valued than those of domestically educated workers. Valdés and colleagues (2009), for example, note that in Spanish departments in US institutions there is a long-standing hierarchy that defines the relative worth of different Spanish dialects. Dávila (2001), furthermore, notes that in the Spanish language television industry in the United States, there is a noticeable hierarchy in which Latin Americans educated abroad are privileged in comparison with United States–educated Latinos. Wright (2007) also notes the lament of a federal employer over the inability of heritage learners to perform sufficiently well on interpreter competency exams: "I think that as I look back on the last 30 years of testing interpreter candidates, it's very clear to me that the attempt made in our private and public schools to annihilate any knowledge of the language spoken at home has been very successful, and I think we've got to overcome that" (cited by Wright 2007, 17).

Another study, by Villa and Villa (2005), sheds additional light on the value of bilingualism in the southern New Mexico border region. This study consisted of a survey of a large sample of businesses, educational institutions, and government agencies in the Las Cruces area. The survey asked managers to indicate the relative value of bilingual skills in their place of employment. The findings indicated that overall bilingual skills do not translate into economic benefits for Spanish speakers in this border region. Instead, they found that bilingual skills were seen as most useful in the positions in the organization that were the lowest

paying and most customer service oriented. They found that bilingualism normally results in heavier workloads for Spanish-speaking employees. They
reported that workers were not given additional compensation for these heavier
workloads resulting from their ability to speak Spanish. They also reported that
bilingualism is generally not a requirement for a position, but instead that it
is normally listed as a preference. These data lead the authors to surmise that,
rather than contributing to upward mobility and economic advancement, the
ability to speak Spanish may actually prevent workers from ascending into management positions. The great need for Spanish speakers in the lower ranks of
the organization and the heavy workloads experienced by Spanish speakers both
contribute to a pattern of economic stagnation for bilingual workers.

FUTURE DIRECTIONS FOR POLICY AND PLANNING
RESEARCH FOR SPANISH AS A HERITAGE LANGUAGE

The language-as-resource orientation that has recently gained traction in SHL
policy and planning research has confronted heritage language researchers with
very important questions. What administrative barriers prevent greater integration of Spanish heritage learners and Spanish second-language learners? What
policy adjustments can be made in teacher training and credentialing to ensure
that SHL teachers can emerge as leaders in the academic achievement of Latino
youth and in the integration of Latino parents into the American educational
system? How can ingrained ideologies about the value of bilingualism be contested in order to carve out an effective leadership role for heritage language
workers in the United States? Future research in SHL policy and planning will
certainly shed light on these questions while introducing a new set of questions
that may be just as vexing.

In response to the research findings that are already available, two areas will
increasingly become focal points of future research and curriculum development.
The first is the area of heritage language teaching for the professions. The professions of foreign language teaching and English as a second language have made
great strides in the development of custom-tailored programs for medical personnel, law enforcement officers, school personnel, and business professionals.
Heritage language teaching, however, has not followed suit. At the University of
Texas–Pan American, a program in medical Spanish for heritage learners is
breaking new ground in this important area. This program is premised on the
idea that the elimination of language barriers in health care requires the infusion
of a new workforce that not only has proficiency in the language of patients but
also has a deep cultural understanding of the particular challenges faced by
patients with a limited proficiency in English. The program thus integrates direct
instruction in the language of biomedical sciences with a broad public health
perspective on the often-insurmountable barriers that populations with a limited

proficiency in English face in accessing quality health care. In doing so, it not only builds on essential linguistic skills in the areas of medical interpreting, patient interviewing, and medical terminology but also develops an enriched understanding of how ideologies of language can shape patient–provider interactions. Through a cooperative agreement with a local community health center that serves 90 percent of the county's patients who are indigent, undocumented, and have a limited proficiency in English, students in the program also gain hands-on experience in the provision of high-quality medical services in Spanish. The intent of the program is to develop a new bilingual and bicultural leadership for the health professions that will have the linguistic proficiency and the cultural competence needed to advocate and effectuate change for the millions of patients with a limited proficiency in English who receive substandard care in the current health delivery system (www.utpa.edu/medicalspanish). Other initiatives across the country have also made great strides in this area. At the University of Arizona, for example, an interdisciplinary major in translation and interpretation has been created that was designed to tap into the linguistic dexterities and cultural knowledge of Spanish heritage learners (www.coh.arizona.edu/spanish/trans_interp/translation.cfm). At the John Jay College of Criminal Justice in New York City, furthermore, the Department of Foreign Languages and Literatures offers specialized Spanish courses in law enforcement. The faculty has designed a unique course in Spanish for criminal investigation that is geared toward both bilingual students in criminal justice and political science majors.

The second area of development is connected to the first, inasmuch as heritage language instruction for the professions is tied to leadership development. There is a need to communicate the benefits of Spanish heritage language education and its ongoing successes beyond the realm of the language teaching profession. There is a need to actively shape public opinion through the professional endeavors of SHL teachers and researchers. Today, unfortunately, open hostility to Spanish and its speakers is intensifying. The voices that peddle these uninformed positions, however, seem to have taken the airwaves hostage and to resonate profoundly with the American public. The voices of heritage language educators and proponents, conversely, are not being heard in today's policy environment. Although the profession could strategize and develop mechanisms for its own voice to be heard, what is more urgent today is that the voices of SHL students be heard. In this respect the profession has failed both its students and itself. SHL programs have now existed in American universities for more than thirty years. Where are those legions of students who came through SHL programs and went on to become leading surgeons, lawyers, politicians, policemen, and teachers? I have no doubt that they exist, and I have no doubt that they would readily support the cause if given the opportunity to do so. The problem is that the profession has not yet created these opportunities. Therefore, the profession must begin to envision a strong network of former students who can provide a unified voice well into the future. It must envision an organization that brings together heritage language students from all walks of life and from around the country to support innovations in teaching and research that will benefit their own children. This is a direction that SHL policy and planning research and advocacy could profitably take in the future.

CONCLUSION

Returning for a moment to the stories told at the beginning of this chapter, one cannot help but wonder what the fate of Marta Laureano or of Dame Edna, for that matter, would have been if the heritage language community would have been proactive rather than reactive. Maybe a proactive stance on the positive value of bilingualism and bilingual upbringing would have earned Laureano the praise of the court rather than its scorn. Maybe Dame Edna's joke would have been taken as the nonsense rambling of a buffoon. Although King (2009) has expressed a guarded optimism about a bright future for Spanish language education in the United States, the profession has now gained sufficient momentum and critical mass to make it even brighter for the nation's children and communities. Wiley (2001, 2010) has consistently and vigorously insisted on the importance of community participation in any effective heritage language policy in this country. Inasmuch as SHL teachers and researchers are part of this community, they must do everything in their power to ensure that bottom-up policy and planning occur. By endeavoring to develop tomorrow's leaders and to strategically place them throughout the professions and by participating in the organization and mobilization of former, current, and future students in a long-term, sustainable association that provides a unified voice and that successfully and continuously communicates the successes of heritage language learners, I believe that the profession is now in a position to plant the fecund seeds of bottom-up, community-driven policy and planning.

REFERENCES

Baker, Pauline. 1966. *Español para los hispanos.* Skokie, IL: National Textbook Company.
Carreira, María. 2007. "Spanish for Native Speakers Matters: Narrowing the Latino Achievement Gap through Spanish Language Instruction." *Heritage Language Journal* 5 (1). Available at www.heritagelanguages.org.
Carreira, María, and Regla Armengol. 2001. "Professional Opportunities for Heritage Language Speakers." In *Heritage Languages in America: Preserving a National Resource,* edited by Joy Kreeft Peyton, Scott McGinnis, and Dennis Ranard. McHenry, IL: Center for Applied Linguistics and Delta Systems.
Chabram Denersesian, Angie. 1993. "The Role of Chicano Literature in Teaching Spanish to Native Speakers." In *Language and Culture in Learning: Teaching Spanish to Native Speakers of Spanish,* edited by Barbara Merino, Henry Trueba, and Fabián Samaniego. Washington, DC: Falmer Press.

Colomer, Soria. 2010. "Dual Role Interpreters: Spanish Teachers in New Latino Communities." *Hispania* 93 (3): 490–503.

Cooper, Robert. 1989. *Language Planning and Social Change*. Cambridge: Cambridge University Press.

Dávila, Arlene. 2001. *Latinos, Inc: The Marketing and Making of a People*. Berkeley: University of California Press.

Draper, Joan, and June Hicks. 2000. "Where We've Been; What We've Learned." In *Teaching Heritage Learners: Voices from the Classroom*, edited by John Webb and Barbara Miller. New York: American Council on the Teaching of Foreign Languages.

Emery, David. 2003. "Dame Edna Insults Hispanics in *Vanity Fair*." http://urbanlegends .about.com/library/bl-dame-edna.htm.

Fishman, Joshua. 1974. "Language Modernization and Planning in Comparison with Other Types of National Modernization and Planning." In *Advances in Language Planning*, edited by Joshua Fishman. The Hague: Mouton.

Gándara, Patricia, and Frances Contreras. 2009. *The Latino Education Crisis: The Consequences of Failed School Policies*. Cambridge, MA: Harvard University Press.

García, Ofelia. 1993. "From Goya Portraits to Goya Beans: Elite Traditions and Popular Streams in US Spanish Language Policy." *Southwest Journal of Linguistics* 12:69–86.

Hernández-Chávez, Eduardo. 1993. "Native Language Loss and Its Implications for Revitalization of Spanish in Chicano Communities." In *Language and Culture in Learning: Teaching Spanish to Native Speakers of Spanish*, edited by Barbara Merino, Henry Trueba, and Fabián Samaniego. Washington, DC: Falmer Press.

Hidalgo, Margarita. 1997. "Criterios normativos e ideología lingüística: Aceptación y rechazo del español de los Estados Unidos." In *La Enseñanza del español a hispanohablantes: Teoría y praxis*, edited by M. Cecilia Colombi and Francisco Alarcón. Boston: Houghton Mifflin.

Kaplan, Richard, and Robert Baldauf. 1997. *Language Planning: From Practice to Theory*. Clevedon, UK: Multilingual Matters.

King, Kendall. 2009. "Spanish Language Education Policies in the US: Paradoxes, Pitfalls, and Promises." In *Español en Estados Unidos y otros contextos de contacto: Sociolingüística, ideología y pedagogía*, edited by Manel Lacorte and Jennifer Leeman. Madrid: Iberoamericana.

Kloss, Heinz. 1998. *The American Bilingual Tradition*. McHenry, IL: Center for Applied Linguistics and Delta Systems.

Leeman, Jennifer, and Glenn Martínez. 2007. "From Identity to Commodity: Ideologies of Spanish in Heritage Language Textbooks." *Critical Inquiry in Language Studies* 4 (1): 35–65.

MacGregor-Mendoza, Patricia. 2000. "Aquí no se habla español: Stories of Linguistic Repression in Southwest Schools." *Bilingual Research Journal* 24:355–67.

Martínez, Glenn. 2008. "Language Wars on the Texas Frontier." In *Recovering the US Hispanic Linguistic Heritage*, edited by Alejandra Balestra, Glenn Martínez, and Maria Irene Moyna. Houston: Arte Público Press.

McGroarty, Mary, and Alfredo Urzúa. 2009. The Relevance of Bilingual Proficiency in US Corporate Settings. In *Heritage Language Education: A New Field Emerging*, edited by Donna Brinton, Olga Kagan, and Susan Bauckus. New York: Routledge.

Quintana-Sarellana, Rosalinda, Thom Huebner, and Anne Jensen. 1997. "La utilización de nuestros recursos lingüísticos: Los estudiantes hispanohablantes como tutores de español como idioma extranjero." In *La Enseñanza del español a hispanohablantes: Teoría y praxis*, edited by M. Cecilia Colombi and Francisco Alarcón. Boston: Houghton Mifflin.

Ricento, Thomas. 2000. "Historical and Theoretical Perspectives in Language Policy and Planning." *Journal of Sociolinguistics* 4 (2): 196–213.

———. 2009. "Problems with the Language as Resource Discourse in the Promotion of Heritage Languages in the US." In *Language Allegiances and Bilingualism in the US*, edited by Máximo Rafael Salaberry. Clevedon, UK: Multilingual Matters.

Ruiz, Richard. 1988. "Orientations in Language Planning." In *Language Diversity: Problem or Resource?* edited by Sandra McKay and Sau-ling Cynthia Wong. Boston: Heinle and Heinle.

———. 2010. "Reorienting Language as Resource." In *International Perspectives on Bilingual Education*, edited by John Petrovic. Charlotte: Information Age.

Shohamy, Elana. 2006. *Language Policy: Hidden Agendas and New Approaches*. New York: Routledge.

Spolsky, Bernard. 2004. *Language Policy*. Cambridge: Cambridge University Press.

Teschner, Richard. 2000. "Trade Secrets: Advising, Tracking, Placing, and Progressing through the College-Level Spanish for Native Speakers Sequence." In *Spanish for Native Speakers*, edited by American Association of Teachers of Spanish and Portuguese. Fort Worth: Harcourt College.

Tollefson, James. 1991. *Planning Language, Planning Inequality: Language Policy in the Community*. London: Longman.

Valdés, Guadalupe. 1981. "Pedagogical Implications of Teaching Spanish to the Spanish-Speaking in the United States." In *Teaching Spanish to the Hispanic Bilingual: Issues, Aims, and Methods*, edited by Guadalupe Valdés, Antony Lozano, and Rodolfo García-Moya. New York: Teachers College Press.

———. 2000a. "The ACTFL–Hunter College FIPSE Project and Its Contributions to the Profession." In *Teaching Heritage Learners: Voices from the Classroom*, edited by John Webb and Barbara Miller. New York: American Council on the Teaching of Foreign Languages.

———. 2000b. "Introduction." In *Spanish for Native Speakers*, edited by American Association of Teachers of Spanish and Portuguese. Fort Worth: Harcourt College.

Valdés, Guadalupe, Sonia González, Dania García, and Patricio Márquez. 2009. "Heritage Languages and Ideologies of Language: Unexamined Challenges." In *Heritage Language Education: A New Field Emerging*, edited by Donna Brinton, Olga Kagan, and Susan Bauckus. New York: Routledge.

Verhovek, Sam Howe. 1995. "Mother Scolded by Judge for Speaking Spanish." *New York Times*, August 30. www.nytimes.com/1995/08/30/us/mother-scolded-by-judge-for-speaking-in-spanish.html.

Villa, Daniel, and Jennifer Villa. 2005. "Language Instrumentality in Southern New Mexico: Implications for the Loss of Spanish in the Southwest." *Southwest Journal of Linguistics* 1–2:169–84.

Wiley, Terrence. 2001. "Policy Formation and Implementation." In *Heritage Languages in America: Preserving a National Resource*, edited by Joy Peyton, Dennis Ranard, and Scott McGinnis. McHenry, IL: Center for Applied Linguistics and Delta Systems.

———. 2004. "Language Planning, Language Policy and the English-Only Movement." In *Language in the USA: Themes for the Twenty-First Century*, edited by Edward Finnegan and John Rickford. Cambridge: Cambridge University Press.

————. 2010. "Language Policy in the USA." In *Language Diversity in the USA*, edited by Kim Potowski. Cambridge: Cambridge University Press.

Wright, Wayne. 2007. "Heritage Language Programs in the Era of English-Only and No Child Left Behind." *Heritage Language Journal* 5 (1). Available at www.heritage languages.org.

CHAPTER 4

Key Concepts for Theorizing Spanish as a Heritage Language

Andrew Lynch, University of Miami

URING THE 1970S, in the aftermath of the civil rights movement and the formation of La Raza, a critical mass of studies on Spanish in the United States emerged. The scholars who undertook these studies were different than their early-twentieth-century predecessors, who had developed detailed descriptions of language use and form. Instead, many scholars in the 1970s and early 1980s took up ideological and theoretical issues (e.g., language "loyalty," as discussed by Sánchez 1972; and "diglossia," as proposed by Fishman, Cooper, and Ma 1971).[1] With the growing presence of "native speaker" students in university Spanish courses, the phenomena of fluent vernacular bilingualism and language "loss" posed pedagogical challenges. At that time, Valdés (1978, 103) affirmed that "defining native language instruction for the profession . . . is simply a question of deciding exactly *what* teaching a standard dialect of a language involves" (emphasis in the original). The first premise that she posited for a "comprehensive language development program" for bilingual speakers was "a dedication to bringing about the acquisition of 'educated' language use to include an overall development of total proficiency as characteristic of educated speakers of any language" (p. 106).

This philosophical premise seems to have remained at the heart of the emerging field of Spanish as a heritage language (SHL). Key to its interpretation are the concepts of "educated" or "standard" language, which is the concern of sociolinguistic inquiry; and "proficiency," which is a construct borrowed mostly from the field of second-language acquisition (SLA). This chapter presents a brief, critical overview of these central concepts as they relate to SHL, highlighting their connection to the theory of diglossia and the phenomena of language register, social agency, and generational continuity of the language. Clearly, all these theoretical notions have been intricately bound up together in the conceptualization of SHL: "Diglossia" is concomitant with notions of "register" and "standard language"; "register" appears as a crucial (albeit at times implicit) dimension of the "proficiency" of heritage language learners; "agency" provides an ideological basis for hypotheses (again, at times implicit) regarding the processes of acquisition and use generally correlated with degrees of "proficiency"; and in the great majority of studies about these processes, "generation" appears as the fundamental extralinguistic variable. Because the still-nascent field of SHL lacks a cohesive theoretical framework, the aim of this chapter is to generate further dialogue in advancement of this agenda by shedding critical light on several principal concepts that have guided the field thus far. First, however, a historical perspective on the notion of "diglossia" is in order, given that it seems to have provided the basis for Valdés's initial ideas regarding a "standard dialect" and to have laid the ground for the major theoretical proposals and research agendas that were to follow.

A HISTORICAL PERSPECTIVE ON DIGLOSSIA

In her seminal publications on teaching Spanish to US Hispanic bilinguals, Valdés (1976, 1977, 1978) made an argument that was characterized by a sort of "language deficit" model—that is, the notion that heritage speakers (who were at that time called native speakers) lack some aspects of an idealized "complete" repertoire, relative to a "high" or "formal" variety, suggestions that evoke Ferguson's (1959, 325) theory of diglossia. Adapting the French *diglossie*, Ferguson elaborated "diglossia" as a model for societies in which "two or more varieties of the same language are used by some speakers under different conditions, . . . with each having a different role to play." He took the situations of Arabic, Modern Greek, Swiss German, and Haitian Creole as the basis for his proposal, observing that, in all these cases, one variety ("high," or H) serves public, formal functions and is highly standardized, whereas another variety ("low," or L) of the same language, which is limited to orality, serves private and informal functions and lacks prestige and standardization.

In Fishman's (1967) extension of this model to bilingual societies—that is, societies where two different languages are used rather than two varieties of the same language—five important characteristics of diglossia, as defined by Ferguson, were disregarded: (1) speakers' feeling that H is more prestigious than L is sometimes "so strong that H alone is regarded as real and L is reported 'not to exist'" (Fishman 1967, 329–30); (2) H has a literary heritage but L does not (pp. 330–31); (3) "H has grammatical categories not present in L and has an inflectional system of nouns and verbs which is more reduced or totally absent in L" (p. 333); (4) "the bulk of the vocabulary of H and L is shared" (p. 334);

and (5) "the sound systems of H and L constitute a single phonological struc-ture" (p. 335). Although all these conditions hold true in most of the Arab world, they do not characterize the situation of Spanish and English in the United States. Nonetheless, Fishman's theory—which he and his colleagues applied in their widely cited sociological research on bilingualism among Puerto Ricans in New York City (Fishman, Cooper, and Ma 1971)—made an indelible impression on scholars of Spanish in the United States, some of whom continue to think of Spanish-English bilingualism as a diglossic sort of social arrangement (cf. Klee and Lynch 2009).

Silva-Corvalán (2001, 280), however, urged caution with regard to this theo-retical concept in the study of Spanish in the United States. She affirmed that

> no es recomendable . . . extender el concepto de tal manera que abarque cualquier comunidad en la que se empleen dos o más variedades en difer-entes circunstancias ya que perdería totalmente el valor que tiene en socio-lingüística como término clasificatorio de ciertas comunidades. . . . El gran número de hablantes de inglés y español en algunos estados de los Estados Unidos conduce al uso de las dos lenguas sin restricciones temáticas y situacionales: las dos cumplen funciones públicas y privadas. En estos casos, no se puede hablar fácilmente de una situación diglósica.

> it is not recommendable . . . to extend the concept in such a way that it takes on any community in which two or more varieties are used in different circumstances because, in doing so, it would totally lose the value that it has in sociolinguistics as a classificatory term for certain communities. . . . The great number of English and Spanish speakers in some states of the United States leads to the use of both languages without thematic and situational restrictions: both languages serve public and pri-vate functions. In these cases, one cannot readily refer to a diglossic situation.

According to Silva-Corvalán, "diglossia" in the macro-level sociological sense does not rightly pertain to the present-day context of the Spanish-speaking United States, because Spanish can be amply observed in numerous formal domains of public life. Her research (Silva-Corvalán 1994, 2003, 2006) during the past two decades suggests that the problem of "total proficiency" (Valdés 1978) might be conceptualized more aptly in terms of "reduced input" and a restricted use of Spanish in general among United States–born Hispanics/La-tinos—leading to stages of an incomplete acquisition of the language—rather than in terms of "nonstandard" varieties limited to given "domains." The model of diglossia, then, has perhaps misrepresented to some extent the sociolinguistic realities of Spanish in the United States. It is nonetheless true that schooling and literacy among United States–born Spanish speakers are largely—and in many cases exclusively—realized in English, a fact that led SHL researchers to look to the field of SLA when conceptualizing and describing (for applied purposes) the sorts of linguistic phenomena that these bilinguals present in Spanish. The construct they looked to was "proficiency."

OVERVIEW OF KEY CONCEPTS IN CURRENT RESEARCH

This section gives an overview of key concepts in current research. These include proficiency, register, agency, and generation.

Proficiency

Debates have been ongoing in SLA since the so-called proficiency movement began in the 1980s (Kramsch 1986). Valdés (1989), Barnwell (1993), and Valdés and Figueroa (1994) expressed serious concerns regarding the second language (L2) proficiency construct in the realm of bilingualism, arguing that the demonstration—and thus measurement—of "abilities" in the less dominant language of the bilingual are of a substantially different nature than in the case of the L2 speaker. Valdés and Figueroa pointed to the "monolingual bias" in the field of bilingualism, an argument similar to one that was later made by Firth and Wagner (1997, 293) regarding the idealization of the "native speaker" in SLA. They wrote that "IL [interlanguage] studies remain locked into a pattern of explaining variability and anomalous usage by recourse to notions of underdeveloped grammatical competence." In this way, the L2 speaker is perpetually "a deficient communicator struggling to overcome an underdeveloped L2 competence, striving to reach the "target" competence of an idealized NS [native speaker]," in the Chomskyan sense of the term (Firth and Wagner 1997, 295–96).[2]

To date, "proficiency," "competence," and "ability" have been gauged in most SHL studies vis-à-vis "native speaker" norms through one or more of the following measures: oral production in a conversational interview situation (e.g., Fairclough 1999; Fairclough and Mrak 2003; Lynch 2008; Sánchez-Muñoz 2007) or in a structured task (e.g., Beaudrie 2009; Montrul 2009; Pease-Álvarez, Hakuta, and Bayley 1996), grammaticality judgment (e.g., Mikulski 2010; Montrul 2009, 2010; Potowski, Jegerski, and Morgan-Short 2009), sentence completion or cloze tasks (e.g., Lynch 1999; Montrul 2004, 2005; Silva-Corvalán 1994), vocabulary identification (Montrul 2004, 2005; Pease-Álvarez, Hakuta, and Bayley 1996; Potowski and Matts 2008), delayed imitation or story retelling (e.g., Merino 1983; Potowski and Matts 2008), role-playing (e.g., Gutiérrez-Rivas 2007), or self-reporting (e.g., Lambert and Taylor 1996; Montrul 2004). Much the same as in SLA studies, SHL researchers have offered largely morphological and syntactic accounts of speaker ability. Aspects of phonology (Alvord 2010;

Lynch 2009; Phillips 1982), the lexicon (Mendieta 1999; Otheguy 1993; Silva-Corvalán 1994; Torres Cacoullos and Aaron 2003), and discourse-pragmatic features (see chapter 6 in this volume, by Pinto) have been considered more in variationist terms than as issues of proficiency per se. For institutional assessment purposes to date, little distinction seems to have been made between heritage and L2 learners. Two very important cases in point—the American Council on the Teaching of Foreign Languages' *Oral Proficiency Interview* Guidelines, which have in no way been modified for heritage learners; and the Spanish Advanced Placement examinations, which are administered by the Educational Testing Service for college-level credit—employ the same test materials and the same scoring criteria for both groups.

The present author has argued elsewhere (Lynch 2003a, 2003b) that the research questions and theoretical paradigms of SLA provide a meaningful basis upon which to build in SHL, and that heritage learners, particularly those at lower levels of proficiency, bear important linguistic similarities to intermediate and advanced L2 learners (Lynch 2008). Morphosyntactic and lexical-syntactic commonalities are quite salient among these two groups, as Lipski (1993) noted. Important grammatical differences also emerge, however (see chapter 5 in this volume, by Montrul). Beaudrie (2009) and Potowski, Jegerski, and Morgan-Short (2009) have also noted both similar and different outcomes for heritage and L2 learners in classroom settings. As for the theoretical premise of these sorts of comparative studies, Montrul (2005, 201) reasoned that "in many respects, L1 [first language] loss in a bilingual context is the flip side of the L2 acquisition coin." Similarly, Silva-Corvalán (1990, 167–68) observed several years earlier that "it is arresting to note that language attrition in societal bilingualism is in fact to a large extent the mirror image of development in creolization, and in first- and second-language acquisition. . . . This correspondence may in fact reflect the freezing . . . of the bilingual's secondary language."

The supposition that L1 and L2 are inversely and necessarily related dates to earlier theories of creolization. Indeed, there was serious debate during the 1970s regarding the analogousness of "interlanguage" (Selinker 1972) to pidginization and creolization (Anderson 1983; Schumann 1974, 1978). Although the great majority of scholars today would no longer say that L2 or HL speech reflects creolization (cf. Otheguy 2003), the concept of interlanguage—which was founded on Selinker's notion of "fossilization" and was implied in Silva-Corvalán's (1990, 1994) use of the term "freezing"—has remained part and parcel of SLA. This concept, however, has entered into very few discussions of HL acquisition. One example of those few is Valdés and Geoffrion-Vinci's (1998, 494) widely cited treatment of the notion of "register," which is discussed in the following section. These authors observe that Chicano bilinguals manifest an "approximative register" or "interregister" in formal, academic settings—in their words, "a variety that has characteristics similar to those discussed in Selinker."

It seems unclear how much theoretical parallelism Valdés and Geoffrion-Vinci (1998, 478) wished to establish with SLA on conceptual grounds. At the outset of their study, they state that they "do not consider Chicano speakers of Spanish to be learners of Spanish as a second language," yet they ultimately conclude that "bilinguals can be classified as analogous to L2 learners" in that their nondominant language is stable and continues to develop and change over time (p. 495). In 1995 Valdés affirmed that "we know enough . . . to make us suspect that the process of further development of a first language is fundamentally different from the process of L2 acquisition" (Valdés 1995, 317), thus reiterating her earlier stance (Valdés 1978). By 2005, however, Valdés was calling for "the reconceptualization and expansion of the field of SLA by using the teaching of heritage languages to L1/L2 users as a lens through with such a reconceptualization and expansion might be envisioned" (Valdés 2005, 422). Her most recent proposal, that heritage learners be conceptualized as "L1/L2 users," reflects an apparently hybrid sort of speaker based on Cook's (1992; 2002, 413–14) notion of the "L2 user" in his revision of SLA theory.

What surely has been different in theoretical discussions of SLA and SHL is the great lack of concern regarding the phenomenon of "register" or "style" in the former (cf. Tarone 1988) versus its centrality in the latter. Although traditional SLA is concomitant with the use of academic language in the written mode, the nature of HL acquisition is rather the opposite, given that the majority of learners begin the process of acquiring formal literacy in Spanish with an already-existent capacity to use the language (to varying degrees) in noninstitutional social settings and with particular interlocutors.

Register

The notion of "register"—bound up in "educated" language—is invoked by SHL researchers seemingly as a dimension of proficiency, the argument being that heritage learners lack knowledge and productive skill relative to formal, academic varieties of the language. This thinking is in line with deficit theories of language (cf. MacSwan 2000), such as Bernstein's (1971) seminal treatise on restricted versus elaborate codes and Cummins's (1979) theoretical distinction between "BICS" (i.e., basic interpersonal communication skills) and "CALP" (cognitive academic language proficiency), which formed the basis of his highly criticized Threshold Hypothesis for bilingual education. Although Valdés and Geoffrion-Vinci (1998) do not cite Bernstein in their analysis of the "underdeveloped code" of Chicano bilinguals, or clarify if "code" is meant to be synonymous with "register," "the problem" that they describe appears as more of a social class phenomenon (as in Bernstein's sense of "code") than as a language "style" phenomenon (in the Labovian sense).[3]

Valdés and Geoffrion-Vinci (1998, 477) observed that "because in Mexico these [first-generation Chicano] speakers did not have access to the range of situations and contexts in which formal high varieties of Spanish are used, their language is characterized by a somewhat narrower range of lexical and syntactic alternatives than is the language of upper-middle-class speakers." They affirmed that Chicano communities are "characterized by diglossia (the functional differentiation of languages) and bilingualism" and "also reflect the social class origins of their residents," that is, lower social status (p. 476). After a careful comparison of the speech produced by ten second-, third-, and fourth-generation bilingual Chicano students giving classroom presentations in Spanish at an elite university in the Western United States and that produced by six same-age monolingual Mexican university students in Ciudad Juárez making the same types of presentations (autobiographical and argumentative), the authors concluded that "both the working-class Mexican students and the Chicano students used varieties of the academic register of Spanish that they were still in the process of acquiring. . . . Even though they were native speakers, the Mexican students had not developed the ability to use consistently the high varieties of the language" (p. 494). They noted that all ten Chicano students "were aware of register differences and that they attempted, as far as possible, to produce suitably academic speech for classroom activities" (p. 493). In sum, because the phenomenon at hand did not appear largely attributable to a lack of awareness of the differential "registers" of Spanish, one could suppose that a fundamental condition for acquisition was already met, whether from within or outside the academic context.

Perhaps key to a clearer understanding of "register" for purposes of HL acquisition are the notions of "activity" and "task." Halliday (1978) identified three different dimensions of "register": the nature of the topic at hand ("field"), the nature of the social relations between the individuals involved ("tenor"), and the medium of the interaction ("mode"). Applying Halliday's (1994) ideas about functional grammar to SHL, Colombi (2002, 2003) and Achugar (2003, 2009) considered the ways in which heritage learners manifest and develop "functions" of language in academic or classroom discourse, for example, ideational, interpersonal, textual, expansion (elaborating, extending, enhancing), and projection (direct speech, indirect speech, etc.). These sorts of analyses, centered on the idea of "function" rather than the more abstract "register," could prove quite fruitful in the future (for more on functional grammar, see chapter 12 in this volume, by Colombi and Harrington).[4] It is particularly important that this idea is much less bound up in the ideological and somewhat artificial dichotomy of "formal" versus "informal" varieties, a dichotomy that seems to have been perpetuated in SHL by the theory of diglossia. One wonders to what extent this theory may at times influence researchers and educators to assume a priori that heritage speakers are "deficient" in formal styles of language yet "proficient" in informal styles, when in reality they are also "deficient" in informal styles in some respects—something clearly demonstrated by Silva-Corvalán (1994)—and "proficient" in formal styles by some measures (Sánchez-Muñoz 2007). Language deficit, then, following MacSwan's (2000) reasoning, would not be necessarily register- or domain-specific.[5]

"Agency," as attributed to individual learners in their social and cultural milieus, appears in some studies as a central problem in the acquisition and use of other registers of Spanish. Urciuoli (2008, 270) suggests that "Spanish that is adequate at home may be experienced at school as inadequate or fragmentary; students . . . find themselves pushed into often uncomfortable metalinguistic reflection at school, where correctness is a constant concern. Such circumstances complicate, even inhibit, rather than enhance its significance as a cultural marker." As in Valdés and Geoffrion-Vinci's (1998) study, heritage learners were in fact aware of linguistic differences. Urciuoli (2008, 261) characterizes the "correctness model" as a "recasting of Spanish itself" inherent in "the reworking of Latino identity that takes place in college." In this way, "correct" Spanish is imbued with agency, "a goal worth striving for," because of its market value, that is, cultural and symbolic capital (p. 273). The ideological notion of agency in sociolinguistic conceptualizations of SHL is discussed in what follows.

Agency

Urciuoli's study is a good example of interpretation of the macro-level social relationship of Spanish and English in the United States through the theoretical lens of the autonomous individual actively making conscious choices and forging a social identity. Her conclusions illustrate the centrality of the notion of agency (cf. Giddens 1984, 276) to her argument: "For students striving toward a rethinking of Latinidad, the internalization of correct Spanish can be empowering, a realization of an identity encompassing both one's local origins and a sense of elite generic belonging; in this identity, Spanish and the rethought Latinidad are a bulwark against class/race marking." One could venture that classroom exposure to forms that heritage learners perceive as more "correct" or "generic"—that is, less socially marked—leads to the acquisition and use of a theoretically distinctive variety in psychosocial terms. On these grounds, this variety would be the vehicle for dissociation or detachment from the negative connotations of a variety that is partially and informally acquired, or in some cases stigmatized. The act of HL acquisition thus might not be self-perceived by learners as compensation for an "incomplete" or "underdeveloped code"—or ultimate "completion" of that code in an idealized linguistic sense—but rather acquisition of a "different" variety.

Although Fairclough (2005) conceptualizes SHL explicitly as a process of second-dialect acquisition in grammatical terms, Vilar Sánchez (1995) casts the issue more on perceptual grounds in her case study of a second-generation Spanish speaker in Germany. This seventeen-year-old boy, who was born and raised in Germany, was the son of immigrants from a small Andalusian village. Vilar

Sánchez explained that "when he spoke Spanish [in Spain], he had a good chance of being considered illiterate and therefore an object of derision. On the other hand, if he were taken as a German by the same group, he would receive a more positive evaluation, and any linguistic deficiency would be considered natural" (Vilar Sánchez 1995, 7). The author noted that "when speaking Spanish he distinguished two different codes: (1) a strongly dialectal variety, which he used inside the family; . . . [and] (2) the typical interlanguage of a native speaker of German with all the interferences that normally arise between the two languages." She affirmed that he "obviously considered the latter superior. Consequently, he consistently used it to communicate in more formal situations." (p. 8). The mental basis seemed laid, then, for conscious acquisition of a "second" variety of Spanish rather than a "completed" or more "developed" variety of the original L1, at least in psychosocial (i.e., perceptual and attitudinal) terms, as some of the students quoted in Urciuoli's study seem to suggest. This may perhaps be the reason why some Spanish HL learners in the United States self-identify as L2 learners of Spanish and feel more comfortable with that label (cf. Carreira 2004; Lynch 2008).

However, ethnic identity remains as an often-crucial aspect of agency in SHL. For example, Scott Shenk (2007, 195) described how English-dominant Mexican-origin university students in California use Spanish in spontaneous playful speech as a means of ethnic "authentication"—"a dialogic process linking social action and ideology with interactionally negotiated identity stances" —in relation to three apparent ideological constructs: bloodline, nationality, and Spanish fluency. With regard to the latter, Scott Shenk (2007, 210–11) observed how, when a less-fluent speaker said *joves* (hoves) referring to the day of the week, she was emphatically corrected by a more fluent peer, "JUEVES [ɣueßes] GUEY," who then laughingly mocked her and told her that she was "gonna revoke [her] Mexican privileges." Scott Shenk affirmed that this example reflects "language disfluency treated as cultural inadequacy and inauthenticity" and showed how "the participant who speaks Spanish without error acts as a cultural gatekeeper." In other words, "being Mexican is a privilege that can be taken away by more culturally proficient community members" (p. 212).[6] With regard to the ontological debate about agency versus structure, more emphasis on "community" may be in order. Scott Shenk suggested that "to make our investigations fruitful, we should abandon the notion that authenticity resides in the speaker and can be determined by the analyst, and instead promote the idea that authenticity is a social construct" (pp. 213–14).

In Sánchez's (1983) seminal treatise *Chicano Discourse*, the forces of collective life appear more powerful than the individual. Social and material conditions determine patterns of language acquisition, variation, use, and choice. For Sánchez, language choice is "both conscious and subconscious, as is evident in many Chicano homes where parents address their children in Spanish and they

respond in English" (Sánchez 1983, 12). This theoretical perspective seems crucial to the understanding of SHL. One of the New York City Puerto Rican students quoted by Urciuoli is a case in point: "'I understand a lot of Spanish but
in terms of speaking it, I just feel uncomfortable with it because I feel like I
sound silly. After spending so much time with my family, like me even trying
would just like—'" (Urciuoli 2008, 265). Clearly, this student's conscious decision to try speaking Spanish with his family had been impeded by the perceived
"silliness" of doing so. In Miami, highly fluent second- and third-generation
bilinguals have responded similarly when asked by the present author (Lynch)
why they do not speak Spanish with each other more often. "Because it's just
unnatural," they say; "because I feel ridiculous"; "because people will think I'm
a *ref*" (meaning "refugee," a term commonly used by adolescents and young
adults to refer pejoratively to recently arrived immigrants in Miami who do not
know much English or prefer Spanish); or "I get tired of being corrected by
others who speak it better," which is reminiscent of Scott Shenk's (2007) observation above. Yet when asked if they want their children and grandchildren to
be bilingual, these same bilinguals respond with a resounding "yes." Given the
substantial socioeconomic and cultural prestige of Spanish and the positive
macro-level attitudes toward bilingualism in Miami (cf. Lynch 2000; López
Morales 2003), it seems likely that if individual agency were the principal force
driving language use, many more second- and third-generation bilinguals in
South Florida would speak Spanish more often than they do. This proposition
remains somewhat of a conundrum for SHL theory; that is, it could not be
validated unless apparently "real" and present language ideologies in US society
at large were to change.

Nonetheless, a more profound and elaborate exploration of "community" in
SHL and sociolingusitics might constitute a firm step toward reconciling linguistic theory and empirical evidence in this regard. Otheguy, Zentella, and Livert's
(2007, 797) variationist study offers interesting insights into linguistic constraint
hierarchies in Spanish-speaking New York City, but an exploration of the social
construct(ion) of "community" is precluded by the authors' affirmation that
"because the bilingualism of . . . NYC Latinos tends to last for only two or three
generations, settings of [this] sort . . . have not been favored in the search for the
structural consequences of bilingualism." After reading their provocative conclusion that "the NYBR [New York–born and/or –raised] generation constitute[s]
a better delineated speech community than do newcomers to the City" (p. 797),
one is left asking, What happens to this "community" beyond the third generation? Does it disappear without a trace from the sociolinguistic landscape of New
York City in the following couple of decades, to then be replaced by another one,
which may be characterized by different variable linguistic constraint hierarchies?
Or might there be some sort of continuity underlying such apparent discontinu-
ity? Could the "community" be continuous in some other respect? It may be

that linguistic discontinuities are, in fact, a defining feature of bilingual Spanish-speaking communities in the United States, as Mougeon and Nadasdi (1998) have suggested in the case of French-English bilingual communities in Canada.

In the end, the uniformity of structural patterns by Labovian design may not be the key to the theoretical conceptualization of bilingual communities but rather acts of positioning, as stated by Lemke (2002, 74): "Communities, like other ecosystems, are not defined by what their participants have in common, but by how their interdependence on one another articulates across differences of viewpoint, beliefs, values, and practices." Likewise, a linear model of intergenerational language transmission may not be valid for highly dynamic and sometimes cyclical Spanish-English bilingualism in the United States. In their proposed revision of a model for language maintenance in the Southwest, Villa and Rivera-Mills (2009, 30) emphasize the notion of "community," affirming that "it is the need to connect with a particular speech community that requires a change in the traditional unidirectional, linear pattern of change to a more circular one, in which at any given point and with any generation there is the opportunity to recapture the HL, thereby promoting a more stable bilingualism." The notion of "generation" in SHL research is taken up in the following section.

Generation

Almost all SHL researchers to date have adhered to an age-of-immigration criterion to isolate groups of speakers for linguistic analysis. For example, Otheguy, Zentella, and Livert (2007, 780) identified the "newcomer" as "someone who arrived in New York at age seventeen or older and has lived in the City for no more than five years." In her cross-generational analysis of Mexican Spanish in Los Angeles, Silva-Corvalán (1994, 15–16) defined "group 1" speakers as those born in Mexico who immigrated to the United States sometime after age eleven; the members of "group 2" were those born in the United States or those who immigrated before age six. Similarly, Pease-Álvarez, Hakuta, and Bayley (1996, 139) differentiated between those "born in Mexico, parents born in Mexico"; those "born in the United States, parents born in Mexico; mother immigrated at age 15 or older"; and those "born in the United States, mother born in Mexico, mother immigrated at age 10 or younger." This age-of-immigration criterion implicitly asserts the validity of Lenneberg's (1967) hypothesis—which has been restated in various ways by others as a "sensitive period" or a "fundamental difference hypothesis" (Bley-Vroman 1990)—that language acquisition is constrained by the age at which learning or exposure begins; specifically, ultimate attainment or "proficiency" is negatively correlated with the age of the onset of acquisition.

Researchers have posited different biological and neurocognitive limits for language acquisition, anywhere between six and sixteen years of age. In a highly influential study of Korean and Chinese L2 learners of English, Johnson and Newport (1989, 79) posited that after eight to ten years of age, ultimate attainment would be "non-native-like." Of particular importance, they observed "no systematic relationship to age of exposure, and a leveling off of ultimate performance, among those exposed to the language after puberty." In other words, the "critical period" extended to puberty, but beyond puberty there was no further basis for maturational effects, that is, a seventeen-year-old would stand no better chance at ultimate "native-like" attainment than a forty-year-old. Johnson and Newport's study—based on a grammaticality judgment task—was replicated by Birdsong and Molis (2001) with native Spanish-speaking learners of L2 English. Two important differences were observed: (1) A significant decline in performance appeared around seventeen years of age, much later than in Johnson and Newport's study (Birdsong and Molis 2001, 240); (2) the effects of age continued past the presumed end of maturation (p. 246). There was a significantly higher incidence of "near-nativeness" among subjects in their twenties than among those in their thirties (p. 239). Brain-imaging studies from the rapidly emerging field of neurolinguistics have also shown that the degree of proficiency and extent of language use in bilingualism have a significantly greater impact on cerebral activity than does age of acquisition (Abutalebi, Cappa, and Perani 2007).

As Montrul (2008, 261) has cogently demonstrated, age "is very relevant to L1 attrition in language minority speakers." But the compelling evidence presented by Birdsong and Molis (2001) and others (e.g., Bialystok and Hakuta 1994) who have cast doubt on the "critical period," demonstrating variable "cutoff" points and maturational effects well beyond puberty, suggests that we may need to refine the concept of "generation" or "speaker group" in HL acquisition studies by taking into account other sorts of factors, that is, nonbiological ones. In most studies of Spanish in the United States to date, someone who immigrated at the age of seventeen falls into the same category as someone who arrived at the age of forty. Likewise, those who arrived at the age of six—and, in some studies, as high as at the age of ten or eleven—figure into the same group as those who were born in the United States to parents who immigrated at some "adult" age. Such a priori groupings may be fallacious in some respects. Although most would agree that "age" is quite clear-cut, unidimensional, and empirically unproblematic as a biological construct, few would argue the same regarding "age" as a social, mental, cultural, or pedagogical construct (cf. Vygotsky 1978). Indeed, sociolinguists have begun to demonstrate through longitudinal variationist studies that language does not become "fixed" at a particular age and then remain static throughout the rest of one's life span (cf. research being conducted by Lanchart in Denmark: lanchart.hum.ku.dk). As Sankoff and Blondeau (2007, 584) have noted, "Change is dramatic in childhood, but it does not stop there. To understand the dynamics of change in the speech community, we must follow language across the life span." This phenomenon seems central to future theory building in SHL.

CONCLUSION

Heller (2007, 342) has remarked that bilingualism is "a kind of fault line, a space that is particularly sensitive to and revealing of social change, both in terms of how we understand it and in terms of the phenomena we see when we orient our gaze in the ways we have learned to do, and which we need to find new ways of describing and explaining, because the older frame no longer holds so well." With "diglossia" as part of that "older frame," predating globalization and the rise of mass media and communication technologies, language researchers must turn to issues of "agency" and "activity" (in the sense of language "practice") to guide theory building in the years ahead. As language varieties become increasingly delocalized and reconceptualized through emerging new paradigms of communication and literacy (cf. Martín Barbero 1987; New London Group 1996), SHL researchers must look to less linear and dichotomous theoretical concepts of Spanish in the United States. "Register," as a social and institutional discourse phenomenon (cf. Bourdieu 1991), must be deconstructed in terms of actual language use, that is, "function," in relation to specific sorts of activities. As a result, "proficiency" should emerge as more of a variable, task-based construct and less of an idealized, fixed measure based upon literacy practices in traditional SLA. Villa and Rivera-Mills's (2009) proposal for a circular (or cyclical) model of bilingual phenomena in the United States points to very interesting avenues for future investigation, particularly of what pertains to "identity." Along these same lines, the field should also focus more on questions of subjectivity (cf. Carter 2009) and affect (cf. Pavlenko 2006) in SHL, because these hold valuable insights into heritage learners' choices to speak Spanish (or not), and to speak it in certain ways; the perceptions they have of themselves as members of a "community"; and the ideological, political, and global economic construction of the United States as a "Spanish-speaking community" (cf. Del Valle 2007).

NOTES

1. Sánchez argued that there are at least three dimensions of language choice and use: the linguistic level, the utterance level, and the social level. Each of these reflects language "loyalty" as an ideological, political, and material phenomenon. Sánchez (1983, 178) affirmed that "the fact that dynamic and transitional bilingualism persists in communities of the Southwest . . . is a sign of the contradictory material conditions under which Chicanos live. The continued presence of Spanish in verbal interaction that gradually becomes more and more English dominant reflects both language maintenance and loss, both acculturation and cultural resistance, both maintenance of class boundaries and occupational mobility, both a highly urban population and a large population of rural roots, both recent immigrants from Mexico and third, fourth, and fifth Mexican-origin generations in the United States, both largely segregated barrios and highly integrated multi-ethnic urban communities. . . . The role that language choice can play in social

transformation is secondary but undoubtedly significant as language is our principal means of communicating ideas to others."

2. Haugen (1978, 34) remarked that the juxtaposition of bilingual and monolingual speech for purposes of linguistic inquiry is "merely a descriptive convenience" and "not a denial of its [the bilingual variety's] status as an independent variety."

3. Indeed, the anecdotal case of "Estela," which provides Valdés and Geoffrion-Vinci's introduction, could fit seamlessly into Bernstein's (1971, 474) treatise: "Given her family's position in the social structure, her access to English academic discourse has been limited. Her access to academic Spanish, on the other hand, has also been limited, both because of her family background and because of the characteristics of the community in which she acquired Spanish."

4. As Sánchez-Muñoz (2007, 169) concludes, agreeing with Biber (1995), "distinctive indicators of register are rare."

5. In his criticism of language deficit models in educational linguistics and, in particular, Cummins's Threshold Hypothesis, MacSwan (2000, 34) observed that "Cummins defines school literacy as one component of language proficiency. Taking literacy and related school knowledge to be the locus of the deficiency in L1, rather than language itself, makes the Threshold Hypothesis tautological, or trivially true, and it may therefore be said to have no empirical content." He concluded that "although L1 literacy and knowledge of academic discourse and vocabulary are certainly relevant to *academic* achievement, they are not relevant to *linguistic* achievement" (MacSwan 2000, 35; emphasis in the original).

6. It is interesting to note here that, in a survey study on language-related uses of humor, Vaid (2006, 165–66) observed that bilingual Mexican Americans perceived humorous teasing to be more a part of their "culture" than a part of their "self" repertoire.

REFERENCES

Abutalebi, Jubin, Stefano Cappa, and Daniela Perani. 2007. "The Bilingual Brain as Revealed by Functional Neuroimaging." In *The Bilingualism Reader, Second Edition*, edited by Li Wei. London: Routledge.

Achugar, Mariana. 2003. "Academic Registers in Spanish in the US: A Study of Oral Texts Produced by Bilingual Speakers in a University Graduate Program." In *Mi lengua: Spanish as a heritage language in the United States*, edited by Ana Roca and Cecilia Colombi. Washington, DC: Georgetown University Press.

———. 2009. "Constructing a Bilingual Professional Identity in a Graduate Classroom." *Journal of Language, Identity, and Education* 8:65–87.

Alvord, Scott. 2010. "Variation in Miami Cuban Spanish Interrogative Intonation." *Hispania* 93:235–55.

Anderson, Roger, ed. 1983. *Pidginization and Creolization as Language Acquisition*. Rowley, MA: Newbury House.

Barnwell, David. 1993. "Oral Proficiency Testing and the Bilingual Speaker." In *Spanish in the United States: Linguistic Contact and Diversity*, edited by Ana Roca and John Lipski. Berlin: Mouton de Gruyter.

Beaudrie, Sara. 2009. "Receptive Bilinguals' Language Development in the Classroom: The Differential Effects of Heritage versus Foreign Language Curriculum." In *Español en Estados Unidos y otros contextos de contacto*, edited by Manel Lacorte and Jennifer Leeman. Madrid: Iberoamericana/Vervuert.

Bernstein, Basil. 1971. *Class, Codes and Control, Volume 1: Theoretical Studies toward a Sociology of Education*. London: Routledge & Kegan Paul.

Bialystok, Ellen, and Kenji Hakuta. 1994. *In Other Words: The Science and Psychology of Second Language Acquisition*. New York: Basic Books.

Biber, Douglas. 1995. *Dimensions of Register Variation: A Cross-Linguistic Comparison*. Cambridge: Cambridge University Press.

Birdsong, David, and Michelle Molis. 2001. "On the Evidence for Maturational Constraints in Second-Language Acquisition." *Journal of Memory and Language* 44:235–49.

Bley-Vroman, Robert. 1990. "The Logical Problem of Foreign Language Learning." *Linguistic Analysis* 20:3–49.

Bourdieu, Pierre. 1991. *Language and Symbolic Power*, edited by John Thompson. Cambridge, MA: Harvard University Press.

Carreira, Maria. 2004. "Seeking Explanatory Adequacy: A Dual Approach to Understanding the Term 'Heritage Language Learner.'" *Heritage Language Journal* 2 (1). Available at www.heritagelanguages.org.

Carter, Phillip. 2009. "Speaking Subjects: Language, Subject Formation, and the Crisis of Identity." PhD diss., Duke University.

Cook, Vivian. 1992. "Evidence for Multicompetence." *Language Learning* 42:557–91.

———. 2002. "Background of the L2 User." In *Portraits of the L2 User*, edited by Vivian Cook. Clevedon, UK: Multilingual Matters.

Colombi, M. Cecilia. 2002. "Academic Language Development in Latino Students' Writing in Spanish." In *Developing Advanced Literacy in First and Second Languages: Meaning with Power*, edited by Mary Schleppegrell and M. Cecilia Colombi. Mahwah, NJ: Lawrence Erlbaum Associates.

———. 2003. "Un enfoque funcional para la enseñanza del ensayo expositivo." In *Mi lengua: Spanish as a Heritage Language in the United States*, edited by Ana Roca and Cecilia Colombi. Washington, DC: Georgetown University Press.

Cummins, James. 1979. "Cognitive/Academic Language Proficiency, Linguistic Interdependence, the Optimum Age Question and Some Other Matters." *Working Papers on Bilingualism* 19:121–29.

Del Valle, José. 2007. "La lengua, patria común: la *hispanofonía* y el nacionalismo panhispánico." In *La lengua, ¿patria común?* edited by José Del Valle. Madrid: Iberoamericana/Vervuert.

Fairclough, Marta. 1999. "Discurso directo vs. discurso indirecto en el español hablado en Houston." *Bilingual Review* 24:217–29.

———. 2005. *Spanish and Heritage Language Education in the United States: Struggling with Hypotheticals*. Madrid: Iberoamericana/Vervuert.

Fairclough, Marta, and N. Ariana Mrak. 2003. "La enseñanza del español a los hispanohablantes bilingües y su efecto en la producción oral." In *Mi lengua: Spanish as a Heritage Language in the United States*, edited by Ana Roca and Cecilia Colombi. Washington, DC: Georgetown University Press.

Ferguson, Charles. 1959. "Diglossia." *Word* 1:325–40.

Firth, Alan, and Johannes Wagner. 1997. "On Discourse, Communication, and (Some) Fundamental Concepts in SLA Research." *Modern Language Journal* 81:285–300.

Fishman, Joshua. 1967. "Bilingualism with and without Diglossia; Diglossia with and without Bilingualism." *Journal of Social Issues* 23:29–38.

Fishman, Joshua, Robert Cooper, and Roxana Ma. 1971. *Bilingualism in the Barrio.* Bloomington: Indiana University Press.

Giddens, Anthony. 1984. *The Constitution of Society.* Berkeley: University of California Press.

Gutiérrez-Rivas, Carolina. 2007. "Variación pragmática del español de los cubanos y cubanoamericanos en Miami: El efecto de género y generación en el uso de estructuras discursivas." PhD diss., University of Florida.

Halliday, M. A. K. 1978. *Language as Social Semiotic: The Social Interpretation of Language and Meaning.* London: Edward Arnold.

———. 1994. *An Introduction to Functional Grammar, Second Edition.* London: Edward Arnold.

Haugen, Einar. 1978. "Bilingualism, Language Contact and Immigrant Languages in the United States. A Research Report 1956–1970." In *Advances in the Study of Societal Multilingualism,* edited by Joshua Fishman. The Hague: Mouton.

Heller, Monica. 2007. "The Future of Bilingualism." In *Bilingualism: A Social Approach,* edited by Monica Heller. New York: Palgrave Macmillan.

Johnson, Jacqueline, and Elissa Newport. 1989. "Critical Period Effects in Second Language Learning: The Influence of Maturational State on the Acquisition of English as a Second Language." *Cognitive Psychology* 21:60–99.

Klee, Carol, and Andrew Lynch. 2009. *El español en contacto con otras lenguas.* Washington, DC: Georgetown University Press.

Kramsch, Claire. 1986. "Proficiency versus Achievement: Reflections on the Proficiency Movement." *ADFL Bulletin* 18:22–24.

Lambert, Wallace, and Donald Taylor. 1996. "Language in the Lives of Ethnic Minorities: Cuban American Families in Miami." *Applied Linguistics* 17:477–500.

Lemke, Jay. 2002. "Language Development and Identity: Multiple Timescales in the Social Ecology of Learning." In *Language Acquisition and Language Socialization: Ecological Perspectives,* edited by Claire Kramsch. London: Continuum.

Lenneberg, Eric. 1967. *The Biological Foundations of Language.* New York: John Wiley & Sons.

Lipski, John. 1993. "Creoloid Phenomena in the Spanish of Transitional Bilinguals." In *Spanish in the United States: Linguistic Contact and Diversity,* edited by Ana Roca and John Lipski. Berlin: Mouton de Gruyter.

López Morales, Humberto. 2003. *Los cubanos de Miami: Lengua y sociedad.* Miami: Ediciones Universal.

Lynch, Andrew. 1999. "The Subjunctive in Miami Cuban Spanish: Bilingualism, Contact, and Language Variability." PhD diss., University of Minnesota.

———. 2000. "Spanish-Speaking Miami in Sociolinguistic Perspective: Bilingualism, Recontact, and Language Maintenance among the Cuban-Origin Population." In *Research on Spanish in the United States: Linguistic Issues and Challenges,* edited by Ana Roca. Somerville, MA: Cascadilla Press.

————. 2003a. "The Relationship between Second and Heritage Language Acquisition: Notes on Research and Theory Building." *Heritage Language Journal* 1. Available at www.heritagelanguages.org.

————. 2003b. "Toward a Theory of Heritage Language Acquisition: Spanish in the United States." In *Mi lengua: Spanish as a Heritage Language in the United States*, edited by Ana Roca and M. Cecilia Colombi. Washington, DC: Georgetown University Press.

————. 2008. "The Linguistic Similarities of Spanish Heritage and Second Language Learners." *Foreign Language Annals* 41:252–81.

————. 2009. "A Sociolinguistic Analysis of Final /s/ in Miami Cuban Spanish." *Language Sciences* 31:767–90.

MacSwan, Jeff. 2000. "The Threshold Hypothesis, Semilingualism, and Other Contributions to a Deficit View of Linguistic Minorities." *Hispanic Journal of Behavioral Sciences* 22:3–45.

Martín Barbero, Jesús. 1987. *De los medios a las mediaciones*. Barcelona: Gustavo Gili.

Mendieta, Eva. 1999. *El préstamo en el español de los Estados Unidos*. New York: Peter Lang.

Merino, Barbara. 1983. "Language Loss in Bilingual Chicano Children." *Journal of Applied Developmental Psychology* 4:277–94.

Mikulski, Ariana. 2010. "Receptive Volitional Subjunctive Abilities in Heritage and Traditional Foreign Language Learners of Spanish." *Modern Language Journal* 94:217–33.

Montrul, Silvina. 2004. "Subject and Object Expression in Spanish Heritage Speakers. A Case of Morpho-Syntactic Convergence." *Bilingualism: Language and Cognition* 7:125–42.

————. 2005. "Second Language Acquisition and First Language Loss in Adult Early Bilinguals: Exploring Some Differences and Similarities." *Second Language Research* 21:199–249.

————. 2008. *Incomplete Acquisition in Bilingualism. Re-Examining the Age Factor.* Amsterdam: John Benjamins.

————. 2009. "Knowledge of Tense-Aspect and Mood in Spanish Heritage Speakers." *International Journal of Bilingualism* 13:239–69.

————. 2010. "How Similar Are Second Language Learners and Heritage Speakers? Spanish Clitics and Word Order." *Applied Psycholinguistics* 31:167–207.

Mougeon, Raymond, and Terry Nadasdi. 1998. "Sociolinguistic Discontinuities in Minority Language Communities." *Language* 74:40–55.

New London Group. 1996. "A Pedagogy of Multiliteracies: Designing Social Futures." *Harvard Educational Review* 66:60–92.

Otheguy, Ricardo. 1993. "A Reconsideration of the Notion of Loan Translation in the Analysis of US Spanish." In *Spanish in the United States: Linguistic Contact and Diversity*, edited by Ana Roca and John Lipski. Berlin: Mouton de Gruyter.

————. 2003. "Las piedras nerudianas se tiran al norte: Meditaciones lingüísticas sobre Nueva York." *Ínsula* 679–80:13–19.

Otheguy, Ricardo, Ana Celia Zentella, and David Livert. 2007. "Language and Dialect Contact in Spanish in New York: Toward the Formation of a Speech Community." *Language* 83:770–802.

Pavlenko, Aneta. 2006. *Bilingual Minds: Emotional Experience, Expression and Representation.* Clevedon, UK: Multilingual Matters.

Pease-Álvarez, Lucinda, Kenji Hakuta, and Robert Bayley. 1996. "Spanish Proficiency and Language Use in a California Mexicano Community." *Southwest Journal of Linguistics* 15:137–51.

Phillips, Robert. 1982. "Influences of English on /b/ in Los Angeles Spanish." In *Spanish in the United States. Sociolinguistic Aspects*, edited by Jon Amastae and Lucía Elías-Olivares. Cambridge: Cambridge University Press.

Potowski, Kim, and Janine Matts. 2008. "MexiRicans: Interethnic Language and Identity." *Journal of Language, Identity and Education* 7:137–60.

Potowski, Kim, Jill Jegerski, and Kara Morgan-Short. 2009. "The Effects of Instruction on Linguistic Development in Spanish Heritage Language Speakers." *Language Learning* 59:537–79.

Sánchez, Rosaura. 1972. "Nuestra circunstancia lingüística." *El Grito* 6:45–74.

———. 1983. *Chicano Discourse: Socio-Historic Perspectives*. Houston: Arte Público Press. Reprinted 1994.

Sánchez-Muñoz, Ana. 2007. "Style Variation in Spanish as a Heritage Language. A Study of Discourse Particles in Academic and Non-Academic Registers." In *Spanish in Contact: Policy, Social and Linguistic Inquiries*, edited by Kim Potowski and Richard Cameron. Amsterdam: John Benjamins.

Sankoff, Gillian, and Hélène Blondeau. 2007. "Language Change across the Lifespan: /R/ in Montreal French." *Language* 83:560–88.

Schumann, John. 1974. "The Implications of Interlanguage, Pidginization and Creolization for the Study of Adult Second Language Acquisition." *TESOL Quarterly* 8:145–52.

———. 1978. *The Pidginization Process: A Model for Second Language Acquisition*. Rowley, MA: Newbury House.

Scott Shenk, Petra. 2007. " 'I'm Mexican, Remember?' Constructing Ethnic Identities via Authenticating Discourse." *Journal of Sociolinguistics* 11:194–220.

Selinker, Larry. 1972. "Interlanguage." *International Review of Applied Linguistics* 10:209–31.

Silva-Corvalán, Carmen. 1990. "Current Issues in Studies of Language Contact." *Hispania* 73: 162–76.

———. 1994. *Language Contact and Change. Spanish in Los Angeles*. Oxford: Oxford University Press.

———. 2001. *Sociolingüística y pragmática del español*. Washington, DC: Georgetown University Press.

———. 2003. "Linguistic Consequences of Reduced Input in Bilingual First Language Acquisition." In *Linguistic Theory and Language Development in Hispanic Languages*, edited by Silvina Montrul and Francisco Ordóñez. Somerville, MA: Cascadilla Press.

———. 2006. "El español de Los Ángeles: ¿Adquisición incompleta o desgaste lingüístico?" In *Estudios sociolingüísticos del español de España y América*, edited by Ana María Cestero, Isabel Molina, and Florentino Paredes. Madrid: Arco Libros.

Tarone, Elaine. 1988. *Variation in Interlanguage*. London: Edward Arnold.

Torres Cacoullos, Rena, and Jessi E. Aaron. 2003. "Bare English-Origin Nouns in Spanish: Rates, Constraints, and Discourse Functions." *Language Variation and Change* 15:287–326.

Urciuoli, Bonnie. 2008. "Whose Spanish? The Tension between Linguistic Correctness and Cultural Identity." In *Bilingualism and Identity: Spanish at the Crossroads with*

Other Languages, edited by Mercedes Niño-Murcia and Jason Rothman. Amsterdam: John Benjamins.

Vaid, Jyotsna. 2006. "Joking across Languages: Perspectives on Humor, Emotion, and Bilingualism." In *Bilingual Minds: Emotional Experience, Expression and Representation*, edited by Aneta Pavlenko. Clevedon, UK: Multilingual Matters.

Valdés, Guadalupe. 1989. "Teaching Spanish to Hispanic Bilinguals: A Look at Oral Proficiency Testing and the Proficiency Movement." *Hispania* 72:392–401.

———. 1995. "The Teaching of Minority Languages as Academic Subjects: Pedagogical and Theoretical Challenges." *Modern Language Journal* 79:299–328.

———. 2005. "Bilingualism, Heritage Language Learners, and SLA Research: Opportunities Lost or Seized?" *Modern Language Journal* 89:410–26.

Valdés Fallis, Guadalupe. 1976. "Pedagogical Implications of Teaching Spanish to the Spanish-Speaking in the United States." In *Teaching Spanish to the Spanish-Speaking: Theory and Practice*, edited by Guadalupe Valdés Fallis and Rodolfo García Moya. San Antonio: Trinity University.

———. 1977. "Spanish Language Programs for Hispanic Minorities: Current Needs and Priorities." In *Minority Language and Literature. Retrospective and Perspective*, edited by Dexter Fisher. New York: Modern Language Association.

———. 1978. "A Comprehensive Approach to the Teaching of Spanish to Bilingual Spanish-Speaking Students." *Modern Language Journal* 62:102–10.

Valdés, Guadalupe, and Richard Figueroa. 1994. *Bilingualism and Testing: A Special Case of Bias*. Norwood, NJ: Ablex.

Valdés, Guadalupe, and Michelle Geoffrion-Vinci. 1998. "Chicano Spanish: The Problem of the 'Underdeveloped' Code in Bilingual Repertoires." *Modern Language Journal* 82:473–501.

Vilar Sánchez, Karin. 1995. "For Want of the Standard Educated Variety of Spanish . . . a German Accent: A Sociolinguistic Case Study." *International Journal of the Sociology of Language* 116:5–16.

Villa, Daniel, and Susana Rivera-Mills. 2009. "An Integrated Multi-Generational Model for Language Maintenance and Shift. The Case of Spanish in the Southwest." *Spanish in Context* 6:26–42.

Vygotsky, Lev. 1978. *Mind in Society: The Development of Higher Psychological Processes*. Cambridge, MA: Harvard University Press.

PART II

Linguistic Perspectives

The Grammatical Competence of Spanish Heritage Speakers

Silvina Montrul, University of Illinois at Urbana-Champaign

A LTHOUGH DEFINITIONS of heritage language speakers vary from very broad to very narrow (Carreira 2004; Hornberger and Wang 2008), those interested in understanding the nature of heritage speakers' proficiency and competence in the heritage language tend to adopt Guadalupe Valdés's (2000, 1) definition: "a student who is raised in a home where a non-English language is spoken, who speaks or merely understands the heritage language, and who is to some degree bilingual in English and the heritage language." In the context of the United States, Spanish heritage speakers are individuals who emigrated in early childhood with their parents and other family members, or children of immigrants from Spanish-speaking countries. Although the parents are either monolingual or dominant in a variety of Spanish, the children grow up in a context where both English and Spanish are spoken.

Valdés's definition of who is a heritage speaker, like many others that are available, is not without problems. Although many would question the term "non-English" if we want to extend this definition to heritage speakers living in other countries or in other language contact situations, others would find Valdés's definition too inclusive of speakers who possess from minimal to advanced proficiency in the heritage language and silent with respect to a person's generation of immigration (first, second, third, etc.). Nonetheless, Valdés's definition is still useful for grammatically oriented studies because it takes into account *knowledge* and *use* of the heritage language (even if minimally) rather than just a cultural connection to the language with no actual knowledge of it. Having some ability in the language is important for studies that look at the grammatical competence of heritage speakers.

Heritage speakers are exposed to the heritage language early in childhood, like monolingual children; but unlike monolingual children, who end up with similar levels of competence in their native language (leaving sociolinguistic variation aside), heritage speakers do not form a linguistically homogeneous group. In fact, the range of linguistic ability and proficiencies reached by heritage language speakers in adulthood varies considerably, from minimal aural comprehension ability to full fluency in written and spoken registers, and everything else in between, as aptly captured by Valdés's (2000) definition. For this reason, it has been claimed that many Spanish heritage speakers do not completely acquire their family language in childhood (i.e., incomplete acquisition), or may have acquired and later lost parts of their language in childhood (attrition) (Montrul 2008; Polinsky 2007; Silva-Corvalán 1994), thus also giving the impression that as a group they speak a different variety of Spanish altogether (Lipski 1993). As a result, the grammatical competence of Spanish heritage speakers may differ in important ways from the grammatical competence of highly fluent bilinguals and native speakers of the language who grew up in a predominantly monolingual environment (regardless of whether they have knowledge of a second language and are also "bilingual" to some extent). Indeed, heritage speakers raise crucial questions about what it means to be a native speaker, what complete acquisition of a language entails, and what are the necessary ingredients for achieving target-like levels of linguistic ability in a language learned in childhood. The extent to which heritage speakers are also native speakers is a matter of much current controversy and debate, but space limitations do not allow me to elaborate on this issue in the depth that it deserves; for a discussion of this issue, see Benmamoun, Montrul, and Polinsky (2010).

OVERVIEW OF THE MAIN ISSUES FOR RESEARCH IN THE SUBFIELD

The wide range of grammatical variation found in Spanish heritage speakers has long been the realm of sociolinguistics, and notably of the field of Spanish in the United States (among many others, Dvorak 1983; Flores-Ferrán 2004; García 1982, 1995; Lipski 1993; Lowther 2005; Lynch 1999; Ocampo 1990; Otheguy, Zentella, and Livert 2007; Poplack 1983; Poplack and Pousada 1981; Potowski 2007; Silva-Corvalán 1994, 2003; Zentella 1997). It is important to clarify that not all these studies have used the term "heritage speaker" that is widely used today; some have referred instead to a person's "generation of immigration" or to the "type of bilingual" person. Still, given the descriptions these researchers provide of the participants investigated, they can all be broadly characterized as heritage speakers. Not all studies of Spanish in the United States within sociolinguistics deal with grammar (phonological variation, language contact in morphosyntax, and variation in discourse structure), because sociolinguistics is also concerned with issues of language and identity, and of language and power (in this volume, for more information about the former, see chapter 9, by Potowski; and about the latter, see chapter 2, by Leeman, and chapter 3, by Martínez). Sociolinguistic studies of grammatical properties have focused on language use by Spanish heritage speakers typically elicited through interviews, spontaneous oral production, translation tasks, completion tasks, or participant observation of naturalistic speech. They describe and quantify how the Spanish produced by Spanish-speaking immigrants differs from the standard variety with respect to different grammatical properties, such as the tense, aspect, and mood system (Lynch 1999; Martínez Mira 2009a, 2009b; Ocampo 1990; Silva-Corvalán 1994, 2003; Zentella 1997), subject pronouns (Flores-Ferrán 2004; Otheguy, Zentella, and Livert 2007; Silva-Corvalán 1994; Lipski 1993), prepositions (García 1995; Lipski 1993), the copulas *ser* and *estar* (Silva-Corvalán 1994), and gender agreement in noun phrases (García 1998; Lipski 1993). These studies have focused on describing the language of heritage speakers as examples of different emerging regional and community varieties of Spanish in the United States (e.g., the Spanish of Los Angeles, of New York, of Miami, and of the Southwest), and they most frequently address theoretical issues of language contact and change as a sociohistorical phenomenon.

From the perspectives of formal linguistics and psycholinguistics, interest in Spanish heritage speakers has surged more recently (Anderson 1999; Au et al. 2002; Bruhn de Garavito 2002; Bowles 2011b; Cuza and Frank 2011; Foote 2010, 2011; Keating, VanPatten, and Jegerski 2011; Lynch 2008; Montrul 2002, 2004, 2007, 2009, 2010; Montrul and Potowski 2007; Montrul, Foote, and Perpiñán 2008; Montrul and Bowles 2009; Montrul and Ionin 2010, 2012; Mueller-Gathercole 2002; Zapata, Sánchez, and Toribio 2005). These formal linguistic and psycholinguistic studies have also investigated knowledge of several grammatical properties examined in sociolinguistic studies, including subject–verb agreement (Bruhn de Garavito 2002; Foote 2010, 2011), tense, aspect, and mood (Montrul 2002, 2007); the copulas *ser* and *estar* (Bruhn de Garavito and Valenzuela 2006); subject pronouns (Montrul 2004; Keating, VanPatten, and Jegerski 2011); prepositions (Montrul and Bowles 2009); gender agreement (Montrul, Foote, and Perpiñán 2008; Montrul and Potowski 2007; Mueller-Gathercole 2002); articles and genericity (Montrul and Ionin 2010, 2012); and word order (Cuza and Frank 2011; Montrul 2010; Luján and Parodi 1996; Zapata, Sánchez, and Toribio 2005). But because the focus of these studies is on knowledge of language and processing, not just patterns of language use, these studies involve experimental investigations of heritage speakers' grammatical competence and processing using a variety of aural, oral, and written controlled tasks, following the quantitative methodologies used in monolingual and bilingual first-language acquisition, adult second-language acquisition, bilingualism, and adult psycholinguistics. There has also been a very recent surge of studies comparing the grammatical development of heritage language speakers and second-language learners in the classroom (Bowles 2011b, in press; Fairclough 2005; Hislope 2005; Lynch 2008; Mikulski 2010; Montrul and Bowles 2010; Potowski, Jegerski, and Morgan-Short 2009).

Sociolinguistic Studies

Sociolinguistics focuses on the social forces that shape language structure and use, and it sees language as an inherently variable phenomenon. It also pays attention to the internal linguistic processes that are involved in language change, such as simplification, transfer, analysis, and reanalysis. To date, the most complete sociolinguistic study of Spanish heritage speakers has been, without a doubt, Carmen Silva-Corvalán's seminal study of the Spanish of Los Angeles. Other sample studies from different parts of the United States include Lipski (1993), about the Spanish in Houston; and Otheguy, Zentella, and Livert's (2007) research conducted in New York City.

Silva-Corvalán (1994) investigated the linguistic production of a cohort of Mexican Americans living in Los Angeles between 1983 and 1988 in order to understand language change in progress as a result of Spanish speakers being in contact with English. In particular, Silva-Corvalán investigated stable changes in language maintenance and changes generally characteristic of language shift or loss. Her sample consists of Mexican American bilinguals, as she calls them, including adolescents and adults from three generations of immigrants. Rather than using a proficiency measure, as understood in experimental and pedagogically oriented studies, she considers a person's generation of immigration as an indirect indication of his or her functional proficiency in Spanish. First-generation speakers, the members of group I, were born in Mexico and had immigrated to the United States after age eleven. These speakers had a native command of Spanish, and their command of English ranged from near native to poor. The speakers in group II were either born in the United States or had arrived there before the age of eleven. Group III speakers were also born in the United States, but at least one parent had to be classified as a speaker in group II. All the United States–born bilinguals had been exposed to the two languages from birth and had a native command of English, and their ability in Spanish ranged from near-native to poor. All speakers were interviewed, and the conversations were later transcribed for analysis. (In addition, all speakers completed fill-in-the-gap questionnaires designed to elicit supplementary information about the choice of tenses.)

Silva-Corvalán studied potential language attrition in the tense-aspect and mood verb system across the three generations, documenting seven implicationally ordered stages of progression of simplification and loss. The first stage affected the use of the future perfect and the conditional (as a tense), and the last stage represented the loss of the present subjunctive. The simplification (but not loss) of the preterit and imperfect forms of the past tense occurred in stage three, with simplification of the preterit (with a closed class of stative verbs) occurring before simplification of the imperfect indicative. The researcher documented speech samples showing that speakers often confused the preterit and imperfect forms, using one for the other: *En la casa mi mamá era la única que* **habló** *español y las demás* **hablaron** *en ingles*; "At home my mom was the only one who spoke Spanish and the other ones only spoke English" (Silva-Corvalán 1994, 44).

With respect to the other tenses, Silva-Corvalán documented the absence of the morphological future, the conditional, and the pluperfect indicative, starting with the speakers of the second generation. Simplification was also observed in the use of the indicative for the subjunctive (*Lo voy a guardar antes que* **llega**; "I am going to keep it before he arrives"—example from a speaker in group III).

Other changes observed in the adult heritage speakers studied by Silva-Corvalán (1994) were the extension of the copula *estar* to cases where *ser* should be used, as with predicative adjectives (*la recámara* **está** *pequeñito*; *yo* **estoy** *inteligente*); omission of the complementizer *que* in complement clauses (*Yo creo ø no la quiere ver*), and the loss of semantic-pragmatic constraints on subject–verb—phrase word order (*una señora entró y me preguntó si conocía*). Finally, Silva-Corvalán also observed that overt pronominal subjects were used in cases where null subjects are more pragmatically appropriate (e.g., *Yo pienso que* **yo** *me olvido el español*).

For Silva-Corvalán the loss or simplification of tenses in the adults studied is not the result of transfer from English—the superordinate language—but rather a result of reduced exposure and the use of Spanish and other cognitive and interactional factors. She claimed that the patterns of simplification and loss of tense morphology evident in her data appear to be the mirror image of development in creolization and in first- and second-language acquisition. Silva-Corvalán views these changes as well as other morphophonological changes in verb forms as driven by an accelerated process of internal change already inherent in other monolingual Spanish regional varieties.

Lipski (1993) also offered a comprehensive descriptive study of what he calls Spanish-English "semifluent" bilingual speakers or "transitional bilinguals," noting that while they usually produce errors similar to those of adult second-language learners and child first-language (L1) learners of Spanish, they appear to have high levels of linguistic abilities in Spanish, similar to those of native speakers. He lists several grammatical areas where these bilinguals show divergences from native speakers and fluent bilinguals, including instability of gender and number agreement in noun phrases (*Mi blusa es blanco*), errors with verb paradigms (*Yo bailo y come*), an incorrect use of definite and indefinite articles (*Yo iba a escuela*), errors with prepositions (*¿Tienes oportunidad en hablar el español?*), and redundant uses of pronominal subjects (*Yo sé las palabras pero cuando yo tengo que encontrar las palabras es cuando yo tengo problemas*).

Unlike Silva-Corvalán's study, which included specific groups of speakers matched on a number of variables and systematic analyses of all the speakers' productions within the framework of variationist sociolinguistics (Labov 1963, 1994), Lipski's data are isolated examples of different speakers with apparently very different bilingual profiles and from different Hispanic backgrounds. There is also no quantification of the data, so it is hard to estimate the prevalence of the errors he points out in a speaker or in a group of speakers. Nonetheless, as we will see in the next section, Lipski's observations have been confirmed in subsequent experimental studies comparing Spanish heritage speakers and second-language learners of Spanish.

Most recently, Otheguy, Zentella, and Livert (2007) conducted a state-of the-art variationist study of pronominal subject use in New York City. The data come from groups of first-, second-, and third-generation immigrants from Puerto Rico, the Dominican Republic, Cuba, Ecuador, Colombia, and Mexico living in New York City. These Spanish linguistic varieties differ in their rates of pronominal subject use; the Caribbean dialects (Puerto Rico, Cuba, and the Dominican Republic) are known to exhibit higher percentages of overt subject pronouns than non-Caribbean varieties (Colombia, Ecuador, and Mexico). At the same time, the rate of pronominal subject use varies in Spanish and English, because Spanish is a pro-drop language and English is not. Otheguy, Zentella, and Livert were interested in issues of both dialect contact and language contact with respect to this particular linguistic variable. What they found was solid evidence of transfer from English: The longer the speakers had been in the United States, and especially those of the second generation (or heritage speakers), the higher was the rate of overt subject pronoun production in Spanish. Although the first-generation speakers produced 30 percent overt pronouns, the United States–born speakers produced 38 percent, a difference that was statistically significant. Unlike Silva-Corvalán (1994) and Flores-Ferrán (2004), Otheguy, Zentella, and Livert concluded that these changes in the second generation are primarily due to less use of Spanish and transfer from English. Finally, when they compared first- and second-generation speakers from Caribbean and non-Caribbean dialects, they observed an increase of overt subject production in the two dialect zones in the second generation, which gave rise to a new variety of US Spanish where dialectal variation is also neutralized. All immigrants show evidence of an impact from English use on their pronoun rates. Dialect leveling in the Spanish of New York City involves greater movement in the direction of Caribbean usage than in the direction of non-Caribbean usage due to influence from English, which only has overt subjects.

In conclusion, these sociolinguistically oriented studies show divergences in the grammars of heritage speakers of Spanish with respect to the norm or the standard varieties of Caribbean and non-Caribbean varieties. Debate exists as to whether these changes follow diachronic developments already in place in the language or are the result of direct contact and transfer from English, the major-ity language.

Formal Linguistic and Psycholinguistic Studies

Since the 2000s there has been increasing interest in heritage speakers of Spanish from a formal linguistics and pyscholinguistics perspective, where language change is seen as an individual phenomenon in the mind of the speaker. One of the goals of linguistic theory is to understand the nature of native speakers' knowledge of language and how this knowledge is acquired and used. It is widely assumed in the generative linguistics tradition, for example, that any normally developing child brought up in a predominantly monolingual speech commu-nity eventually acquires the language of the environment completely at age-appropriate levels and, once acquired, the person's mature linguistic competence remains relatively stable throughout his or her life span (Crain and Lillo-Martin 1999; Chomsky 1981). Although the sociolinguistic studies discussed in the pre-vious section did not address the issue of language acquisition by bilingual heri-tage speakers of the second generation directly, they all mention that language contact and restricted language use cause linguistic change. Formal linguists and psycholinguists look at these changes at the levels of knowledge, representation, and use by individuals.

Changes observed in bilingual grammar are seen as a result of the process of language acquisition at the individual level. Even though the complete acquisi-tion of the phonology, morphology, syntax, and discourse properties of the lan-guage is the most natural outcome of monolingual acquisition in childhood (i.e., one's vocabulary keeps growing throughout one's entire life span), the same is not necessarily true for bilingual acquisition, where one of the languages may lag behind in development and end up incompletely acquired at the levels of pho-nology, morphology, syntax, and discourse pragmatics. Montrul (2008) defines an individual's grammar as incomplete when it fails to reach age-appropriate linguistic levels of proficiency as compared with the grammar of monolingual or fluent bilingual speakers of the same age, cognitive development, and social group.

Incomplete, partial, or interrupted acquisition (Montrul 2002, 2006; Polinsky 2007; Silva-Corvalán 1994, 2003) is a specific case of language loss that differs from L1 attrition in both the time in life when the language is affected and the extent of the loss. Attrition implies that a grammatical system had a chance to develop completely into adolescence and remained stable for a while before some grammatical aspects later on eroded. Incomplete acquisition, conversely, occurs primarily in childhood due to insufficient input to develop the full L1 system.

The factors that distinguish whether the linguistic outcome of heritage lan-guage acquisition is due to attrition, incomplete acquisition, or both can only be teased apart with longitudinal or well-designed experimental studies. For more discussion, see Montrul (2008). Within this context, several studies of Spanish heritage speakers have been carried out in the last few years. These studies have investigated the incomplete acquisition or attrition of many of the same grammatical domains discussed in the sociolinguistics literature—such as tense, aspect, and mood (Mikulski 2010; Montrul 2002, 2007, 2009; Potowski, Jegerski, and Morgan-Short 2009); subject expression and word order (Montrul 2004, 2006); and object expression and differential object marking (Montrul and Bowles 2009)—utilizing instead experimental methodologies drawn from linguistics theory, psycholinguistics, and second-language acquisition.

These methodologies involve oral narrative tasks, oral and written elicited production tasks, grammaticality judgment tasks, and truth value judgment tasks, in addition to other online techniques measuring speed of processing in real time. Groups of heritage speakers whose members differ in their age of onset of bilingualism are compared with a control group of native speakers born and raised in Spanish-speaking countries where the heritage speakers trace their roots; they either reside in the country of origin or are very recent arrivals in the United States. Like the sociolinguistic studies discussed, all these psycholinguistically oriented studies have also found significant differences in the performance of heritage speakers as compared with native speakers. These studies have also shown that incomplete acquisition affects several areas of grammatical competence, particularly inflectional morphology and complex syntax, depending on the age of the onset of bilingualism: The earlier the age of acquisition of the second language (in this case, English) by heritage speakers and concomitant disuse of the L1, the more severe the loss in the L1 (Montrul 2008).

The findings from these studies show that Spanish heritage speakers display significant gaps in their grammatical development, and these gaps are typically interpreted as being the result of incomplete acquisition. However, these findings cannot address *directly* whether the mature bilingual grammar is due to incomplete acquisition, attrition, or both, because the grammatical competence of the subjects is evaluated synchronically, at a specific stable point in time and after the fact, and by comparing their knowledge to what speakers of the same age and level of linguistic development typically know. The ideal way to investigate attrition and incomplete acquisition is by following bilingual children longitudinally and documenting their language development and regression. Three studies that focus on Spanish-speaking children and address these issues to some extent are those by Anderson (1999), Silva-Corvalán (2003), and Merino (1983), but many more should be done.

In addition to issues related to potential language loss at the individual level and as a function of the age of the onset of bilingualism, another leading theme in the study of Spanish heritage speakers in the last few years has been to investigate the potential similarities and differences between heritage language learners and second-language learners, as noted by Lipski (1993) and advocated by Lynch

(2003). Not only is this comparison theoretically significant for debates on the role of age and input in bilingual language acquisition and regression, but such a comparison also has important pedagogical implications for the field of heritage language teaching. In recent years, traditional college-level foreign language classrooms have been accommodating heritage speakers who wish to learn, reacquire, or expand their proficiency of the family language. Debate exists about whether special classes and programs need to be developed for heritage language learners or whether it is appropriate to instruct them together with typical second-language learners (Bowles 2011a, in press; Lynch 2008; Mikulski 2010; Potowski, Jegerski, and Morgan-Short 2009). Thus, in order to develop effective materials, programs, and outcomes assessments for these different types of learners, it is crucial to understand what types of linguistic knowledge second-language learners and heritage speakers bring to the classroom, how they process the target language as a result of their language experience, and how they react to formal language instruction.

Many of these studies have extended theories and methodologies of second-language acquisition to investigate differences and similarities between second-language learners and heritage language learners (Montrul 2005). For example, Montrul (2011) looked at a perennial problem in second-language acquisition and its theoretical significance: the issue of morphological variability and the source of morphological errors. A recurrent finding is that postpuberty second-language learners often omit or use the wrong affix for nominal and verbal inflections in oral production, but less so in written tasks. According to the Missing Surface Inflection Hypothesis (Prévost and White 2000), second-language learners have intact abstract representations for this morphology, but errors stem from problems during production only (a mapping or processing deficit) under communicative pressure. Montrul (2011) discusses the collective findings from her work with her colleagues showing that variability and instability with gender agreement, tense, aspect, and mood morphology are also characteristic of heritage speakers' grammars (Montrul, Foote, and Perpiñán 2008; Montrul 2010; Montrul and Perpiñán 2011). However, because morphological errors by heritage speakers are more frequent in written than in oral tasks, unlike the pattern found in second-language learners, the Missing Surface Inflection Hypothesis does adequately capture heritage speakers' errors. Montrul concludes that experience with the language and mode of acquisition (predominantly through written input in second-language acquisition vs. aural input in heritage language acquisition) contributes to how the language is processed and represented differently by the two types of learners. Although second-language learners seem to do better on explicit tasks that maximize metalinguistic knowledge, heritage speakers seem to do better on implicit tasks that minimize metalinguistic knowledge. This issue is further developed and actually confirmed by Bowles's (2011b) validation of a battery of tests, ranging from more to less metalinguistic. Results showed that second-language learners of Spanish scored highest on a metalinguistic knowledge test, whereas the heritage language learners scored the lowest on the metalinguistic knowledge test and highest on the oral narration test (a less metalinguistic task). Bowles's results confirm that heritage language learners seem to have more implicit than explicit knowledge of their language by virtue of having acquired the language early in childhood and in a naturalistic setting.

The question of whether early language experience confers advantages to heritage speakers as opposed to second-language learners who acquire the language much later in their life has been at the heart of several studies comparing second-language learners and heritage speakers' grammatical knowledge (Au et al. 2002; Montrul 2010; Montrul, Foote, and Perpiñán 2008). Results for phonology indicate advantages for heritage speakers, who exhibit different but still more native-like pronunciation than second-language learners (Au et al. 2002). Results for morphosyntactic knowledge are mixed, with some studies finding no advantages (Au et al. 2002) and others finding some advantages depending on the proficiency level, type of structure, and type of task (Mikulski 2010; Montrul 2010; Montrul, Foote, and Perpiñán 2008).

Keating, VanPatten, and Jegerski (2011) investigated this same question with structures subsumed under the syntax–discourse interface. They asked whether adult Spanish heritage speakers and adult second-language learners of Spanish utilize the same antecedent assignment strategies as monolingually raised Spanish speakers when processing overt versus null subject pronouns and whether an early exposure to and use of Spanish confers advantages on Spanish heritage speakers relative to second-language learners. Spanish speakers raised without English contact, Spanish heritage speakers, and second-language learners of Spanish completed an offline questionnaire made up of complex sentences such as *Juan vio a Carlos mientras* pro/*él caminaba en la playa*; "John saw Charles while *pro*/he was walking on the beach."

Comprehension questions probed participants' preferences regarding the antecedent of null and overt pronouns. The results indicated that the monolingually raised Spanish speakers showed an antecedent bias, but the heritage speakers and the second-language learners did not. Furthermore, the two experimental groups differed from the control group in different ways; the heritage speakers displayed a stronger subject bias for the overt pronoun, whereas the second-language learners did not exhibit any clear antecedent biases. As found in the sociolinguistic literature with patterns of language use, Keating, VanPatten, and Jegerski's results confirmed that heritage speakers differ from native speakers in their representation of overt/null subjects in Spanish.

Whether the patterns of language change or incomplete acquisition observed in heritage speakers are at least partly due to transfer from English, the psycholinguistically stronger language, is a matter of debate in both the sociolinguistic and psycholinguistic traditions. Montrul and Ionin (2012) investigated dominant language transfer (from English) in adult Spanish second-language learners and Spanish heritage speakers by focusing on the interpretation of definite articles in Spanish, a grammatical domain that Lipski (1993) also identified as problematic from the perspective of use. Spanish plural noun phrases with definite articles can express generic reference (*Los elefantes tienen colmillos de marfil*), or specific reference (*Los elefantes de este zoológico son marrones*). English plurals with definite articles can only have specific reference (*The elephants in this zoo are brown*), whereas a generic reference is expressed with bare plural noun phrases (*Elephants have ivory tusks*). Furthermore, the Spanish definite article is preferred in inalienable possession constructions (*Pedro levantó la mano*; "Peter raised the hand"), whereas in English the use of a definite article typically means that the body part belongs to somebody else (alienable possession). A group of adult Spanish heritage learners and a group of second-language learners of Spanish each completed four written tasks (acceptability judgment, truth value judgment, picture–sentence matching, and sentence–picture acceptability judgment). Montrul and Ionin found that both the Spanish heritage speakers and the second-language learners exhibited transfer from English with the interpretation of definite articles in generic contexts, and were not statistically significant from each other. They tended to interpret *Los tigres comen carne* as referring to a particular group of tigers rather than to tigers in general, as the Spanish native speaker controls tended to interpret these sentences. However, the two groups were similar in their interpretation of articles in inalienable possession constructions in Spanish.

To sum up, linguistic and psycholinguistic studies of Spanish heritage speakers have focused on describing the grammatical system of these bilingual grammars and on identifying potential gaps in linguistic knowledge and processing. Although some of these studies compare heritage language grammars to the grammars of fully fluent and competent monolingually raised native speakers of the standard variety, other studies seek to trace areas of differences and similarities between heritage language grammars and adult second-language grammars. Although many questions remain about the individual internal and external factors that contribute to heritage speakers' grammatical development and stabilization in young adulthood, these studies have added much to our current understanding of the grammatical competence of heritage language speakers and learners.

Classroom-Oriented Studies

If heritage language learners and second-language learners have difficulty with the same grammatical areas, a logical next step is to investigate whether they react to instruction in the classroom in the same way, and to study what type of instruction may be most beneficial to the two groups of learners. Unfortunately, classroom-based research on heritage language learners and on their comparison with second-language learners is still very scarce (Beaudrie 2009; Fairclough 2005; Hislope 2005; Lynch 2008; Mikulski 2010; Montrul and Bowles 2010; Potowski, Jegerski, and Morgan-Short 2009), although highly needed, and I hope that future work will continue to delve deeper into this comparison.

Montrul and Bowles (2009) documented problems with differential object marking, or "a-personal," in Spanish heritage speakers; Montrul and Bowles (2010) followed up on these findings by developing an instructed intervention with a focus on form to see whether heritage speakers would notice the gaps in their linguistic knowledge and improve their grammatical accuracy with respect to this feature of Spanish as a result of the instruction. In general, Spanish objects that are animate and specific are obligatorily marked with the preposition a (*Juan conoce a tu hermana*; "Juan knows your sister"), whereas inanimate objects are unmarked (*Juan escuchó la radio*; "Juan listened to the radio"). The study also included *gustar*-type psych verbs with dative experiencers, obligatorily marked with the dative preposition a and a dative clitic (*A Juan le gusta el rugby*; "Juan likes rugby"), and investigated the effects of instruction on the acquisition of differential object marking and *gustar* verbs. Although the study was originally conceived to compare second-language learners and heritage language learners, only heritage language learners were retained for this study. A group of forty-five heritage speakers completed a pretest, an instructional treatment with a focus on form delivered through computer-assisted instruction, and a posttest. The instructional treatment consisted of an explicit grammatical explanation of the uses of a followed by three practice exercises, for which participants received immediate, explicit feedback, including negative evidence. The results of the heritage learners' pretest confirmed that their recognition and production of a with animate direct objects and dative experiencers is probabilistic, compared with a baseline group of twelve native speakers of Spanish. Posttest results revealed highly significant gains by heritage learners in both intuitions and production, which suggests that instruction, including both positive and negative evidence, facilitated classroom heritage language acquisition, at least in the short term.

Potowski, Jegerski, and Morgan-Short (2009) were able to directly compare adult college-level second-language learners and heritage language learners of Spanish. Unlike Montrul and Bowles, who were simply interested in the question of whether heritage speakers react positively to a focus on form in the classroom and improve their grammatical accuracy in the language, Potowski and her colleagues went a step further and evaluated the role of two types of instruction (traditional and input-processing) in the acquisition of the Spanish imperfect subjunctive of the two groups of learners. The learners were administered production, interpretation, and grammaticality judgment tasks. All groups were pretested on day one, and they later received either type of instruction on days two and three and were subsequently tested on day four. They found significant improvements in comprehension, production, and grammaticality judgments in both groups, regardless of the type of instruction, although the overall gains were greater for the second-language learners than for the heritage language learners. After exposure to instruction, both types of learners showed significant improvement on interpretation and production tasks. But only the second-language learners showed significant improvement in grammaticality judgments, which is not surprising in light of recent findings by Bowles (2011b) that heritage language speakers do not do very well on tasks that maximize metalinguistic knowledge of the language. Although the second-language learners in this study outperformed the heritage learners, the results suggest that heritage speakers can benefit from focused grammar instruction.

Summarizing, classroom-oriented studies so far have sought to determine whether heritage language learners would benefit from explicit, form-focused instruction in the first place. Other related questions are whether they would react to instruction as second-language learners and whether the specific type of instruction makes a difference in their grammatical learning.

LIMITATIONS OF EXISTING RESEARCH AND DIRECTIONS FOR FUTURE STUDIES

Although the sociolinguistic and the psycholinguistic traditions focus on different properties and manifestations of language and use different research methodologies, the studies conducted to date on the grammatical knowledge and use of Spanish in Spanish-English bilinguals or Spanish heritage speakers point to the same facts: Their grammatical knowledge and use of Spanish diverge in significant ways from the norm. Of course, this raises the question of what the norm is, which unfortunately varies from study to study. In some cases first-generation speakers of the same regional variety are the comparison group, as for Silva-Corvalán (1994) and Otheguy, Zentella, and Livert (2007); and in other cases groups of monolingually raised native speakers (immigrants or not) from Spanish-speaking countries are used for comparison, as in many of the psycholinguistic studies discussed (e.g., Keating, VanPatten, and Jegerski 2011; Montrul, Foote, and Perpiñán 2008). Ideally, the norm should be speakers of the same age and socioeconomic status who speak the same regional variety and were raised in a monolingual situation, rather than generation. What the generational comparison allows us to see is whether the Spanish of the first-generation speakers—the input to the second-generation heritage speakers—is already undergoing the changes observed in the second-generation speakers.

Differences are attested in the command of nominal and verbal inflectional morphology, subject pronouns, prepositions copulas, articles, word order, and more. What differ are the interpretations of the data; whereas sociolinguists tend to emphasize mature and developing ability in language use, language change, and the emergence of new varieties, psycholinguists tend to focus on divergences at the level of language acquisition in individuals, cognitive processing, and the organization of the bilingual grammar. Future research should strive to integrate these two approaches in the study of heritage speakers, because the sociolinguistic situation plays a significant role in how the language is actually learned or fails to fully develop. We also need to understand whether and how, in fact, these incompletely acquired systems in individuals spread at the society level to give rise to new varieties acquired by the next generation.

With the exception of Zentella (1997), Silva-Corvalán (2003), Mueller-Gathercole (2002), and Montrul and Potowski (2007), most of the existing studies of heritage speakers so far have focused on adults who are of college age or older. But in order to understand why the language of heritage speakers undergoes certain changes and displays well-attested gaps, what causes these changes, and the linguistic processes at play in these changes (incomplete acquisition, attrition, transfer, simplification, etc.), research should start to focus more on bilingual children who speak minority languages. Most of the changes observed in heritage speakers are triggered by reductions in the use of the language, which typically coincide with the school-age period in second-generation heritage speakers. To understand these changes, it would be ideal to conduct cross-sectional studies of children from kindergarten to grade twelve as well as longitudinal observational studies—like those conduced by Anderson (1999), Merino (1983), and Silva-Corvalán (2003) from early childhood to adolescence—to observe more closely the fluctuations in the bilingual balance of these children in response to changes in the sociolinguistic environment. Although longitudinal studies spanning so many years are difficult to carry out and impractical, Kohnert and her colleagues offer an example of a possible research design that could circumvent these difficulties by looking at five groups of bilingual children cross-sectionally and by integrating a longitudinal design that spans two years for one of the age groups (Kohnert, Bates, and Hernández 1999; Kohnert and Bates 2002).

Although trying to integrate sociolinguistic and formal approaches to the study of heritage language speakers' grammatical systems may be fruitful, this integration raises a number of issues related to subject selection and comparison norms. One is the issue of proficiency in the heritage language, which is addressed in different ways in existing studies. For example, sociolinguistic studies tend to use a person's generation of immigration as an indirect indicator of his or her proficiency, whereas formal and pedagogically oriented studies have indeed employed independent measures of proficiency (written proficiency tests, oral tests, placement tests, lexical decision tasks, etc.). Independent proficiency measures of this sort, however suitable or unsuitable they may be judged to be, allow us to see that even within the second generation of heritage speakers there can be a wide variation in proficiency, especially if both written and aural comprehension skills are considered.

Another problem that arises in comparing how the two approaches have dealt with heritage speakers is that whereas sociolinguistic studies tend to describe the grammars of heritage speakers who are "in the wild"—to use Polinsky and Kagan's (2007) term—formal linguistic studies include heritage speakers who may or may not be taking classes for heritage speakers. In addition, pedagogically oriented studies tend to focus on what are more accurately referred to as "heritage language learners" because these speakers are relearning the language in a formal setting. To what extent are all these types of heritage speakers comparable? It is possible that instructed heritage speakers may have already advanced in their language development through their instruction (hopefully), and they may be reacting differently to input in the heritage language from heritage speakers who have not received formal instruction. In other words, the metalinguistic awareness of the language and implicit knowledge for heritage speakers in the "wild" may be different from these same characteristics for heritage speakers in the classroom. Future research should also strive to tease apart the factors that explain whether the linguistic knowledge of heritage speakers who have never received instruction in their heritage language is different from the linguistic abilities of those who have received or are currently receiving instruction. This would be another way to evaluate the role and impact of language instruction in heritage speakers' linguistic development.

Finally, the issue of how heritage language learners learn in the classroom is very timely, because it would allow us to address the specific pedagogical needs of this population. Although classroom research with heritage speakers is just emerging, more studies are needed to shed light on how heritage speakers may react to different types of instruction in the classroom, and in which areas they would benefit from a focus on form as opposed to other less explicit methods. We also know very little about the actual gains that heritage speakers make—in grammatical accuracy, in communicative competence, in expansion of the bilingual repertoire, and in acquisition of different registers in the heritage language, among many other goals of heritage language education—after completing the required courses in a heritage language or regular foreign language program. Robust research findings from studies of this sort are important in order to be able to advocate for evidence-based practice or language programs for heritage speakers.

CONCLUSION

Research efforts to explain the grammatical competence of Spanish heritage speakers carry great theoretical and practical significance. On the one hand, the study of heritage speakers' grammatical systems allows us to address key issues in linguistics, such as the nature of language knowledge and use in language contact situations and with suboptimal input conditions. On the other hand, the study of heritage speakers' grammatical systems allows us to address how language experience shapes language acquisition and the resulting adult use of grammar. It also helps us understand how these experiences play out in a classroom environment.

REFERENCES

Anderson, Raquel. 1999. "Noun Phrase Gender Agreement in Language Attrition. Preliminary Results." *Bilingual Research Journal* 23:318–37.

Au, Terry, Leah Knightly, Sun-Ah, Jun, and Janet Oh. 2002. "Overhearing a Language during Childhood." *Psychological Science* 13:238–43.

Beaudrie, Sara. 2009. "Receptive Bilinguals' Language Development in the Classroom: The Differential Effects of Heritage versus Foreign Language Curriculum." In *Español en Estados Unidos y otros contextos de contacto: Sociolingüística, ideología y pedagogía*, edited by Manel Lacorte and Jennifer Leeman. Madrid: Iberoamericana/Vervuert.

Benmamoun, Elabbas, Silvina Montrul, and Maria Polinsky. 2010. "White Paper: Prolegomena to Heritage Linguistics." Manuscript, University of Illinois at Urbana-Champaign and Harvard University.

Bowles, Melissa A. 2011a. "Exploring the Role of Modality: Second Language–Heritage Learner Interactions in the Spanish Language Classroom." *Heritage Language Journal* (Special Issue on the Heritage Acquisition of Spanish) 8 (1). Available at www.heritagelanguages.org.

———. 2011b. "Measuring Implicit and Explicit Linguistic Knowledge: What Can Heritage Language Learners Contribute?" *Studies in Second Language Acquisition* (Special Issue on the Linguistic Competence of Heritage Speakers) 33 (2): 247–71.

———. In press. "Task-Based Interactions of Second Language–Heritage Learner Pairs in Spanish Language Classrooms." *Modern Language Journal*.

Bruhn de Garavito, Joyce. 2002. "Verb Raising in Spanish, a Comparison of Early and Late Bilinguals." In *Proceedings of the 26th Annual Boston University Conference on Language Development*. Somerville, MA: Cascadilla Press.

Bruhn de Garavito, Joyce, and Elena Valenzuela. 2006. "The Status of *Ser* and *Estar* in Late and Early Bilingual Second Language Spanish." In *Selected Proceedings of the 7th Conference on the Acquisition of Spanish and Portuguese as First and Second Languages*, edited by Carol Klee and Timothy Face. Somerville, MA: Cascadilla Press.

Carreira, Maria. 2004. "Seeking Explanatory Adequacy: A Dual Approach to Understanding the Term 'Heritage Language Learner.'" *Heritage Language Journal* 2:1–25. Available at www.heritagelanguages.org.

Chomsky, Noam. 1981. *Lectures on Government and Binding*. Dordrecht: Foris.

Crain, Stephen, and Diane Lillo-Martin. 1999. *An Introduction to Linguistic Theory and Language Acquisition*. Oxford: Blackwell.

Cuza, Alejandro, and Joshua Frank. 2011. "Transfer Effects at the Syntax-Semantics Interface: The Case of Double-*Que* Questions in Heritage Spanish." *Heritage Language Journal* (Special Issue on the Heritage Acquisition of Spanish) (8) 1. Available at www.heritagelanguages.org.

Dvorak, Trisha. 1983. "Subject-Object Reversals in the Use of *Gustar* among New York Hispanics." In *Spanish in the US Setting: Beyond the Southwest*, edited by Lucía Elías-Olivares. Rosslyn, VA: National Clearinghouse for Bilingual Education.

Fairclough, Marta. 2005. *Spanish and Heritage Language Education in the United States: Struggling with Hypotheticals*. Madrid: Iberoamericana/Vervuert.

Flores-Ferrán, Nidia. 2004. "Spanish Subject Personal Pronouns Use in New York City Puerto Ricans: Can We Rest the Case of English Contact?" *Language Variation and Change* 16:49–73.

Foote, Rebecca. 2010. "Age of Acquisition and Proficiency as Factors in Language Production: Agreement in Bilinguals." *Bilingualism: Language and Cognition* 13 (2): 99–118.

———. 2011. "Integrated Knowledge of Agreement in Early and Late English-Spanish Bilinguals." *Applied Psycholinguistics* 32:187–220.

García, MaryEllen. 1982. "Syntactic Variation in Verb Phrases of Motion in US Mexican Spanish." In *Spanish in the United States. Sociolinguistic Aspects*, edited by Jon Amastae and Lucía Elías-Olivares. Cambridge: Cambridge University Press.

———. 1995. "En los sábados," "En las mañanas," "En veces": A Look at "En" in the Spanish of San Antonio." In *Spanish in Four Continents: Studies in Language Contact and Bilingualism*, edited by Carmen Silva-Corvalán. Washington, DC: Georgetown University Press.

———. 1998. "Gender Marking in a Dialect of Southwest Spanish." *Southwest Journal of Linguistics* 17:49–58.

Hislope, Kristi. 2005. "A Present Subjunctive Focus-on-Form Study of Heritage Speakers of Spanish." In *Contactos y contextos lingüísticos: El español en los Estados Unidos y en contacto con otras lenguas*, edited by Luis A. Ortiz López and Manel Lacorte. Madrid: Iberoamericana/Vervuert.

Hornberger, Nancy, and Shuhan Wang. 2008. "Who Are Our Heritage Language Learners?" In *Heritage Language Education: A New Field Emerging*, edited by Donna Brinton, Olga Kagan, and Susan Bauckus. New York: Routledge.

Keating, Gregory D., Bill VanPatten, and Jill Jegerski. 2011. "Who Was Walking on the Beach? Anaphora Resolution in Spanish Heritage Speakers and Adult Second-Language Learners." *Studies in Second-Language Acquisition* (Special Issue on the Linguistic Competence of Heritage Speakers) 33 (2): 193–221.

Kohnert, Kathryn, and Elizabeth Bates. 2002. "Balancing Bilinguals II: Lexical Comprehension and Cognitive Processing in Children Learning Spanish and English." *Journal of Speech, Language, and Hearing Research* 45:347–59.

Kohnert, Kathryn, Elizabeth Bates, and Arturo Hernández. 1999. "Balancing Bilinguals, Lexical-Semantic Production and Cognitive Processing in Children Learning Spanish and English." *Journal of Speech, Language and Hearing Research* 42:1400–1413.

Labov, William. 1963. "The Social Motivation of a Sound Change." *Word* 19:273–309.

———. 1994. *Principles of Linguistic Change, Volume I: Internal Factors*. Oxford: Blackwell.

Lipski, John. 1993. "Creoloid Phenomena in the Spanish of Transitional Bilinguals." In *Spanish in the United States*, edited by Ana Roca and John Lipski. Berlin: Mouton.

Lowther, Kelly. 2005. "Variation in Heritage Language Learner Spanish: Ser or Estar? That Is the Question." *Divergencias: Revista de Estudios Lingüísticos y Literarios* 3 (2): 1–19.

Luján, Marta, and Clauda Parodi. 1996. "Clitic Doubling and the Acquisition of Agreement in Spanish." In *Perspectives on Spanish Linguistics*, vol. 1, edited by Javier

Gutiérrez-Rexach and L. Silva Villar. Los Angeles: Department of Linguistics, University of California, Los Angeles.

Lynch, Andrew. 1999. "The Subjunctive in Miami Cuban Spanish. Bilingualism, Contact and Language Variability." PhD diss., University of Minnesota.

———. 2003. "The Relationship between Second and Heritage Language Acquisition: Notes on Research and Theory Building." *Heritage Language Journal* 1:1–18. www.international.ucla.edu/languages/heritagelanguages/journal.

———. 2008. "The Linguistic Similarities of Spanish Heritage and Second-Language Learners." *Foreign Language Annals* 41 (2): 252–81.

Martínez Mira, Maria Isabel. 2009a. "Position and the Presence of Subjunctive in Purpose Clauses in US-Heritage Spanish." *Sociolinguistic Studies* 3 (1): 61–91.

———. 2009b. "Spanish Heritage Speakers in the Southwest: Factors Contributing to the Maintenance of the Subjunctive in Concessive Clauses." *Spanish in Context* 6 (1): 105–26.

Merino, Barbara. 1983. "Language Loss in Bilingual Chicano Children." *Journal of Applied Developmental Psychology* 4:277–94.

Mikulski, Ariana. M. 2010. "Receptive Volitional Subjunctive Abilities in Heritage and Traditional Foreign Language Learners of Spanish." *Modern Language Journal* 94 (2): 217–33.

Montrul, Silvina. 2002. "Incomplete Acquisition and Attrition of Spanish Tense/Aspect Distinctions in Adult Bilinguals." *Bilingualism: Language and Cognition* 5:39–68.

———. 2004. "Subject and Object Expression in Spanish Heritage Speakers. A Case of Morpho-Syntactic Convergence." *Bilingualism: Language and Cognition* 7:125–42.

———. 2005. "Second Language Acquisition and First Language Loss in Adult Early Bilinguals, Exploring Some Differences and Similarities." *Second Language Research* 21:199–249.

———. 2006. "On the Bilingual Competence of Spanish Heritage Speakers. Syntax, Lexical-semantics and Processing." *International Journal of Bilingualism* 10:37–69.

———. 2007. "Interpreting Mood Distinctions in Spanish as a Heritage Language." In *Spanish Contact: Policy, Social and Linguistic Inquiries*, edited by Kim Potowski and Richard Cameron. Amsterdam: John Benjamins.

———. 2008. *Incomplete Acquisition in Bilingualism: Re-Examining the Age Factor*. Amsterdam: John Benjamins.

———. 2009. "Incomplete Acquisition of Tense-Aspect and Mood in Spanish Heritage Speakers." *International Journal of Bilingualism* (Special Issue) 13 (2): 239–69.

———. 2010. "How Similar Are Second-Language Learners and Heritage Speakers? Spanish Clitics and Word Order." *Applied Psycholinguistics* 31:167–207.

———. 2011. "Morphological Errors in Spanish Second Language Learners and Heritage Speakers." *Studies in Second Language Acquisition* (Special Issue on the Linguistic Competence of Heritage Speakers) 33 (2): 163–92.

Montrul, Silvina, and Melissa Bowles. 2009. "Back to Basics: Differential Object Marking under Incomplete Acquisition in Spanish Heritage Speakers." *Bilingualism: Language and Cognition* 12 (3): 363–83.

———. 2010. "Is Grammar Instruction Beneficial for Heritage Language Learners: Dative Case Marking in Spanish." *Heritage Language Journal* 7 (1): 47–73.

Montrul, Silvina, and Silvia Perpiñán. 2011. "Assessing Differences and Similarities between Instructed Second Language Learners and Heritage Language Learners in

Their Knowledge of Spanish Tense-Aspect and Mood (TAM) Morphology." *Heritage Language Journal* 8 (1). Available at www.heritagelanguages.org.

Montrul, Silvina, and Kim Potowski. 2007. "Command of Gender Agreement in School-Age Spanish Bilingual Children." *International Journal of Bilingualism* 11:301–28.

Montrul, Silvina, Rebecca Foote, and Silvia Perpiñán. 2008. "Gender Agreement in Adult Second-Language Learners and Spanish Heritage Speakers: The Effects of Age and Context of Acquisition." *Language Learning* 58 (3): 503–53.

Montrul, Silvina, and Tania Ionin. 2010. "Transfer Effects in the Interpretation of Definite Articles by Spanish Heritage Speakers." *Bilingualism: Language and Cognition* 13 (4): 449–73.

———. 2012. "Dominant Language Transfer in Spanish Heritage Speakers and Second-Language Learners in the Interpretation of Definite Articles." *Modern Language Journal* 96 (1): 70–94.

Mueller-Gathercole, Virginia. 2002. "Grammatical Gender in Monolingual and Bilingual Acquisition. A Spanish Morphosyntactic Distinction." In *Language and Literacy in Bilingual Children*, edited by Kim Oller and Rebecca Eilers. Clevedon, UK: Multilingual Matters.

Ocampo, Francisco. 1990. "El subjuntivo en tres generaciones de hablantes bilingües." In *Spanish in the United States: Sociolinguistic issues*, edited by John Bergen. Washington, DC: Georgetown University Press.

Otheguy, Ricardo, Ana Celia Zentella, and David Livert. 2007. "Language and Dialect Contact in Spanish in New York: Toward the Formation of a Speech Community." *Language* 83:770–802.

Polinsky, Maria. 2007. "Incomplete Acquisition: American Russian." *Journal of Slavic Linguistics* 14:191–262.

Polinsky, Maria, and Olga Kagan. 2007. "Heritage Languages: In the 'Wild' and in the Classroom." *Language and Linguistics Compass* 1 (5): 368–95.

Poplack, Shana. 1983. "Bilingual Competence: Linguistic Interference or Grammatical Integrity?" In *Spanish in the US Setting: Beyond the Southwest*, edited by Lucía Elías-Olivares. Rosslyn, VA: National Clearinghouse for Bilingual Education.

Poplack, Shana, and A. Pousada. 1981. "No Case for Convergence: The Puerto Rican Spanish Verb System in a Language Contact Situation." In *Bilingual Education for Hispanic Students in the United States*, edited by Gary Keller and Joshua Fishman. New York: Teachers College Press.

Potowski, Kim. 2007. "Characteristics of the Spanish Grammar and Sociolinguistic Proficiency of Dual Immersion Graduates." *Spanish in Context* 4 (2):187–216.

Potowski, Kim, Jill Jegerski, and Kara Morgan-Short. 2009. "The Effects of Instruction on Linguistic Development in Spanish Heritage Language Speakers." *Language Learning* 59:537–79.

Prévost, Philippe, and Lydia White. 2000. "Missing Surface Inflection or Impairment in Second Language Acquisition? Evidence from Tense and Agreement." *Second Language Research* 16:110–33.

Silva-Corvalán, Carmen. 1994. *Language Contact and Change: Spanish in Los Angeles*. Oxford: Oxford University Press.

———. 2003. "Linguistic Consequences of Reduced Input in Bilingual First-Language Acquisition." In *Linguistic Theory and Language Development in Hispanic Languages*, edited by Silvina Montrul and Francisco Ordóñez. Somerville, MA: Cascadilla Press.

Valdés, Guadalupe. 2000. "Introduction." In *Spanish for Native Speakers, Volume I. AATSP Professional Development Series Handbook for Teachers K–16.* New York: Harcourt College.

Zapata, Gabriela, Liliana Sánchez, and Almeida Jacqueline Toribio. 2005. "Contact and Contracting Spanish." *International Journal of Bilingualism* 9:377–95.

Zentella, Ana Celia. 1997. *Growing Up Bilingual: Puerto Rican Children in New York.* Malden, MA: Blackwell.

CHAPTER 6

Pragmatics and Discourse

DOING THINGS WITH WORDS IN SPANISH AS A HERITAGE LANGUAGE

Derrin Pinto, University of Saint Thomas

WHEN TAKEN SEPARATELY, linguistic studies on Spanish as a heritage language (SHL) and those involving pragmatics and discourse analysis represent two research trends that have both flourished during the past two or three decades. It is somewhat surprising, then, that when considered together, the body of research in pragmatics/discourse that incorporates SHL is still in the developing stages. One explanation for this may simply be a matter of time, because relatively speaking these are both young areas of enquiry that do not belong to long-standing research traditions. The same could be said for research on SHL, which did not fully come into its own until the 1980s and 1990s. Another contributing factor could be that the interdisciplinary fields of pragmatics/discourse cover such a vast range of topics and theoretical perspectives that no single line of research on SHL has been particularly prominent. Taking into consideration this disparateness, in order to locate a homogeneous focus among diverse areas of research that are often only loosely interrelated, this chapter only addresses pragmatic/discourse issues linked to how heritage speakers (HS) in the United States use Spanish in oral interaction.

Pragmatics/discourse research on different varieties of Spanish has progressed greatly during the past two decades. Márquez Reiter and Placencia (2005) dedicate an entire book to summarizing research on Spanish pragmatics—encompassing speech acts, politeness, and conversation analysis—and not only was the bibliography already substantial at the time of publication, it has continued to grow since then. There are also academic journals, among them the internationally reputable *Spanish in Context*, that are dedicated largely to Spanish pragmatics and closely related interdisciplinary fields. Although bilingual and multilingual perspectives on Spanish in contact with other language communities only make up a small portion of the research, there are indications that this area is going to thrive in the years to come. Just to cite a few examples in the existing literature, investigators have examined Spanish in contact with Basque in northern Spain (Barnes 2001); Zapotec in Oaxaca, Mexico (Schrader-Kniffki 2004); Quechua in Ecuador and southern Peru (Hurley 1995; Harvey 1991); and numerous other indigenous languages throughout Latin America (Brody 1995; Torres 2006).

TOPICS THAT ARE RELEVANT TO SHL

Because there is not enough space to provide an overview of the history and development of the interdisciplinary fields and subfields of pragmatics and discourse analysis, this section is limited to a brief discussion of the major lines of research most pertinent to SHL. The threads that appear to be attracting the most interest thus far are speech acts, discourse markers, and personal pronouns, whereas other topics such as oral academic registers and spontaneous oral discourse have also received some attention. Certain other issues that overlap with discourse/pragmatics, especially code-mixing and identity, are addressed in chapters 7 and 9, respectively.

Perhaps the unit of linguistic expression most typically associated with pragmatics is the speech act. The notion of the speech act was primarily developed in the writings of two language philosophers, John Austin and John Searle, particularly *How to Do Things with Words* (Austin 1962), *Speech Acts* (Searle 1969), and *Expression and Meaning* (Searle 1979). Briefly, speech acts can be understood as attempts by language users to perform specific actions, such as making statements, asking questions, making promises, expressing gratitude, requesting, and apologizing (Searle 1969). During the last thirty years, there has been great interest in examining the production and interpretation of speech acts in the hybrid fields of cross-cultural and interlanguage pragmatics. Although speech act studies in cross-cultural pragmatics generally compare and contrast the linguistic behavior of two or more (native) speech communities, the interlanguage focus incorporates second language (L2) learners and often compares their linguistic performance to one or more native-speaker groups. Two influential edited collections that have contributed to the international visibility of these avenues of research are *Cross-Cultural Pragmatics: Requests and Apologies* (Blum-Kulka, House, and Kasper 1989) and *Interlanguage Pragmatics* (Kasper and Blum-Kulka 1993). Many studies on speech acts also concern (im)politeness, another topic that interconnects disciplines and subdisciplines. The most prominent theories on politeness have stemmed from Brown and Levinson's work (1978, 1987), which attempted to establish a universal framework for politeness based on the notion of "face." Although widely influential, this paradigm has been criticized by scholars for various reasons, ranging from claims that it does not apply universally to all cultures to criticism that it underplays how (im)politeness develops in actual language interaction (for in-depth discussions, see Eelen 2001; Watts 2002). With regard to politeness phenomena exclusively in the Spanish-speaking world, a recent edited volume by Placencia and García (2007) attests to the growing body of research in this area.

Another basic component of pragmatics includes temporal, spatial, and personal indexical expressions (e.g., "here, now, I"), words that directly encode elements of the context. However, this area is not particularly relevant to the present volume on SHL, with the exception of personal pronouns. The use of formal and informal second-person pronouns has been studied in Spanish and other languages that make a similar distinction between formal and informal address. Brown and Gilman (1960) published what has now become a classic work on the topic, and their study highlights the historical development of second-person pronouns in different cultures, based on the evolving notions of power and solidarity.

The term "discourse analysis" is essentially a catchall for studies from an array of disciplines in the humanities that analyze oral or written texts, although distinctions are often made between different approaches. For example, investigators such as Emanuel Schegloff and Harvey Sacks were pioneers in the area of conversation analysis, a research focus that specifically targets the interactional element of speech and the co-construction of talk. Another popular line of investigation has been referred to as Critical Discourse Analysis, which is particularly useful in the analysis of written texts. More pertinent to this chapter on SHL is the topic of discourse markers, which are single or multiword expressions that have been investigated under a variety of labels (e.g., pragmatic markers, discourse particles, gambits, sentence connectives), covering a gamut of languages, genres, and theoretical approaches. One common thread is the attempt to determine the function(s) that an expression has in a given context; in fact, researchers such as Brinton (1996) and Schiffrin (1987) highlighted the multifunctional nature of discourse markers, stressing that no single function is necessarily predominant in a particular context.

Although not all the studies summarized below incorporate bilingual speakers who are prototypical heritage speakers, they are relevant to understanding the development and speech habits of Spanish speakers residing in the United States. This wider panorama, which includes studies that target adult subjects with varying degrees of English proficiency, allows us to consider the members of the larger Hispanic community with whom heritage learners are in contact.

OVERVIEW OF RESEARCH: MAIN ISSUES

This section discusses speech acts, pronoun usage, discourse markers, and other discourse-related issues. Most of the research cited are published studies rather than doctoral dissertations.

Speech Acts

One group of studies on the speech act production of Spanish-English adult bilinguals in the United States involves university students. Valdés (1981) considers the role that code-switching plays in forty-five direct and indirect requests taken from the conversations of college students in New Mexico. She reports that the participants utilize code-switching as a strategy for mitigating and aggravating requests. In some cases the head act of the request was in English, with a mitigating code-switch inserted in Spanish, as in *Mira mano* ("Look man"), *you just have to do it till it's okay*, . . . whereas in other cases the softening element was in English, such as *No toques eso* ("Don't touch that"); *I don't want it broken*. García Pastor (1999) applies a "cultural approach" to examine how directives were used by a group of graduate students in Iowa City. The results indicate that directives in this community sustain and enact relationships of *confianza* ("trust"), a type of close family-like affiliation based on the premises of helping one's neighbor, solidarity, and equality. Consequently, members perceive direct requests (e.g., imperatives) as a sincere way of enhancing relationships, a finding that is similar to what has been reported for other Spanish-speaking communities (Fitch 1994; Fitch and Sanders 1994). Even though these informants appear to be Spanish-dominant, the article is still significant due to the unique methodology and the fact that the subjects were residing in the United States.

Pinto and Raschio (2007) examine how twenty-one university-level HS in California perform requests in an online written questionnaire. The data, which were compared with both first language (L1) English and L1 Spanish groups, show that the HS did not employ as many direct strategies as their monolingual counterparts from Mexico. Although the monolingual group used some direct strategies, such as *por favor limpia el cuarto* ("please clean the room") for making a request to a roommate, the HS were more similar to the monolingual English speakers, resulting in indirect requests like *¿Me podrías hacer el favor de hacerlo tú?* ("Could you do me the favor of doing it?"). Contrary to the informants for García Pastor (1999), discussed above, and Arellano (2000), below, Pinto and Raschio's participants were prototypical HS who were further toward the English-dominant end of the spectrum. Therefore, the use of direct imperatives as a marker of *confianza* and solidarity among peers may be in tension with the preference in English for indirectness. When request strategies and downgrading (i.e., softening devices) were examined together, the HS group trended towards differentiating itself from both monolingual groups, although the difference was not statistically significant. The qualitative analysis also indicated a unique intercultural style for the HS; for instance, they used some strategies identical to those of L2 learners, including indirect requests such as *¿Es posible que me prestes tus apuntes de clase?* ("Is it possible for you to lend me your class notes?") and *Quisiera ver si me pudieras dar las notas* ("I would like to see if you could give me the notes"). In a follow-up study, Pinto and Raschio (2008) look at HS complaints from three questionnaire scenarios. Similar to their article on requests, the HS group displays a unique intercultural style, which is characterized by similarities to monolingual Spanish speakers in some aspects, including a higher number of complaints with no downgraders, and to monolingual English speakers in other aspects, as demonstrated in their selection of semantic formulas and use of more subjectivizers, such as *quisiera saber* in <u>*quisiera saber* *si me*</u> <u>*podrías pagar el dinero que te presté*</u> ("<u>I wanted to know if</u> you could pay me the money I lent you"). The heritage group also employed more words per complaint than both monolingual groups, comparable to the findings reported for the members of some L2 groups, who tend to overcompensate for a perceived lack of proficiency.

Through oral role-plays, Dumitrescu (2005) compares expressions of gratitude between twenty L1 Spanish speakers, thirty-five L2 Spanish learners, and sixty-five university heritage learners in California. The HS group made various pragmatic errors, ranging from grammar mistakes (*Gracias por me llevar*; "Thanks for me taking") to inappropriate English transfer (e.g., *Espero hacer esto de nuevo*; "I hope to do it again," when thanking a friend for dinner). Overall, the author affirms that the most distinctive feature of the HS speech is the persistent influence of English, either through code-switching or calques (e.g., *Gracias por un buen tiempo*; "Thanks for a good time").

The last group of studies entails adult speech in nonacademic environments. Arellano (2000) investigated the request preferences of 100 monolingual and bilingual Mexican American farmworkers in the Central Valley of California. On a multiple-choice questionnaire, these informants indicated a preference for imperatives with *por favor* while disfavoring bare imperatives. Furthermore, the variables of authority and level of imposition had an effect on the request; when the hearer was the authority, higher levels of indirectness and mitigation were favored, and when the request involved less imposition, the participants were more direct. Only the gender variable did not elicit a significant difference. Through observations and recordings of natural interactions, Valdés and Pino (1981) investigated compliment responses produced by Mexican monolinguals from Ciudad Juárez and Mexican American bilinguals in southern New Mexico. For the bilingual group, all the response patterns reported by Pomerantz (1978) for English surface in the data, including various subcategories of acceptances, rejections, and self-praise avoidance mechanisms. The most obvious difference between the monolingual and bilingual groups is the use of code-switching, which the authors attribute primarily to momentary memory lapses, formulaic expressions, and bilingual style. The monolingual group also used more politeness formulas, such as *muy a la orden* ("at your orders") and *estoy para servirla* ("I'm here to serve you"), whereas the bilinguals only employed two partial formulas, perhaps due to a lack of culture-specific formulas in their Spanish repertoire. Yáñez (1990) analyzes compliments and responses produced in Spanish and English by Chicano women from southern New Mexico. Notable findings include confirming the formulaic nature of complimenting (and responding), which is similar to the structures reported for monolingual English speakers (Wolfson 1983; Pomerantz 1978), the limited variety of adjectives (more than half contained *bonito*, "nice"), and the fact that compliments praising a food item, when not directed specifically to the cook (e.g., *El arroz está muy bueno*; "The rice is very good"), did not trigger a response. The author was surprised at the lack of code-switching in her data, especially given the findings of Valdés and Pino (1981). However, a limitation of this study is the scarcity of data examined, which are restricted to forty-one utterance pairs.

García (1981) performs a conversation analysis of leave-taking in the context of a Mexican American family in Los Angeles. The results indicate four different phases within the larger speech event: initiation, preparation, joking interchanges, and final leave-taking. The author also highlights certain cultural aspects of the interaction that she describes as uniquely Mexican American, including the closeness and importance of family, the authority given to male members in decision making, the dynamic and emotionally charged nature of the talk exchange (e.g., verbal overlapping, simultaneous interchanges, and loud voices), the use of Spanish and English with nonstandard features (e.g., *¿Ónde está Juan*; "Where is Juan?"), and switching between Spanish and English names (e.g., *Elena*/Helen; *Consuelo*/Connie). The author ends by speculating that a similar exchange in Mexico would have had different characteristics, although she does not specify any details and emphasizes the need for cross-cultural studies.

Using role-plays, Gutiérrez-Rivas (2008) studies the requests of ten first-generation, Spanish-dominant Cubans living in Miami. The data indicate that the informants largely employed strategies of positive politeness, to establish solidarity or camaraderie with their interlocutor, and relatively direct strategies, similar to the findings in García Pastor (1999) and consistent with the tendencies reported for directives throughout the Spanish-speaking world in general (see Márquez Reiter and Placencia 2005).

The number of studies summarized in this section is modest at best, and only a few investigate the prototypical heritage speaker. Hopefully, these initial explorations will inspire further research on speech acts in order to uncover more details about how these bilingual speakers disentangle the inevitable discrepancies between Spanish and English speech norms. Finally, to complete this overview on speech acts, some readers may also be interested in consulting studies that target bilingual children in the United States (e.g., Walter 1981; García and Leone 1984; Bhimji 2002).

Pronoun Usage

In an early study on *tú/usted* ("you" informal/formal) reported in a short squib, Brown (1975) discusses data compiled from a questionnaire distributed to fifty-nine Mexican American undergraduate students at the University of Arizona.

The results reveal that more than twice as many students employ *usted* (63 percent) than *tú* (30 percent) with their parents, a finding that the author found surprising. Jaramillo (1990) examines the use of *tú/usted* in interviews with fifty adult Spanish-speaking residents of Tomé, New Mexico. The results yielded two domain clusters: *tú* (informal), including nuclear family and friendship domains, and *usted* (formal), consisting of ceremonial family, employment, and low-and high-status professionals. Overall, though the patterns reported are consistent with those described for other Spanish-speaking communities, Jaramillo detects a slightly more conservative trend, especially regarding *compadrazgo* interactions between a child's parents and godparents, where up to 88 percent of the participants reported giving and receiving *usted*. Also, 96 percent attest to giving *usted* exceedingly to godparents, while only receiving *tú*, illustrating "the importance placed on respect and formalized social interaction among *compadres* and godparents" (Jaramillo 1990, 19), even though they are usually close friends or relatives. In another study using fifty Spanish-speaking residents of the same town, Jaramillo (1995) looks at the use of *tú/usted* and finds that the participants older than fifty-one years of age, and those who had between zero and eight years of education, reported using and receiving more instances of *usted*. In addition, she noted that *tú* is gradually taking over in both informal and formal contexts, a trend that coincides with what has been reported for Spain and Latin America.

Through oral interviews and a written questionnaire, Schreffler (1994) examines the usage of second-person singular pronouns by twenty-five Salvadorians, representing different ages, living in Houston. Of particular interest is the novelty of exploring how the children of immigrants will adapt the tripartite system—*tú, vos* ("you" informal), and *usted*—in the face of contact with other varieties of Spanish and English. The results of the study indicate that *voseo* is used decreasingly by members of this community, in favor of *tuteo*, which can be attributed primarily to extended contact with the local Mexican population and the desire to blend in. The use of *vos* is still common in some contexts, such as when parents converse with children, although they usually receive *usted*, and among siblings. *Usted* continues to be the pronoun of choice to show respect and deference. Finally, Schreffler reports an attitude change regarding *vos*, in that *tuteo* is perceived as a mark of higher education.

Sigüenza-Ortiz (1996) carries out an in-depth analysis of *tú/usted* in eastern Los Angeles County. Her methodology consists of responses from a self-report questionnaire, interviews, observations, and recorded speech, with a special focus on the language use of thirty participants at home and in church. The author finds that for the English-dominant speakers, the second-person singular pronoun system appears to be syncretizing into a one-person system, with *tú* edging out *usted*. For the home-versus-church domains, all participants self report a higher use of *usted* at church, although the observations showed that those who were less proficient in Spanish employed *tú* more than *usted*, which draws into question the accuracy of self-report data. These less fluent informants also preferred more symmetry, whether *tú-tú* or *usted-usted*, which the author attributes to cognitive simplification. With regard to first encounters, the results indicate that *tú* was preferred by the United States–born participants, compared with *usted* by those born in Mexico. Among her conclusions, the author believes that English is a possible external influence on the expansion of *tú*, due to its similarities with "you" in English. Although difficult to prove, contact with English could speed up the process of a general linguistic change occurring in Spanish and other Romance languages.

Gervasi (2007) applies a pragmatic approach to the use of impersonal pronouns and compares bilingual oral data from the southwestern United States with monolingual data from Mexico City. This analysis considers the influence of certain discourse tasks on the use of *se* (pronominal "one"), *uno* ("one"), *tú*, and the second-person plural (-n). The results indicate that both groups use these impersonal forms in a similar fashion, with either an inclusive meaning (including the speaker) or an exclusive one (excluding the speaker). However, there was a significant difference in the use of *se* because the monolingual group used exclusive *se* with a higher frequency. The author stresses that the findings are preliminary and that more research is needed to determine if the bilingual system of impersonal pronouns in the southwestern United States is indeed unique. This point by Gervasi is well taken and underscores the need for more comparative research on pronoun usage in SHL.

Discourse Markers

Researchers have investigated the role of both Spanish and English discourse markers in the Spanish interactions of bilingual speakers in the United States. With regard to research on adults, García (1999) analyzes *nomás* in the Spanish of southern Texas, a discourse marker that, in addition to its adverbial meaning of "just/only," can enter the pragmatic/discourse domain by expressing the speaker's strong commitment to the proposition. This is especially evident when *nomás* co-occurs with redundant equivalents such as *solamente* ("only") (e.g., *no nomás* solamente "not only just"). There are no claims, however, that the use of *nomás* in this part of the United States differs from that of Latin America. Torres (2002) investigates both English and Spanish discourse markers in the oral Spanish language narratives produced by a group of thirty bilingual Puerto Rican adults in New York. One of the questions Torres considers is whether the English markers such as "so" and "y'know" in Spanish discourse are cases of borrowing or code-switching, and she concludes that they indicate characteristics of both phenomena; they enter as code-switches and eventually acquire the status of borrowings. Aaron (2004) examines 413 uses of both *entonces* ("so/then") and "so" in two corpora of interviews with Spanish/English bilingual speakers in

New Mexico. Although both "so" and *entonces* fulfilled similar functions, "so" triggered code-switches more frequently. The author also reported that "so" is employed similarly in monolingual English, monolingual Spanish, and switched discourse. In a similar study, Torres and Potowski (2008) analyze "so" and *entonces* in Mexican, Puerto Rican, and MexiRican Spanish in Chicago, using fifty-one interviews with speakers representing three generations and varying proficiency levels. The data indicate that "so" was employed more frequently than *entonces* by all speakers, and the functions of both markers proved fairly consistent across the three generations. Some notable differences are that the third generation used "so" more than the other two, and the most proficient speakers preferred *entonces* over "so." Finally, among the three groups, the Puerto Rican and MexiRican informants used "so" twice as often as the Mexican subjects. Overall, the authors believe that only time will tell if "so" entirely displaces *entonces* in Chicago Spanish, but they predict that it is more likely that future generations will not maintain significant proficiency in Spanish.

The articles by Said-Mohand cited here appear to be based on Said-Mohand (2006), a dissertation focusing on *como* ("like/as"), *entonces* ("so/then"), and *tú sabes* ("you know"). In one article, Said-Mohand (2007) concentrates on *tú sabes* in informal interviews with fifty-six university students in Florida. The results indicate that narrative progression was the most frequent function of the marker, accounting for 62 percent of the occurrences, followed by conclusion (22 percent) and reformulation (16 percent). In addition, a higher frequency of *tú sabes* was employed by speakers of Caribbean Spanish, who often use the marker to reduce social distance. Given the absence of studies on monolingual *tú sabes*, no comparisons were possible with other varieties of Spanish.

In another article, Said-Mohand (2008) studies *como* using the same data corpus discussed above for Said-Mohand (2007). In 71.5 percent of the cases, *como* was employed for an approximate numeric value (*pasó como a las nueve y diez*; "it happened around ten after nine"), a general approximation (*pero, es como raro*; "but, it's like rare"), or for presenting an example of something mentioned in the discourse (*puedes hablar como francés, español, italiano*; "you can talk like French, Spanish, Italian"). The intermediate-level third generation also used *como* as a connector on the sentence level, such as the following example: *Pero ellos nunca hablaron en español a los dos menos, ellos, como mi padre llamó a mi madre cielo pero no, nunca hablaron, y conmigo tampoco en español* ("But they never spoke Spanish to the two [of us] except, they, like my father called my mother *cielo* but no, they never spoke, and with me neither in Spanish"). The author points out that this use of *como* in monolingual Spanish, without some combination with *por ejemplo* ("for example") or *que* ("that"), would not be common. Another notable finding was the preference by females for *como* to indicate a direct quotation (*él estaba como ¿qué estás haciendo?* "he was like, what are you doing?"), although no conclusions were made regarding the possible influence of "like" in English.

In the Spanish of six university heritage students of Mexican origin, Sánchez-Muñoz (2007) examines "so," *así que* ("so/then"), *entonces*, and *como*, as well as the fillers "you know," "I don't know," "I mean," *sabes* ("you know"), *o sea* ("that is"), *no sé* ("I don't know"), and *este* ("um"). For *como*, the author focuses primarily on its quotative use and its function as an empty punctor, a meaningless interjection or hesitation device, two uses that only occur in casual registers and are considered by the author to indicate a noncanonical practice transferred from English "like." For "so," *así que*, and *entonces*, no variation across registers was observed, although certain speakers showed a strong preference for a particular marker. In addition, though hesitation devices were not used for formal presentations, *no sé* occurred with the highest frequency in the informal interactions. Finally, the English "you know," "I don't know," and "I mean" also surfaced in the informal Spanish data.

After speech acts, the study of discourse markers in SHL is one of the research topics most likely to prosper during the next few years. This may be attributed to their high frequency, their relative salience in oral discourse, their occurrence in both Spanish and English, the ease with which they are incorporated into speech, and their susceptibility to variation across different Hispanic communities. In addition, the use of these mechanisms by bilingual children is an area that warrants further attention (Andersen et al. 1999; Brizuela, Andersen, and Stallings 1999).

Other Discourse-Related Issues

Elías-Olivares (1995) examines the different discourse strategies of the members of a small group of Spanish speakers in the Mexican American community in Chicago, although eleven of the participants are predominantly Spanish monolinguals and only three are bilingual. Unfortunately, the author does not separate the two groups and the results are somewhat diluted. The author concludes that in spite of the adult speakers' limited proficiency in English, they still demonstrate evidence of language contact (loanwords, calques, etc.). The group also employs various discourse strategies—such as paraphrasis, repetition, direct citation, and taboo words—all features that the author associates with a style of participatory discourse characterized by honesty, emotion, shared experiences, and involvement.

Oral academic discourse, a form of interaction that often occurs in long stretches of monologue, is investigated by Valdés and Geoffrion-Vinci (1998) and Achugar (2003). Valdés and Geoffrion-Vinci (1998) explore the oral presentations of ten first-, second-, third-, and fourth-generation Chicano students at a university in the western United States. A comparable set of data was collected from a monolingual group of six students in Mexico. The results indicate that the bilingual group is aware of register differences, and they attempt to adjust their speech according to the academic context by avoiding code-switching and limiting their use of stigmatized features such as archaisms and ruralisms. The requirements of the task also pushed the HS beyond their ability, which compelled them to invent nonexistent words (e.g., *ojalamente*, "hopefully"; *arruinamiento*, "ruin"; and *mayoridad*, "majority"). Overall, their vocabulary was much more restricted than that of the monolingual group and contained fewer strategies for managing academic discourse. The authors conclude that when compared with the monolinguals, the bilingual participants "appear to be young, unsophisticated, and sometimes even inarticulate" (Valdés and Geoffrion-Vinci 1998, 494). However, the study also highlights different ways in which the Mexican group was unsuccessful at sustaining a formal register.

Achugar (2003) analyzes the oral presentations of two graduate students; one bilingual with an English-dominant education and the other with a Spanish-dominant background. She applies a systemic-functional approach and primarily focuses on the logico-semantic relationships and use of code-switching. Because the English-dominant subject lacked experience in a Spanish academic setting, he did not demonstrate the same level of discursive expertise as the other student. For example, the Spanish-dominant speaker employed expansions to elaborate, extend, and enhance the information presented; projections (e.g., *creo que*, "I believe that"), which served to mark her authority; and conjunctions. The combination of these discursive features allowed her to take a critical stance, make connections between ideas and the source being discussed, and establish logical relations between the ideas. In contrast, the bilingual participant did not make use of these linguistic resources in an appropriate fashion. Furthermore, although both speakers employed code-switching, the English-dominant speaker relied on English to clarify and expand the information presented in Spanish, which undermined his academic legitimacy. Finally, for studies on bilingual children's discourse, Cashman (2005, 2006) delves into some interesting questions regarding the potentially conflictive side of verbal interaction.

LIMITATIONS IN EXISTING RESEARCH AND SUGGESTIONS FOR THE FUTURE

As mentioned in the introduction, SHL research in pragmatics/discourse is still very much a work in progress. In fact, here we opted to extend the focus beyond SHL in order to provide a more complete picture of the existing research on Spanish/English bilingual communities in the United States, but the body of research as a whole is still inconsistent. Apart from the most obvious shortcoming concerning the limited number of studies, the following are some additional limitations that simultaneously indicate opportunities for future research.

Numerous studies do not incorporate comparisons between SHL and monolingual Spanish, although the idea of establishing a monolingual norm or standard baseline as a point of comparison is in itself problematic. One of the difficulties is the fact that many SH speakers do not strive to obtain a monolingual-like proficiency because they are satisfied being functioning bilinguals (Valdés et al. 2000). Nevertheless, whereas Valdés and Geoffrion-Vinci (1998) point out that many scholars reject the idea of a monolingual norm, incorporating a comparable monolingual group of Spanish speakers is crucial to anchoring the research in a wider cross-cultural context. Furthermore, when the influence of English is under consideration, a monolingual English-speaking group should also be included. In the event that collecting three sets of data is not a viable option, researchers should build off existing studies in L1 Spanish and/or English so that the findings are more meaningful and are better integrated into the growing body of research in pragmatics/discourse. There are even instances when replicating L1 Spanish studies on SHL would yield the most informative results because a baseline for comparison is already established.

A substantial methodological limitation is the lack of studies offering a balance between quantitative and qualitative approaches. Some researchers elicit data from large groups via instruments such as questionnaires or role-plays, but one must weigh the benefits of carrying out quantitative analyses with the fact that the data collected through these measures may not represent speech that is entirely authentic. Conversely, with qualitative analyses of naturally occurring discourse, the subjects are often limited in number, and regardless of the amount of detail revealed though a descriptive analysis, it can be impossible to collect comparable instances of the phenomenon under investigation, which leads to inconclusive results. Ideally, the field could benefit from studies combining quantitative and qualitative measures, in addition to more follow-up studies that would allow topics to be analyzed from a range of methodological perspectives.

Thus far the field has primarily been dominated by studies that look at speech production, although this trend will likely change as researchers increasingly consider the receptive/interpretive perspective in order to determine how certain linguistic phenomena are perceived by regular language users (Bernal 2008; Boretti 2003; Hernández-Flores 2003; Lewin 2005). One advantage to eliciting reactions from others is that it allows the researcher to avoid applying his or her own subjective interpretation of the linguistic behavior being analyzed.

Although not unique to the field of pragmatics/discourse, the amount of dialectical variation within the SHL community warrants special attention. For example, research has begun to highlight pragmatic variation between native speaker groups (Márquez Reiter and Placencia 2005); thus it would be productive to explore variations between HS groups that represent diverse backgrounds, namely, speakers from different Spanish dialects who are in contact with dissimilar varieties of English (Torres 1997).

Other topics that have yet to be explored in much detail are linguistic (im)politeness, including mitigation strategies and face work, a wider range of speech acts, interactions between HS and L2 Spanish learners (e.g., Blake and Zyzik

2003, but with a focus on pragmatics/discourse), temporal and spatial deixis, and the pedagogical effects of teaching pragmatics/discourse strategies to HS. Although this last issue has not been investigated for SHL, research in second-language acquisition has shown some promising results for the explicit teaching of pragmatics in the classroom (Rose and Kasper 2001).

CONCLUSION

Blum-Kulka and Sheffer (1993) propose that in situations of language contact, it is likely that the realm of pragmatics will be the primary domain affected. If this is true, it could be attributed to the fact that the pragmatic and discourse levels often entail lexical devices, from single-word discourse markers to conventionalized expressions, which can be transferred across languages or dialects with minimal effort. In addition, with pragmatics and discourse the prescriptive norms are often rather ambiguous, resulting in a malleable model for linguistic behavior and perhaps less resistance to change within a speech community. Therefore, if we take into consideration the permeability of the pragmatic/discursive component of language, might we expect not only a high level of interference in contact situations, as Blum-Kulka and Sheffer (1993) predict, but also a substantial amount of variation between dialects, which research is starting to reveal.

Concerning the brief literature review in this chapter, the role of English interference is undoubtedly a fundamental issue, although some studies lack sufficient comparisons with monolingual Spanish and/or English data to provide compelling evidence. Among the above-mentioned findings regarding English interference, Sánchez-Muñoz (2007) reports what appears to be the influence of the English marker "like" on the use of *como*, especially with the quotative use, and researchers also discuss the persistent use of other English expressions ("you know," "so," "I mean," etc.) in bilingual Spanish (Aaron 2004; Said-Mohand 2007; Sánchez-Muñoz 2007; Torres 2002). Sigüenza-Ortiz (1996) believes that among bilingual English-dominant Spanish speakers born in the United States, the extended use of *tú* over *usted* may be at least partially influenced by the phonetically similar and deferentially neutral "you" in English. Pinto and Raschio (2007, 2008) found that their HS subjects produced requests and complaints that indicated characteristics of English speech acts. With regard to these findings indicating English influence, one of the challenges in corroborating language interference is that contact with English may accelerate internal changes that are already under way in Spanish, similar to what Silva-Corvalán (1994, 2001) has reported for the distinction between indicative and subjunctive moods. So, for example, although Pinto and Raschio (2007) observe noncanonical uses of *si* + conditional in HS requests, it is not clear to what extent exposure to

English can be considered the primary factor, because the same usage has also been reported for monolingual Spanish (e.g., Silva-Corvalán 1985).

Another matter that surfaces concerns gaps in knowledge due to only partial exposure to the same richness of pragmatic and discourse conventions that a monolingual context offers. From the studies summarized above, some of the linguistic consequences of this inconsistent contact include a limited use of devices and strategies unique to formal registers (Valdés and Geoffrion-Vinci 1998; Achugar 2003), a restricted range of politeness formulas and adjectives for complimenting (Valdés and Pino 1981; Yáñez 1990), and potential unease with monolingual-like directness for requesting (Pinto and Raschio 2007). Undoubtedly, for many English-dominant bilinguals living in the United States, both English interference and a limited exposure to monolingual Spanish interact together to produce what Blum-Kulka (1990) refers to as a bicultural hybrid system. A more detailed account of what this emerging hybrid system entails, however, is left for future researchers to uncover.

To conclude this overview of pragmatics/discourse and anchor the discussion in an educational context, perhaps a suitable question to ask is the following: To what extent should we attempt to teach heritage speakers to speak like monolingual Spanish speakers? Undoubtedly there is no definitive answer to this question, but two general objectives could guide us in our pedagogical approach to SHL. The first goal would be to facilitate heritage learners in achieving an oral proficiency that is not potentially detrimental to their own professional success, whereas the second goal would entail minimizing the possibility of being misunderstood by Spanish monolinguals who are unfamiliar with SHL. For instance, given that the inability to speak in an academic register can undermine one's academic legitimacy (Achugar 2003), or make a person sound inarticulate (Valdés and Geoffrion-Vinci 1998), this is an area that warrants pedagogical intervention, especially because the same linguistic deficiencies would likely surface in certain professional contexts. Finally, with regard to effective teaching strategies for pragmatics and discourse-related phenomena, these approaches should include various types of consciousness-raising activities that highlight potential areas of English interference and language-specific expressions or discourse strategies in Spanish.

REFERENCES

Aaron, Jessi Elana. 2004. "So respetamos una tradición del uno al otro." *Spanish in Context* 1 (2): 161–79.

Achugar, Mariana. 2003. "Academic Registers in Spanish in the US: A Study of Oral Texts Produced by Bilingual Speakers in a University Graduate Program." In *Mi lengua: Spanish as a Heritage Language in the United States, Research and Practice*, edited by Ana Roca and M. Cecilia Colombi. Washington, DC: Georgetown University Press.

Andersen, Elaine, Maquela Brizuela, Beatrice DuPuy, and Laura Gonnerman. 1999. "Cross-Linguistic Evidence for the Early Acquisition of Discourse Markers as Register Variables." *Journal of Pragmatics* 31:1339–51.

Arellano, Silvia. 2000. "A Hierarchy of Requests in California Spanish: Are Indirectness and Mitigation Polite?" In *Research on Spanish in the U.S.*-edited by Ana Roca. Somerville, MA: Cascadilla Press.

Austin, John. 1962. *How to Do Things with Words.* Cambridge, MA: Harvard University Press.

Barnes, Julia. 2001. "Politeness in English, Basque and Spanish: Evidence from a Trilingual Child." *Jakingarriak* 45:40–45.

Bernal, María. 2008. "El test de hábitos sociales aplicados al estudio de la cortesía." In *Tercer Coloquio Internacional del Programa EDICE,* edited by Antonio Briz, Antonio Hidalgo, M. Albelda, Josefa Contreras, and Nieves Hernández-Flores. Valencia: Programa EDICE.

Bhimji, Fazila. 2002. "'Dile Family': Socializing Language Skills with Directives in Three Mexican Families in South Central Los Angeles." PhD diss., University of California, Los Angeles.

Blake, Robert, and Eve Zyzik. 2003. "Who's Helping Whom: Learner/Heritage-Speakers' Networked Discussion in Spanish." *Applied Linguistics* 24 (4): 519–44.

Blum-Kulka, Shoshana. 1990. "Don't Touch Your Lettuce with Your Fingers." *Journal of Pragmatics* 14:259–88.

Blum-Kulka, Shoshana, Juliane House, and Gabriele Kasper. 1989. *Cross-Cultural Pragmatics: Requests and Apologies.* Norwood, NJ: Ablex.

Blum-Kulka, Shoshana, and Hadass Sheffer. 1993. "The Metapragmatic Discourse of American-Israeli Families at Dinner." In *Interlanguage Pragmatics,* edited by Gabriele Kasper and Shoshana BlumKulka. New York: Oxford University Press.

Boretti, Susana. 2003. "Test de hábitos sociales y la investigación de la cortesía." In *Actas del I Coloquio del Programa EDICE,* edited by Diana Bravo. Stockholm: Stockholms Universitet.

Brinton, Laurel J. 1996. *Pragmatic Markers in English.* Berlin: Mouton de Gruyter.

Brizuela, Maquela, Elaine Andersen, and Lynne Stallings. 1999. "Discourse Markers as Indicators of Register." *Hispania* 82 (1): 128–41.

Brody, Jill. 1995. "Lending the 'Unborrowable': Spanish Discourse Makers in Indigenous American Languages." In *Spanish in Four Continents: Studies in Language Contact and Bilingualism,* edited by Carmen Silva-Corvalán. Washington, DC: Georgetown University Press.

Brown, Dolores. 1975. "The Use of 'Tú' and 'Usted' with Parents by Some Mexican American Students." *Hispania* 58 (1): 126–27.

Brown, Penelope, and Steven Levinson. 1978. "Universals in Language Use: Politeness Phenomena." In *Questions and Politeness,* edited by Esther N. Goody. Cambridge: Cambridge University Press.

———. 1987. *Politeness.* Cambridge: Cambridge University Press.

Brown, Roger W., and Albert Gilman. 1960. "The Pronouns of Power and Solidarity." In *Style in Language,* edited by Thomas Sebeok. Cambridge, MA: MIT Press.

Cashman, Holly R. 2005. "Aggravation and Disagreement: A Case Study of a Bilingual, Cross-Sex Dispute." *Southwest Journal of Linguistics* 24 (1): 31–51.

———. 2006. "Impoliteness in Children's Interactions in a Spanish/English Bilingual Community of Practice." *Journal of Politeness Research* 2:217–46.

Dumitrescu, Domnita. 2005. "Agradecer en una interlengua." In *ACTAS, II Coloquio Internacional del Programa EDICE*, edited by Jorge Murillo Medrano. San Pedro, Costa Rica: Programa EDICE.

Eelen, Gino. 2001. *A Critique of Politeness Theories*. Manchester: St. Jerome.

Elías-Olivares, Lucía. 1995. "Discourse Strategies of Mexican American Spanish." In *Spanish in Four Continents. Studies in Language Contact and Bilingualism*, edited by Carmen Silva-Corvalán. Washington, DC: Georgetown University Press.

Fitch, Kristine. 1994. "A Cross-Cultural Study of Directive Sequences and Some Implications for Compliance-Gaining Research." *Communication Monographs* 61 (3): 185–209.

Fitch, Kristine, and Robert Sanders. 1994. "Culture, Communication, and Preferences for Directness in Expression of Directives." *Communication Theory* 4 (3): 219–45.

García, MaryEllen. 1981. "Preparing to Leave: Interaction at a Mexican-American Family Gathering." In *Latino Language and Communicative Behavior*, edited by Richard P. Durán. Norwood, NJ: Ablex.

———. 1999. "Nomás in a Mexican American Dialect." In *Advances in Hispanic Linguistics*, edited by Javier Gutiérrez-Rexach and Fernando Martínez-Gil. Somerville, MA: Cascadilla Press.

García, MaryEllen, and Elizabeth Leone. 1984. *The Use of Directives by Two Hispanic Children: An Exploration of Communicative Competence*. Report 25. Los Alamitos, CA: National Center of Bilingual Research.

García Pastor, Maria D. 1999. "Directive Use and Performance in a US Hispanic Community: A Cultural Approach." *Studies in English Language and Linguistics* 1:147–70.

Gervasi, Kareen. 2007. "The Use of Spanish Impersonal Forms in Monolingual and Bilingual Speech." *Hispania* 90 (2): 342–53.

Gutiérrez-Rivas, Carolina. 2008. "Actos de habla mixtos: Reflexiones sobre la pragmática del español en referencia a la teoría y métodos actuales de análisis." *Núcleo* 25:149–71.

Harvey, Penelope. 1991. "Drunken Speech and the Construction of Meaning: Bilingual Competence in the Southern Peruvian Andes." *Language in Society* 20 (1): 1–36.

Hernández-Flores, Nieves. 2003. "Los tests de hábitos sociales en el estudio de la cortesía: una introducción." In *Actas del I Coloquio del Programa EDICE*, edited by Diana Bravo. Stockholm: Stockholms Universitet.

Hurley, Joni. 1995. "Pragmatics in a Language Contact Situation: Verb Forms Used in Requests in Ecuadorian Spanish." *Hispanic Linguistics* 6–7:225–64.

Jaramillo, June. 1990. "Domain Constraints on the Use of Tú and Usted." In *Spanish in the United States: Sociolinguistic Issues*, edited by John J. Bergen. Washington, DC: Georgetown University Press.

———. 1995. "Social Variation in Personal Address Etiquette." *Hispanic Linguistics Journal* 6–7:191–224.

Kasper, Gabriele, and Shoshana Blum-Kulka. 1993. *Interlanguage Pragmatics*. New York: Oxford University Press.

Lewin, Beverly. 2005. "Hedging: An Exploratory Study of Authors' and Readers' Identification of 'Toning Down' in Scientific Texts." *Journal of English for Academic Purposes* 4:163–78.

Márquez Reiter, Rosina, and María Elena Placencia. 2005. *Spanish Pragmatics*. New York: Palgrave Macmillan.

Pinto, Derrin, and Richard Raschio. 2007. "A Comparative Study of Requests in Heritage Speaker Spanish, L1 Spanish, and L1 English." *International Journal of Bilingualism* 11 (2): 135–55.

———. 2008. "Oye, ¿qué onda con mi dinero? An Analysis of Heritage Speaker Complaints." *Sociolinguistic Studies* 2 (2): 221–49.

Placencia, María Elena, and Carmen García. 2007. *Research on Politeness in the Spanish-Speaking World*. Mahwah, NJ: Lawrence Erlbaum Associates.

Pomerantz, Anita. 1978. "Compliment Responses." In *Studies in the Organization of Conversational Interaction*, edited by Jim Schenkein. New York: Academic Press.

Rose, Kenneth, and Gabriele Kasper. 2001. *Pragmatics in Language Teaching*. Cambridge: Cambridge University Press.

Said-Mohand, Aixa. 2006. "Estudio sociolingüístico de los marcadores 'como,' 'entonces' y 'tú sabes' en el habla bilingüe estadounidense." PhD diss., University of Florida.

———. 2007. "A Sociolinguistic Approach to the Discourse Marker *Tú Sabes* 'You Know' in the Speech of Young US bilinguals." *Southwest Journal of Linguistics* 26 (2): 67–93.

———. 2008. "Aproximación sociolingüística al uso de 'entonces' en el habla de jóvenes bilingües estadounidenses." *Sociolinguistic Studies* 2 (1): 97–130.

Sánchez-Muñoz, Ana. 2007. "Style Variation in Spanish as a Heritage Language: A Study of Discourse Particles in Academic and Non-Academic Registers." In *Spanish in Contact: Policy, Social and Linguistic Inquiries*, edited by Kim Potowski and Richard Cameron. Amsterdam: John Benjamins.

Schiffrin, Deborah. 1987. *Discourse Markers*. Cambridge: Cambridge University Press.

Schrader-Kniffki, Martina. 2004. "Speaking Spanish with Zapotec Meaning: Requests and Promises in Intercultural Communication in Oaxaca, Mexico." In *Current Trends in the Pragmatics of Spanish*, edited by Rosina Márquez Reiter and María Elena Placencia. Amsterdam: John Benjamins.

Schreffler, Sandra B. 1994. "Second-Person Singular Pronoun Options in the Speech of Salvadorans in Houston, TX." *Southwest Journal of Linguistics* 13 (1–2): 101–19.

Searle, John. 1969. *Speech Acts*. Cambridge: Cambridge University Press.

———. 1979. *Expression and Meaning: Studies in the Theory of Speech Acts*. New York: Cambridge University Press.

Sigüenza-Ortiz, Consuelo. 1996. "Social Deixis in a Los Angeles Spanish-English Bilingual Community: Tú and Usted Patterns of Address." PhD diss., University of Southern California.

Silva-Corvalán, Carmen. 1985. "Modality and Semantic Change." In *Historical Semantics: Historical Word Formation*, edited by Jacek Fisiak. Berlin: Mouton.

———. 1994. "The Gradual Loss of Mood Distinctions in Los Angeles Spanish." *Language Variation and Change* 6:255–72.

———. 2001. *Sociolingüística y pragmática del español*. Washington, DC: Georgetown University Press.

Torres, Lourdes. 1997. *Puerto Rican Discourse: A Sociolinguistic Study of a New York Suburb*. Mahwah, NJ: Lawrence Erlbaum Associates.

———. 2002. "Bilingual Discourse Markers in Puerto Rican Spanish." *Language in Society* 31 (1): 65–83.

————. 2006. "Bilingual Discourse Markers in Indigenous Languages." *International Journal of Bilingual Education and Bilingualism* 9 (5): 615–24.

Torres, Lourdes, and Kim Potowski. 2008. "A Comparative Study of Bilingual Discourse Markers in Chicago Mexican, Puerto Rican, and MexiRican Spanish." *International Journal of Bilingualism* 12 (4): 263–79.

Valdés, Guadalupe. 1981. "Codeswitching as Deliberate Verbal Strategy: A Microanalysis of Direct and Indirect Requests among Bilingual Chicano Speakers." In *Latino Language and Communicative Behavior*, edited by Richard P. Durán. Norwood, NJ: Ablex.

Valdés, Guadalupe, Christina Chávez, Claudia Angelelli, Kerry Enright, Marisela Gonzalez, Dania García, and Leisy Wyman. 2000. "Bilingualism from Another Perspective: The Case of Young Interpreters from Immigrant Communities." In *Research on Spanish in the United States: Linguistic Issues and Challenges*, edited by Ana Roca. Somerville, MA: Cascadilla Press.

Valdés, Guadalupe, and Michelle Geoffrion-Vinci. 1998. "Chicano Spanish: The Problem of the 'Underdeveloped' Code in Bilingual Repertoires." *Modern Language Journal* 82 (4): 473–501.

Valdés, Guadalupe, and Cecilia Pino. 1981. "Muy a tus órdenes: Compliment Responses among Mexican-American Bilinguals." *Language in Society* 10:53–72.

Walter, Joel. 1981. "Variation in the Requesting Behavior of Children." *International Journal of the Sociology of Language* 27:77–92.

Watts, Richard. 2002. *Politeness*. Cambridge: Cambridge University Press.

Wolfson, Nessa. 1983. "An Empirically Based Analysis of Complimenting in American English." In *Sociolinguistics and Language Acquisition*, edited by Nessa Wolfson and Elliot Judd. Rowley, MA: Newbury House.

Yáñez, Rosa H. 1990. "The Complimenting Speech Act among Chicano Women." In *Spanish in the United States: Sociolinguistic Issues*, edited by John Bergen. Washington DC: Georgetown University Press.

CHAPTER 7

Code-Switching

FROM THEORETICAL TO PEDAGOGICAL CONSIDERATIONS

Ana M. Carvalho, University of Arizona

THIS CHAPTER REVIEWS the major issues in the study of code-switching (CS), which is defined as the alternate use of two or more languages in the same utterance. Initially, CS was seen as aberrant linguistic behavior (Weinreich 1953), but the current consensus is that bilinguals code-switch simply because they can, and they use it to serve a variety of functions, as is demonstrated in this chapter. CS is a routine linguistic behavior among bilinguals when they interact with community members in numerous bilingual contexts around the world, and it is a well-established bilingual practice among Spanish-speaking immigrants and their offspring in the United States. As such, the main findings regarding the nature of, functions of, and attitudes toward CS merit the attention of anyone involved with heritage language pedagogy.

Of all bilingual practices, CS is the most salient, and thus it is frequently perceived by both insiders and outsiders as indicative of disfluency or an inability to speak only one language at a time. These popular views treat CS as the result of incomplete acquisition (i.e., a failure to master both languages) or of language convergence (an inability to separate the languages). In contrast, the last thirty years of research have consistently shown not only that fluent CS is a hallmark of bilingual competence (not lack thereof) but also that it is rule-governed, serves a plethora of discourse functions, and functions as an important marker of group membership.

This chapter aims to inform heritage language pedagogues, teachers, and developers of curricula and material about this essential characteristic of the linguistic repertoire that students bring to class. It presents a brief historical overview of CS research, followed by a discussion of the differences between CS and other language contact phenomena; the relationships between contact

139

phenomena and language competence; and the most important linguistic, social, and discursive aspects of this language practice. Finally, it addresses the use of CS in the heritage language classroom and explores the main implications of research findings for heritage language education.

THE HISTORY OF RESEARCH ON CS

Erica Benson (2001, 26), in reviewing the history of CS research, stated that the term was probably first used in Vogt's 1954 review of Weinreich's *Languages in Contact*, but that both Baker and Espinosa had already documented and studied the phenomenon itself in the first half of the twentieth century (Benson 2001, 27). Both seminal works investigated Spanish-English bilingual communities in the US Southwest. Baker (quoted by Benson 2001) examined the linguistic behavior of Mexican American bilinguals in Tucson. He observed that Mexican Americans used English to speak with Anglo-Americans and Spanish to speak with family members, but that communication among bilinguals was characterized by frequent shifting from one language to the other (Benson 2001, 29). Interestingly, the conclusions that Baker reached in the 1940s—that CS was more frequent among youth, varied depending on the topic of conversation, and served as a strong marker of group membership—still hold true, given that numerous studies since Baker's have identified these factors as characteristic of CS behavior.

The other seminal research on CS was conducted by Espinosa, whose series of studies on New Mexican Spanish (1909–17, cited by Benson 2001, 34) detected CS behavior predominantly in the cities (where English-Spanish bilingualism was more common) and among schoolchildren (usually more fluent bilinguals than their parents). Both educated and uneducated speakers used CS; the important factor was whether they spoke English well (Benson 2001, 30–31). Espinosa's and Baker's early descriptive perspective that identified CS as a common bilingual behavior contrasted sharply with Haugen's (1953, 1956) and Weinreich's (1953) later prescriptive view of CS as an aberrant behavior. Unfortunately, as Benson (2001, 33) pointed out, subsequent scholars have been more influenced by Haugen and Weinreich than by Espinosa and Baker.

The late 1970s and early 1980s saw the emergence of systematic studies of the sociolinguistics of US Spanish and, concurrently, investigations on CS in Spanish-English bilingual conversation (Amastae and Elías-Olivares 1982; Bowen and Ornstein 1976; Durán 1981; Hernández-Chávez, Cohen, and Beltramo 1975). Timm (1975), Pfaff (1979), and Poplack (1980) completed seminal work on English-Spanish CS, demonstrating that this bilingual practice not only serves social functions but is also governed by linguistic constraints. These papers showed that by switching at syntactic boundaries that are equivalent in both languages, speakers maintain grammaticality in both languages. These studies continue to be a must-read for anyone interested in the syntactic constraints of CS.

Zentella's (1981) first exploration of the sociolinguistics of bilingualism among New York Puerto Ricans was based on observations of bilingual classes. Through analyzing student–teacher interactions, she detected that CS served clear didactic functions. In later works (Zentella 1982a, 1982b) she expanded her corpus to incorporate conversations among bilinguals outside the classroom and reported preliminary results that were later incorporated into her 1997 study, which was the most complete longitudinal ethnography of US Spanish-English bilingual behavior to date.

The first modern sociolinguistic studies of CS among Spanish-English bilinguals in the Southwest were done by Valdés (1981) and Silva-Corvalán (1983). Using a large corpus of recorded conversations among bilinguals in New Mexico, Valdés looked at the role of CS in a single speech act—requests—and found that CS played an important role as an interactional strategy (e.g., as mitigation), a claim that was later confirmed by several other studies. In California, Silva-Corvalán (1983, 71) studied CS behavior among Chicano bilinguals and proposed a distinction between "code-shifting," which she defined as changing languages to compensate for a gap in knowledge of one language, and "code-switching," which she defined as a deliberate sociolinguistic strategy. Although later researchers have not utilized her differentiation between code-shifting and code-switching, relationships between bilingual proficiency and CS behavior continue to be a subject of great interest in current CS research (e.g., Bullock and Toribio 2009, 7–9).

In the thirty years since these seminal works, studies on CS have multiplied, delving into four main areas of linguistic research: sociolinguistics, conversation analysis, psycholinguistics, and syntax. Sociolinguistic research has revealed predictable relationships between CS and social factors, such as identity marking, stylistic variation, and interactional functions (Blom and Gumperz 1972; Myers-Scotton 1993; and Zentella 1997, to name only a few). Conversation analysis, although related to sociolinguistics, emphasizes not the social context in which conversation takes place but rather how CS is constrained by the sequential organization of a conversation (Auer 1995, 1998; Cashman 2006; Gafaranga 2005, 2009; Moyer 1998). Departing from the question of why bilinguals code-switch and turning to the question of how, psycholinguistic studies have researched speakers' grammaticality judgments and eye movements during CS in order to explain how they can process CS so rapidly and intricately (Dussias 2001, 2003; Toribio 2000). Research on the syntactic aspects of CS has also been extremely prolific. On the basis of the assumption that there are grammatical restrictions on the ways in which languages can be mixed, such research has observed, analyzed, and generalized the structural constraints of CS. Scholars have tried to explain these constraints within the formal theories of the minimalist approach (MacSwan 1999), X-bar theory (Belazi, Rubin, and Toribio 1994), government relations (Di Sciullo, Muysken, and Singh 1986), and the matrix language frame model (Myers-Scotton 1993).

Structural accounts of CS have devoted a great deal of effort to differentiating CS from other language contact phenomena. Lexical borrowing, also a very common consequence of language contact, entails the incorporation of lexical elements from one language into another. CS, in contrast, is the ephemeral departure from one linguistic system to an entirely different one, or, as Grosjean (1995, 263) put it, "shifting completely to the other language for a word, a phrase, or a sentence." CS is easily identified when an entire phrase or more is spoken in the donor language, because the phrase is internally consistent with the morphology, syntax, and phonology of that other language, but the intrusion of a single word from another language presents a challenge for classification, because usually there is not enough information to reveal a pattern. Degree of integration and frequency of use are criteria often used to distinguish a lexical borrowing from a one-item switch. Established borrowings are morphologically and phonologically assimilated to the recipient language, to the point that they even appear in monolingual speech (e.g., "burrito" in English or "software" in Spanish). However, as Poplack (2004, 590) pointed out, "Distinguishing a nonce borrowing [i.e., one used only sporadically] from CS of a lone lexical item is conceptually easy but methodologically difficult, especially when this item surfaces bare, giving no apparent indication of language membership."

Although phonological integration is generally seen as a sufficient criterion to distinguish CS from lexical borrowing, Poplack (1980) claimed that lexical borrowing requires morphological or phonological adaptation, not necessarily both. This view is shared by Bullock (2009, 166), who argued that it is now clear that borrowing is not necessarily fully phonologically integrated, and thus it should not be considered a sine qua non criterion for distinguishing a borrowed word from CS. Poplack and Meechan (1998) suggested a detailed quantitative method for the disambiguation of language contact phenomena in general, and of one-item CS versus lexical borrowing in particular, whereas others believe that the difference between CS and lexical borrowing is better described as a matter of degree, on a continuum from nonassimilated to assimilated forms (Gardner-Chloros 2009; Myers-Scotton 1993; Treffers-Daller 1991). Although the complexities of the distinction between lexical borrowing and CS are not particularly relevant to heritage language pedagogy, an awareness of the types of language contact phenomena is useful for preparing educators to better understand the bilingual repertoires of heritage language students.

THE MYTH OF *NI UNO NI OTRO*

CS is typically present in contact varieties, and consequently it sets them apart from the more prestigious, standard dialects spoken in monolingual societies.

This evaluation that standard dialects are superior to contact ones is due, in part, to the inaccurate but common comparison of bilinguals to two monolinguals (Grosjean 1995). Although speakers in bilingual communities usually command bilingual and multidialectal linguistic repertoires, when compared with monolinguals, they are often perceived as not speaking either language well but rather as using a random mixture popularly labeled *ni uno ni otro* (neither one nor the other).

Despite the evidence that CS, more often than not, is a sign of proficient bilingualism, a purist ideology prevails that interprets isolated mixed utterances as representative of failure to master either language. In fact, bilinguals often command a range of styles ranging from mixed, bilingual utterances to ones that are close to standard, monolingual dialects. Bilingual and multidialectal speakers are frequently denigrated as speakers of a degenerate mixed language (e.g., "Spanglish"), even though the creation of a third language is an uncommon outcome of language contact (Garrett 2006, 53).[1]

CS carries a clear, solidarity-based covert prestige among code-switchers, but overall community attitudes toward the practice provide important contextual information about the surrounding sociolinguistic reality. Accordingly, language attitudes are fundamental to understanding how CS affects the heritage-language-speaking population. In educational settings, CS is often perceived as a form of semilingualism that must be eradicated from the classroom (Bullock and Toribio 2009, 11).

Studies that attempt to unveil language attitudes examine how speakers react to language varieties. Direct methods include openly questioning people about their assessment of forms of speaking, whereas indirect methods use matched-guise techniques that ask people to judge speakers' personal attributes based solely on a sample of their speech. Montes-Alcalá (2000) used direct methods to explore attitudes towards CS among young college-educated US Latino bilinguals and found that they had generally positive attitudes, and thus they interpreted CS as an important identity marker. Fernández (1990), conversely, found very negative attitudes toward CS and that it was seen as a sign of linguistic deficiency. To assess bilinguals' attitudes toward different language contact phenomena, Anderson and Toribio (2007) presented bilinguals with language texts that ranged from standard, monolingual speech, to texts with commonly used borrowings and CS, to ones with less frequently attested borrowings and infelicitous CS. Bilinguals could detect the differences among these texts and evaluate them accordingly as being produced by monolingual, heritage language, or second-language speakers of Spanish. Anderson and Toribio's research confirmed, first, the general tendency among bilinguals to positively value monolingual dialects. It also brought additional evidence to the assertion that CS behavior is not erratic but rule-governed, by showing that bilinguals were able to make fine-grained distinctions between felicitous and infelicitous language contact phenomenon.

Intrinsically related to the negative attitudes toward CS is the idea that it is the result of a language deficit. Although CS is commonly found among proficient bilinguals in stable bilingual communities where neither language shift or language attrition is occurring, it is also found in less stable bilingual communities among speakers of Spanish as a heritage language who have a wide range of bilingual proficiency, ranging from highly productive to basically receptive. Among this population, whose dominant language is English and whose receding language is Spanish, one may expect to find, in addition to CS, a great deal of calquing, semantic extensions, and convergence. Bilinguals who are clearly dominant in one language show different CS patterns than do more balanced bilinguals. Both Poplack (1980) and Zentella (1997) have shown that bilinguals who are dominant in one language tend to switch more intersententially (i.e., between sentences) by means of taglike phrases, whereas those with stronger bilingual skills favored intrasentential switches (i.e., switches within the sentence). Poplack (2004, 594) explained that speakers who are less proficient favor switches that require less knowledge of the donor language's grammar—thus, of permissible CS sites—and result in a use of tags and frozen phrases. Use of short Spanish insertions was also common among Silva-Corvalán's (1994) third-generation Mexican American speakers in Los Angeles, whom she classified as residual speakers with limited Spanish that only allowed them to switch using emblematic phrases. In Zentella's (1997) ethnography of immigrants in New York City, code-switchers indeed represented the last generation of Spanish speakers before the shift to English took place. However, CS may not be indicative of a language shift in border communities, where bilingualism has a longer life span than the three generations typical of immigrant communities, and where consecutive generations of code-switchers are found.

For all types of bilinguals, CS may sporadically have compensatory functions; that is, a switch may be triggered by difficulty recalling words. Compensatory CS, or "crutches," were investigated by Zentella (1997), who analyzed each switch as a known word, an unknown word, a momentary lapse, or no evidence (i.e., the cause was not identifiable). She verified that, in general, the children did not code-switch to compensate for a lack of linguistic knowledge, because they knew how to say three-fourths of their switches in both languages. Interestingly, these children perceived that they used CS mainly for compensatory reasons, when "they couldn't remember a word." Zentella (1997, 99) convincingly explained this apparent contradiction by arguing that effortless CS in conversation is unconscious, whereas a switch for an unknown or forgotten segment is likely to be a conscious choice and, hence, more easily perceived and remembered. It is thus plausible that, although bilinguals occasionally code-switch to compensate for a lack of linguistic knowledge, most CS behavior originates from the simple fact of being bilingual. Anyone involved in heritage language education should be aware of the myth of *ni uno ni otro* and its potentially detrimental consequences in the community and in the classroom.

FUNCTIONS AND RULES OF CS

As has been repeatedly demonstrated in the literature, CS is not only the expected result of language contact but also follows syntactic rules and performs social and interactional functions, as noted by Zentella (1997, 80; emphasis added):

> All native speakers demonstrate a tacit cultural knowledge of how to speak their language appropriately in different speech situations, in keeping with their community's "ways of speaking" (Hymes 1974). Whereas monolinguals adjust by switching phonological, grammatical, and discourse features within one linguistic code, bilinguals alternate between languages in their linguistic repertoire as well. Children in bilingual speech communities acquire two grammars and the rules for communicative competence which prescribe not only *when* and *where* each language may be used, but also *whether* and *how* the two languages may be woven together in a single utterance.

In this section, I concentrate on the when, where, and how of language alternation in bilingual speech: first, the main structural constraints at work; then, the social functions and interactional meaning performed by CS. The awareness that CS is rule-governed and may serve important functions in the community is critical in understanding the linguistic repertoire and practices that heritage language learners bring to the classroom, which is the base on which heritage language educators are expected to build.

Linguistic Aspects of CS

Myers-Scotton (1993) proposed the matrix language framework model. Under this influential model, one language serves as the matrix and thus provides the grammatical frame, including grammatical morphemes, whereas the other language is embedded and thus supplies content morphemes that are incorporated into the matrix (equivalent to Muysken's notion of insertion). The two languages may switch between matrix and embedded roles throughout the course of a conversation. Some scholars (e.g., Auer 2000) have, however, questioned whether there must be a matrix language in each and every utterance.

Muysken (1995) proposed a three-part typology of patterns of language mixture: alternation, congruent lexicalization, and insertion. Alternation corresponds to classic CS, in which the two languages remain relatively separate. Congruent lexicalization, more commonly found when the languages are typologically similar, represents cases in which the languages share a common grammatical structure that is filled with lexical elements from either language. Finally, an insertion involves the incorporation of a constituent (a word or phrase) into the recipient language, which, as Poplack (2004) correctly stated, better fits the definition of lexical borrowing than CS.

In her seminal works on Spanish-English CS, Poplack (1980, 1981) laid important groundwork for the definition of linguistic constraints on CS by proposing the free morpheme and equivalence constraints. The free morpheme constraint predicts that CS will occur only between words, never between free and bound morphemes in a single word (e.g., *comer + ing*), unless the switch is integrated phonologically. The equivalence constraint requires that CS take place only at points where the order of constituents coincides in both languages. Zentella (1997) tested the equivalence constraint against her data, and she found that it was violated by only 3 percent of the switches; she also found correlations between the application of grammatical constraints and her participants' ages and dominant languages. Although counterarguments and counterexamples to the free morpheme and equivalence constraints exist, these concepts are still invoked in the current literature due to their explanatory power (Chan 2009, 184), especially if they are seen, as proposed by Poplack (2004, 589), more as general principles than absolute rules.

Although formal accounts of CS engage in the analysis of mixed-language utterances in the same way that monolingual language production is analyzed (MacSwan 1999), Poplack (2004, 589) argued that one should not assume the principles that apply in monolingual syntax apply the same way in bilingual syntax. In addition, she argued against the formal predictability usually associated with isolated examples, grammaticality judgments, and introspection (p. 592), and proposed, instead, a production-based explanation that derives from recurrent patterns of everyday bilingual interactions and thus departs substantially from explanations deduced from universal constraints. Finally, she argued against the generalization of the same principles for different language pairs and communities (pp. 592–94), and she thus emphasized locally relevant patterns and minimized the relevance of universal principles upon which generative grammar and the Matrix Language Frame Model are based.[2]

Social Aspects of CS

From the beginning, CS has been studied mainly in the framework of sociolinguistics. Gumperz's work, especially his distinctions between situational and metaphorical CS and between we-code and they-code, continue to be influential (Gardner-Chloros 2009, 104). Blom and Gumperz's (1972) seminal work on the functions of switching between dialectal varieties in Norway led them to distinguish situational and metaphorical CS. Situational CS occurs when speakers alternate between standard and local dialects according to changes in the setting, whereas metaphorical CS takes place when the setting remains the same but the switch itself evokes a change in formality or topic. Also based on direct associations between language choice and socially indexed meaning, Gumperz (1982) proposed a distinction between we-code, which is associated with the minority language and is used in within-group and informal activities, and they-code, which is associated with the majority language and is used in out-of-group relations in more formal settings.

Further research problematized this firm dichotomy by adopting more fluid, nuanced, and complex concepts of social identity and, thus, its relation to linguistic behavior (Auer 1984, 1998; Li 1994; Rampton 1995). Cashman (2005b), for example, in her analysis of bilingual conversation among Latinos in Michigan, demonstrated how speakers "make" social identities by constructing, maintaining, and crossing ethnic boundaries when switching languages. She concluded that "language alternation in conversation may be seen as constituting and changing, not merely reflecting, social structure" (Cashman 2005b, 313).

CS is clearly a group behavior that both insiders and outsiders recognize as such, although it is important to keep in mind recent trends in language studies that have rejected simple and straightforward links between linguistic behavior and social identity, and thus have rightly problematized one-to-one correspondence between certain codes and certain identities (Mendoza-Denton 2002). Gonzales (1999), in her study of language choice among US Latina bilinguals at a bridal shower, clearly showed that in-group cohesiveness among participants was conducive to CS. Poplack (1993) discussed the difficulties of collecting CS data in sociolinguistic interviews because the interviewer needs not only to be bilingual but also a community member in order for speakers to code-switch in his or her presence. Therefore, the status of CS as an in-group language practice and identity marker, learned and practiced during language socialization in one's community and household (Delgado 2009), has important implications for the heritage language classroom, where teachers and curriculum designers are expected to respect and validate learners' backgrounds.[3]

Because CS is a bilingual practice based on personal relationships, the social network framework has been particularly fruitful for its investigation (e.g., Karadan 2004; Raschka, Wei, and Lee 2002; Rocchi 2008; Sabec 1997). This method involves compiling a list of an individual's daily contacts and identifying whether a strong or weak tie exists with each contact. Milroy and Wei's (1995) work on Chinese-English bilinguals in England is an excellent illustration of how a social network study is able to detect the sociolinguistics of fast-changing immigrant communities and intergenerational patterns of CS, particularly because in immigrant societies one cannot rely on traditional social categories, such as socioeconomic class and status, that usually are better suited for stable, nonimmigrant communities. To the best of my knowledge, social network studies of this scope are rarely reproduced among the US Latino bilingual population (a welcome exception is the study by Cashman 2003).

Conversational Functions

CS serves as an extraconversational tool among bilinguals who—in addition to switching tones, volume, and style to fulfill conversational functions like monolinguals do—also switch languages. Zentella (1997) presented a comprehensive list of the conversational strategies CS accomplished in her corpus, including realignment strategies (topic shift, quotation, role shift, narrative break, etc.), appeal or control (mitigating requests, attracting attention, etc.), and clarification or emphasis (translations, appositions, requests, etc.). Although 48 percent of the switches were associated with clear communicative intents, Zentella (1997, 90) clarified that "not every switch could be identified with a particular function, and every change in communicative function was not accomplished by a shift in language."

The genre of narratives has been the subject of studies that focus on interactional meanings of CS. Both Koike (1987) and Alvarez (1991) have analyzed narratives and confirmed that most CS occurred at the transitions between the main structural components of the narratives—abstract, orientation, complicating actions, evaluations, resolution, and coda.

From the viewpoint of strict conversation analysis, where the meaning is locally derived from the text itself, the meaning of CS is dependent on its sequential environment. Auer (1984, 1995, 1998) has been an important proponent of the application of conversational analysis to the study of CS. He advocated that instead of relying on external constraints or social meanings, researchers should focus on the sequence of turns and analyze CS in terms of the utterances that precede and follow it. This approach has been applied by Torras and Garafanga (2002) in their analysis of Spanish-Catalan CS, by Moyer (1998) in her analysis of Spanish-English CS in Gibraltar, by Cashman (2005a, 2006) in her analyses of peer interaction in classrooms in Phoenix, and by Delgado (2009) in her analysis of CS among Mexican American family members in Tucson.

Analyses of the interactional meanings of CS, such as the studies mentioned in this section, could be the basis for a discussion in the heritage language classroom. Teachers and students should understand that CS can be and often is used strategically in conversation. Based on the premise that students' bilingual repertoire should be the point of departure for heritage language education, I now turn to the implications of CS research for classroom practice.

CODE-SWITCHING IN THE
HERITAGE LANGUAGE CLASSROOM

Schools usually promote language standardization, and teachers often promote the monolingual standard language ideology in their teaching, in the belief that they are getting students ready for the real world, where vernaculars are marginalized. Educational institutions (or "local elites," in Barreto's 1998 terminology), embrace second-language teaching in order to promote elite bilingualism but look down on bilingual practices that do not conform to the idealized use of one language at a time. As well stated by Heller (1999, 5), what is valued is multilingualism as a set of parallel monolingualisms, not a hybrid system. As a consequence, the heritage language classroom usually operates in a monolingual mode instead of a bilingual one. Grosjean (2001) has proposed a monolingual–bilingual continuum where the bilingual mode at one end is characterized by simultaneous activation of the bilingual speaker's two languages, whereas at the other end is a totally monolingual language mode in which the speaker is interacting with individuals who are monolingual in one of the two languages. The usual policy in the heritage language classroom is a monolingual mode where Spanish is activated while English is deactivated, disregarding the fact that this environment is not the most conducive to learning among bilinguals who often engage in CS in their daily interactions. Fitts (2006) showed that dual-immersion programs emphasize the development of parallel monolingualisms, whereas Shannon (1995) demonstrated that some teachers do resist the hegemony of English in the classroom.[4] Fuller (2009c) presented a comprehensive synthesis of research done on the use of CS in the classroom in terms of its functions in discourse, its use as an identity marker, and the language ideologies that surround it.

Several scholars of heritage language education have argued that teachers should accept CS in the classroom (De Meija 2002; Edmondson 2004; Gumperz and Cook-Gumperz 2005; Nichols and Colón 2000; Palmer 2009; Timm 1993; Valdés-Fallis 1978), in order to capitalize on the oral skills students bring to class and promote a relaxed classroom atmosphere that is more conducive to learning. Gibson (2009, 221–23) detailed three types of pedagogic functions of CS in the classroom: CS for pedagogic reasons (e.g., clarification, mediation of meaning), CS for classroom management (e.g., transitions between activities), and CS for interpersonal relations (i.e., to index different identities and create solidarity). Martin-Jones (1995, 90–91) pointed out that whereas early studies of bilingual classrooms tended to focus on the frequency and functions of CS in the classroom, more recent studies have explored how CS contributes to the flow of communication and promotes interactions among students and teachers. Riegelhaupt (2000, 213) argued that teachers should be informed about the value and roles of CS in the community so that they can use this knowledge to "help make the classroom a place where we promote equality and try to avert the prejudices often found outside the school."

Lippi-Green (1997, 66) explained that when speakers of stigmatized varieties assimilate the standard ideology, they incorporate negative attitudes about their language and themselves. As they encounter overt social denigration of their linguistic behavior outside their communities, they start to look down on their way of speaking even as they continue to use it. According to Nichols and Colón (2000, 500), bilinguals who engage in CS often experience even greater disdain for their linguistic behavior than do speakers of nonstandard dialects. To combat negative attitudes toward CS, the authors argued that an examination of CS should be incorporated into the heritage language curriculum, in order to promote students' and teachers' recognition of the practice as a resource with social value rather than a deficiency (p. 501), a case also made by Sayer (2008). Nichols and Colón went on to report on their observation of a bilingual high school class in California, where the students and teacher freely used CS; the supportive and interactive climate thereby created in the classroom promoted students' academic achievement.

Analyses of CS in the classroom have highlighted its usefulness as a pedagogic tool in elementary school (Fuller 2009a, 2009b; Gort 2006; Palmer 2009; Potowski 2009; Reyes 2004), both middle school (Unamuno 2008) and high school (Nichols and Colón 2000). Although several universities currently offer Spanish as a heritage language (see chapter 10 in this volume, by Beaudrie), there is little research documenting language use in the postsecondary heritage language classroom (but see Lowther 2009; Sanchez Muñoz 2007).

After thirty years of research, the consensus is that CS and lexical borrowing are unavoidable language practices among bilingual US Latinos. Consequently, heritage language pedagogy, whose objective is to promote the maintenance and development of Spanish, should embrace this emblematic behavior and allow it in the classroom. Common goals of heritage language education are the expansion of the learners' vernacular base, that is, the incorporation of other linguistic styles and registers into the learners' existing repertoires. To this end, a common practice has been the development of dialectal awareness through contrastive analysis activities, so that learners come to understand the differences between their vernacular and the standard variety. Texts for contrasting native dialects with their standard counterparts can be found in the community or, alternatively, in the recent, prolific literature on written CS. CS occurs in song lyrics (Ohlson 2007), e-mail correspondence (Goldbarg 2009; Montes-Alcalá 2005), blogs (Montes-Alcalá 2007), personal letters (Montes-Alcalá 2005), fiction (Callahan 2004), and cellphone text messages (Carrier and Benitez 2010)—all of which provide ample sources for corpus analysis of authentic CS in the classroom. Using and discussing CS in the heritage language classroom is consistent with the two decades of heritage language research, which have demonstrated that efforts to promote students' linguistic confidence, language, and cultural pride are factors that are highly conducive to minority language maintenance and expansion.

CONCLUSION

Sociolinguistics can play an important role in informing heritage language pedagogy. It is well known that when a mismatch occurs between the linguistic environment of the community and that of the school, students are at a disadvantage. To remedy this situation, I hope that the major findings of the extensive research on CS presented in this chapter will inform heritage language education practices and goals. Hélot (2004) pinpointed the disconnects between home practices and the language used in school, and thus highlighted an urgent need for educators to understand bilingual socialization—a claim echoed by Zentella (2005). In the past, as Starks (2005, 534) pointed out, "educationalists and sociolinguists have, with a few notable exceptions, tended to work in relative isolation from each other." Only by undertaking interdisciplinary research that considers learners' sociolinguistic reality will the field of heritage language education continue to flourish on a solid foundation. A thorough description of learners' linguistic repertoire is an essential step for the development of a pedagogy that is sensitive to students' sociolinguistic background; in the case of bilingual US Latinos, CS constitutes an essential characteristic of their background.

The continued development of a research agenda to advance scholars' understanding of the role of CS in heritage language education should include detailed ethnographies of classrooms at all levels. Gibson (2009, 234) claimed that this type of research should "move beyond documentation of the pedagogic functions of classroom CS to investigate, and demonstrate, effects on learning and classroom behavior, on the affective climate of the classroom, and on processes of identity formation and negotiation, all this, in turn, implying greater recourse to more interventionist, controlled research designs." He went on to emphasize that such research should investigate and describe good practices in the area of teacher education and CS awareness so that scholars will begin to better understand the impact of CS on learning and achievement. The findings of CS research summarized here can constitute a foundation for this research agenda.

NOTES

1. See Otheguy (2007) for criticism of the term "Spanglish." Although the formation of a third language that departs significantly from the language pair that are in contact is not frequent, the idea that discrete codes coexist and can be discretely categorized has been disputed by Gardner-Chloros (1995) and Swigart (1992), among others.

2. See MacSwan (2009) for an overview of the main generativist approaches to CS. See Myers-Scotton and Jake (2009) for a summary of the Matrix Language Frame Model.

3. For a comprehensive discussion of identity and heritage language education, see chapter 9 in this volume, by Potowski.

4. For a comprehensive discussion of ideology and heritage language education, see chapter 2 in this volume, by Leeman.

REFERENCES

Alvarez, Celia. 1991. "Code-Switching in Narrative Performance: Social, Structural, and Pragmatic Functions in the Puerto Rican Speech Community in East Harlem." In *Sociolinguistics of the Spanish-speaking World: Iberia, Latin America, United States*, edited by Carol Klee. Tempe: Bilingual Press.

Amastae, Jon, and Lucía Elías-Olivares, eds. 1982. *Spanish in the United States: Sociolinguistic Aspects.* New York: Cambridge University Press.

Anderson, Tyler Kimball, and Almeida Jacqueline Toribio. 2007. "Attitudes towards Lexical Borrowing and Intra-Sentential Code-Switching among Spanish-English Bilinguals." *Spanish in Context* 4 (2): 217–40.

Auer, Peter. 1984. *Bilingual Conversation.* Amsterdam: John Benjamins.

———. 1995. "The Pragmatics of Code-Switching: A Sequential Approach." In *One Speaker, Two Languages: Cross-Disciplinary Perspectives on Code-Switching,* edited by Leslie Milroy and Peter Muysken. Cambridge: Cambridge University Press.

———, ed. 1998. *Code-Switching in Conversation: Language, Interaction and Identity.* London: Routledge.

———. 2000. "Why Should We and How Can We Determine the 'Base Language' of a Bilingual Conversation?" *Estudios de Sociolingüística* 1 (1): 129–44.

Barreto, Amílcar A. 1998. *Language, Elites, and the State: Nationalism in Puerto Rico and Quebec.* Westport, CT: Praeger.

Belazi, Heidi, Edward Rubin, and Almeida Jacqueline Toribio. 1994. "Code-Switching and X-Bar Theory: The Functional Head Constraint." *Linguistic Inquiry* 25 (2): 221–37.

Benson, Erica J. 2001. "The Neglected Early History of Codeswitching Research in the United States." *Language and Communication* 21:23–36.

Blom, Jan-Petter, and John J. Gumperz. 1972. "Social Meaning in Linguistic Structures: Code-Switching in Norway." In *Directions in Sociolinguistics,* edited by John J. Gumperz and Dell Hymes. New York: Holt, Rinehart & Winston.

Bowen, Donald, and Jacob Ornstein, eds. 1976. *Studies in Southwest Spanish.* Rowle, MA: Newbury House.

Bullock, Barbara E., and Almeida Jacqueline Toribio. 2009. "Themes in the Study of Code-Switching." In *The Cambridge Handbook of Linguistic Code-Switching,* edited by Barbara Bullock and Almeida Jacqueline Toribio. Cambridge: Cambridge University Press.

Bullock, Barbara E. 2009. "Phonetic Reflexes of Code-Switching." In *The Cambridge Handbook of Linguistic Code-Switching,* edited by Barbara E. Bullock and Almeida Jacqueline Toribio. Cambridge: Cambridge University Press.

Callahan, Laura. 2004. *Spanish/English Codeswitching in a Written Corpus.* Philadelphia: John Benjamins.

Carrier, L. Mark, and Sandra Benitez. 2010. "The Effect of Bilingualism on Communication Efficiency in Text Messages (SMS)." *Multilingua* 29 (2): 167–83.

Cashman, Holly. 2003. "Social Networks and English/Spanish Bilingualism in Detroit, Michigan." *Revista Internacional de Linguistica Iberoamericana* 1 (2): 59–78.

———. 2005a. "Aggravation and Disagreement: A Case Study of a Bilingual, Cross-Sex Dispute in a Phoenix Classroom." *Southwest Journal of Linguistics* 24 (1–2): 31–51.

———. 2005b. "Identities at Play: Language Preference and Group Membership in Bilingual Talk in Interaction." *Journal of Pragmatics* 37:301–15.

———. 2006. "Impoliteness in Children's Interactions in a Spanish/English Bilingual Community of Practice. "*Journal of Politeness Research* 2: 217–46.

Chan, Brian Hok-Sching. 2009. "Code-Switching between Typologically Distinct Languages." In *The Cambridge Handbook of Linguistic Code-Switching,* edited by Barbara E. Bullock and Almeida Jacqueline Toribio. Cambridge: Cambridge University Press.

Delgado, Rocio. 2009. "Spanish Heritage Language Socialization Practices of a Family of Mexican Origin." PhD diss., University of Arizona, Tucson.

De Meija, Anne-Marie. 2002. *Power, Prestige and Bilingualism: International Perspectives on Elite Bilingual Education.* Clevedon, UK: Multilingual Matters.

Di Sciullo, Anne-Marie, Pieter Muysken, and Rajendra Singh. 1986. "Government and Code-Mixing." *Journal of Linguistics* 22 (1): 1–24.

Durán, Richard P., ed. 1981. *Latino Language and Communicative Behavior.* Norwood, NJ: Ablex.

Dussias, Paola. 2001. "Psycholinguistic Complexity in Codeswitching." *International Journal of Bilingualism* 5 (1): 87–100.

———. 2003. "Spanish-English Code Mixing at the Auxiliary Phrase: Evidence from Eye-Movement Data." *Revista Internacional de Lingüística Iberoamericana* 1 (2): 7–34.

Edmondson, Willis. 2004. "Code-Switching and World-Switching in Foreign Language Classroom Discourse." In *Multilingual Communication,* edited by Juliane House and Jochen Rehbein. Amsterdam: John Benjamins.

Fernández, Rosa. 1990. "Actitudes hacia los cambios de código en Nuevo México: Reacciones de un sujeto a ejemplos de su habla." In *Spanish in the United States: Sociolinguistics Issues,* edited by John J. Bergen. Washington, DC: Georgetown University Press.

Fitts, Shanan. 2006. "Reconstructing the Status Quo: Linguistic Interaction in a Dual-Language School." *Bilingual Research Journal* 29:337–65.

Fuller, Janet M. 2009a. "Gendered Choices: Code-Switching and Collaboration in a Bilingual Classroom." *Gender and Language* 3 (2): 181–208.

———. 2009b. "How Bilingual Children Talk: Strategic Codeswitching among Children in Dual-Language Programs." In *First-Language Use in Second-Language and Foreign Language Learning,* edited by Miles Turnbull and Jennifer Daily O'Cain. Bristol, UK: Multilingual Matters.

———. 2009c. "Multilingualism in Educational Contexts: Ideologies and Identities." *Language and Linguistics Compass* 3 (1): 338–58.

Gafaranga, Joseph. 2005. "Demythologising Language Alternation Studies: Conversational Structure vs. Social Structure in Bilingual Interaction." *Journal of Pragmatics* 37 (3): 281–300.

———. 2009. "The Conversation Analytic Model of Code-Switching." In *The Cambridge Handbook of Linguistic Code-Switching,* edited by Barbara E. Bullock and Almeida Jacqueline Toribio. Cambridge: Cambridge University Press.

Gardner-Chloros, Penelope. 1995. "Code-Switching in Community, Regional and National Repertoires: The Myth of the Discreteness of Linguistic Systems." In *One Speaker, Two Languages: Cross-Disciplinary Perspectives on Code-Switching,* edited by Leslie Milroy and Peter Muysken. Cambridge: Cambridge University Press.

———. 2009. "Sociolinguistic Factors in Code-Switching." In *The Cambridge Handbook of Linguistic Code-Switching,* edited by Barbara E. Bullock and Almeida Jacqueline Toribio. Cambridge: Cambridge University Press.

Garrett, Paul B. 2006. "Language Contact and Contact Languages." In *A Companion to Linguistic Anthropology,* edited by Alessandro Duranti. Malden, MA: Blackwell.

Gibson, Ferguson. 2009. "What Next? Towards an Agenda for Classroom Codeswitching Research." *International Journal of Bilingual Education and Bilingualism* 12 (2): 231–41.

Goldbarg, Rosayn Negron. 2009. "Spanish-English Codeswitching in Email Communication. *Language@Internet*, 2009, 6.

Gonzales, María Dolores. 1999. "Crossing Social and Cultural Borders: The Road to Language Hybridity." In *Speaking Chicana. Voice, Power, and Identity*, edited by D. Letticia Galindo, and María Dolores Gonzales. Tucson: University of Arizona Press.

Gort, Mileidis. 2006. "Strategic Codeswitching, Interliteracy, and other Phenomena of Emergent Bilingual Writing: Lessons from First Grade Dual-Language Classrooms." *Journal of Early Childhood Literacy* 6 (3): 323–54.

Grosjean, François. 1995. "A Psycholinguistic Approach to Code-Switching: The Recognition of Guest Words by Bilinguals. In *One Speaker, Two Languages: Cross-Disciplinary Perspectives on Code-Switching*, edited by Lesley Milroy and Pieter Muysken. Cambridge: Cambridge University Press.

———. 2001. "The Bilingual's Language Modes." In *One Mind, Two Languages: Bilingual Language Processing*, edited by Janet Nicol. Oxford: Blackwell.

Gumperz, John J. 1982. *Language and Social Identity*. Cambridge: Cambridge University Press.

Gumperz, John J., and Jenny Cook-Gumperz. 2005. "Making Space for Bilingual Communicative Practice." *Intercultural Pragmatics* 2 (1): 1–23.

Haugen, Einar. 1953. *The Norwegian Language in America: A Study of Bilingual Behavior*. Philadelphia: University of Pennsylvania Press.

———. 1956. *Bilingualism in the Americas: A Bibliography and Research Guide*. American Dialect Society Publication 26. Tuscaloosa: University of Alabama Press.

Heller, Monica. 1999. *Linguistic Minorities and Modernity: A Sociolinguistic Ethnography*. London: Longman.

Hélot, Christine. 2004. "Bilingual Language Socialization in the Family: What Teachers Should Know." In *Bilingualism and Education: From the Family to the School*, edited by Xoán Paulo Rodríguez-Yáñez, Anxo M. Lorenzo Suárez, and Fernando Ramallo. Frankfurt: Lincom Europa.

Hernández-Chávez, Eduardo, Andrew D. Cohen, and Anthony F. Beltramo. 1975. *El lenguaje de los Chicanos*. Arlington, VA: Center for Applied Linguistics.

Hymes, Dell H. 1974. *Foundations in Sociolinguistics: An Ethnographic Approach*. Philadelphia: University of Pennsylvania Press.

Karadan, Firdeys. 2004. "Ethnolinguistic Vitality, Attitudes, Social Network and Code-Switching: The Case of Bosnian-Turks Living in Sakarya, Turkey." *International Journal of the Sociology of Language* 165:59–92.

Koike, Dale. 1987. "Code-Switching in the Bilingual Chicano Narrative." *Hispania* 70:148–54.

Li, Wei. 1994. *Three Generations, Two Languages, One Family: Language Choice and Language Shift in a Chinese Community in Britain*. Clevedon, UK: Multilingual Matters.

Lippi-Green, Rosina. 1997. *English with an Accent: Language, Ideology, and Discrimination in the United States*. London: Routledge.

Lowther, Kelly. 2009. "Spanish Heritage Learner Variation and the Role of Language Ideology in the Heritage Learner Classroom." PhD diss., University of Arizona, Tucson.

MacSwan, Jeff. 1999. *A Minimalist Approach to Intrasentential Code-Switching*. New York: Garland.

———. 2009. "Generative Approaches to Code-Switching." In *The Cambridge Handbook of Linguistic Code-Switching*, edited by Barbara E. Bullock and Almeida Jacqueline Toribio. Cambridge: Cambridge University Press.

Martin-Jones, Marilyn. 1995. "Code-Switching in the Classroom: Two Decades of Research." In *One Speaker: Two Languages: Cross-Disciplinary Perspectives on Code-Switching*, edited by Lesley Milroy and Pieter Muysken. Cambridge: Cambridge University Press.

Mendoza-Denton, Norma. 2002. "Language and Identity." In *The Handbook of Language Variation and Change*, edited by J. K. Chambers, Peter Trudgill, and Natalie Shilling-Estes. Oxford: Blackwell.

Milroy, Lesley, and Li Wei. 1995. "A Social Network Approach to Code-Switching: The Example of a Bilingual Community in Britain." In *One Speaker, Two Languages: Cross-Disciplinary Perspectives on Code-Switching*, edited by Lesley Milroy and Pieter Muysken. Cambridge: Cambridge University Press.

Montes-Alcalá, Cecilia. 2000. "Attitudes towards Oral and Written Codeswitching in Spanish-English Bilingual Youths." In *Research on Spanish in the United States,* edited by Ana Roca. Somerville, MA: Cascadilla Press.

———. 2005. "Dear Amigo: Exploring Code-Switching in Personal Letters." In *Selected Proceedings of the Second Workshop on Spanish Sociolinguistics*, edited by Lotfi Sayahi and Maurice Wetmoreland. Somerville, MA: Cascadilla Proceedings Project.

———. 2007. "Blogging in Two Languages: Code-Switching in Bilingual Blogs." In *Selected Proceedings of the Third Workshop on Spanish Sociolinguistics*, edited by Jonathan Holmquist. Somerville, MA: Cascadilla Proceedings Project.

Moyer, Melissa. 1998. "Bilingual Conversation Strategies in Gibraltar." In *Code-Switching in Conversation: Language, Interaction and Identity*, edited by Peter Auer. London: Routledge.

Muysken, Pieter. 1995. "Code-Switching and Grammatical Theory." In *One Speaker, Two Languages: Cross-Disciplinary Perspectives on Code-Switching*, edited by Lesley Milroy and Pieter Muysken. Cambridge: Cambridge University Press.

Myers-Scotton, Carol. 1993. *Social Motivations for Code-Switching: Evidence from Africa.* Oxford: Oxford University Press.

Myers-Scotton, Carol, and Janice Jake. 2009. "A Universal Model of Code-Switching and Bilingual Language Processing and Production." In *The Cambridge Handbook of Linguistic Code-Switching*, edited by Barbara E. Bullock and Almeida Jacqueline Toribio. Cambridge: Cambridge University Press.

Nichols, Patricia C., and Manuel Colón. 2000. "Spanish Literacy and the Academic Success of Latino High School Students: Codeswitching as a Classroom Resource." *Foreign Language Annals* 33 (5): 498–511.

Ohlson, Linda. 2007. "Soy el brother de dos lenguas: Code-Switching in Contemporary Popular Music of the Latinos in the United States." PhD diss., Goteborgs Universitet, Sweden.

Otheguy, Ricardo. 2007. "La filología del unicornio: El verdadero referente del vocablo Spanglish y su función como adjudicador de posiciones de poder en la población de origen hispano en los EEUU." In *La incidencia del contexto en los discursos*, edited by Enric Serra. Lynx Monograph Series. Valencia: Servicio de Publicaciones de la Universidad de Valencia.

Palmer, Deborah K. 2009. "Code-Switching and Symbolic Power in a Second-Grade Two-Way Classroom: A Teacher's Motivation System Gone Awry." *Bilingual Research Journal* 32 (1): 42–59.

Pfaff, Carol W. 1979. "Constraints on Language Mixing: Intrasentential Code-Switching and Borrowing in Spanish/English." *Language* 55 (2): 291–318.

Poplack, Shana. 1980. "Sometimes I'll Start a Sentence in Spanish *y termino en español*: Toward a Typology of Code-Switching. *Linguistics* 18 (7–8): 581–618.

———. 1981. *Syntactic Structure and Social Function of Code-Switching*. In *Latino Language and Communicative Behavior*, edited by R. Duran, 169–84. NJ: Albex Publishing Corp.

———. 1993. "Variation Theory and Language Contact." In *American Dialect Research*, edited by Dennis Preston. Amsterdam: John Benjamins.

———. 2004. "Code-Switching." *Soziolinguistik: An International Handbook of the Science of Language*, 2nd ed., edited by Ulrich Ammon, Norbert Dittmar, Klaus J. Mattheier, and Peter Trudgill. Berlin: Walter de Gruyter.

Poplack, Shana, and Marjory Meechan. 1998. "How Languages Fit Together in Codemixing." *International Journal of Bilingualism* 2 (2): 127–38.

Potowski, Kim. 2009. "Forms and Functions of Codeswitching by Dual-Immersion Students: A Comparison of Heritage Speaker and L2 Children." In *First-Language Use in Second-Language and Foreign Language Learning*, edited by Miles Turnbull and Jennifer Daily O'Cain. Bristol, UK: Multilingual Matters.

Rampton, Ben, 1995. *Crossing: Language and Ethnicity among Adolescents*. London: Longman.

Raschka, Christine, Li Wei, and Sherman Lee. 2002. "Bilingual Development and Social Networks of British-Born Chinese Children." *International Journal of the Sociology of Language* 153:9–25.

Reyes, Iliana. 2004. "Functions of Code-Switching in Schoolchildren's Conversations." *Bilingual Research Journal* 28 (1): 77–98.

Riegelhaupt, Florencia. 2000. "Codeswitching and Language Use in the Classroom." In *Research on Spanish in the United States*, edited by Ana Roca. Somerville, MA: Cascadilla Press.

Rocchi, Lorenzo. 2008. "Social Networks and Linguistic Choices of Italian Emigrants in an Anglophone Environment." *Studi Linguistici e Filologici Online* 6:219–74.

Sabec, Nada. 1997. "Slovene-English Language Contact in the USA." *International Journal of the Sociology of Language* 124:129–83.

Sanchez Muñoz, Ana. 2007. "Register and Style Variation in Speakers of Spanish as a Heritage and as a Second Language." PhD diss., University of Southern California, Los Angeles.

Sayer, Peter. 2008. "Demystifying Language Mixing: Spanglish in School." *Journal of Latinos and Education* 7 (2): 94–112.

Shannon, Sheila. 1995. "The Hegemony of English: A Case Study of One Bilingual Classroom as a Site of Resistance." *Linguistics and Education* 7:175–200.

Silva-Corvalán, Carmen. 1983. "Code-Shifting Patterns in Chicano Spanish." In *Spanish in the US Setting: Beyond the Southwest*, edited by Lucía Elías-Olivares. Rosslyn, VA: National Clearinghouse for Bilingual Education.

———. 1994. *Language Contact and Change: Spanish in Los Angeles*. Oxford: Oxford University Press.

Starks, Donna. 2005. "The Effects of Self-confidence in Bilingual Abilities on Language Use: Perspectives on Pasifika Language Use." *Journal of Multilingual and Multicultural Development* 26:533–50.

Swigart, Leigh. 1992. "Two Codes or One? The Insiders' View and the Description of Codeswitching in Dakar." *Journal of Multilingual and Multicultural Development* 13 (1–2): 83–102.

Timm, Eleonora. 1975. "Spanish-English Code-Switching: El porque y How Not to." *Romance Philology* 28 (4): 473–82.

———. 1993. "Bilingual Code-Switching: An Overview of Research." In *Language and Culture in Learning: Teaching Spanish to Native Speakers of Spanish*, edited by Barbara J. Merino, Henry T. Trueba, and Fabián A. Samaniego. San Diego, Calif.: Institute for Cultural Pluralism.

Toribio, Almeida Jacqueline. 2000. "Once Upon a Time en un lugar muy lejano: Spanish–English Codeswitching across Fairy Tale Narratives." In *Research on Spanish in the United States*, edited by Ana Roca. Somerville, MA: Cascadilla Press.

Torras, Maria-Carme, and Joseph Gafaranga. 2002. "Social Identities and Language Alternation in Non-Formal Institutional Bilingual Talk: Trilingual Encounters in Barcelona." *Language in Society* 31:527–48.

Treffers-Daller, Jeanine. 1991. "Towards a Uniform Approach to Code-Switching and Borrowing." In *Papers for the Workshop on Constraints, Conditions, and Models*. Strasbourg: European Science Foundation.

Unamuno, Virginia. 2008. "Multilingual Switch in Peer Classroom Interaction." *Linguistics and Education* 19 (1): 1–19.

Valdés, Guadalupe. 1981. "Codeswitching as Deliberate Verbal Strategy: A Microanalysis of Direct and Indirect Requests among Bilingual Chicano Speakers." In *Latino Language and Communicative Behavior*, edited by Richard Durán. Norwood, NJ: Ablex.

Valdés-Fallis, Guadalupe. 1978. "Codeswitching in the Classroom." *Language in Education: Theory and Practice* (Center for Applied Linguistics, Eric Clearinghouse on Language and Linguistics) 4.

Weinreich, Uriel. 1953. *Languages in Contact*. The Hague: Mouton.

Zentella, Ana Celia. 1981. "Tá bien, You Could Answer Me en cualquier idioma: Puerto Rican Codeswitching in Bilingual Classrooms." In *Latino Language and Communicative Behavior*, edited by Richard Durán. Norwood, NJ: Ablex.

———. 1982a. "Code-Switching and Interactions among Puerto Rican Children." In *Spanish in the United States: Sociolinguistic Aspects*, edited by Jon Amastae and Lucía Elías-Olivares. Cambridge: Cambridge University Press.

———. 1982b. "Spanish and English in Contact in the United States: The Puerto Rican Experience." *Word: Journal of the International Linguistic Association* 33 (1–2): 41–57.

———. 1997. *Growing up Bilingual: Puerto Rican Children in New York City*. Oxford: Blackwell.

———. 2005. *Building on Strengths: Language and Literacy in Latino Families and Communities*. New York: Teachers College Press.

PART III

Learners' Perspectives

SHL Learners' Attitudes and Motivations

RECONCILING OPPOSING FORCES

Cynthia M. Ducar, Bowling Green State University

JOSÉ WAS A SECOND-GENERATION MEXICAN AMERICAN, studying Spanish to avoid being made fun of every time he went "home" to Mexico to see his extended family. He did not want to speak *pocho* Spanish anymore; he wanted to speak real Spanish.[1] After all, Spanish was an integral part of his identity, and being accepted by his family as a true Mexican motivated him to study Spanish. A story such as this one is all too common in Spanish heritage language (SHL) classrooms, and it barely touches on the complexity of the issues that this chapter aims to address, namely, the role of attitudes and motivation in the SHL context. Though research in the field of second-language acquisition (SLA) has long established the important, albeit arguably indirect, relationship that attitudes and motivation have on language learning (for overviews, see Baker 1992; Dörnyei 2001; Gardner 1985); corresponding research in the SHL field remains in its infancy (Lynch 2003). Despite the continued boom in SHL research, few studies have undertaken an analysis of the role that SHL learners' motivations and attitudes play in the acquisition of their heritage language.

After defining attitude and motivation from a social psychology perspective, this chapter introduces the reader to the widely researched roles of these two constructs in the field of SLA. The chapter next addresses the important differences that surround both constructs when approached from a heritage language (HL) orientation as opposed to an SLA orientation. After synthesizing the research on attitudes and motivations in the HL and SHL fields, a call to critically revisit the methodologies employed to study the constructs is issued. The limitations of the current body of research are addressed, and suggestions for future research are offered.

MOTIVATION AND ATTITUDE IN SLA

It is undeniable that the vast amount of research on the role of motivations and attitudes in SLA has been dominated by Gardner's (1985) socioeducational model of second-language learning. Before delving into the major findings of that body of research, however, it is imperative to first define the two constructs that this chapter and that research investigate. Motivation, following Gardner (1985, 10), is defined as "the combination of effort plus desire to achieve the goal of learning the language, plus favorable attitudes toward the language." Thus, it is understood that motivation subsumes the idea of attitudes, and, as such, has a stronger role in final achievement in language learning than do attitudes (Masgoret and Gardner 2003). That said, the role of attitudes has also been widely investigated and found to have a robust, albeit indirect, correlational effect on ultimate acquisition (Baker 1992; Dörnyei 2001; Gardner 1985). Here, attitude refers to "an evaluative reaction to some referent or attitude object, inferred on the basis of the individual's belief or opinions about the referent" (Gardner 1985, 9). Though the roles of attitudes and motivation have been studied in an array of different subject areas and learning contexts within the sociopsychological framework, the roles of both constructs have been found to be stronger in language learning contexts than in other academic subjects (Gardner 1985).

Since the seminal publications of Gardner and Lambert (1959, 1972) and Gardner (1985) on motivation, the topic has frequently been treated in the SLA literature as a dichotomous construct involving two distinct yet not necessarily separate ideas, namely, integrative and instrumental motivation. Following Gardner (1985), integrative motivation refers to an interest in the second language (L2) due to a desire to associate with people who use the language; clearly, this idea is relevant to the SHL field, given that SHL students are often members of the "target-language community." Instrumental motivation, conversely, refers to the practical value associated with L2 acquisition: increased job or business opportunities, passing a class, meeting a requirement, and so on.[2] Although at first glance instrumental motivation may intuitively appear to play a lesser role in SHL (re)acquisition, and indeed has often been found to play a lesser role in the previous SLA literature, this construct and its combined role with that of integrative motivation have been highlighted in recent research, particularly in the HL field. Although much of the SLA and HL research has continued to treat all the above-mentioned concepts as static, discrete, noninteracting entities, recent studies have stressed the need to further explore the interrelationships of these constructs and their role in SLA (Csizér and Dörnyei 2005). Even Gardner himself has stated that it is imperative to understand that "motivation itself is dynamic" (Gardner and Tremblay 1994, 360). Despite this recognition, the strictly quantitative nature of studies realized in this vein of research has limited researchers' ability to describe the dynamic nature of motivation in both SLA and SHL contexts.

In the more recent SLA literature, the construct of motivation has often been treated using two additional concepts: intrinsic and extrinsic motivation. Much as their names imply, intrinsic motivation refers to "doing something because it is inherently interesting or enjoyable" (Ryan and Deci 2000, 55), where learners choose to study a language because, for example, they think it will be both interesting and fun (Noels 2001). Intrinsic motivation is, of particular importance, not synonymous with integrative motivation; the former refers to a desire to study the language because it is viewed as inherently fun, whereas the latter addresses one's desire to become a part of the target language community. Extrinsic motivation, conversely, "leads to a separable outcome" (Ryan and Deci 2000, 55), such as tangible rewards or a job (Noels 2001). Thus extrinsic motivation maps onto the constructs of both integrative and instrumental motivation, from a Gardnerian perspective (Ryan and Deci 2000; Noels 2001). Researchers who use this terminology explicitly state that the terms are distinct from and not synonymous with the Gardnerian constructs (Noels 2001).

Finally, though research on anxiety does not precisely fall under the domain of attitude and motivational research, it is hard to negate the role that negative attitudes, as evidenced through anxiety, can have on the language learning context (Horwitz and Young 1999; MacIntyre 1999; Sparks and Ganschow 2007). Often, the factors investigated in this line of research represent the polar opposites of what is investigated in research on attitudes and motivation; namely, instead of investigating why students continue their study of a language, this line of research is more focused on factors that may lead them to discontinue their studies. Clearly, these studies should be in dialogue with those on attitude and motivation. Though the link between the areas is not direct, the interaction of anxiety, attitude, and motivation is unquestionable.

Before exploring these ideas from an HL perspective, several central tenets of SLA motivation and attitude studies need to be addressed. First, the majority of research indicates a robust, positive correlation between motivation and second-language achievement (for a review of seventy-five independent studies, see Masgoret and Gardner 2003). Researchers no longer debate whether or not motivation plays a role in language learning; this role is well established. Today's research grapples with what exactly is encompassed within the idea of motivation and how individual, social, and cognitive factors interplay to create motivation. One major point of contention lies in the fact that the majority of research in the field has been carried out in the Canadian context by Gardner and his colleagues using similar instruments (primarily the Attitude/Motivation Test Battery) and is therefore, arguably, not generalizable across different learning contexts. Indeed, some have gone so far as to state that Gardner's socioeducational model "was too influential" (Dörnyei 1994). Of particular importance for the SHL research agenda, the field of SLA has called for a more socioculturally informed understanding of the role of motivation and attitudes (McGroarty 2001; Ushioda 2008). Though Gardner and colleagues' contribution to the field is undeniable, the social nature of SHL learning, the recurrent issue of identity as a motivating factor, and the attitudes toward Spanish in society at large demand a more socioculturally informed approach to these constructs.

Overall, researchers agree that SLA research, and I would argue SHL research as well, must move beyond the sociopsychological paradigm to include a more socioculturally informed perspective. Sociocultural theory holds that the individual cannot be separated from the social, arguing that "the individual emerges from social interaction and as such is always a fundamentally social being" (Lantolf and Thorne 2007, 217). Given the nature of the SHL context, and the inherent connection between the learner and the larger Spanish-speaking community, it is clear that the treatment of both attitude and motivation in the SHL context requires a socially informed framework that understands the individual learner as both shaping and being shaped by the larger social context.

RESEARCH ON ATTITUDE AND MOTIVATION IN THE HL FIELD

This new sociocultural perspective is particularly relevant to the HL field; it is disappointing, however, that to date there has been little research dedicated to the roles of attitude and motivation in the HL context. Furthermore, the majority of the research continues to operationalize the constructs of attitude and motivation following Gardner (1985). This is not surprising, given the tremendous influence and contribution of Gardner's work in the SLA field, the relative newness of the study of HLs in general, and the virtual lack of research on the roles of attitudes and motivation vis-à-vis SHL learners, specifically.

In both the HL and SHL contexts, research has shown time and again that separating attitude from motivation in order to quantify the force of each is a task fraught with difficulty. The interacting nature of these two concepts is exemplified in Kondo-Brown's (2001) extensive survey of 145 Japanese HL learners, who demonstrated variation across proficiency levels in addition to showing a multiplicity of motivational forces.[3] Although all survey participants cited the integrative motive of language maintenance, 80 percent of first- and second-year students stressed an additional, instrumental principal motivator, namely, meeting a language requirement.[4] In terms of attitudes, the majority of participants found studying their HL to be "interesting, challenging and important" (Kondo-Brown 2001, 447). Yet differences were obtained across proficiency levels, with more first- and second-year students reporting that Japanese is frustrating (62.5 percent). Virtually all students, however, recognized the job advantages associated with bilingualism in Japanese and English (more than 90 percent).

These findings are important because they highlight the interaction of motivation and attitudinal factors in the HL field in general, and they remind us that students' attitudes may change over time. Though Kondo-Brown's (2001) study was not longitudinal, by analyzing students at varying levels in the Japanese HL program, her research begs the question of whether students' attitudes evolved over time and, if so, what role (if any) the HL classes played in that evolution. To my knowledge, no studies have undertaken a longitudinal look at the role an HL or SHL program might have in the evolution of student attitudes and motivation toward the HL (for a similar call to action, see Allen 2010). The multiplicity of factors involved in HL learning represent a complex interplay of learner- and societal-level variables that interact to give rise to student attitudes and motivations.

Researchers and pedagogues in HL and SHL contexts seem drawn to the idea of integrative motivation, and they often relegate instrumental motivations to the L2 context. Yet, as shown in Kondo-Brown's study, an extensive body of research from East Asian HLs alone refutes this assumption. Of particular importance, a growing body of research supports this same claim in the SHL context. For instance, in a study investigating the roles of attitude and motivation for both L2 and HL Chinese learners, Wen (2011) reports survey results from 317 students across three public universities, with supplementary interview information, finding statistically significant differences between L2 and HL learners of Chinese. Contrary to much speculation in the SLA literature, the study found instrumental motivation to be the prime motivator for these Chinese HL students; indeed, Cho (2000) arrived at the same results for Korean HL students as did Carreira and Kagan (2011) for several other Asian languages (though see also Yang 2003). Wen (2011) found that both a genuine interest in Chinese culture and a career advantage associated with being bilingual combined to motivate students' desire to study the HL. Wen also found that positive attitudes toward learning can be used to predict motivational magnitude for all learners. Finally, identity as a Chinese individual and the role of identity in motivation were also cited by participants (see chapter 9 in this volume, by Potowski). Clearly, all these constructs overlap. Given the increasing monetary value attached to a bilingual workforce, and the overwhelming recognition that Spanish-English bilingualism represents increased job opportunities (US Bureau of Labor Statistics 2009; also see US Census Bureau 2009), it would be detrimental to ignore the power of instrumental motivation in the SHL context.

In a combined study of both L2 and HL learners, Reynolds, Howard, and Deák (2009) analyzed survey data from 401 students of nineteen different languages. The study looked at students in introductory foreign language courses to discover the goals of HL learners enrolled in such classes. Overall findings indicated a clear difference between SLA learners and HL learners. Integrative motivation, coupled with positive attitudes, was highest in the HL group whereas instrumental motivation was highest for the SLA group. This finding concurs with previous research on Russian HL learners, who also were found to have stronger integrative motivations than their L2 peers (Geisherik 2004). The study undertaken by Reynolds and colleagues emphasized the important connection between identity formation and language study, along with the desire to engage with the HL/L2 language community; clearly, these are factors that language educators must consider when attempting to increase student motivation for continued study of the language (see also Beaudrie, Ducar, and Relaño Pastor 2009).

Noels (2005) investigated the intrinsic, extrinsic, integrative, and instrumental motivations for learning German both for L2 ($N = 55$) and HL ($N = 41$) students. Her socioculturally informed perspective stressed both the important role that potential contact with the target language community and the ethnolinguistic vitality (or lack thereof) of said language community can have in terms of motivating students; though Noels's study focused on German HL learners, these two concerns are of primary importance particularly in the SHL context.[5] Additionally, Noels's (2005, 299) research highlighted the importance of identity as a principal motivator for HL students who were "more likely to be oriented to learn German because they felt it was an important part of their self-concept or because they wished to integrate into the German community." Perhaps most important, Noels's research stressed that the social milieu has "important implications for motivation, particularly for heritage language learners" (p. 302). She concluded that HL learners, from a social psychological perspective, indeed represent a distinct group from their L2 peers. This recognition alone begs further research. What role does HL learners' participation in the HL community play in motivating students and changing their attitudes? How are attitudes affected by such interactions? Does participation in the HL community lead to an increase in both integrative and instrumental motivation? Must these two ideas continue to be understood as distinct, or is better terminology available to address the complex intricacies observed, specifically in the SHL context? All these questions represent venues for future research.

To summarize, though research on the roles that attitudes and motivation play in the HL learning context is somewhat scant, various conclusions can be drawn. First, in the larger HL context, the role of social milieu and identity as motivating factors demands a thorough analysis. The issue of identity formation is inevitably intertwined with motivation in the HL context, as evidenced in all the studies reviewed. Finally, the results as to what the principal motivators are in the HL context seem to be mixed, with much research citing the primacy of integrative motivators whereas others, though less numerous, have found instrumental motivation and other constructs, such as Noels's "identified regulation reasons" (a.k.a. self-concept) for language study, to have primary roles. It is clear that additional research in this area is required to resolve the conflicts in the data. As Ely (1986, 28) states, "The difficulty of teasing apart integrativity and instrumentality" is nowhere more apparent than in the context of the study of

Spanish as a heritage language. The complexity of the constructs is augmented by the fact that the underlying natures of the social and pragmatic dimensions of motivation are "always dependent on *who* learns *what* languages *where*" (Dörnyei 1994, 275; emphasis in the original); nowhere is this tenet more imperative than in the study of attitudes and motivations of SHL learners.

RESEARCH ON ANXIETY, ATTITUDE, AND MOTIVATION AMONG SHL LEARNERS

Despite the growing power and presence of the Spanish language in the United States (Castillo 2004; Potowski and Carreira 2010), or perhaps in light of it, there is an equally powerful negative stigma attached to the language from the dominant English-speaking community along with internal stigmas attached to US varieties of the language, stemming from both the speakers of US varieties of Spanish themselves and outsider, Spanish-monolingual attitudes toward the language. To date, twenty-eight states have implemented English-only laws (http://englishfirst.org/englishstates/). As Zentella and numerous other researchers have pointed out, the Hispanophobia associated with a growing minority population that maintains the first language in any way represents a danger to the US status quo (Schreffler 2007; Urciuoli 2008; Zentella 1997). Additionally, as Bills (2005, 71) indicates, internal linguistic prejudices also play an important role in belittling the importance of Spanish. Several quotations from participants in his study exemplify the negative attitudes that some US speakers of Spanish have toward other members of this heterogeneous language community; as one Cuban American stated, "Yo odio como hablan los puertorriqueños" (I hate how Puerto Ricans talk); and yet another participant stated, "Yo no quiero que mi hijo aprenda a hablar como un mexicano" (I don't want my child to learn to speak like a Mexican). Clearly, the power of strong linguistic prejudices from the US Spanish-speaking community itself, the larger Spanish-speaking world, and the US English-speaking community cannot be ignored when researching SHL students' attitudes and motivations.

That said, it is to the detriment of SHL students, teachers, and researchers alike that the current body of research has focused so heavily on the negative attitudes surrounding Spanish, while virtually ignoring the growing power of the language in the US context. The complex reality of the role of Spanish and Spanish speakers in the United States needs to be addressed in the research on attitudes and motivations in the SHL context. Ignoring the larger social milieu in which the Spanish of our students resides simultaneously ignores a plethora of factors that contribute to both their attitudes toward the language and their motivation to (dis)continue studying it.

SHL studies on attitude and motivation concur that SHL learners have distinct motivational and affective needs as compared with their L2 peers (Beaudrie and Ducar 2005; Carriera 2000, 2004; Ducar 2008; Lynch 2003; Oh and Au 2005; Potowski and Carriera 2004; Reynolds, Howard, and Deák 2009; Schreffler 2007; Schwarzer and Petrón 2005; Tallon 2009; Villa and Villa 1998; though see also Coryell and Clark 2009). In what follows, the topic of language anxiety is briefly discussed, followed by a more complete discussion of attitude and motivational variables specific to the SHL context. These data serve as a starting point for delineating an agenda for future research.

Language Anxiety in the SHL Context

Language anxiety, as defined by MacIntyre (1999, 27), is "the worry and negative emotional reaction aroused when learning or using a second language." Such a definition, when modified to fit the SHL context, necessarily incorporates what Tallon (2009, 114) terms the "fear of negative evaluation." The centrality of anxiety in the SHL context should not be surprising, given that it is not uncommon to find SHL students who share this type of attitude: "I don't feel my Spanish is that good. I talk '*pocha*' Spanish" (participant cited by Beaudrie and Ducar 2005, 13). Attitudes toward Spanish in the desert Southwest and in other communities throughout the United States combine to create linguistic insecurities (Lippi-Green 2004), which lead to cases of language anxiety or language shyness (Krashen 1998).

Research in this area by Tallon (2009) found that SHL learners exhibited significantly less anxiety when speaking than their L2 peers, as measured by the Foreign Language Classroom Anxiety Scale.[6] Yet, in spite of experiencing less anxiety than their L2 peers, it is important to note the finding that some SHL students did experience anxiety. This finding was corroborated in research done by Beaudrie and Ducar (2005), though students expressed a positive association with listening to Spanish, their attitudes toward speaking the language were reported to be both anxious and insecure. The role of anxiety, particularly with regard to receptive bilinguals, begs additional research due to the higher level of linguistic insecurities evidenced in this group (Beaudrie and Ducar 2005), as does the issue of anxiety in the SHL context in general. Future studies could examine how students' attitudes in other areas, combined with local society-level attitudes toward the language, interact to promote or diminish student anxiety and motivation.

One study addressing this gap is that of Coryell and Clark (2009), who investigated the issue of language anxiety in an online environment. After analyzing learners' narratives for an explanation of students' motivations, the authors conclude that both L2 and SHL students understand language learning to be the acquisition of the "one right way" to communicate in Spanish. In their narratives, participants discussed the disjuncture between "book" Spanish and community Spanish (see Barbara's example; Coryell and Clark 2009, 494). In addition to their anxiety in the classroom, participants mentioned the anxiety they felt when speaking in the community and with Spanish speakers from foreign nations. Yet in spite of this anxiety, participants remained "committed to acquiring a culturally sensitive, communicative competence in Spanish" (p. 498). Their primary motivation was an integrative one: They wanted to gain access to the local Spanish-speaking community—a community in which these L2 and SHL learners alike felt like outsiders due to a perceived language barrier. These findings attest to the importance of social milieu and anxiety in the research on attitude and motivation, in both the L2 and the SHL contexts. It is clear that the role of anxiety as a (de)motivator in the SHL context merits future investigation.

Attitudes toward the HL

In a summary of past research on HLs in general, Cho, Shin, and Krashen (2004) found that attitudes toward HLs are generally positive. In the SHL context in particular, numerous researchers have found overwhelmingly positive attitudes toward Spanish across diverse SHL learning contexts (Alarcón 2010; Beaudrie 2009; Beaudrie and Ducar 2005; Beckstead and Toribio 2003; Carrasco and Riegelhaupt 2003; Rivera-Mills 2000), though it bears mentioning that there have been mixed findings as to the strength of those positive attitudes. For example, though Bell-Corales's (2006) study corroborates these findings, it also shows that positive attitudes toward Spanish decline as students' length of time in the United States increases. Beaudrie's (2009) research touches on the complexity of the issue of attitude and language in the SHL context, and highlights the fact that though students overwhelmingly associate Spanish with prestige, the results are more mixed when it comes to the prestige of their own dialect.

In a similar line of research, Ducar's (2008) study of SHL students' opinions and attitudes regarding language use in the SHL classroom corroborates the findings of the Coryell and Clark (2009) study, namely, students want their instructors to correct their Spanish (96 percent, $N = 152$), and indeed 91 percent of those surveyed feel that their Spanish is being corrected in the classroom; it is important, however, that a vast majority (93 percent) feel their Spanish is respected by their instructor, a finding that diverges from the Coryell and Clark (2009) study. Students' linguistic insecurities are respected in this SHL environment and students' desire to learn a *personally relevant variety* of Spanish echoes Coryell and Clark's (2009) call for further investigation of intercultural competence as a motivator specifically in SHL contexts.

Mikulski (2006) performed an in-depth case study of the motivations, attitudes, and goals of four SHL speakers using a triangulated methodology of class observations, questionnaires, and interviews. As in previous research, participants in the study unanimously expressed positive attitudes toward both their Spanish class and Spanish in general. Most germane to the present discussion, however, is the fact that student attitudes changed during the semester, with students developing more positive attitudes toward "Spanglish," or code-switching, as the semester progressed. These positive attitudes fostered the desire to continue studying the language, thus resulting in more motivation. Once again, "motivation, attitudes, and goals interacted in complex ways" (Mikulski 2006, 671).

SHL students clearly recognize the vitality of Spanish as a world language, and as a key to their future success. Yet simultaneously, students reflect an awareness of the stigmatization afforded to their own variety of Spanish, as evidenced in the body of research on language and anxiety, and also in the studies undertaken by Beaudrie (2009) and Mikulski (2006). This is but the tip of the iceberg that surrounds the complex nature of the sociolinguistic and sociocultural contexts and their effects on student attitudes. Further studies should strive to examine these issues in a wider array of SHL learning contexts, with larger sample sizes. In light of the findings of Beaudrie (2009) and Mikulski (2006), as well as Kondo-Brown's (2001) findings in the Japanese HL context, future research in this area should undertake a thorough investigation of the evolution of language and dialect attitudes of SHL learners by means of a multimethod, longitudinal analysis. Such a task is daunting, no doubt; yet it would demonstrably advance scholars' understanding of these issues in the SHL context.

Motivation and the Role of Identity

Instrumental motivation, though often overlooked in the SHL context, has been found time and again to play an important role in motivating SHL students. Given the overwhelmingly positive attitude toward the Spanish language, it is not surprising that Beaudrie (2009) found that students associated Spanish with prestige. Nor is it surprising that Beaudrie and Ducar (2005) and Alarcón (2010) found that students connect Spanish speaking ability with increased job opportunities. A recent comprehensive survey of multiple heritage languages found that SHLs "along with Japanese, Mandarin, and Cantonese HLLs [heritage language learners], were the only respondents for whom professional goals outranked personal goals. Specifically, 71.1 percent of Spanish speakers said they were studying their HL with a future career or job in mind" (Carreira and Kagan 2011, 51).

Indeed, students' intuitions are accurate; there are in fact more job opportunities for bilinguals. As the *Occupational Outlook Handbook* (US Bureau of Labor Statistics 2009) states, bilingual jobseekers "should enjoy excellent opportunities" not only in the field of customer service representatives but also in the realm of education and service jobs in general. Clearly, students have internalized the societal value associated with Spanish in this respect. These studies barely scratch the surface of the contributing factors behind an instrumental motivation, however. Given the growth in the job market for bilinguals, researchers cannot continue to ignore the power of instrumental motivation as one among myriad extrinsic motivators related to the economic futures of students.

The role of integrative motivation, which has been more well studied and is thought to be more powerful, naturally cannot be ignored either. Research overwhelmingly supports the idea that high integrative motivation leads to increased successes in the language classroom (for an overview, see Yanguas 2010). Given this tendency, it is not surprising that many SHL researchers have underscored the role of identity formation and participation in the local Spanish-speaking community as prime factors influencing integrative motivation (Alarcón 2010; Beaudrie 2009; Beaudrie and Ducar 2005; Beaudrie, Ducar, and Relaño-Pastor 2009; Beckstead and Toribio 2003; Carrasco and Riegelhaupt 2003; Mikulski 2006; Oh and Au 2005; and chapter 9 in this volume, by Potowski).

At both ends of the bilingual spectrum, integrative motivation has been found to play a leading role. Beaudrie and Ducar's (2005) study of beginning-level SHL students found that students demonstrated a strong connection between the study of Spanish and the desire to be a part of the Spanish-speaking community. In a parallel study of advanced SHL learners, Alarcón (2010) found SHL learners were "intrinsically invested in Spanish." Though the sample size in both studies is small, the clear parallels between Alarcón's findings and Beaudrie and Ducar's findings cannot be underscored enough. In recent research by Carreira and Kagan (2011), an array of SHL students also cited improving communication with friends and family in the United States as well as learning about their cultural and linguistic roots (48.9 percent) as primary motivators for study. In this case, research has brought to light the fact that regardless of proficiency level, learners across the bilingual spectrum share more similarities with each other than with their L2 classmates. Here, the importance to attitude and motivation research is clear—for it is precisely this type of research that has emphasized the need to include both beginning and advanced SHL learners in scholars' definition of SHL students, and, moreover, in the classes and programs directed to serve these students.

Additionally, Beaudrie's (2009, 94) study of beginning-level SHL students enrolled in both L2 and SHL classes found that even in the case of so-called passive bilinguals, competence in Spanish is viewed as central to their identity. In fact, students indicated that "they sometimes feel 'less' Hispanic or Mexican-American for not being able to communicate in Spanish." As Beaudrie asserts, these findings "suggest that the students' motivation for being in a language class may be substantially related to their need to reconnect with their Hispanic identity" (p. 96; see also Beaudrie, Ducar, and Relaño-Pastor 2009).

Yanguas was the first to fully assess SHL motivation directly following in the Gardnerian tradition, utilizing the Attitude/Motivation Test Battery as well as incorporating additional questions to account for the factor of social milieu. Yanguas (2010, 658) concludes that "the more attachment there is between participants and their language/community, the more motivation they display to improve their Spanish." Of particular importance, integrativeness was found to be a significant predictor of motivation. These results attest to the need to incorporate issues of the social milieu and remind one that students' motivation can be increased by offering them additional opportunities for language use in the target community (Beaudrie, Ducar, and Relaño-Pastor 2009). Though Yanguas suggests that promoting positive attitudes toward Spanish in the classroom may aid in increasing motivation, it should be noted that increased motivation does not necessarily translate into guaranteed success in the language-learning context.

Conclusions from SHL Research

This overview of current research has underscored several common themes across both the HL and SHL literature. First, SHL (and HL) learners are clearly distinct from their L2 peers in terms of what motivates their study of the language. One of the concepts that clearly separates the two groups is that of identity formation. Additionally, both SLA and SHL research on attitudes and motivations needs to further address the role of social milieu, both in terms of language attitudes stemming from social contexts and also individual-level extrinsic motivators that may originate in the specific social network of the learner.

As Schwarzer and Petrón (2005, 569) state, "Nowhere is the lack of information concerning heritage speakers more apparent than in the area of student attitudes and perceptions." Though the research is scant, the findings can be synthesized into two distinct camps that parallel the complexity of the larger sociolinguistic picture of Spanish speakers in the United States. Namely, students have generally positive attitudes toward the Spanish language, and yet often simultaneously devalue their own variety of Spanish. This devaluation of the language variety results in linguistic insecurities, which contribute to language anxiety in the SHL context (Beaudrie 2009; Beaudrie and Ducar 2005; Coryell and Clark 2009; Tallon 2009). In spite of this, students are clearly motivated to learn the language, particularly in order to (re)connect with the larger Spanish-speaking community (Beaudrie 2009; Beaudrie, Ducar, and Relaño-Pastor 2009). As Coryell and Clark (2009, 491) found, both L2 and SHL learners "had passionate motivations to study Spanish . . . (in order) to improve their capacity to participate meaningfully with the Spanish-speaking cultural community." It is notable that these SHL learners felt that being Hispanic necessitated the ability to speak Spanish; Schwarzer and Petrón (2005, 571) echo these findings, asserting that cultural ties serve as "a catalyst for Spanish language development."

LIMITATIONS AND DIRECTIONS FOR FUTURE RESEARCH

The contributions of the research reviewed here are clear; nevertheless, the small quantity of studies and the relative newness of this vein of research in the SHL literature do result in several limitations. First, there is a pressing need to break from the confines of a strictly quantitative approach toward these concepts. Though the bulk of research continues to follow a Gardnerian-style analysis, and though the contribution of such research is unquestionable, it is imperative that this field of study incorporate more qualitative and mixed-methods approaches to more fully understand attitude and motivation in the SHL context. Second, given the complex sociopolitical reality of Spanish in the United States and the heterogeneous nature of SHL learners, it is crucial that the study of attitude and motivation take on a more socioculturally informed perspective. To adequately account for the multifaceted and fluid nature of the variables under investigation, the role that sociocultural factors play in influencing both students' attitudes and motivations must be addressed (McGroarty 2001; Noels 2001; Ushioda 2008).

In light of these limitations, the following research agenda is proposed as a starting point for future studies. This agenda is not intended to be comprehensive; rather, it should be used to generate ideas for future research while providing a clear path to respond to Lynch's (2003) call to investigate the role attitudes and motivations play in the SHL context. First, the subtleties of language anxiety in the SHL context merit further research. In analyzing this situation, both societal (e.g., anti-Spanish sentiments, English-only laws, prejudices against US varieties of Spanish) and learner-specific variables should be considered (e.g., classroom-based stressors, test anxiety, speaking anxiety). The interplay of these variables and their relationship with both students' attitudes and motivations should then be addressed.

Those interested in the study of language attitudes need to bear in mind two factors: (1) Positive attitudes toward Spanish do not necessarily translate into positive attitudes toward the students' specific variety of Spanish; and (2) attitudes toward Spanish in the United States need to be considered from multiple perspectives. At the very least, such research must consider the role of individual SHL students' attitudes, SHL teachers' attitudes, local Spanish-speaking community attitudes toward Spanish and toward the specific dialect of Spanish spoken in the area, the attitudes of Latin American and Spanish speakers of Spanish, and attitudes toward Spanish in the English-dominant society. The multiplicity of contexts and attitudes that are related to Spanish in the United States calls for a multifaceted approach that acknowledges the power of both internal and external attitudes toward US Spanish.

In terms of motivational factors, the growing recognition of the instrumentality of Spanish should serve as a catalyst for increased research in this area. Teasing out the intricacies of this motivational orientation is a clear next step for future research. A continued effort toward understanding the role of integrative motivation and intrinsic and extrinsic motivation in the SHL context calls for research that looks at the role of identity formation and community participation as motivators for SHL students. Does integrative motivation promote increased interaction with the community, or vice versa? What results in higher achievement: a high level of integrative motivation or actual increased participation in community activities? All these issues beg the question: Does motivation to connect to Latino culture cause students to seek out more opportunities with this culture and therefore improve their overall language skills, or does increased contact with the culture lead to increased motivation? Oh and Au (2005, 238) emphasize that "the relationships among the sociocultural background variables themselves reveal that their relationships with HLLs' mastery of the language may be more complicated than simple bivariate relationships." Clearly, the need for research that goes beyond the existing paradigms, allowing for interaction among these and other factors while bridging quantitative data with qualitative data, is necessary. Specifically, I suggest that future SHL researchers follow Dörnyei's lead in this area and thus allow for a consideration of the simultaneous and ever-changing interaction of issues involving the language (Spanish), the learners (SHL students), the learning context, and the longitudinal effects of motivation (Dörnyei 2001; see also Allen 2010; Ushioda 2008).

The interaction of attitude and motivation and the strong influence of social context can be traced all the way back to Labov's (1963) seminal study of the centrality of attitude in societally motivated language change on Martha's Vineyard. The plethora of questions that continue to plague this area of study should come as no surprise in light of the dynamic and interactive nature of the variables under study. Add to that the complexities of the sociolinguistic reality of Spanish in the United States today and the intricate interplay of these variables is complicated even further. In order to grapple with these complexities, researchers must revisit the premises upon which the vast majority of past and current data and research is based; this requires a broader approach to understanding the role of attitude and motivation by incorporating more multimethods and qualitative approaches to the study of language, attitudes, and motivation in the SHL context, thereby adding to the base of quantitative research. Only if scholars recognize the tug-of-war over attitudes toward Spanish in the United States, in both the larger society and students' social networks, will they be able to tackle the complexity of this situation. Ideally, this will lead to a more socioculturally informed approach to the study of attitudes and motivation in the SHL context; what motivates students must also now motivate scholars' research.

NOTES

1. For those unfamiliar with the term, *pocho*, as defined in *Urban Dictionary* (2012), refers to an "Americanized Mexican, or Mexican who has lost their culture. (Which largely refers to losing the Spanish.) It is a derogatory term."

2. Despite the limitations of this terminology, its use is so prevalent that it is impossible to discuss these constructs without employing the very terminology that is simultaneously being critiqued.

3. The author recognizes the very distinct sociocultural contexts in which Japanese and Spanish exist in the United States; however, this research demonstrates the important interplay of numerous learner and societal valuables, which, though distinct, are also at work in the SHL context.

4. Though see Ely (1986, 31) for a separate consideration of this issue. His results indicate that despite a strong tendency to mention a language requirement as a motivator, correlational cluster analysis revealed that taking a course for a university requirement actually "negatively predicts strength of motivation."

5. Though it is important to note that Noels, like the majority of researchers cited here, comes from a sociopsychological perspective and does not categorize her approach as a sociocultural one. Indeed, the reference made here is the only reference in the text to this end. Nevertheless, this acknowledgment is an important one and bears mentioning.

6. However, he acknowledges that this measure was designed for the L2 context.

REFERENCES

Alarcón, Irma. 2010. "Advanced Heritage Learners of Spanish: A Sociolinguistic Profile for Pedagogical Purposes." *Foreign Language Annals* 43 (2): 269–88.

Allen, Heather. 2010. "Language Learning Motivation during Short-Term Study Abroad: An Activity Theory Perspective." *Foreign Language Annals* 43 (1): 27–49.

Baker, Colin. 1992. *Attitudes and Language*. Philadelphia: Multilingual Press.

Beaudrie, Sara. 2009. "Spanish Receptive Bilinguals: Understanding the Cultural and Linguistic Profile of Learners from Three Different Generations." *Spanish in Context* 6 (1): 85–104.

Beaudrie, Sara, and Cynthia Ducar. 2005. "Beginning-Level University Heritage Programs: Creating a Space for All Heritage Language Learners." *Heritage Language Journal* 3. Available at www.heritagelanguages.org.

Beaudrie, Sara, Cynthia Ducar, and Ana M. Relaño-Pastor. 2009. "Curricular Perspectives in the Heritage Language Context: Assessing Culture and Identity." *Language, Culture and Curriculum* 22 (2): 157–74.

Beckstead, Karen, and Almeaida Toribio. 2003. "Minority Perspectives on Language: Mexican and Mexican-American Adolescents' Attitudes toward Spanish and English." In *Mi Lengua: Spanish as a Heritage Language in the United* States, edited by Ana Roca and Cecelia Colombi. Washington, DC: Georgetown University Press.

Bell-Corales, Maritza. 2006. "The Role of Positive Attitudes and Motivation in Minority Language Maintenance." *Journal of the Georgia Philological Association*, 126–57.

Bills, Garland. 2005. "Las comunidades lingüísticas y el mantenimiento del español en Estados Unidos." *In Contactos y contextos lingüísticos: El español en los Estados Unidos y en contacto con otras lenguas*, edited by Luis Ortiz López and Manel Lacorte. Madrid: Lingüística Iberoamericana.

Carrasco, Roberto, and Florencia Riegelhaupt. 2003. "META: A Model for the Continued Acquisition of Spanish by Spanish/English Bilinguals in the United States." In *Mi lengua: Spanish as a Heritage Language in the United States*, edited by Ana Roca and Cecelia Colombi. Washington, DC: Georgetown University Press.

Carreira, María. 2000. "Validating and Promoting Spanish in the United States: Lessons from Linguistic Science" *Bilingual Research Journal* 24 (4). Available at http://brj.asu.edu.

————. 2004. "Seeking Explanatory Adequacy: A Dual Approach to Understanding the Term 'Heritage Language Learner.'" *Heritage Language Journal* 2 (1). Available at www.heritagelanguages.org.

Carreira, Maria, and Olga Kagan. 2011. "The Results of the National Heritage Language Survey: Implications for Teaching, Curriculum Design, and Professional Development." *Foreign Language Annals* 44 (1): 40–64.

Castillo, Jenny. 2004. "Spanish in the United States: Demographic Changes, Language Attitudes and Pedagogical Implications." *Geolinguistics* 40: 71–83.

Cho, Grace. 2000. "The Role of Heritage Language in Social Interactions and Relationships: Reflections from a Language Minority Group." *Bilingual Research Journal* 24 (4). Available at http://brj.asu.edu.

Cho, Grace, Fay Shin, and Stephen Krashen. 2004. "What Do We Know about Heritage Languages?" *Multicultural Education* 11 (4): 23–26.

Coryell, Joellen, and M. Carolyn Clark. 2009. "One Right Way, Intercultural Participation and Language Learning Anxiety: A Qualitative Analysis of Adult Online Heritage and Nonheritage Language Learners." *Foreign Language Annals* 42 (3): 483–504.

Csizér, Kata, and Zoltán Dörnyei. 2005. "The Internal Structure of Language Learning Motivation and Its Relationship with Language Choice and Language Effort." *Modern Language Journal* 89 (1): 19–36.

Dörnyei, Zoltán. 1994. "Motivation and Motivating in the Foreign Language Classroom." *Modern Language Journal* 78:273–84.

————. 2001. *Teaching and Researching Motivation.* London: Longman.

Ducar, Cynthia 2008. "Student Voices: The Missing Link in the Heritage Language Debate." *Foreign Language Annals* 41 (3): 415–33.

Ely, Christopher. 1986. "Language Learning Motivation: A Descriptive and Causal Analysis." *Modern Language Journal* 70 (1): 28–35.

English First. 2009. *Official English States.* http://englishfirst.org/englishstates/.

Gardner, Robert. 1985. *Social Psychology and Second Language Learning: The Role of Attitudes and Motivation.* London: Edward Arnold.

Gardner, Robert, and Wallace Lambert. 1959. "Motivational Variables in Second Language Acquisition." *Canadian Journal of Psychology* 13:266–72.

————. 1972. *Attitudes and Motivation in Second-Language Learning.* Rowley, MA: Newbury House.

Gardner, Robert, and Paul Tremblay. 1994. "On Motivation, Research Agendas and Theoretical Frameworks." *Modern Language Journal* 78:359–68.

Geisherik, Anna. 2004. "The Role of Motivation among Heritage and Non-Heritage Learners of Russian." *Canadian Slavonic Papers* 46 (1–2): 9–22.

Horwitz, Elaine, and Dolly Young. 1991. *Language Anxiety: From Theory and Research to Classroom Implications.* Upper Saddle River, NJ: Prentice Hall.

Kondo-Brown, Kimi. 2001. "Bilingual Heritage Students' Language Contact and Motivation." In *Motivation and Second Language Acquisition,* edited by Zoltán Dörnyei and Richard Schmidt. Honolulu: Second Language Teaching and Curriculum Center, University of Hawaii at Manoa.

Krashen, Stephen. 1998. "Language Shyness and Heritage Language Development." In *Heritage Language Development,* edited by Stephen Krashen, Lucy Tse, and Jeff McQuillan. Culver City, CA: Language Education Associates.

Labov, William. 1963. "The Social Motivation of a Sound Change." *Word* 19:273–309.

Lantolf, James, and Stephen Thorne. 2007. "Sociocultural Theory and Second Language Acquisition." In *Theories in Second Language Acquisition: An Introduction*, edited by Bill VanPatten and Jessica Williams. Cambridge: Cambridge University Press.

Lippi-Green, Rosina. 2004. "Language Ideology and Language Prejudice." In *Language in the USA: Themes for the Twenty-First Century*, edited by Edward Finegan and John R. Rickford. Cambridge: Cambridge University Press.

Lynch, Andrew. 2003. "The Relationship between Second and Heritage Language Acquisition: Notes on Research and Theory Building." *Heritage Language Journal* 1. Available at www.heritagelanguages.org.

MacIntyre, Peter. 1999. "Language Anxiety: A Review of the Research for Language Teachers." In *Affect in Foreign Language and Second Language Learning: A Practical Guide to Creating a Low-Anxiety Classroom Atmosphere*, edited by Dolly Young. Boston: McGraw-Hill College.

Masgoret, Anne-Marie, and Richard Gardner. 2003. "Attitudes, Motivation and Second Language Learning: A Meta-Analysis of Studies Conducted by Gardner and Associates." *Language Learning* 58 (1): 123–63.

McGroarty, Mary. 2001. "Situating Second Language Motivation." In *Motivation and Second Language Acquisition*, edited by Zoltán Dörnyei and Richard Schmidt. Honolulu: Second Language Teaching and Curriculum Center, University of Hawaii at Manoa.

Mikulski, Ariana. 2006. "Accent-uating Rules and Relationships: Motivations, Attitudes, and Goals in a Spanish for Native Speakers Class." *Foreign Language Annals* 39:660–82.

Noels, Kimberly. 2001. "New Orientations in Language Learning Motivation: Towards a Model of Intrinsic, Extrinsic and Integrative Orientations and Motivation." In *Motivation and Second Language Acquisition*, edited by Zoltán Dörnyei and Richard Schmidt. Honolulu: Second Language Teaching and Curriculum Center, University of Hawaii at Manoa.

———. 2005. "Orientations to Learning German: Heritage Language Learning and Motivational Substrates." *Canadian Modern Language Review/La Revue canadienne des langues vivantes* 62 (2): 285–312.

Oh, Janet, and Terry Kit-Fong Au. 2005. "Learning Spanish as a Heritage Language: The Role of Sociocultural Background Variables." *Language, Culture and Curriculum* 18 (3): 229–41.

Potowski, Kim, and María Carreira. 2004. "Teacher Development and National Standards for Spanish as a Heritage Language." *Foreign Language Annals* 37 (3): 427–38.

———. 2010. "Spanish in the USA." In *Language Diversity in the United States*, edited by Kim Potowski. New York: Cambridge University Press.

Reynolds, Rachel, Kathryn Howard, and Julia Deák. 2009. "Heritage Language Learners in First-Year Foreign Language Courses: A Report of General Data across Learner Subtypes." *Foreign Language Annals* 42 (2): 250–69.

Rivera-Mills, Susana V. 2000. "Intraethnic Attitudes among Hispanics in a Northern California Community." In *Research on Spanish in the United States: Linguistic Issues and Challenges*, edited by Ana Roca. Somerville, MA: Cascadilla Press.

Ryan, Richard, and Edward Deci. 2000. "Intrinsic and Extrinsic Motivations: Classic Definitions and New Directions." *Contemporary Educational Psychology* 25:54-67.

Schreffler, Sandra. 2007. "Hispanic Heritage Language Speakers in the United States: Linguistic Exclusion in Education." *Critical Inquiry in Language Studies* 4 (1): 25–34.

Schwarzer, David, and María Petrón. 2005. "Heritage Language Instruction at the College Level: Reality and Possibilities." *Foreign Language Annals* 38 (4): 568–78.

Sparks, Richard, and Leonore Ganschow. 2007. "Is the Foreign Language Classroom Anxiety Scale Measuring Anxiety or Language Skills?" *Foreign Language Annals* 40:260–87.

Tallon, Michael. 2009. "Foreign Language Anxiety and Heritage Students of Spanish: A Quantitative Study." *Foreign Language Annals* 42 (1): 112–37.

US Bureau of Labor Statistics. 2009. "Customer Service Representatives." In *Occupational Outlook Handbook, 2010–2011 Edition*. www.bls.gov/oco/ocos280.htm.

US Census Bureau. 2009. "News: Facts for Figures—Hispanic Heritage Month." www.census.gov/newsroom/releases/archives/facts_for_features_special_editions/cb09-ff17.html.

Urban Dictionary. 2012. www.urbandictionary.com/define.php?term=Pocho.

Urciuoli, Bonnie. 2008. "Whose Spanish? The Tension between Linguistic Correctness and Cultural Identity." In *Bilingualism and Identity: Spanish at the Crossroads with Other Languages*, edited by Mercedes Niño-Murcías and Jason Rothman. Philadelphia: John Benjamins.

Ushioda, Ema. 2008. "Motivation and Good Language Learners." In *Lessons from Good Language Learners*, edited by Carol Griffiths. Cambridge: Cambridge University Press.

Villa, Daniel, and Jennifer Villa. 1998. "Identity Labels and Self-Reported Language Use: Implications for Spanish Language Programs." *Foreign Language Annals* 31 (4): 505–16.

Wen, Xiaohong. 2011. "Chinese Language Learning Motivation: A Comparative Study of Heritage and Non-Heritage Learners." *Heritage Language Journal* 8 (3): 41–66. Available at www.heritagelanguages.org.

Yang, Jean. 2003. "Motivational Orientations and Selected Learner Variables of East Asian Language Learners in the United States." *Foreign Language Annals* 36:44–55.

Yanguas, Áñigo. 2010. "A Quantitative Approach to Investigating Spanish HL Speakers' Characteristics and Motivation: A Preliminary Study." *Hispania* 93 (4): 650–70.

Zentella, Ana Celia. 1997. "The Hispanophobia of the Official English Movement in the US." *International Journal of the Sociology of Language* 127:71–86.

CHAPTER 9

Identity and Heritage Learners

MOVING BEYOND ESSENTIALIZATIONS

Kim Potowski, University of Illinois at Chicago

C ITIBANK AIRED A SERIES of television commercials in 2003 to promote awareness of the risks of identity theft. Each commercial features a fictional victim of identity theft engaged in an activity common to their daily lives—a forty-something female Asian dentist attending to a patient, a thirtyish African American man working out at the gym, a pair of white, sixtysomething women sitting on a couch having coffee. However, these individuals speak with the voices of the identity thieves, who talk about the luxuries they bought with the victims' money. The incongruity of the things the perpetrators purchased—the woman dentist bought self-tanning cream and hair plugs to become a "babe magnet" at an upcoming singles' retreat; the bald man working out at the gym got hair extensions and lip injections to launch a Hollywood singing career; and the elderly women bragged about how loud their new motorcycles were—are almost as funny as the voices with which they speak. A husky male voice comes forth from the petite, Asian dentist; a young Valley Girl voice emanates from the burly African American man; southern male voices typically identified as "hillbilly" are drawled by the elderly, coffee-sipping ladies. Citibank effectively utilized the crucial role played by language in the enactment of identity to make their point: We rely on language as a key variable in identifying each other's gender, age, socioeconomic status, and other factors. The Citibank examples, however, involve varieties of the same language; identity enactments become even more complex when more than one language is available to speakers.

Language, indeed, plays a crucial role in the construction of identity, which as a construct has seen a large body of research in the social sciences accumulate during the past thirty years. The first approaches that arose in sociology in the late nineteenth century held that individuals' identities were largely determined by their membership in groups determined by social class, religion, educational background, and peer networks. However, this formulation has been criticized as "essentializing" individuals–that is, reducing them to a set of basic social or cultural characteristics—and as assuming that they all have those characteristics in common. Although it seems obvious that, for example, not all Christians are alike, or all Jews, or all college graduates or all plumbers, essentializing views of identity are still common and are formulated in such a way that individuals' commonalities are sought and are assumed to be stronger than their differences.

Theorists now search for "more nuanced, multileveled and ultimately complicated framings" of identity (Block 2007, 13), which constitutes a poststructuralist attempt to move beyond a search for universals. This introductory section seeks to lay out some of the basic tenets of modern approaches to the study of identity, drawing largely from Block (2007) and Pavlenko and Blackledge (2004). This includes definitions of terms such as "performativity," "ambivalence," "hybridity," and "communities of practice." After laying out these concepts, the chapter turns to work on heritage speaker identities generally, and then specifically focuses on bilingual Latinos in the United States.[1] Some of the questions I explore include: What identities have been ascribed to these groups, both from within their own communities as well as by the hegemonic mainstream, and how do these groups respond to such positionings? In what ways are these identities relevant for these individuals both as speakers of and as students of Spanish? The chapter concludes with a consideration of the concrete ways in which heritage speaker classrooms might profitably incorporate knowledge about the identities of US Spanish speakers and directions for future research.

Table 9.1 displays seven common contemporary dimensions of an individual's identity as summarized by Block (2007). Although "language identity" is listed as its own category in this table, language in fact does a lot of work in constructing the other facets of identity, as demonstrated in the Citibank commercials cited above. In addition to invoking one or more of these categories, modern conceptualizations of identity often utilize several key terms. One is "performativity," which means that identity is constantly performed. In particular, Butler's (1990) work on gender identity emphasizes that individuals continually stylize their appearance, language, and body movements as they "do" being women or men. That is, though all individuals are born with a biological sex, gender is largely socially constructed and must be constantly performed. Likewise, other aspects of identity are upheld through multiple ongoing performances. As noted by Bucholtz and Hall (2004, 476), "Identity inheres in actions, not in people." This chapter reviews work that explores various ways in which US Spanish speakers "perform" being US Spanish speakers, as opposed to monolinguals or Spanish speakers from other places.

Table 9.1 Individual and Collective Identity Types

Ascription/Affiliation	Based on
Ethnic identity	Shared history, descent, belief systems, practices, language and religion, all associated with a cultural group
Racial[a] identity	Biological/genetic makeup, i.e., racial phenotype
National identity	Shared history and practices associated with a nation-state
Migrant identity	Ways of living in a new country, on a scale ranging from classic immigrant to transmigrant
Gender identity	Nature of conformity to socially constructed notions of femininities and masculinities
Social class identity	Income level, occupation, education, and symbolic behavior
Language identity	Relationship between one's sense of self and different means of communication

[a] Although anthropologists dispute the notion of race as having any biological reality, most people do utilize a concept of race as a meaningful category.
Source: Block (2007).

Another important construct in identity theory is the fact that identity can often involve "ambivalence," which is sometimes resolved through "hybridity." When belonging comes naturally to a given individual, identity is usually not given a second thought. However, when identity is somehow under threat or viewed as problematic by the hegemonic majority, identity is questioned and ambivalence often emerges. Thus, a woman who does not perform femininity in ways commonly accepted by her community, for example, can have her identity as a woman called into question. Similarly, a person who speaks one variety of Spanish, or no Spanish at all, can have his identity as a Latino called into question. Block (2007, 22) explains that individuals generally attempt to resolve the conflicts that underlie their ambivalence in order to create a coherent life narrative. Particularly when one moves across geographical and sociocultural borders, as do the families of many US Spanish speakers, individuals "often find that any feelings they might have of a stable self are upset and that they enter a period of struggle to reach a balance" (Block 2007, 20).

One way to resolve such a potential crisis of identity and ambivalence is through the creation of a hybrid identity. An example is the "hyphenated American," such as "Pakistani-American" or "Mexican-American," which is more common now than in past discourses on Americanness (the literal hyphen is now often dropped from these types of identifying terms, usually as a gesture of political sensitivity and to recognize that these dual identities are now permanent and accepted). Zhou (2004) asserts that today "there is no contradiction between an ethnic identity and an American identity." Below, we consider the role of hybridized identity terms, and of hybridized linguistic practices, in the identities of US Latinos, as well as the role of transnationalism in current debates about identity in today's increasingly globalized world.

Finally, the concept of communities of practice, defined as "an aggregate of people who come together around mutual engagement in an endeavor" (Eckert and McConnell-Ginet 1992, 464), has played an important role in explaining issues of identity. This is because communities of practice offer subject positions that individuals can adopt "on a moment-to-moment and day-to-day basis, and indeed throughout their lifetimes, depending on who they are with" (Block 2007, 25). For example, a fifty-year-old man who begins riding a motorcycle and becomes deeply involved with a motorcycle group (one example of a community of practice) can be said to acquire an identity as a biker. To return to the issue of performativity, however, a relevant question for this particular example is: Does this man get tattoos *because* he is a biker, or does he *become* a biker through getting tattoos? To consider two linguistic examples: Does a gay man produce a strident /s/ because he is gay, or does he enact an identity as a gay man by producing a strident /s/ (Podesva, Roberts, and Campbell-Kibler 2001)? Mendoza-Denton (2008) provides compelling evidence that Latina high school girls pronounced "nothing" as "nuhteen" once they had joined a gang; they did not join a gang after beginning to produce this variant. Theorists now acknowledge that performativity plays an important role in identity.

A critical point here is the fact that, unlike tattoos, clothing, hairstyle, or the pronunciation of individual phonemes, an entire linguistic system is not very easily acquired. This is why multilingualism plays such a primary role in the construction and perception of identities, and even more so in a country like the United States that is 80 percent monolingual in English (according to the 2000 US census). The next section examines connections between identity, language, and ethnicity in greater depth, before turning specifically to heritage Spanish students.

CONNECTIONS AMONG IDENTITY, LANGUAGE, AND ETHNICITY

Identity is not considered static or monolithic, even in monolingual contexts. Monolingual individuals often make choices in register and dialect for different purposes, thus enacting different identity performances. In multilingual situations, identity is in an even more active state of reevaluation and renegotiation, as attested to by volumes such as that by Pavlenko and Blackledge (2004, 1): "In multilingual settings, language choice and attitudes are inseparable from political arrangements, relations of power, language ideologies, and interlocutors' views of their own and others' identities." These researchers also note that globalization and transnational migration have led to shifts in language ideologies as well as in the range of identities available to individuals. Language choice is never neutral; it is always imbued with ideology. Thus negotiation is constantly taking place between speakers of different languages who share the same geopolitical space. If the United States were not 80 percent monolingual in English, the Citibank commercials cited above would likely have employed multiple languages.

Bourdieu's (1999) notion of the "linguistic market" explains this struggle using economic metaphors. Mainstream society assigns greater value to mainstream/majority languages than to peripheral/minority languages. This legitimizes the use of the majority language while devaluing the use of minority languages or heritage languages (HLs). In the United States, the language with valued cultural capital is English. Other languages are not only not assigned as much value, they are often stigmatized and suppressed. One common result is loss of languages other than English by the third generation (Potowski 2010).[2] It is due in part to this linguistically repressive context that we see a wide variety of identity configurations and levels of Spanish proficiency among US Spanish speakers. Unfortunately, as Val and Vinogradova (2010, 5) note, this devaluing of language also occurs among minority language speakers themselves, reflecting language norms and attitudes about more and less prestigious dialects. Thus, a more prestigious variety of a minority language is valued over others (below, we will see specific examples from Spanish). In sum, the development of a dual language identity "depends on the degree to which heritage speakers are able to find coherence and continuity in multiple discursive worlds. It also depends on whether HL speakers are able to develop hybrid situated nonconflicted identities within the dominant and heritage sociocultural discourses" (Val and Vinogradova 2010, 5).

In a novel quantitative study seeking to correlate minority language proficiency with ethnic identity, Phinney and others (2001) administered questionnaires to adolescents and their parents in Southern California. The authors sought to determine the weight of three factors: ethnic language proficiency, cultural maintenance by parents, and social interaction with peers from the same ethnic group. Their model is displayed in figure 9.1.

In this survey, eighty-one Armenian families, forty-seven Vietnamese families, and eighty-eight Mexican families answered questions about ethnic language proficiency, in-group peer social interaction, and ethnic identity. The results suggested both common processes as well as group differences in the factors that influence ethnic identity. Although there were substantial differences across the three groups in the pathways and in the strength of the relationships, what these groups had in common included the following three findings. First, ethnic language proficiency had a positive impact on ethnic identity, which was also found by, among others, Kondo (1997); Maloof, Rubin, and Miller (2006); and Caldas

Figure 9.1   Model of Influences on Ethnic Identity

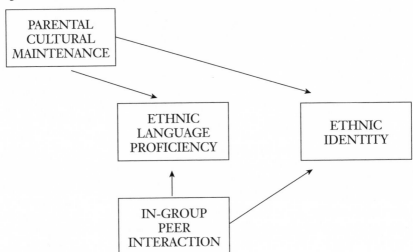

Source: Phinney et al. (2001). Used by permission.

and Caron-Caldas (1999). Second, social interaction with peers from one's own ethnic group was significantly related to ethnic identity (this peer effect was in fact stronger than the effect of ethnic language). And third, behaviors reported by parents to promote cultural maintenance had a significant positive effect on ethnic language proficiency. The second finding, about interacting with peers from one's own ethnic group, is reminiscent of the claims of García-Bedolla (2003) that many children of immigrants "selectively disassociate" from their HL and ethnic group when negative associations are forced on them by the hegemonic majority, but they desire close identification with the group when their heritage is positioned more positively. When enough same-group peers are around, it seems more likely that positive associations can be fostered and negative ones rejected.

Among the Mexican youth in particular, highly significant correlations obtained between parental encouragement of cultural maintenance and Spanish proficiency, which, along with in-group peer social interactions, influenced ethnic identity.[3] Thus proficiency in Spanish contributed to their sense of ethnic identity. The next section returns to this idea through the following question: Do US Latinos consider it necessary to speak Spanish in order to claim an identity as a US Latino?

IDENTITIES OF US SPANISH SPEAKERS

He (2006, 7), in a seminal piece on heritage learner identity, argues that learner identity is "the centerpiece rather than the background of HL development" and that "identity formation and transformation is symbiotic with [HL] development." He's study documenting the experiences of a Chinese heritage learner named Jason clearly illustrates the meanings he assigned to studying Chinese as well as his ongoing self-assessment of his own identity and how his identity fit within the community of Chinese speakers represented by his parents, teachers, imagined future employment in China, and what it meant to him to be Chinese American.

The implications of He's (2006) proposals for HL teaching will be revisited in the section below on identity in the Spanish heritage speaker classroom. In this section I attempt to unpack the concept of "what it means to be Chinese American" but changing the focus to Spanish speakers. In the United States, Spanish is spoken by close to 35 million individuals with different countries of origin, socioeconomic status, races, concentrations of local Hispanic communities, connections to homeland Spanish-speaking countries, proficiency in Spanish and English, and educational experiences—all of which can influence each other and contribute to an individual's sense of identity. To begin, there is no agreement among the members of US Spanish-speaking communities about how to refer to themselves; it is more difficult to conceive of a macro group identity if the group cannot agree on a name. The 1970 census was the first that used the term "Hispanic," and the terminology has been modified in each successive census. The 2000 census asked, "Is this person Spanish/Hispanic/Latino?"—which was modified in 2010 to "Is this person of Hispanic, Latino, or Spanish origin?" Although the wording changed slightly, the basic approach is the same: People are counted as Spanish/Hispanic/Latino if that is what they say they are, and their responses are not subject to any independent checks.[4]

As mentioned above, and despite such terms not appearing among the census choices, Zhou (2004) notes that it is increasingly common to "live on the hyphen" and utilize terms such as "Mexican American" or "Colombian American." However, surveys conducted by the Pew Hispanic Center (Passel 2009) indicate that this terminology, too, is far from widely embraced. It seems the most common term (preferred by 52 percent of respondents in 2009) is taken from the country of family origin, such as "Mexican" or "Salvadoran," without the "American" following it.[5] When asked to choose "Hispanic" or "Latino," 43 percent said they use the two terms equally, 36 percent preferred "Hispanic," and 21 percent chose "Latino" (Passel 2009). Other terms include "Spanish," which is common among New Mexicans (Nieto-Phillips 2000) and among the diverse Spanish-speaking community in Providence (Bailey 2000).

These terms result in a fair amount of debate in both academic and public discourse (Fears 2003), with people on all sides expressing angry rejections of different terms. But whatever terms they use to identify themselves, US Latinos, like the members of many ethnic groups in the United States, are subject to stereotypes. These stereotypes constitute a national discourse that Hispanic groups can either accept or resist. In the process, they help shape and define their identities both through who they are and, of particular importance, who they are not. In addition, it is important to engage in a "careful examination of the discourses on linguistic and cultural diversity that are present within and outside the [heritage] classroom" in order to determine "how to foster an environment that promotes empowered [positive] identities" (Showstack 2012, 9).

A good place to look for contemporary stereotypes is popular culture, and in particular the work of comedians (Pacheco 2008). If George Lopez (see Markert 2004) and Carlos Mencia can be said to provide a window into today's mainstream stereotypes of US Latinos, the following are at the top of the list (Pacheco 2008):[6]

- ► laziness
- ► poverty;
- ► alcoholism;
- ► being illegal immigrants, taking jobs, working as day laborers;
- ► having many children, living in extended families, many in a house; driving with many passengers in a vehicle;
- ► speaking English poorly or with an accent;
- ► being devoutly Catholic;[7]
- ► belonging to gangs; and
- ► wearing sombreros and pointy boots.

In fact, García-Bedolla (2003, 276) was surprised by "the consistency of the [ninety-seven Latino] respondents' answers regarding what kind of images they felt Euro Americans had of Latinos," including gang member, wetback, uneducated, dirty, and lazy. These negative stereotypes and the concomitant discrimination faced by many Hispanics—by some estimates, nearly 40 percent of young Latinos say they or a relative or close friend has been a victim of ethnic or racial discrimination (Olson 2009)—can clearly affect their self-identification and identity development. I will return to this point in the concluding section because such stereotypes can be profitably addressed in heritage speaker classrooms.

Discrimination can also come from within the Latino community itself. US Latinos hail from a number of different places (see table I.1 in the introduction to this volume), and today 60 percent of them are actually born in the United States.[8] Although Morales (2003) and others insist that there is more in common among US Chicanos, *cubanos*, *nuyoricans*, *quisqueyas*, *tejanos*, and so on than what divides them, many scholars in Latino studies focus precisely on the ways in which immigrant status, class, citizenship, skin color, and other factors position Hispanic groups differently, both within the hegemonic white mainstream and also within an intra-Latino hierarchy.[9] Typically, those individuals with a higher socioeconomic status, documented legal status, knowledge of English, and lighter skin usually seek to distance themselves from other Latinos without these qualities (De Genova and Ramos-Zayas 2003; García-Bedolla 2003; Gorman 2010; Ochoa 2004; Mendoza-Denton 2008; Bailey 2000).

Transnational communities, which are formed by individuals who engage in networks beyond national borders, are also becoming increasingly common. Smith (2006) and Farr (2006) give ethnographic portraits of the transnational Mexican communities in New York and Chicago, respectively, whereas Pérez (2004) portrays the transnational lives of Puerto Ricans in Chicago. Clachar (1997) describes the linguistic identity difficulties of United States–raised Puerto Ricans who returned to the island after the age of fourteen. Romaine (2011) posits that transnationalism, with its accompanying travel and Internet-facilitated communication, opens new avenues for maintaining language, culture, and identity and thus plays an important role in current discussions about identity.

Finally, the concentration of Hispanics in a given area can radically affect how these individuals construct their identities. For example, Alba and his colleagues (2002) determined that a child of Cuban origin growing up in Miami is twenty times more likely to develop bilingual proficiency than a child living in an area where just 5 percent of the residents speak Spanish. Similarly, Mexicans along the border were five times more likely to report home Spanish use than those in other areas. Given that bilingualism is usually accompanied by biculturalism (recall Phinney et al. 2001), and taking into account the very different experiences of young Latinos growing up in predominately Hispanic neighborhoods compared with those who are "the only Mexicans in town," Latino demographic density and the resulting local community of practice exert an important influence on identity development.

This leads us to a more focused discussion of the role of the Spanish language in the creation of US Latino identity. As posited in the introduction to this chapter, knowledge of another linguistic system is a very strong identity marker because learning another language, along with its concomitant social and pragmatic norms, requires considerable time and exposure; it is often the case that native-like attainment is not possible for postpuberty learners. What role does the Spanish language—including proficiency, dialect variety, and the degree of English influence—play in Latino identity constructions? This question is not restricted to linguists and educators. Koike and Graham (2006), for example, analyzed a political debate between two Hispanic gubernatorial candidates in Texas, and they highlighted how one candidate appealed to his knowledge of Spanish as a marker of cultural authenticity, whereas the other candidate, who was less proficient in Spanish, sought to disassociate the Spanish language from Hispanic ethnicity.

Spanish Proficiency

According to the 2000 census, about 75 percent of all Hispanics speak Spanish in the home. However, a shift to monolingualism in English by the third generation has also been widely documented around the country (in the Southwest,

Bills and Vigil 1999, and Bills, Hudson, and Hernández-Chávez 2000; in California, Rivera-Mills 2001, and Hurtado and Vega 2004; in New York City, Zentella
1997; in Miami, García and Otheguy 1988; and in Chicago, Potowski 2004; also
see chapter 1 in this volume, by Rivera-Mills). There are many reasons for this
shift, including the strong hegemonic force of English in education and daily life
mentioned above. But also relevant are (1) low proficiency, often caused by a
lack of input, which is exacerbated by parental exogamy; (2) the absence of
Spanish-dominant adults in the home; and (3) distance from monolingual countries.[10] Attempts to understand shift and proficiency lead to a chicken-or-egg
question: Do individuals shift to English because of a lack of proficiency in Spanish, or do they fail to develop strong Spanish proficiency due to shifting patterns
of input and use? Both factors are probably at work.

As noted by Val and Vinogradova (2010), the loss of the HL can result in a
loss of communication among family members (as happened to Rodriguez
2004), and negative childhood experiences associated with the language (e.g.,
misunderstandings, embarrassments, or humiliation) can lead to decreased identification with the HL and heritage culture. Many young Hispanics say that they
are ashamed of their Spanish, frustrated that it does not fulfill all their communicative needs, and convinced that it is not proper. Their ways of speaking Spanish
are often mocked by their own family members and others when they spend
time in their families' country of origin (Clachar 1997; Potowski 2011), and they
are often particularly embarrassed when nonnatives develop stronger proficiency
than they have (Potowski 2002; Edstrom 2005).

Despite the causes of differing levels of Spanish proficiency, a principal question for identity is: Do Hispanics with less proficiency in Spanish construct identity differently than those with greater proficiency? The answer seems to be "yes,"
although the ability to speak Spanish is neither required nor sufficient for Hispanic identity.

Despite documented connections between the Spanish language and identity,
there is also a strong sense among many US Latinos that Spanish is not necessary
to be Latino. Phinney and colleagues (2001), whose model is cited above, found
that among Mexican adolescents, proficiency in Spanish was not very strongly
correlated with ethnic identity. Rivera-Mills (2000) studied fifty Hispanics of
various nationalities representing three generations of immigration to the United
States, finding that only 30 percent strongly agreed with the sentiment that a
person needs to speak Spanish in order to be Hispanic; the same percentage
moderately disagreed. Potowski and Matts (2008) found that 88 percent of the
twenty-five Chicago Latinos they surveyed claimed that Spanish was not necessary to be Latino; a larger corpus of ninety-six Mexicans and Puerto Ricans in
Chicago suggests a similar trend (Potowski and Torres, unpublished manuscript).
In northwest Indiana, Attinasi (1985) found less insistence on Spanish among Latinos than did their counterparts in New York City (Pedraza 1985). Pease-Alvaréz
(2002), studying the language socialization experiences of Mexico-origin families

in California, found a multifaceted construction of bilingualism that did not require Spanish to be considered Mexican American. And Toribio (2003), in a study of Dominicans in New York, found that all the immigrant parents viewed Spanish as an important feature of Dominican identity, but several United States–born participants expressed the opinion that Spanish was not necessary to be Dominican. Thus, many Latinos—typically those with weak proficiency themselves—are unwilling to require Spanish for group membership.

Interestingly, however, when a third-generation Latino has Spanish proficiency, this does not guarantee acceptance among other Latinos. Valdés (2011, 139), documenting the dual immersion schooling experiences of her granddaughters, demonstrates how knowledge of Spanish did not result in a bilingual and bicultural ethnolinguistic identity: "As a light-skinned girl who personified all the characteristics of a middle-class, nerdy, politically and environmentally correct background, [Marisa] was seen as an outsider by her Latino classmates"—which, in turn, affected the quality of her interactions with native Spanish-speaking classmates.

Spanish Dialect Variety

In a study that shed light on the roles of both proficiency and dialect variety of Spanish, De Genova and Ramos-Zayas (2003, 158) showed how Mexicans and Puerto Ricans living in Chicago understand the connections between their ethnic groups and Spanish proficiency, finding that (1) many first-generation Mexican immigrants were suspicious of United States–born Latinos who did not know Spanish; (2) although politically active Puerto Ricans saw Spanish as inseparable from notions of cultural authenticity, many Puerto Ricans in fact did not speak Spanish; and (3) the Spanish language "in no way automatically provided a shared space for the creation of a mutual Latinidad between Mexicans and Puerto Ricans," because both groups tended to devalue Puerto Rican Spanish. Urciuoli (2008, 261) presents a fascinating account of the experiences of bilingual Latinos from urban working-class neighborhoods who, while attending an elite college, rework a Latino identity that "reflects who they are becoming as college students and may well include a recasting of Spanish itself" relative to perceptions of correctness and cultural value. Zentella (1990, 1102), too, found a hierarchy of Spanish dialects in New York City related to race, education, and class. The Spanish spoken by middle-class, better-educated, and lighter-skinned Cubans and Colombians was "not as stigmatized as that of their darker poorer Caribbean sisters and brothers," the Dominicans and Puerto Ricans.

A brief aside about race is in order. Bailey (2000, 556) notes that many Dominicans who are phenotypically indistinguishable from African Americans will often invoke Spanish to counter assumptions that they are African American. Similarly, Toribio (2003) found evidence that Dominicans' language loyalty is related to their phenotype, with black Dominicans using Spanish to distinguish themselves from their African American neighbors, but that among light-skinned Dominicans, there was a sense that Spanish could hinder their acculturation into the dominant social structure.[11]

Dialect features can also play an interesting role in the identities of individuals of mixed Latino heritage, such as "MexiRicans." Potowski (2008) found that MexiRicans in Chicago claimed to be equally Mexican and Puerto Rican, yet 74 percent of them spoke a variety of Spanish that converged more closely on one dialect (usually that of their mother's ethnolinguistic group). Thus, despite their solid ethnocultural identification with both backgrounds, MexiRicans' Spanish accents strongly marked them as either Mexican or Puerto Rican. And, as noted by Urciuoli (2008, 271), "Accents are not simply phonetic variation produced by a speaker's place or language of origin. Accents are semiotic complexes through which people locate each other."

Amount of English Influence

It would be a mistake to restrict our consideration of Spanish along a continuum of more to less proficient, and study identity performances at different points along the continuum. Researchers have long documented novel linguistic practices that enable individuals to enact identities as US Spanish speakers. For example, Zentella (1997) has emphasized that code-switching serves important functions of performing bilingual ethnolinguistic identity, documenting the ways that New York Puerto Ricans "do being bilingual" using the theoretical performative identity frameworks cited above. Otheguy and García (1993) have documented the need to create English-origin words in US Spanish in order to express new cultural concepts. Within the pop culture realm, Santiago (2008, 7) writes, "Spanglish" is "very pro-Spanish.[12] I wage it as an act of *resistencia* against the assimilate-or-else mentality *todavía bastante presente* in a land where Spanish is far from the official *idioma*." Anzaldúa (1999, 77) is widely quoted on the hybridity inherent in US Spanish:

> For a people who are neither Spanish nor live in a country in which Spanish is the first language; for a people who live in a country in which English is the reigning tongue but who are not Anglo; for a people who cannot entirely identify with either standard (formal, Castilian) Spanish nor standard English, what recourse is left to them but to create their own language? A language which they can connect their identity to, one capable of communicating the realities and values true to themselves—a language with terms that are neither *español ni inglés*, but both. We speak a patois, a forked tongue, a variation of two languages.

To summarize this section, Spanish language maintenance is not always considered a fundamental part of Latino identity within the Latino community itself; nor does knowledge of Spanish constitute automatic acceptance as a group member by other Latinos. In addition, hybridized language and linguistic practices often characterize and stigmatize bilingual US Latinos. The next section attempts to explain what these factors suggest for the heritage speaker classroom.

IDENTITY IN THE SPANISH HERITAGE SPEAKER CLASSROOM

The previous section explored several roles of the Spanish language in the construction of US Latino identity. This section asks somewhat of an inverse question: What role do heritage speakers' identities play in the study of Spanish in a heritage speaker classroom? He (2006, 2) underscores that "to a greater extent than the [second-language] learner, the HL learner is likely to be motivated by an identification with the intrinsic cultural, affective, and aesthetic values of the language" and that "the propositional contents . . . conveyed in the HL (e.g., the contents of HL textbooks) and the ways in which HL is used (e.g., how HL instructors communicate with students in everyday classroom interaction) have a direct impact on how the HL learner perceives the language/culture and how s/he consequently positions him/herself."

According to Hornberger and Wang (2008, 6), educators must understand "who heritage language learners are in various contexts and how they see, perceive, interpret, present and represent themselves in those contexts" before they can develop appropriate pedagogical theories and approaches. As a step toward this goal, Showstack (2012) examined how bilingual Hispanic students constructed their linguistic and cultural identities as well as notions of different kinds of Hispanics and Spanish speakers in a heritage classroom in central Texas. She found that the students generally privileged what they considered "standard" Spanish while delegitimizing what they considered nonstandard varieties; they held essentialized notions of linguistic and cultural identity; and they marginalized individuals who did not fit into their cultural and linguistic categories. Valdés and Geoffrion-Vinci (1998) also report how heritage speakers whose Spanish reflects characteristics of working-class speech are often stigmatized by instructors.

For these and other reasons associated with the often deeply significant connections between learners' identity and the language, the heritage speaker instructor plays a very important role. Instructors can assist students in deconstructing such essentializations and finding positive connections between their variety of Spanish and a healthy sense of ethnolinguistic identity. He (2006) reminds us that the language learner's ultimate success lies in the degree to which they acculturate/accommodate to the target language group.[13] This is best achieved when there is a relatively low degree of social and psychological distance between the learner and the target culture. These relationships are dynamic and ever shifting, according to the evolving view of identity that each group has of the other (He 2006, 11). When teachers respect students, their differing backgrounds, and their language varieties, a positive affective situation can be achieved. Velez-Rendon (2006) highlights several examples of students recounting how their Spanish instructor validated their sense of cultural identity. Conversely, instructors like those considered by Potowski (2002), who are critical and disdainful toward heritage speakers' varieties of Spanish, damaged many students' sense of identity as Spanish speakers. It is of crucial importance that heritage instructors receive appropriate professional preparation that includes familiarity with the sociolinguistic realities of US Latinos in order to work effectively with heritage speakers (Potowski and Carreira 2004). As shown by Edstrom (2005) and Potowski (2002), this sensitivity is not automatically present among Spanish-speaking instructors, whether native or nonnative.

Another fruitful area in which to explore "how the HL learner perceives the language/culture and how s/he consequently positions him/herself" (He 2006, 2) is the study abroad context. We currently know very little about how heritage Spanish speakers experience studying abroad in Spanish-speaking countries. Carrasco and Riegelhaupt (2003) related cases of Mexican host families expecting native-like social and linguistic behavior from their Mexico-origin US Latino students and, in cases in which this did not occur, they requested Anglo students instead, which resulted in "an identity crisis as the result of a language and culture clash with their Guanajuato host families." The authors found that it was beneficial to provide sociohistorical, cultural, and sociolinguistic knowledge to the heritage learners and, of particular importance, to the host families. Finding more positive results, Gorman (2011) worked with twenty-three New Mexican students in Nicaragua on a program specifically designed for heritage speakers.[14] Although some were forced to reconceptualize themselves as "gringos" in the eyes of the locals, they were often praised for interacting more than the Anglo students with the host families, which they described as very familiar to them.

Textbooks clearly merit an examination for themes related to identity because they often drive course curricula. As cited above, a large proportion of US Latinos are victims of discrimination (Olson 2009), and the heritage speaker classroom—including the instructor, classmates, textbook, and assignments—offers ideal sites to explore and contest such practices. Several critical analyses of heritage speaker textbooks (Leeman and Martínez 2007; Ducar 2009) indicate how they can both reinforce and contest ideologies. Showstack (2012, 21) asserts that the students in her study did not seem aware of how their classroom discourse supported "monoglossic language ideologies and essentialist models of language and identity" and suggested that solid pedagogy can deconstruct such discourses, "making them less opaque and thus creating the possibility for the construction of empowering discourses in the [heritage] classroom." Thus, textbooks, which are often seen as an official source of legitimization, can and should assist instructors in encouraging students to examine critically issues of language and power.

A final note about identity in the heritage speaker classroom comes from Beaudrie, Ducar, and Relaño-Pastor (2009), who propose that students' voices need to play a more crucial role in program and curricular decisions. Surveys like theirs can be used very profitably to incorporate student perspectives about what they want to study; a recent survey conducted in Illinois revealed, among other things, that students wanted to improve their grammar and writing, and they wanted to study topics related to culture and to US Latinos.[15]

How do identity issues play out when heritage speakers find themselves not in heritage speaker courses but in Spanish courses with second-language learners? Potowski (2002) found that Anglo students were intimidated by the oral proficiency of heritage speakers, and heritage speakers were intimidated by the grammatical knowledge of Anglo students. As mentioned above, some heritage speakers indicated embarrassment that second-language learners "knew Spanish better than they did." However, Bowles (2011) found that carefully structured tasks involving heritage–L2 student pairs can be mutually beneficial, both linguistically and regarding students' confidence.

CONCLUSION

US Latino youth face complex issues as they construct an ethnolinguistic identity within a predominately English-speaking society. On the basis of the three-part model developed by Leung, Harris, and Rampton (1997, 555), Klee (2011) proposes that many Latino youth have Spanish language inheritance (family affiliation) but may not have language expertise (proficiency) in Spanish, and they may have a high or weak degree of affiliation toward their HL. Thus, in contrast to He (2006), I propose that assuming an intimate link between the development and maintenance of an HL and a core sense of identity is a kind of essentialization that runs the risk of homogenizing heritage speakers, who vary on this and a number of other primary identity constructs.

To further address the many facets of heritage speakers' identities, more classroom-based research is needed. This includes heritage speaker courses, mixed classes, and study abroad, with interpretive lenses like those of Urciuoli (2008) and Showstack (2012), and also documenting instructor efforts to challenge students' conceptions about language. Powerful motivations for this research direction are found in He's (2006, 7) argument that studying an HL "means not merely to *inherit* one's HL and *maintain* one's heritage cultural identity but also to *transform* the heritage language [by changing its script, accent discourse norms, etc.] . . . and *recreate* one's identity" (emphasis added). It is a very basic and incontrovertible fact that individuals change language, forming a core principle of the field of sociolinguistics, and it should be respected not only by HL teachers but also by the misguided prescriptivist organizations that, in their efforts to codify Spanish, admonish US Spanish speakers and their linguistic innovations (Lynch and Potowski, unpublished manuscript). Other ways to advance the field of identity studies among Latinos involve the kind of qualitative scholarship common in Latino studies, which can enable educators to understand "who heritage language learners are in various contexts and how they see, perceive, interpret, present and represent themselves in those contexts" (Hornberger and Wang 2008, 7). This is critically important for heritage speaker instructors who wish to understand and help students examine negative stereotypes, intra-Latino hierarchies, and the relationships between language and culture.

NOTES

1. As is discussed below in the text, there is considerable debate about the terms "Latino" and "Hispanic" in the United States; in this chapter, I use these terms interchangeably. I also use the terms "bilingual Spanish speaker" and "heritage speaker" synonymously (see García 2005 for a criticism of the term "heritage speaker").

2. This is with the exception of extremely isolated religious communities, e.g., the Amish and the Hassidic Jews.

3. It is unclear whether authors did not find, or did not look for, an influence of ethnic identity on language proficiency.

4. However, this still left many of my Latino students confused about whether they should mark "white" or fill in "Mexican" under "some other race."

5. An individual's answer about self-identification terms likely depends on who is asking the question and in what context.

6. Pacheco (2008) asserts that the humor of such comedians is an attempt to contest these stereotypes.

7. In the United States, 70 percent of Hispanics/Latinos report being Catholic and 23 percent are Protestant, with 6 percent having no affiliation (Espinosa, Elizondo, and Miranda 2003).

8. This represents a significant shift from fifteen years ago, when nearly half of US Hispanics were immigrants.

9. Chicanos are US citizens of Mexican descent, particularly in the Southwest; *quisqueya* = of Dominican descent; *tejanos* = Texans of Mexican and/or Latin American descent.

10. Exogamy is marriage outside one's ethnolinguistic group. Alba et al. (2002) found that if a marriage crosses a language boundary—i.e., a bilingual marries an English monolingual—the odds that a third-generation child will speak only English are increased. Several studies indicate that, in an exogamous marriage, if the *mother* speaks the minority language, there is a better chance that the offspring will acquire it (see Potowski 2008). Shin (2010) offers insight on language and identity among heritage speakers of mixed heritage (resulting from exogamous marriages).

11. It remains to be documented empirically whether phenotype correlates with Spanish proficiency or usage patterns.

12. The term "Spanglish" is also contentious; see the debate between Ana Celia Zentella and Ricardo Otheguy at http://potowski.org/debate-spanglish.

13. However, in our case, who exactly is the "target language group"? It should *not* be our goal to make bilingual heritage speakers pass for monolinguals from their families' countries of origin; a bilingual is not two monolinguals rolled into one. This question is of acute importance in the field of HL education.

14. There are several such programs in countries, including Spain (Academic Language Institute 2006).

15. This is from an unpublished report from the Department of Spanish, Italian, and Portuguese, at the University of Illinois at Urbana-Champaign. However, we should keep in mind that not all undergraduates are equipped to decide what they want and need to study, nor know the best way to achieve their academic goals.

REFERENCES

Academic Language Institute. 2006. "En busca de nuestras raíces: A Course for Heritage Speakers of Spanish." www.ali-cante.com/heritage.html.

Alba, Richard, John Logan, Amy Lutz, and Brian Stults. 2002. "Only English by the Third Generation? Loss and Preservation of the Mother Tongue among the Grandchildren of Contemporary Immigrants." *Demography* 39 (3): 467–84.

Anzaldúa, Gloria. 1999. *Borderlands/La Frontera: The New Mestiza*. San Francisco: Aunt Lute Books.

Aparicio, Frances. 1997. "La enseñanza del español para hispanohablantes y la pedagoía multicultural." In *La enseñanza del español a hispanohablantes: Praxis y teoría*, edited by Cecilia Colombi and Francisco Alarcon. Boston: Houghton Mifflin.

Attinasi, John. 1985. "Hispanic Attitudes in Northwestern Indiana and New York." In *Spanish Language Use and Public Life in the USA*, edited by Lucia Elías-Olivares, Elizabeth Leone, Rene Cisneros, and John Gutierrez. Berlin: Mouton.

Bailey, Benjamin. 2000. "Language and Negotiation of Ethnic/Racial Identity among Dominican Americans." *Language in Society* 29 (4): 555–82.

Beaudrie, Sara, and Cynthia Ducar. 2005. "Beginning-Level University Heritage Programs: Creating a Space for All Heritage Language Learners." *Heritage Language Journal* 3 (1). Available at www.heritagelanguages.org.

Beaudrie, Sara, Cynthia Ducar, and Ana María Relaño-Pastor. 2009. "Curricular Perspectives in the Heritage Language Context: Assessing Culture and Identity." *Language, Culture and Curriculum* 22 (2): 157–74.

Bills, Garland, Alan Hudson, and Eduardo Hernández-Chávez. 2000. "Spanish Home Language Use and English Proficiency as Differential Measures of Language Maintenance and Shift." *Southwest Journal of Linguistics* 19 (1): 11–27.

Bills, Garland, and Neddy Vigil. 1999. "The Spanish Language of New Mexico and Southern Colorado: A Linguistic Atlas." *Journal of Sociolinguistics* 16 (2): 292–94.

Block, David. 2007. *Second Language Identities*. New York: Continuum.

Bourdieu, Pierre. 1999. *Language and Symbolic Power*. Cambridge, MA: Harvard University Press.

Bowles, Melissa A. 2011. "Exploring the Role of Modality: L2-Heritage Learner Interactions in the Spanish Language Classroom." *Heritage Language Journal* 8 (1). Available at www.heritagelanguages.org.

Bucholtz, Mary, and Kira Hall. 2004. "Theorizing Identity in Language and Sexuality Research." *Language in Society* 33:469–515.

Butler, Judith. 1990. *Gender Trouble: Feminism and the Subversion of Identity.* New York: Routledge.

Caldas, Steven, and Suzanne Caron-Caldas. 1999. "Language Immersion and Cultural Identity: Conflicting Influences and Values." *Language, Culture and Curriculum* 12 (1): 42–58.

Carrasco, Roberto, and Florence Riegelhaupt. 2003. "META: A Model for the Continued Acquisition of Spanish by Spanish/English Bilinguals in the United States." In *Mi lengua: Spanish as a Heritage Language in the United States,* edited by Ana Roca and Cecilia Colombi. Washington, DC: Georgetown University Press.

Clachar, Arlene. 1997. "Ethnolinguistic Identity and Spanish Proficiency in a Paradoxical Situation: The Case of Puerto Rican Return Migrants." *Journal of Multilingual and Multicultural Development* 18(2): 107–24.

De Genova, Nicolas, and Yolanda Ramos-Zayas. 2003. *Latino Crossings: Mexicans, Puerto Ricans, and the Politics of Race and Citizenship.* New York: Routledge.

Ducar, Cynthia. 2009. "The Sound of Silence: Spanish Heritage Textbooks' Treatment of Language Variation." In *Español en Estados Unidos y otros contextos,* edited by Manel Lacorte and Jennifer Leeman. Madrid: Iberoamericana/Vervuert.

Eckert, Penelope, and Sally McConnell-Ginet. 1992. "Think Practically and Look Locally: Language and Gender as Community-Based Practice." *Annual Review of Anthropology* 21:461–90.

Edstrom, Anne. 2005. "'A "Gringa" Is Going to Teach Me Spanish!'" A Nonnative Teacher Reflects and Responds." *ADFL Bulletin* 36 (2): 27–31.

Espinosa, Gaston, Virgilio Elizondo, and Jesse Miranda. 2003. "Hispanic Churches in American Public Life: Summary of Findings." Interim Report 2, January. Institute for Latino Studies, University of Notre Dame.

Farr, Marcia. 2006. *Rancheros in Chicagoacán: Language and Identity in a Transnational Community.* Austin: University of Texas Press.

Fears, Darryl. 2003. "Latinos or Hispanics? A Debate about Identity." *Washington Post,* August 25.

García, Ofelia. 2005. "Positioning Heritage Languages in the United States." *Modern Language Journal* 89 (4): 601–5.

García, Ofelia, and Ricardo Otheguy. 1988. "The Language Situation of Cuban Americans." In *Language Diversity: Problem or Resource?* edited by S. McKay and S. Wong. New York: Harper & Row.

García-Bedolla, Lisa. 2003. "The Identity Paradox: Latino Language, Politics and Selective Dissociation." *Latino Studies* 1: 264–83.

Gorman, Lillian. 2010. "'Paisas, bracers, and nacos': Ethnic Identification and Linguistic Perceptions among Second-Generation Mexicans in Chicago." Unpublished manuscript.

———. 2011. "'Es como si ya nos conociéramos': Spanish Heritage Learners and Ethnolinguistic Identity in the Study Abroad Context." Paper delivered at the Twenty-Second Conference on Spanish in the United States, Sacramento, March.

He, Agnes. 2006. "Toward an Identity Theory of the Development of Chinese as a Heritage Language." *Heritage Language Journal* 4 (1). Available at www.heritage languages.org.

Hornberger, Nancy, and S. C. Wang. 2008. "Who Are Our Heritage Language Learners? Identity and Biliteracy in Heritage Language Education in the United States." In *Heritage Language Education: A New Field Emerging*, edited by Donna Brinton, Olga Kagan, and Susie Backus. Mahwah, NJ: Lawrence Erlbaum Associates.

Hurtado, Alda, and Luis Vega. 2004. "Shift Happens: Spanish and English Transmission between Parents and Their Children." *Journal of Social Issues* 60 (1): 137–55.

Klee, Carol. 2011. "Migration, Ethnic Identity and Heritage Language Maintenance of Spanish-Speaking Youth in English-Speaking Societies: A Reexamination." In *Bilingual Youth: Spanish Speakers in English-Speaking Societies*, edited by Kim Potowski and Jason Rothman. Amsterdam: John Benjamins.

Koike, Dale, and Clayton Graham. 2006. "Who Is More Hispanic?: The Co-Construction of Identities in a US Hispanic Political Debate." *Spanish in Context* 3 (2): 181–213.

Kondo, Kimi. 1997. "Social-Psychological Factors Affecting Language Maintenance: Interviews with Shin Nisei University Students in Hawaii." *Linguistics and Education* 9 (4): 369–408.

Leeman, Jennifer, and Glenn Martínez. 2007. "From Identity to Commodity: Ideologies of Spanish in Heritage Language Textbooks." *Critical Inquiry in Language Studies* 4 (1): 35–65.

Leung, Constant, Roxy Harris, and Ben Rampton. 1997. "The Idealized Native Speaker, Reified Ethnicities, and Classroom Realities." *TESOL Quarterly* 31:543–60.

Lipski, John. 2008. *Varieties of Spanish in the United States*. Washington, DC: Georgetown University Press.

Lynch, Andrew, and Kim Potowski. Unpublished manuscript. "La valoración del habla bilingüe en Estados Unidos: Criterio sociolingüístico y voz pedagógica en *Hablando bien se entiende la gente*."

Maloof, Valerie, Donald Rubin, and Ann Neville Miller. 2006. "Cultural Competence and Identity in Cross-Cultural Adaptation: The Role of a Vietnamese Heritage Language School." *International Journal of Bilingual Education and Bilingualism* 9 (2): 255–73.

Markert, John. 2004. "George Lopez: The Same Old Hispano?" *Bilingual Review* 28 (2): 148–65.

Mendoza-Denton, Norma. 2008. *Homegirls: Language and Cultural Practice among Latina Youth Gangs*. Hoboken, NJ: Wiley Blackwell.

Morales, Ed. 2003. *Living in Spanglish: The Search for Latino Identity in America*. New York: St. Martin's Press.

Nieto-Phillips, John. 2000. "Spanish American Ethnic Identity and New Mexico's State-hood Struggle." In *The Contested Homeland: A Chicano History of New Mexico*, edited by Erlinda Gonzales-Berry and David Maciel. Albuquerque: University of New Mexico Press.

Ochoa, Gilda. 2004. *Becoming Neighbors in a Mexican American Community: Power, Conflict, and Solidarity*. Austin: University of Texas Press.

Olson, David. 2009. "Most Young Latinos US-Born, Feel Labeled as Immigrants, Study Finds." www.pe.com/localnews/inland/stories/PE_LN_20091211_latinoyouth.351935672.html.

Otheguy, Ricardo, and Ofelia García. 1993. "Convergent Conceptualizations as Predictors of Degree of Contact in US Spanish." In *Spanish in the US: Linguistic Contact and Diversity*, edited by Ana Roca and John Lipski. New York: Mouton de Gruyter.

Pacheco, George. 2008. "Rhetoric with Humor: An Analysis of Hispanic/Latino Comedians' Uses of Humor." PhD diss., University of Southern Mississippi.

Passel, Jeffrey Paul Taylor. 2009. "Who's Hispanic? Pew Hispanic Center." http://pew hispanic.org/reports/report.php?ReportID = 111.

Pavlenko, Aneta, and Adrian Blackledge. 2004. *Negotiation of Identities in Multilingual Contexts*. Clevedon, UK: Multilingual Matters.

Pease-Alvaréz, Lucinda. 2002. "Moving beyond Linear Trajectories of Language Shift and Bilingual Language Socialization." *Hispanic Journal of Behavioral Sciences* 24 (2): 114–37.

Pedraza, Pedro. 1985. "Language Maintenance among New York Puerto Ricans." In *Spanish Language and Public Life in the United States*, edited by Lucia Elías-Olivares, Elizabeth Leone, Rene Cisneros, and John Gutierrez. New York: Mouton.

Pérez, Gina. 2004. *The Near Northwest Side Story: Migration, Displacement, and Puerto Rican Families*. Berkeley: University of California Press.

Phinney, Jean, Irma Romero, Monica Nava, and Dan Huang. 2001. "The Role of Language, Parents, and Peers in Ethnic Identity among Adolescents in Immigrant Families." *Journal of Youth and Adolescence* 30 (2): 135–53.

Podesva, Robert, Sara Roberts, and Katherine Campbell-Kibler. 2001. *Sharing Resources and Indexing Meanings in the Production of Gay Styles: Language and Sexuality— Contesting Meaning in Theory and Practice*. Stanford, CA: Center for the Study of Language and Information, Stanford University.

Potowski, Kim. 2002. "Experiences of Spanish Heritage Speakers in University Foreign Language Courses and Implications for Teacher Training." *ADFL Bulletin* 33 (3): 35–42.

———. 2004. "Spanish Language Shift in Chicago." *Southwest Journal of Linguistics* 23 (1): 87–116.

———. 2008. "'I Was Raised Talking Like My Mom': The Influence of Mothers in the Development of MexiRicans' Phonological and Lexical Features." In *Linguistic Identity and Bilingualism in Different Hispanic Contexts*, edited by Jason Rothman and Mercedes Niño-Murcia. Amsterdam: John Benjamins.

———, ed. 2010. *Language Diversity in the USA*. New York: Cambridge University Press.

———. 2011. "Balancing Act: Autobiographical Narratives of Spanish-speaking Youth in the United States." Paper delivered at the Twenty-Second Conference on Spanish in the United States, Sacramento, March.

Potowski, Kim, and Maria Carreira. 2004. "Towards Teacher Development and National Standards for Spanish as a Heritage Language." *Foreign Language Annals* 37 (3): 421–31.

Potowski, Kim, and Janine Matts. 2008. "Interethnic Language and Identity: MexiRicans in Chicago." *Journal of Language, Identity and Education* 7 (2): 137–60.

Potowski, Kim, and Lourdes Torres. Unpublished manuscript. *Spanish in Chicago: Dialect Contact and Language Socialization among Mexicans and Puerto Ricans*.

Rivera-Mills, Susana. 2001. "Acculturation and Communicative Need: Language Shift in an Ethnically Diverse Hispanic Community." *Southwest Journal of Linguistics* 20:211–23.

Rodriguez, Richard. 2004. *Hunger of Memory: The Education of Richard Rodriguez—An Autobiography*. Boston: Dial Press.

Romaine, Suzanne. 2011. "Identity and Multilingualism." In *Bilingual Youth: Spanish in English-Speaking Societies*, edited by Kim Potowski and Jason Rothman. Amsterdam: John Benjamins.

Santiago, Bill. 2008. *Pardon My Spanglish ¡Porque Because!* Philadelphia: Quirk Books.

Shin, Sarah. 2010. "'What About Me? I'm Not Like Chinese but I'm Not Like American': Heritage-Language Learning and Identity of Mixed-Heritage Adults." *Journal of Language, Identity and Education* 9 (3): 203–19.

Showstack, Rachel. 2012. "Symbolic Power in the Heritage Language Classroom: How Spanish Heritage Speakers Sustain and Resist Hegemonic Discourses on Language and Cultural Diversity." *Spanish in Context* 9 (1): 1–26.

Smith, Robert Courtney. 2006. *Mexican New York: Transnational Lives of New Immigrants.* Berkeley: University of California Press.

Toribio, Almeida Jacqueline. 2003. "The Social Significance of Language Loyalty among Black and White Dominicans in New York." *Bilingual Review/La Revista Bilingüe* 27 (1): 3–11.

Urciuoli, Bonnie. 2008. "Whose Spanish? The Tension between Linguistic Correctness and Cultural Identity." In *Bilingualism and Identity: Spanish at the Crossroads with Other Languages*, edited by Mercedes Niño-Murcia and Jason Rothman. Amsterdam: John Benjamins.

Val, Adriana, and Vinogradova, Polina. 2010. *What Is the Identity of a Heritage Language Speaker?* Heritage Brief. Washington, DC: Center for Applied Linguistics. www.cal.org/heritage/research/briefs.html.

Valdés, Guadalupe. 2011. "Ethnolinguistic Identity: The Challenge of Maintaining Spanish-English Bilingualism in American Schools." In *Bilingualism and Identity: Spanish at the Crossroads with Other Languages*, edited by Mercedes Niño-Murcia and Jason Rothman. Amsterdam: John Benjamins.

Valdés, Guadalupe, and Michelle Geoffrion-Vinci. 1998. "Chicano Spanish: The Problem of the Underdeveloped Code in Bilingual Repertoires." *Modern Language Journal* 82:473–501.

Velez-Rendon, Gloria. 2005. "Las autobiografías lingüísticas: Una propuesta metodológica para el desarrollo de la lectoescritura de los alumnos hispanohablantes." *Hispania* 88 (3): 531–41.

———. 2006. "La construcción de identidades: El caso de universitarias hispanas inmigrantes en el contexto estadounidense." *Revista Iberoamericana de Lingüística* 1:51–70.

Zentella, Ana Celia. 1990. "Lexical Leveling in Four New York City Spanish Dialects: Linguistic and Social factors." *Hispania* 73 (4): 1094–1105.

———. 1997. *Growing Up Bilingual.* Malden, MA: Blackwell.

Zhou, Min. 2004. 2004. "Assimilation, the Asian Way." In *Reinventing the Melting Pot: The New Immigrants and What It Means to Be American*, edited by T. Jacoby. New York: Basic Books.

PART IV

Pedagogical Perspectives

Research on University-Based Spanish Heritage Language Programs in the United States

THE CURRENT STATE OF AFFAIRS

Sara M. Beaudrie, University of Arizona

ERITAGE LANGUAGE EDUCATION in the United States currently enjoys the attention of a wide group of researchers, policymakers, administrators, and practitioners. There are the National Heritage Language Resource Center (at the University of California, Los Angeles), which is devoted to heritage language education and research; the *Heritage Language Journal*; the Alliance for the Advancement of Heritage Languages at the Center for Applied Linguistics; conferences and workshops devoted to heritage language issues; and many journal articles, books, and dissertations. This is a significant change from the 1970s, when Spanish heritage language (SHL) education began as a grassroots effort of concerned educators in public institutions who realized that traditional foreign language courses did not meet the needs of heritage language learners (Valdés, Lozano, and Garcia-Moya 1981).[1] Unlike in countries such as Canada (Duff 2008) and Australia (Elder 2005, 2009), where heritage language instruction garnered early government support, the US government did not fund large-scale programs or provide other support to spearhead the teaching of heritage languages (Valdés, Lozano, and Garcia-Moya 1981), nor did many communities create Spanish language schools to maintain their language. In fact, some Latinos have objected to their children receiving bilingual education (Barnwell 2008).

Yet despite this lack of support, many pioneering professors in higher education institutions began creating special courses to better serve the specific language-learning needs of Spanish speakers. The huge expansion of the US Latino population in the 1980s and 1990s, especially in institutions of higher education (see the introduction to this volume, by Beaudrie and Fairclough), greatly increased the need to respond to this new student population in the language classroom.

The beginning of Spanish instruction for heritage language learners was not without challenges. There were no instructional objectives, no instructors trained in how to teach Spanish to Spanish-speaking individuals, no curriculum guidelines, and no appropriate textbooks for such courses (Valdés 1997; Valdés et al. 1981). The main focus of early SHL courses was remedial, and thus they were aimed at teaching learners standard Spanish to "repair the damage done at home" (Valdés-Fallis 1977, 90). According to Valdés, very few programs focused on developing proficiency in reading and writing Spanish, the skills with which SHL learners typically need the most help. As SHL researchers continued to debate the appropriate content of SHL courses, they sought answers to basic and fundamental questions, such as Who are SHL learners? What should the objectives of SHL instruction be? What materials should we use to teach these learners?

By the turn of the twenty-first century, the field of SHL education had moved forward by incorporating innovative pedagogical approaches geared for heritage language instruction (Anderson 2008; Carreira 2007; Kondo-Brown 2010; Potowski 2005; Roca and Colombi 2003; Trujillo 2009; Webb and Miller 2000). These various innovations highlighted the diversity of the SHL population and helped instructors to recognize that drafting a single set of learning objectives and curricular specifications for them is neither possible nor desirable. Whereas some learners need instruction that approximates the content of a foreign language course in certain respects (Beaudrie 2009a; Beaudrie and Ducar 2005; Carreira 2004), others need content similar to that in a language arts class (Potowski and Carreira 2004). Indeed, a one-size-fits-all pedagogical paradigm is not likely to succeed in educating such a diverse population (see chapter 11 in this volume, by Carreira). Some principles, however, do hold true for SHL education in a variety of contexts: (1) Mixed classes of heritage and foreign language learners are not an ideal learning environment for either group (see Potowski 2002, 2005); (2) the individual student's specific needs must be the point of departure for curricular decisions (Beaudrie and Ducar 2005; Beaudrie, Ducar, and Relaño-Pastor 2009; Romero 2000); (3) it is important to help learners maintain or develop both standard, formal Spanish and nonstandard, informal registers that are of relevance to them (Bernal-Enríquez and Hernández-Chávez 2003; Ducar 2008; Hernández-Chávez 1993; Martínez 2003; Villa 1996); and (4) the main objectives for SHL instruction are language maintenance and development and literacy development (see Valdés 2005). These tenets of SHL instruction are vital to providing high-quality learning experiences for these students, but it is unclear to what extent they have trickled down to actual programmatic practices.

To fully understand these practices, it is essential to examine the current state of SHL education. This chapter therefore first reviews the historical and current research on SHL program offerings nationwide in US postsecondary institutions. It continues with a review of SHL students' perspectives regarding whether their SHL program is serving their needs. Finally, it concludes with a research agenda on SHL programmatic and curricular issues.

RESEARCH ON UNIVERSITY-BASED SHL PROGRAMS

Research on the nature and availability of SHL programs in the United States has been modest. The earliest data came from a nationwide survey of postsecondary institutions that solicited basic information about SHL programs (Wherritt and Cleary 1990). The questionnaire, which was distributed to BA-granting institutions, inquired about policies regarding testing for Spanish language course placements and outcome assessments, as well as whether the institution offered any specialized first-year courses for SHL learners. Of the 126 small and large institutions across the United States that responded to the survey, 18 percent offered courses for native speakers of Spanish (14 percent of small institutions, and 26 percent of large institutions). The main value of this survey is that it provides a glimpse of the availability of SHL courses before the turn of the twenty-first century.

A later survey conducted by Ingold and colleagues (2002) was the first nationwide study specifically assessing the availability and nature of SHL programs, as well as the challenges and specific needs they faced. The survey was sent out to 240 randomly selected higher education Spanish programs across the nation and achieved a 60 percent (146 programs) response rate. Only 17.8 percent of programs offered separate courses for SHL learners, and enrollment in these courses was quite often low. Among the challenges in implementing SHL courses were inadequate program information, a lack of interest among students, and inadequate language-placement procedures. Among programs offering no SHL courses, the major obstacles to initiating this track were insufficient enrollment, a lack of funding, and a lack of trained instructors. A lack of interest from the administration, students, and faculty was also noted as an obstacle. The results showed little change in the number and types of SHL programs since Wherritt and Cleary's 1990 survey.

More recent regional studies have begun to show a different scenario for SHL programs.[2] Valdés and colleagues (2006) conducted a statewide study in California of SHL programs in secondary and postsecondary institutions. The data collection involved two parts: a survey sent out to 173 institutions, and a multiple-case study of six institutions. In the survey thirty-five out of fifty-two (or 62 percent) responding postsecondary institutions (junior colleges, colleges, and universities) offered SHL programs, a sharp difference from previous nationwide findings. Of these programs, 54 percent were recent additions that had been established after 1990. The survey also inquired about language-placement exam-inations, course objectives, effective instructional practices, and the education of instructors, among other things. The majority of institutions surveyed did not have exams to place students in appropriate language courses, so students either self-selected into a course or were advised by counselors (for more information on SHL placement exams, see chapter 13 in this volume, by Fairclough). The primary focus of most SHL programs was the teaching of standard Spanish, primarily because the instructors had no knowledge of language variation and did not value the Spanish varieties spoken by students. Of particular importance, the authors concluded that there was no evidence SHL programs were helping learners maintain their home language or use it outside the classroom, which one might argue should be the main goal of SHL instruction. The problems revealed in this study may very well be generalizable to other areas of the United States. Thus, although more programs are being created, some of them may not be fully equipped to provide successful learning opportunities for all SHL learners.

Beaudrie (2011) conducted a broader study of SHL course offerings in four-year public and private universities in the Southwest that offer Spanish courses and have at least 5 percent Hispanic enrollment. Of the 173 universities reviewed in the study, 66 (38 percent) had SHL programs; once again, this is a much higher proportion than was found in earlier nationwide surveys. Although the results showed an uneven distribution of courses throughout the Southwest, chi-square analysis revealed a direct, positive relationship between the availability of SHL programs and the size of the Hispanic populations in particular universities.

The same study found that existing SHL programs addressed a limited range of instructional goals and only accommodated learners who had a very specific profile. Most programs had a primary focus on improving students' literacy skills, which primarily meant writing, and ignored other language skills and stu-dents' heritage cultures (Beaudrie 2011). In addition, programs were geared toward students who were at about the midpoint of the bilingual continuum (see Valdés 2001) and thus frequently excluded students at the lower or upper end of the bilingual range. Moreover, there was a lack of consistency among university programs regarding the level of courses and the terminology used to describe various proficiency levels. Terms such as "beginning," "intermediate," and "advanced" had program-specific meanings, and courses were arbitrarily placed in the first-, second-, or third-year curriculum.

In the fall of 2010, Beaudrie undertook a nationwide online survey with the primary aim of generating a current account of the number and types of pro-grams offered for SHL learners in US four-year universities.[3] This short survey

solicited information about (1) the availability of Spanish language courses especially designed for heritage or bilingual Spanish speakers, (2) descriptions of
the courses, (3) the number of sections offered and students enrolled, (4) the
identification or course placement exam practices currently in place, and (5)
plans to create new or expand existing SHL courses. All four-year institutions
that had at least 5 percent Hispanic student enrollment and offered Spanish
language courses were contacted.[4] The survey was sent out via e-mail during
August and September 2010 to either a faculty member in charge of teaching
Spanish courses or the director or chair of the Spanish program. At the end of
September, nonrespondents were contacted by telephone. Of the 249 responses
(which constituted an 86 percent response rate), 192 (77 percent) were filled out
online, 15 (6 percent) by e-mail, and 42 (17 percent) by phone. Merging these
surveys with the data for the 173 universities in the US Southwest that Beaudrie
(2011) had previously collected brought the total number of institutions surveyed to 422.

Table 10.1 presents the number of universities offering at least one course for
SHL learners out of the total number of universities contacted, by state and US
region. There are a total of 169 identified SHL programs in the United States (40
percent), a remarkable increase from the previous proportions of 18 percent in
1990 and 17.8 percent in 2002. This finding provides ample evidence that the call
for special courses for heritage language learners has received an overwhelming
response from postsecondary institutions with sizable populations of Hispanic
students. Regarding the distribution of courses across the various US regions,
the Northeast has the highest percentage (50 percent) and the Mountain West
has the lowest (26 percent), whereas the remaining regions display a fairly even
distribution ranging from 31 to 38 percent. These results are somewhat unex-
pected, given that the Northeast ranks third after the Southwest and the South
in number of Hispanic residents (US Census Bureau 2001). Regarding the prevalence of SHL programs in individual states, 85 percent of the 169 SHL programs
are concentrated in ten states: California (thirty-six universities, or 51 percent),
New York (twenty-six, or 59 percent), Texas (twenty, or 32 percent), Illinois
(fourteen, or 28 percent), Massachusetts (eleven, or 44 percent), Florida (ten, or
43 percent), New Jersey (nine, or 50 percent), Connecticut (seven, or 41 percent), Pennsylvania (six, or 43 percent), and New Mexico (five, or 63 percent).

To determine whether there is a significant relationship between the number
of Latino/Hispanic students enrolled at a university and the availability of SHL
courses there, the author classified universities into six groups according to the
size of their Hispanic population, as presented in table 10.2. This table shows the
number of SHL programs as a proportion of the number of universities that
belong to each size grouping.

As table 10.2 shows, course availability increases in strong correlation with
the size of the Hispanic student population. Among universities with up to 500
Hispanic students, only 26 percent offer at least one SHL course, whereas 88

Table 10.1 Number of US Universities Offering SHL Programs (at least 5 percent Hispanic enrollment)

Region[a]	States (SHL programs / total universities)	Total SHL Programs	Total Universities
Northeast	NH 1/1, VT 0/1, MA 11/25, RI 2/4, CT 7/17, NY 26/44, NJ 9/18, PA 6/14	62 (50%)	124
Midwest	IL 14/26, IN 2/8, IA 1/3, KS 0/4, MI 1/2, MN 0/1, MO 0/4, OH 1/1, NE 0/2, WI 1/3	20 (37%)	54
West	AK 0/2, HI 0/2, ID 1/4, MT 0/1, OR 2/5, WA 3/9	6 (26%)	23
Southwest	AZ 2/5, CA 36/71, CO 1/16, NV 2/3, NM 5/8, TX 20/63, OK 0/4, UT 0/3	66 (38%)	173
South	AR 0/1, DE 0/1, DC 2/5, FL 10/23, GA 1/2, LA 0/1, MD 1/5, NC 0/3, SC 0/1, TN 0/2, VA 1/4	15 (31%)	48
Total		169 (40%)	422

[a] States were assigned to regions as follows: *Northeast:* Maine, New Hampshire, Vermont, Massachusetts, Rhode Island, Connecticut, New York, New Jersey, and Pennsylvania. *Midwest:* Illinois, Indiana, Iowa, Kansas, Michigan, Minnesota, Missouri, Ohio, Nebraska, North Dakota, South Dakota, and Wisconsin. *Southwest:* Texas, Nevada, New Mexico, Arizona, California, Oklahoma, Colorado, and Utah. *West:* Alaska, Hawaii, Idaho, Montana, Oregon, Washington, and Wyoming. *South:* Alabama, Arkansas, Delaware, District of Columbia, Florida, Georgia, Kentucky, Louisiana, Maryland, Mississippi, North Carolina, South Carolina, Tennessee, Virginia, and West Virginia.

Source: Author's data.

Table 10.2 Number of SHL Course Offerings Compared with the Size of the Hispanic Student Population

			No. of SHL Programs/No. of Universities				
Region	0–500 HS[a]	501–1,000 HS	1,001–2,500 HS	2,500–5,000 HS	5,001–7,500 HS	7,500–10,000 + HS	Total
Northeast	33/86	14/20	11/13	4/5	0/0	0/0	62/124
Midwest	12/41	3/5	3/6	2/2	0/0	0/0	20/54
West	2/15	3/6	1/2	0	0/0	0/0	6/23
Southwest	16/78	8/25	14/33	17/24	5/6	6/7	66/173
South	2/29	2/5	5/8	4/4	1/1	1/1	15/48
Total	65/251	30/63	34/59	27/34	6/7	7/8	169/422
	(26%)	(48%)	(58%)	(79%)	(86%)	(88%)	(40%)

[a] HS = Hispanic students.
Source: Author's data.

percent of universities with more than 7,500 Hispanic students offer a course. To determine if this relationship was significant, the overall results per region were subjected to a chi-square test (X^2). The results were significant for the Northeast (X^2 [3, $N = 124$] $= 15.22, p < .01$); the Southwest (X^2 [5, $N = 173$] $= 34.58, p < .01$); and the South (X^2 [5, $N = 48$] $= 25.02, p < .01$). The results were not significant for the Midwest (X^2 [3, $N = 54$] $= 6.02, p > .05$) and the West (X^2 [2, $N = 23$] $= 3.64, p > .05$). Overall, there is a direct positive relationship, which indicates that in a majority of states the size of the Hispanic population at a university influences the availability of SHL programs. However, it is important to mention some noteworthy exceptions (Beaudrie 2011). In Arizona, California, Colorado, Texas, and Utah, at least twenty-eight universities with Hispanic student populations of more than 1,000 do not offer any SHL language courses, whereas in California and Texas sixteen universities with Hispanic student populations of less than 500 offer at least one SHL course.

Table 10.3 shows the number of courses offered by US region. The vast majority of programs offer one course (seventy-two universities, or 43 percent) or two courses (sixty-four, or 38 percent), whereas programs with four or more courses are practically nonexistent. The few multicourse programs available are in the Midwest and Southwest. An interesting contrast appears between the two regions with the highest numbers of programs, the Southwest and Northeast; whereas the majority of SHL programs with two courses (thirty-two, or 48 percent) are in the Southwest, the Northeast has a majority of programs with only one course (thirty-eight, or 63 percent). A possible explanation for this difference is that the northeastern universities have relatively newer SHL programs and that their course offerings will expand as interest and demand increase. The Southwest has some of the oldest programs in the nation, so these universities have had more time to develop their offerings.

The survey also asked about each institution's plans to create new or expand existing SHL courses. Of the ninety-seven respondents to this question, twenty-nine (or 30 percent) reported plans for change, with seventeen (or 59 percent) indicating plans to expand the number of SHL courses and six (or 21 percent) indicating plans to revamp existing offerings by renaming the course, redesigning the curriculum, or improving recruitment strategies. Of the 117 responding institutions not currently offering an SHL program, 14 (or 12 percent) reported plans to create a course for SHL learners. The remaining institutions cited two main obstacles to offering a course: (1) a low number of SHL students (14 of 103, or 14 percent), or (2) no faculty trained to teach such a course (5 of 103, or 5 percent).

The survey also contained an item about whether a heritage language placement exam was administered to place students in the appropriate course (for a discussion of SHL placement, see chapter 13 in this volume, by Fairclough). Out of ninety-nine respondents to this item, fifty-one (or 52 percent) stated that some type of placement exam was used, whereas forty-eight (or 48 percent) said

Table 10.3 Number of SHL Courses Offered at Universities in Various US Regions

Regions	No. of Courses							Not Reported	Total
	9	6	5	4	3	2	1		
Northeast	—	—	1	1	1	19	38 (2[a])	1	88
Midwest	1 (1[a])	1	2 (1[a])	1	0	6	9 (1[a])	—	50
West	—	—	—	—	2 (2[a])	2 (1[a])	2 (2[a])	—	14
Southwest	—	3	—	3	10	32	18	—	142
South	—	—	—	1	4	5	5	—	31
Total	1 (0.6%)	4 (2.4%)	3 (1.8%)	6 (3.6%)	17 (10.1%)	64 (38%)	72 (43%)	1 (0.6%)	

[a] Universities following the quarter system.

Source: Author's data.

none was used. As to the procedures used to identify SHL learners, the ninety-six respondents reported using the following methods (in order of frequency): (1) a combination of two or more methods (twenty-five, or 26 percent), (2) self-identification (twenty-two, or 23 percent), (3) a teacher or adviser referral (nine, or 9.4 percent), (4) an interview (nine, or 9.4 percent), and (5) a placement exam.

RESEARCH ON THE PERSPECTIVES OF SHL LEARNERS

Several studies have examined learners' perspectives on their language courses in an effort to provide insights into how to maximize their learning experiences. One of the first scholars to undertake this line of research was Potowski (2002), who used a questionnaire and focus group interviews to solicit the opinions of twenty-five university SHL learners enrolled in either the foreign language track or the SHL track about their course selections and their Spanish learning experiences. The results revealed generalized dissatisfaction among students in foreign language courses. The students believed that teachers frequently had higher expectations of them compared with other students in the class and that they overcorrected their Spanish, correcting nonstandard forms present in regional varieties of Spanish. Despite their high levels of fluency, pronunciation, and comprehension, SHL students felt inferior to the other students in the class, especially in their knowledge of grammar rules, and they believed that they received lower grades than the nonnative Spanish speakers in the class. This early study is important because it underscores the need for separate tracks for Spanish heritage speakers and learners of Spanish as a foreign language. It also highlights the acute need for stronger teacher development programs that include content on how to address the unique needs of SHL learners.

These findings were reinforced by two subsequent studies examining students' perceptions of learning Spanish in foreign language classes. Felix (2004) explored the experiences of thirty-nine adult Spanish speakers enrolled in a traditional foreign language Spanish class for English speakers. Students completed questionnaires, interviews, and group discussions about their Spanish language experience and what they had learned in the class. The results showed that teachers treated the students as language experts and devoted little attention to their need to develop literacy and other language skills. A number of students expressed feelings of inadequacy and embarrassment in the face of preconceptions and high expectations from their peers, who assumed that Spanish speakers should not need to take a language class, and those who did should easily obtain high grades. Felix concluded that foreign language instruction limits HL learners to activities designed for foreign language learners and neglects their particular skills and needs.

Beaudrie (2006) compared the experiences of beginning-level university SHL learners with receptive abilities in Spanish enrolled in SHL and foreign language classes. As part of a larger study of language development, students completed a questionnaire regarding their level of satisfaction with their SHL or foreign language course. Students in the SHL class had the highest levels of satisfaction, giving positive ratings of the course content, their learning about US Latino/ Hispanic and other relevant cultures, the speaking emphasis of the course, and the comfortable atmosphere of being in a classroom with students who had the same cultural and linguistic strengths and needs.

In contrast, the SHL learners in the foreign language class disliked the way culture was taught in their class. Far from fulfilling their cultural needs and bringing them closer to their family roots, it alienated them and forced them to learn cultural information that they considered irrelevant to their situations. Furthermore, the foreign language class reinforced the students' perceptions that their Spanish varieties were full of slang and nonstandard forms (Beaudrie 2006). In some cases the students felt disconnected from their families because of the discrepancies they noted between their home variety of Spanish and standard Spanish. Finally, they were confused by the emphasis on grammar rules. Taken together, these three studies show that traditional foreign language classes are unsatisfactory for SHL students and that separate language courses for heritage language learners are necessary to meet their specific needs.

A second line of research has investigated what content students would like to learn in their SHL courses. Following a qualitative research paradigm, Schwarzer and Petrón (2005) explored in depth three students' opinions of their language-learning experiences in university SHL classes through oral interviews, an analysis of student compositions, class observations, informal instructor interviews, and field notes. The three students expressed common desires for stronger emphasis on (1) relevant vocabulary (and less focus on grammar), (2) culture, and (3) conversation. Although limited in scope, this study points to a discrepancy between what the students expected from their SHL courses and what they received.

Ducar (2008) surveyed 152 students in a large SHL program regarding their perceptions of the teaching and learning of standard and nonstandard varieties of Spanish. The results suggested that learners were not particularly interested in learning academic Spanish, despite the emphasis that SHL educators assign to expanding learners' knowledge of formal and academic Spanish. Students overwhelmingly welcomed their teachers' corrections as a way to improve their Spanish, yet they preferred to learn varieties that were more relevant to their personal goals, which often lay outside the university setting.

A subsequent study conducted by Beaudrie (2009b) yielded some interesting findings. This study examined the perceptions of 213 SHL learners in a large university on the importance of their teachers' language and cultural backgrounds. The findings challenged the widespread practice in SHL education of assigning native Spanish speakers to teach SHL courses. Although the majority of respondents preferred to be taught by a native speaker, this preference varied by course level and past experiences, and students highlighted the different strengths and weaknesses of all types of teachers. Students in higher-level courses expressed stronger preferences for native Spanish-speaking teachers than students in lower-level courses. Prior experience with a particular type of teacher was significantly related to their current teacher preference, suggesting that it is important for students to be exposed to different types of teachers in order to benefit from and appreciate the strengths that both native and nonnative speakers have to offer. Another interesting finding of the study was that students showed a strong preference for teachers with a different cultural background than their own, thus favoring diversity over uniformity. Students also valued having a competent teacher in charge of the classroom.

Beaudrie, Ducar, and Relaño-Pastor (2009) sought to assess whether students' needs were being met at the various course levels of a large SHL program in a US university, specifically in the areas of culture and identity. This study examined the kinds of cultural knowledge students valued the most, and to what extent SHL classroom instruction fostered cross-cultural awareness. Although SHL teachers were very cognizant of fostering intracultural awareness in the classroom, and encouraged students to learn about their heritage culture in relation to other Latino cultures in the United States, the results also revealed the need to assign a more central role to culture within the SHL curriculum. The authors recommended strengthening students' connections with the surrounding Spanish-speaking community, because it is an integral part of their cultural identity formation process. According to students, SHL programs should focus on "little c" culture more frequently (i.e., knowledge of "what to do when and where") (Beaudrie, Ducar, and Relaño-Pastor 2009, 161). The results also underscored the importance of promoting a sense of self-identity and cultural pride, which is a product of knowing the patterns of living and everyday cultural practices in which students engage within their community. The authors concluded by recommending the creation of courses with a specifically cultural focus.

This research on university students' perceptions of their language learning experiences underscores two major themes: First, the foreign language classroom is a less-than-ideal environment for SHL learners; and second, there are discrepancies between what the SHL programs offer and what the students expect. Because what researchers and educators believe to be most important may not always coincide with what the students expect and need, students' voices must be incorporated into the design of SHL programs. A successful SHL program, first and foremost, needs to meet the needs of the students it is intended to serve.

LIMITATIONS AND FUTURE RESEARCH

Existing research has contributed greatly to scholars' understanding of the state of SHL education in the United States. Perhaps the biggest limitation of the research carried out to date is that with only a few exceptions, studies have utilized survey research. A wider range of methodologies, both qualitative and quantitative, is needed to gain comprehensive insights into SHL programs in the United States. Qualitative designs such as ethnographies and case studies can provide in-depth explanations of currently underresearched, complex issues such as students' and teachers' negotiation of roles as language experts in the class- room, especially when the teacher has a different background and experiences than the students do; descriptions of effective teaching practices; and profiles of struggling and exemplary programs to illuminate effective practices in SHL instruction. Quantitative designs, such as pretest/posttest experimental or quasi- experimental studies, can shed light on how much progress students made and, most important, identify their specific areas of growth so as to inform instruc- tional practices. Finally, longitudinal studies should be used to document student progress and the long-term effects of SHL instruction (Beaudrie 2009a). These results can then be compared with program goals and objectives to see how well they fit.

Because research on SHL programmatic and curricular issues is still in its infancy, the possibilities for a future research agenda are extensive. To strengthen and expand current SHL programs in the United States, it is critically important the scholars enhance their understanding of best practices in several interrelated areas: curriculum design and implementation, program design, evaluation of programs and the effectiveness of instruction, and teacher development.

With regard to curriculum design and implementation, much has been pub- lished regarding second-language acquisition (Brown 1995; Nunan 1988) but not SHL learning, which requires consideration of different curricular issues. As Kondo-Brown and Brown (2010) point out, HL learning requires a specific curriculum design because of the great linguistic diversity that derives from stu- dents' different contextual and individual circumstances. For this reason, a one- size-fits-all approach will fail to address the unique needs of this specific popula- tion. Currently, very little is known about whether or how SHL curricula in courses around the country are addressing individual student differences (for further discussion on differentiated instruction in SHL, see chapter 11 in this volume, by Carreira). Meeting students' needs requires innovative and flexible curricula that are adaptable to diverse needs. Researchers also do not know to what extent they can rely on textbooks versus teacher-developed materials in the SHL classroom. Examining curricular choices specific to the SHL classroom should be a priority for future research.

Programmatic issues are equally important, especially with regard to what program structure and content is most likely to facilitate practitioners' and schol- ars' main goal of delivering a comprehensive education in Spanish language and culture to specific subpopulations. Knowledge of the optimal program sequence for learners at different points on the bilingual continuum will enable teachers to prepare students well to use Spanish fluently in their communities, in their professions, or in furthering their university studies. Foreign language education has a fairly established sequence of at least two first-year, two second-year, and sometimes two third-year courses. In contrast, most SHL programs offer only one or two courses at various points in the students' undergraduate curriculum. There are three important questions for future research: (1) What is the minimum proficiency level required for entrance into an SHL course? (2) How many language courses do learners at different proficiency levels need to reach desired proficiency levels? (3) Where should these courses be placed in the undergraduate curriculum? Only after determining how much students can achieve in one semester of instruction and what are realistic ultimate learning outcomes for postsecondary SHL instruction can these questions be answered. In pursuit of a healthy research agenda in this area, it is crucial to examine students' perspectives and learning aspirations.

The area of evaluating programs and the effectiveness of instruction has not received sufficient attention from SHL researchers. Program evaluation—a powerful tool that has been applied to foreign language programs for more than two decades (Lynch 1996; Rea-Dickins and Germaine 1998)—requires systematic data collection in order to analyze the worth of particular instructional sequences. Program evaluation results would allow us to justify continuing or increasing SHL program funding and undertaking more curriculum improvement and professional development opportunities (see Rea-Dickins and Germaine 1998). Akst and Hecht (1980) propose that program evaluation examine five main curriculum areas: (1) the appropriateness of objectives, (2) the appropriateness of content in relation to program objectives, (3) the appropriateness of placement procedures, (4) the effectiveness of instruction, and (5) the efficiency of instruction. Program evaluation will allow us to answer important questions such as, What are the short- and long-term effects of SHL programs? How much can students achieve within the time frame of the current course sequence? What practices are most effective in SHL instruction? What impact does an SHL program have on students' attitudes toward and interest in learning about Spanish language and culture? What impact does the program have on students' language maintenance and development?

As Cumming (1987, 697) pointed out, "Program evaluations may document the actual interrelationships between program policy, rationale, instructional procedures, learning process and outcomes, curricular content, and a specific social milieu in a way that more theoretical research necessarily has to abstract itself away from." Thus, program evaluation is an invaluable tool with the potential to enhance not only professional teaching practices but also practitioners' and scholars' knowledge of how different aspects of instructional, administrative, and curricular activities relate to one another in practice. Effective instructional practices cannot be studied in isolation in laboratory conditions but only in the classroom, where individual and group dynamics and social factors come into play in student outcomes.

In the area of SHL teacher development, a number of issues beg for consideration in future research. Scholars must continue to examine what competencies and types of knowledge can be transferred from the foreign language classroom versus those that must be developed specifically for the SHL classroom. Aside from a few preliminary discussions (e.g., Beaudrie 2009b; Fairclough 2006; Potowski 2002; Potowski and Carreira 2004), these issues have received little attention. Most important, research needs to determine how those competencies are acquired and what should be the content of SHL teacher development programs in order to ensure the development of these competencies. For example, an issue specifically relevant to SHL teachers is linguistic prejudice. Language teachers frequently bring with them unconscious prejudices against nonstandard dialects that are particularly detrimental to SHL instruction (Lippi-Green 2004). Research needs to answer important questions, such as What are SHL teachers' attitudes toward linguistic variation? What types of training would be most beneficial in reducing these linguistic prejudices? What types of training would properly equip instructors to deal with language variation in their classrooms? Other competencies specific to SHL are HL acquisition and instructional approaches, sociolinguistic issues of language contact and bilingualism, critical dialect awareness, and biliteracy development.

Other important issues that deserve further investigation are the identification of the competencies and types of knowledge that teachers of Spanish as a foreign language need to teach mixed groups of heritage and foreign language learners, the relationship between teachers' backgrounds (e.g., country of origin, Spanish language proficiency, teaching experience) and their response to teacher development programs, and how the beliefs and attitudes that SHL teachers bring to the classroom affect instruction and learning outcomes. Considering that the success of an SHL program depends to a large extent on the SHL teacher, it is of utmost importance to undertake further research in this area.

CONCLUSION

The data on university-based SHL programs reviewed in this chapter provide evidence that SHL programs are no longer confined to those regions of the United States with large, long-established Spanish-speaking communities, such as Florida, Arizona, New Mexico, Texas, California, and major urban areas such as New York and Chicago (Ingold et al. 2002). SHL courses are now offered in twenty-six US states, as well as the District of Columbia. This represents a major success for advocates of SHL education, and those responsible for this expansion should be commended for having undertaken the creation of SHL programs under conditions that have often been challenging.

It is also clear that much research remains to be done to ensure that SHL learners across the nation benefit from high-quality instruction and sound curricular and programmatic practices. Both qualitative and quantitative research designs should be used to identify effective teaching practices and curricular and programmatic practices. Students' feedback, as highlighted in this chapter, can be a valuable tool for identifying program weaknesses and strengths and making sound programmatic and curricular decisions. Research has provided important insights into current practices in SHL education; however, it is critical for future research to focus more intensely on SHL program and classroom-related issues in order to continue advancing SHL education in this country.

NOTES

1. Beaudrie (2006) defines an SHL program as any instructional sequence designed to help heritage language learners acquire, develop, or maintain their heritage languages. At the university level, these courses may include learners who consider themselves native speakers of Spanish.

2. The Alliance for the Advancement of Heritage Languages is currently gathering data on the profile of existing heritage language programs in the United States; see www.cal.org/heritage/profiles/index.html.

3. Surveys were not sent out to universities in the US Southwest because Beaudrie (2011) had recently obtained comprehensive information on these programs. The nationwide survey is unpublished; the data are in possession of the author.

4. The data on Hispanic enrollment came from Peterson's (2009).

REFERENCES

Akst, Geoffrey, and Miriam Hecht. 1980. "Program Evaluation." In *Teaching Basic Skills in College*, edited by Alice Stewart Trillin. San Francisco: Jossey-Bass.

Anderson, Jim. 2008. "Towards an Integrated Second-Language Pedagogy for Foreign and Community/Heritage Languages in Multilingual Britain." *Language Learning Journal* 36 (1): 79–89.

Barnwell, David. 2008. "The Status of Spanish in the United States." *Language, Culture and Curriculum* 21 (3): 235–43.

Beaudrie, Sara. 2006. "Spanish Heritage Language Development: A Causal-Comparative Study the Differential Effect of Heritage Versus Foreign Language Curriculum." PhD diss., University of Arizona.

———. 2009a. "Receptive Bilinguals' Language Development in the Classroom: The Differential Effects of Heritage Versus Foreign Language Curriculum." In *Español en Estados Unidos y otros contextos de contacto: Sociolingüística, ideología y pedagogía*, edited by Manuel Lacorte and Jennifer Leeman. Madrid: Vervuert.

———. 2009b. "Teaching Heritage Language Learners and the Nativeness Issue." *ADFL Bulletin* 40 (3): 94–112.

———. 2011. "Spanish Heritage Language Programs: A Snapshot of Current Programs in the Southwestern United States." *Foreign Language Annals* 44 (2): 321–37.

Beaudrie, Sara, and Cynthia Ducar. 2005. "Beginning-Level University Heritage Programs: Creating a Space for All Heritage Language Learners." *Heritage Language Journal* 3 (1). Available at www.heritagelanguages.org.

Beaudrie, Sara, Cynthia Ducar, and Ana Relaño-Pastor. 2009. "Curricular Perspectives in the Heritage Language Context: Assessing Culture and Identity." *Language, Culture, and Curriculum* 22 (2): 157–74.

Bernal-Enríquez, Ysaura, and Eduardo Hernández-Chávez. 2003. "La enseñanza del español en Nuevo México: ¿Revitalización o erradicación de la variedad chicana?" In *Mi lengua: Spanish as a Heritage Language in the United States*, edited by Ana Roca and M. Cecilia Colombi. Washington, DC: Georgetown University Press.

Brown, James. 1995. *The Elements of Language Curriculum: A Systematic Approach to Program Development.* New York: Heinle and Heinle.

Carreira, Maria. 2004. "Seeking Explanatory Adequacy: A Dual Approach to Understanding the Term 'Heritage Language Learner." *Heritage Language Journal* 2 (1). Available at www.heritagelanguages.org.

———. 2007. "Teaching Spanish in the US: Beyond the One-Size-Fits-All Paradigm." In *Spanish in Contact: Policy, Social, and Linguistic Inquiries*, edited by Kim Potowski and Richard Cameron. Amsterdam: John Benjamins.

Colombi, M. Cecilia, and Francisco X. Alarcón, eds. 1997. *La enseñanza del español a hispanohablantes: Praxis y teoría.* Boston: Houghton Mifflin.

Cumming, Alister. 1987. "What Is Second-Language Program Evaluation?" *Canadian Modern Language Review* 43 (4): 678–700.

Ducar, Cynthia. 2008. "Student Voices: The Missing Link in the Spanish Heritage Language Debate." *Foreign Language Annals* 41 (3): 415–33.

Duff, Patricia A. 2008. "Heritage Language Education in Canada." In *Heritage Language: A New Field Emerging*, edited by Donna Brinton, Olga Kagan, and Susan Bauckus. New York: Routledge/Taylor and Francis.

Elder, Catherine. 2005. "Evaluating the Effectiveness of Heritage Language Education: What Role for Testing?" *International Journal of Bilingual Education and Bilingualism* 8 (2–3): 196–212.

———. 2009. "Reconciling Accountability and Development Needs in Heritage Language Education: A Communication Challenge for the Evaluation Consultant." *Language Teaching Research* 13 (1): 15–33.

Fairclough, Marta. 2006. "La enseñanza del español como lengua de herencia: Un curso de preparación para docentes." *Revista Iberoamericana de Lingüística* 1:31–50.

Felix, Angela. 2004. "The Adult Heritage Spanish Speaker in the Foreign Language Classroom." PhD diss., Capella University.

Hernández-Chávez, Eduardo. 1993. "Native Language Loss and Its Implications for Revitalization of Spanish in Chicano Communities." In *Language and Culture in Learning: Teaching Spanish to Native Speakers of Spanish*, edited by Barbara J. Merino, Enrique T. Trueba, and Fabián A. Samaniego. London: Falmer.

Ingold, Catherine W., William Rivers, Carmen Chavez Tesser, and Erica Ashby. 2002. "Report on the NFLC/AATSP Survey of Spanish Language Programs for Native Speakers." *Hispania* 85 (2): 324–29.

Kondo-Brown, Kimi. 2010. "Curriculum Development for Advancing Heritage Language Competence: Recent Research, Current Practices, and a Future Agenda." *Annual Review of Applied Linguistics* 30:24–41.

Kondo-Brown, Kimi, and James Brown. 2010. "Introduction." In *Teaching Chinese, Japanese, and Korean Heritage Language Students: Curriculum Needs, Materials, and Assessment*, edited by Kimi Kondo-Brown and James Brown. New York: Routledge.

Lippi-Green, Rosina. 2004. "Language Ideology and Language Prejudice." In *Language in the USA: Themes for the Twenty-First Century*, edited by Edward Finegan and John Rickford. Cambridge: Cambridge University Press.

Lynch, Brian. 1996. *Language Program Evaluation.* Cambridge: Cambridge University Press.

Martínez, Glenn. 2003. "Classroom-Based Dialect Awareness in Heritage Language Instruction: A Critical Applied Linguistic Approach." *Heritage Language Journal* 1 (1). Available at www.heritagelanguages.org/.

Nunan, David. 1988. *The Learner-Centred Curriculum.* Cambridge: Cambridge University Press.

Peterson's. 2009. *Four Year Colleges.* Lawrenceville, NJ: Peterson's.

Potowski, Kim. 2002. "Experiences of Spanish Heritage Speakers in University Foreign Language Courses and Implications for Teacher Training." *ADFL Bulletin* 33 (3): 35–42.

———. 2005. *Fundamentos de la enseñanza del español a los hablantes nativos en los Estados Unidos* (Foundations in teaching Spanish to native speakers in the United States). Madrid: Arco/Libros.

Potowski, Kim, and Maria Carreira. 2004. "Towards Teacher Development and National Standards for Spanish as a Heritage Language." *Foreign Language Annals* 37 (3):421–31.

Rea-Dickins, Pauline, and Kevin P. Germaine. 1998. "The Price of Everything and Value of Nothing: Trends in Language Program Evaluation." In *Managing Evaluation and Innovation in Language Teaching: Building Bridges*, edited by Pauline Rea-Dickens and Kevin P. Germaine. London: Longman.

Roca, Ana, and M. Cecilia Colombi, eds. 2003. *Mi lengua: Spanish as a Heritage Language in the United States.* Washington, DC: Georgetown University Press.

Romero, Migdalia. 2000. "Instructional Practice in Heritage Language Classrooms." In *Teaching Heritage Learners: Voices from the Classroom*, edited by John Webb and Barbara Miller. New York: American Council on the Teaching of Foreign Languages.

Schwarzer, David, and Maria Petrón. 2005. "Heritage Language Instruction at the College Level: Reality and Possibilities." *Foreign Language Annals* 38 (4): 568–78.

Trujillo, Juan Antonio. 2009. "*Con Todos*: Using Learning Communities to Promote Intellectual and Social Engagement in the Spanish Curriculum." In *Español en Estados Unidos y otros contextos de contacto: Sociolingüística, ideología y pedagogía*, edited by Manuel Lacorte and Jennifer Leeman. Madrid: Vervuert.

US Census Bureau. 2001. *The Hispanic Population: Census 2000 Brief.* Washington, DC: US Government Printing Office.

Valdés, Guadalupe. 1995. "The Teaching of Minority Students as Academic Subjects: Pedagogical and Theoretical Challenges." *Modern Language Journal* 79 (3): 299–328.

———. 1997. "The Teaching of Spanish to Bilingual Spanish-Speaking Students: Outstanding Issues and Unanswered Questions." In *La enseñanza del español a hispanohablantes: Praxis y teoría*, edited by M. Cecilia Colombi and Francisco X. Alarcón. Boston: Houghton Mifflin.

———. 2001. "Heritage Language Students: Profiles and Possibilities." In *Heritage Languages in America: Preserving a National Resource*, edited by Joy Kreeft Peyton, Donald A. Ranard, and Scott McGinnis. McHenry, IL: Delta Systems.

————. 2005. "Bilingualism, Heritage Language Learners, and SLA Research: Opportunities Lost or Seized?" *Modern Language Journal* 89 (3): 410–26.

Valdés, Guadalupe, Joshua A. Fishman, Rebecca Chávez, and William Pérez. 2006. *Developing Minority Language Resources: The Case of Spanish in California*. Buffalo: Multilingual Matters.

Valdés, Guadalupe, Anthony G. Lozano, and Rodolfo Garcia-Moya. 1981. *Teaching Spanish to the Hispanic Bilingual: Issues, Aims, and Methods*. New York: Teachers College Press.

Valdés-Fallis, Guadalupe. 1977. "Spanish Language Programs for Hispanic Minorities: Current Needs and Priorities." In *Minority Language and Literature*, edited by Dexter Fisher. New York: Modern Language Association.

Villa, Daniel J. 1996. "Choosing a 'Standard' Variety of Spanish for the Instruction of Native Spanish Speakers in the US." *Foreign Language Annals* 29 (2):191–200.

Webb, John, and Barbara Miller, eds. 2000. *Teaching Heritage Learners: Voices from the Classroom*. New York: American Council on the Teaching of Foreign Languages.

Wherritt, Irene, and T. Anne Cleary. 1990. "A National Survey of Spanish Language Testing for Placement or Outcome Assessment at BA-Granting Institutions in the United States." *Foreign Language Annals* 22 (2): 157–65.

CHAPTER 11

Meeting the Needs of Heritage Language Learners

APPROACHES, STRATEGIES, AND RESEARCH

Maria M. Carreira, California State University, Long Beach; and National Heritage Language Resource Center, University of California, Los Angeles

T HIS CHAPTER DEALS with instructional issues surrounding Spanish as a heritage language (SHL). It has three overarching goals: (1) to summarize and evaluate historical developments in SHL teaching, (2) to provide a blueprint of best practices, and (3) to identify areas in need of further development. Within this framework, I focus on learner profiles, classroom strategies that support differentiation, and professional development. Other issues of importance to practitioners are also addressed—notably, socioaffective issues, the grammatical competence of SHL learners, and curriculum and program development. However, because these issues are discussed in depth elsewhere in this book, the present discussion limits itself to instructional implications and directs readers to the corresponding chapters for more information. Placement, a critical issue in SHL teaching, is briefly discussed with reference to learner diversity. For an in-depth analysis of this issue, readers should consult chapter 13 in this book.

HISTORICAL OVERVIEW

The first official recognition of the field of SHL teaching dates back to 1972, when the American Association of Teachers of Spanish and Portuguese (AATSP) issued a statement in support of specialized Spanish classes for bilingual Latinos to develop literacy and reinforce other areas of the curriculum at all levels of instruction. The actual teaching of SHL, however, long predates such recognition, with instruction stretching as far back as the 1930s (Valdés-Fallis 1978).

With a prescriptive orientation, early approaches to teaching SHL came under attack in the 1970s and 1980s for contributing to students' linguistic insecurities and for failing to develop general proficiency. These approaches gave way to the Comprehensive Approach, which focused on giving students "the opportunity to grow in their mother tongue, the opportunity to use it in meaningful communication and creative expression" (Valdés, Lozano, and García-Moya 1981, 14).

A seminal volume in 1981 edited by Guadalupe Valdés, Anthony Lozano, and Rodolfo García-Moya laid out research and pedagogical priorities under the Comprehensive Approach. Many of the recommendations made in this volume remain remarkably vital—for example, that the needs of SHL learners are best addressed in specialized HL courses, that instruction should be linguistically and culturally responsive to the needs and goals of US Latinos, that teachers should have solid preparation in reading and writing, and that SHL teaching should contribute to the maintenance of Spanish in the United States. Valdés (1995, 1997) also proposed three other goals for SHL teaching—the acquisition of a prestige variety of Spanish, the transfer of literacy skills from English to Spanish, and the expansion of the bilingual range.

Over the years, SHL textbooks and other teaching resources have evolved according to developments in the profession and in society at large. In keeping with a normative perspective, early textbooks and other materials made widespread use of labels such as "*arcaísmos,*" "*barbarismos,*" and "*anglicismos,*" and they focused on eradicating nonstandard linguistic features. In the wake of the civil rights movement and in keeping with the priorities of the Comprehensive Approach, textbooks in the 1970s and 1980s explored issues of access, inclusion, and social justice as they sought to help Latino students explore their identity vis-à-vis local communities of Spanish speakers. Starting in the 1990s, with the rise of globalization and the expansion of the US Latino market, textbooks tended to construct standard Spanish as a commodity for economic competitiveness in the global market (see chapter 4 in this book).

SOCIOAFFECTIVE NEEDS OF SHL LEARNERS

Problematizing the commodification of Spanish in the HL curriculum, Leeman and Martínez (2007) argue that it leads to a decoupling of Spanish from Latino identity and from local communities of Spanish speakers (see also Hidalgo 1997; Potowski 2005; Villa 1996). Villa (2002) cautions that classroom practices that single out US Spanish as inferior or less adequate than monolingual varieties are pedagogically counterproductive because they foment insecurities among learners. He observes that US Latinos face "double jeopardy" for their use of Spanish, which is criticized on the one hand by those who would eradicate Spanish from the United States, and on the other by some Spanish speakers who deem them to be imperfect speakers of this language (Schreffler 2007).

A well-developed body of literature documents the negative impact on US Latinos of these and other societal attitudes. These include language shyness (Krashen 1998), arrested linguistic and academic development (García 2001; MacGregor-Mendoza 2000; Valenzuela 1999), and the internalization of negative linguistic stereotypes and ideologies (Potowski 2002; Valdés et al. 2003). These studies underscore the importance of attending to affective factors in SHL classes and preparing students to deal with linguistic and cultural prejudice. To this end, proponents of the Critical Approach advocate teaching about the functions, distribution, and evaluation of dialects and raising awareness of language, power, and social inclusion (Fairclough 2005; Leeman 2005; Martínez 2003; Webb and Miller 2000).

The research literature identifies various activities and strategies that support these and other priorities. For example, sociolinguistic surveys train students to apply the methods of linguistic data collection to explore language variation in the United States and the Spanish-speaking world (Pino 1997; Rodriguez-Pino 1994). Linguistic autobiographies help students reflect on their use of language at different points in their life and in different domains. In the process of writing their autobiographies, students explore a range of topics, including identity, societal attitudes toward Spanish and US Latinos, and the factors behind language maintenance and shift (Aparicio 1997; Velez-Rendon 2005).

Ethnographic interviews form the basis of a model curriculum developed by the National Heritage Language Resource Center (NHLRC) at the University of California, Los Angeles. Building on a protocol developed by Roca and Alonso (2006), students interview an elderly member of their community and, using the methods of ethnographic research, they explore a variety of topics about US Latinos and Spanish. The information collected is applied to progressively more demanding writing assignments that start with a transcribed oral history, which is followed by a written interview, a short story, and finally, an academic essay. Students study the properties of each of theses genres and read two or more representative pieces that are topically related to their assignment. Because all assignments have common themes, the vocabulary, grammatical structures, and concepts mastered in one assignment are recycled and put to use in more demanding tasks.[1]

RESEARCH ON GRAMMATICAL COMPETENCE AND TEACHING IMPLICATIONS

Research on SHL learners' grammatical competence points to areas in need of particular instructional attention by virtue of their susceptibility to attrition and/

or incomplete acquisition. These include subject pronouns, gender, the "a personal," copulas, articles, tense/aspect, and mood (see chapter 5 in this book). As a general rule, the earlier an HL learner acquires the dominant language (i.e., English), the more his or her HL grammar will deviate from that of native speakers. Illustrating this, Montrul (2002) found that Spanish-speaking children who learned English before the age of seven had gaps in their knowledge of tense/ aspect, but those who learned Spanish first and English between the ages of eight and twelve performed largely like monolingual speakers of Spanish with respect to this area of grammar (Montrul and Potowski 2007). Thus, insofar as the age of the acquisition of English is an indicator of grammatical competence, it should be taken into consideration for purposes of placement and curriculum design.

Focusing on differences between HL and L2 learners, Montrul, Foote, and Perpiñán (2008) found that L2 and SHL learners both have gaps in their knowledge of gender and make similar types of mistakes. However, they differ with regard to where they make their mistakes: For L2 learners, it is in the oral domain; for HL learners, it is in the written domain. The authors conclude that form-focused instruction is warranted for both types of learners, but for L2 learners the focus should be on increasing accuracy in the oral domain, whereas for HL learners it should be on the written domain. Bowles (2011) and Montrul (2011) found that heritage speakers do better in tasks that tap into implicit knowledge and attribute this to their having learned Spanish in a naturalistic setting. Conversely, L2 learners do better with tasks that tap into metalinguistic knowledge, by virtue of having acquired their L2 in a school setting. Classroom-based research indicates that HL learners benefit from explicit instruction, including negative evidence (Montrul and Bowles 2010), and derive benefit from traditional and input-processing instruction (though not to the same extent as L2 learners) (Potowski, Jegerski, and Morgan-Short 2009).

Fairclough (2005) points out that HL learning is not just about filling in grammatical knowledge; it is also about mastering a second variant—a dialect or register. As a lengthy and complex process, the acquisition of a second variant is mediated by "language distance," a principle that holds that when two systems are very similar, it is more difficult to keep them apart and the tendency is to merge them. Although form-focused instruction appears to be an effective approach for addressing grammatical gaps, it is not as effective for teaching a second variant. For this purpose, Fairclough proposes first validating students' dialect and then calling attention to the relevant differences between the learner's dialect and the target dialect.

FROM RESEARCH TO REALITY: MIXED CLASSES

The previous discussion underscores the need for specialized courses for HL learners. Despite this, the reality is that many Spanish programs do not have such courses. Indeed, as Sara Beaudrie explains in chapter 10 above, 60 percent of college-level programs do not. In general, schools and geographical areas with large Latino populations are more likely to offer such classes. However, this is not always the case. With a student population that is 30 percent Latino (amounting to approximately 750,000 students), California's 100-plus community colleges educate large numbers of Latinos, notably more than the states' two other systems, the California State University (24 percent Latino) and the University of California (14 percent Latino). Despite this, preliminary results from an ongoing survey by the NHLRC indicate that a third of California community colleges that offer associate degrees in Spanish do not have specialized SHL courses in their curriculum or, if they have them, do not offer them on a regular basis. Respondents' commonly cited reasons for this state of affairs include insufficient funding and a lack of qualified instructors (Carreira 2011).

Whether they offer specialized SHL courses, all Spanish programs with HL learners have to contend with mixed classes (i.e., classes that enroll both SHL and L2 learners). For programs without an HL track, all classes with HL and L2 learners are mixed classes. Conversely, for programs with such a track, all non-HL classes (e.g., literature, linguistics) will be mixed. As Valdés (1997, 12) points out, often the expectation for SHL learners in such courses is that they will "pass undetected as 'real' Spanish majors." The consequences of this expectation and, more generally, the experiences of HL learners in content courses and advanced non-SHL language courses are vitally important topics that remain underresearched (see Valdés et al. 2003).

A recent study by Melissa Bowles (2011) underscores the importance of addressing the needs of HL learners in mixed classes. In one experiment, HL and L2 learners worked on an aural information gap. The learners asked each other questions to uncover differences between their pictures of a kitchen. In a follow-up experiment, HL and L2 learners engaged in a similar task, except that the pictures used more general vocabulary. In addition, they collaborated on two written tasks, a crossword puzzle and a collaborative writing task. Despite their many similarities, the experiments yielded tellingly different results. In the first experiment the L2 learners benefited more from their interactions with HL learners than the reverse. The reason for this, according to Bowles, lies in the task itself, which, being aural and involving home vocabulary, had much to teach the L2 learners but little to teach the HL learners.

In the second experiment, both learners benefited equally from their interactions because the tasks addressed areas of needs for each type of learner and tapped into their complementary knowledge and skills. In particular, the HL learners benefited from the L2 learners' knowledge of orthography and accentuation, whereas the L2 learners benefited from HL learners' intuitive knowledge of Spanish. In all, this discussion underscores the importance of developing materials, curricula, and instructional strategies for use in mixed classes.

LEARNER DIVERSITY

SHL learners present a wide range of linguistic needs and abilities, which makes it difficult for instructors to both understand and manage learner differences (Carreira 2003; Valdés 1995, 1997, 2001). Recent research has identified a number of pedagogically significant learner variables. Those that bear on grammatical competency include generational status in the United States, amount and type of exposure to Spanish, and the age of the onset of bilingualism (see also chapter 5 in this book). Other significant variables include (1) motivation (i.e., students' reasons for studying the HL), (2) academic preparedness (students' level of preparedness to engage in language study), (3) cultural connectedness (students' involvement with the HL culture), (4) emotional factors (students' view of themselves in the context of the classroom), and (5) societal factors (students' place in the HL community and larger society) (Webb and Miller 2000).

To examine these factors, the NHLRC recently completed the largest and most comprehensive study of HL learner profiles. The study queried 1,700 college-level HL learners across twenty-two different languages and geographic regions in the United States, including 400 SHL learners. This section summarizes the survey's main findings and implications for SHL teaching.[2]

The Onset of Bilingualism and Language Use at Home

A large majority (78.4 percent) of SHL learners who participated in the NHLRC's survey spoke only Spanish before the age of five years and learned English at about the time they started school. Surprisingly, this is true even though the overwhelming majority are United States–born (75.3 percent). These background factors—that is, speaking only Spanish at home and learning Spanish before English—have been shown to correlate with having a more complete grammatical system in Spanish (Mueller Gathercole 2002; Montrul 2008; Silva-Corvalán 2003; also see chapter 5 in this book).

Input

Besides speaking Spanish at home, nearly all respondents watch television in Spanish (95 percent) and listen to Spanish language music (93.7 percent) and radio (87.3 percent) on a regular basis. Also, a sizable majority (62 percent) visit their country of origin every year or visited this country three to five times during their childhood. These high levels of exposure may explain SHL learners' high proficiency ratings. Most rate their aural skills in the range of advanced to native (99.2 percent for listening and 66 percent for speaking). Conversely, very few rate their aural skills in the low range (0.5 percent for listening and 4.6 percent for speaking).

Literacy and Schooling

The SHL learners who participated in this survey are relatively unschooled in Spanish; 45 percent of respondents did not study Spanish in elementary school, either in the United States or abroad. Despite this, 95 percent rate their reading skills in the intermediate to native-like range, and 86.5 percent rate their writing skills in this range. This is likely due to a combination of two factors: (1) that Spanish, being highly phonetic, is relatively easy to read and write; and (2) that literacy is taught in the home environment (50 percent of respondents learned to read in Spanish before English). Respondents' low levels of schooling may signal deficiencies in specific areas of the grammar, particularly, mood and complex structures. Montrul and Perpiñán (2001) posit that HL learners who lack the type of access to the written registers provided in school may not get the necessary input to fully master these areas of the grammar.

Attitudes, Motivation, and Identity

Survey participants hold overwhelmingly positive linguistic attitudes. They are far more likely to agree with positive characterizations of Spanish than with negative ones, and when asked to relate an experience in school, home, or neighborhood involving this language, many offered examples of when knowing Spanish made it possible to connect better with other Latinos or proved to be of practical value.

A significant majority (71.1 percent) cited career goals as their main reason for studying Spanish. Communicating better with family and friends in the United States and learning about their background were also important. These findings bear on a point made above about instruction: whether SHL teaching should focus on connecting students to their community of residence through their home language, or whether it should promote a standard variant with professional currency in the global economy. These results indicate that attention should be given to both goals (see chapter 8 in this book).

Regarding identity, the majority (51 percent) of SHL learners use a "hyphenated" term to describe themselves, most commonly Mexican American, Hispanic American, and American Latino. In a distant second place, 17 percent of SHL learners identify exclusively by their country of origin (e.g. Mexican, Cuban); 9 percent identify as Hispanic; 6 percent as Latino; 5 percent as American; 4.7 percent as Chicano; 3 percent as Latin, and Central or South American; and 2.3 percent as "other." These labels attest to the range of identities embraced by Latino students (see chapter 9 in this book).

In sum, survey respondents have high levels of exposure to Spanish, high (self-reported) proficiency levels in the aural and written modalities, positive linguistic attitudes, and ambitious goals for their HL. Although this general profile proves valuable for curriculum design, it is important to understand that all curricula must respond first and foremost to the needs of local populations of learners. In addition, because in any given class some students will deviate from the norm, curricula should provide multiple pathways for students to meet instructional goals.

Low Proficiency and Non-Spanish-Speaking Latinos

The near absence of low-proficiency respondents from the survey suggests that these students do not enroll in SHL classes and raises the question of what happens to them in Spanish departments. According to Beaudrie (2009), most universities and colleges with HL courses do not have courses for receptive bilinguals (i.e., individuals with fairly well-developed receptive abilities but low productive abilities). Reynolds, Howard, and Deák (2009) found that these students are often mistakenly placed in beginning- or intermediate-level L2 classes. Beaudrie (2009) argues that this situation hurts SHL learners by keeping them from developing their full linguistic potential and, in some cases, exacerbating their linguistic insecurities (see also Beaudrie and Ducar 2005).

Also missing from the survey are Latinos who lack functional abilities in Spanish. Though these students are generally assumed to be linguistically indistinguishable from L2 learners, research indicates that these may actually have more target-like phonology than L2 learners (Au et al. 2002; Oh and Au 2005). Many of them also fit what Kagan and Polinsky (2008) refer to as a "broad definition" of the term "heritage language learner." Contrasting with narrow definitions, which require some degree of competency in the HL, broad definitions are premised on the existence of familial ties and cultural connections. This is exemplified by Hornberger and Wang's (2008, 27) definition of HL learners as "individuals who have familial or ancestral ties to a particular language that is not English and who exert their agency in determining whether or not they are HLLs (heritage language learners) of that HL (heritage language) and HC (heritage community)." Broad definitions highlight a defining characteristic of all HL learners: They have a personal stake in their study of their HL and their HC by virtue of their identity needs. This is true of all HL learners, irrespective of their linguistic profile.

From this, it follows that low-proficiency and broadly defined SHL learners are best taught in specialized classes where their identity needs can be properly addressed and their linguistic potential can be exploited to maximize learning. Where that is not possible, Carreira (2004) proposes enrolling them in L2 classes and infusing these classes with a "heritage focus." This entails adopting a curriculum that addresses students' identity needs and that taps into their' cultural and linguistic expertise. This may involve, for example, adopting a curriculum that explores the US Latino experience, including issues such as language shift, linguistic prejudice, acculturation, and assimilation. At the other end of the proficiency scale, highly proficiency SHL speakers are also in need of attention, particularly as concerns the development of advanced literacy skills in Spanish that mirror those developed in English (see chapter 12 in this book).

DEALING WITH LEARNERS' DIVERSITY: DIFFERENTIATED TEACHING

With uniform learning objectives, activities, pacing, and assessment tools for all students, foreign language teaching is not well equipped to meet the challenges of learners' diversity. To address these challenges, there must be a paradigmatic change in teaching from a one-size-fits-all approach to a learner-centered/differentiated approach. Differentiated teaching is predicated on the notion that teaching should be responsive to student differences and reach out to learners at their own level of readiness (Tomlinson 1999, 2003). This approach falls under the umbrella of "teaching in multilevel classrooms," a term that covers many different teaching situations, all of which involve learners that differ from each other in pedagogically significant ways (for an overview of this topic, see Berry and Williams 1992; Hess 2001). Many of the concepts and practices of differentiated teaching are actually familiar to foreign language teachers in one form or another, including, for example, portfolios, journals, group work, and independent studies. Still others are easily modifiable for use in language classrooms. By way of introduction, I briefly discuss three tools—agendas, centers, and exit cards. A more extended treatment of differentiated teaching in SHL classes is given by Carreira (2007b) (for general introductions to differentiated teaching, see Tomlinson 1999, 2003).

Agendas—lists of tasks that students must complete in a specified period of time—allow for variable pacing and support self-directed learning and effective classroom management. Typically, agenda items are assignments for the entire week, which students can complete at their own pace and in any order they choose. In mixed classes, agendas make it possible for HL and L2 learners to focus on different aspects of an instructional point, as needed to meet learning standards. Students can engage in agenda work at home or during a designated class time—for example, during the last fifteen minutes of class or when they have finished other work. Having a designated agenda time in class has the advantage that it frees up the instructor to meet with students who need extra help.

Centers are repositories of resources such as extra exercises, reference tools, reading materials, practice tests, and sample writing assignments. Centers make it possible to vary the process whereby students gain mastery of the material—thus differentiating instruction. In mixed classrooms, centers contain materials that help HL and L2 learners with their particular needs. For example, when studying the verb *haber*, HL learners can find practice exercises that focus on spelling, whereas L2 learners can get practice conjugating this verb. In SHL courses, centers allow advanced learners to work independently on their agenda or projects, while the instructor meets with other learners. Centers can have a physical location, as in a corner of a classroom, or they can occupy a virtual space, for example, in an electronic course management system like Blackboard.

Exit cards are very short tasks that students must complete at the end of class and turn in on their way out. Examples of exit card tasks include describing an "Aha!" moment, identifying a point that remains unclear, or responding to an issue raised in class. Exit cards give learners the opportunity to communicate directly, immediately, and discretely with instructors, and they offer a fair way for instructors to assign an attendance and participation grade. Most important, exit cards can give essential feedback during the course of instruction to help both teachers and students reflect on the learning process and adjust their efforts as needed.

This type of feedback, known as "formative assessment," is a key component of differentiated teaching. To maximize its effectiveness, formative assessment should occur regularly throughout the instructional process and, in its purest form, should not be graded, other than with a check mark (Kellough, Kellough, and Kim 1999). In L2 and SHL classes, most assessment is summative; that is, it comes at the end of an instructional unit and serves to evaluate learning and assign a grade. Diagnostic assessment, which evaluates learners before the start of instruction, plays a critically important role in SHL teaching, primarily in the way of placement testing (see chapter 13 in this book). This kind of assessment, however, can and should do more than direct students to the right class. The information gathered from placement tests should inform syllabus design each semester, so that the goals and objectives of SHL courses are fine-tuned to particular student populations. In sum, a three-pronged approach—(1) offering classes that are responsive to different types of SHL learners, (2) designing placement tests that can direct students to such classes, and (3) applying the methods and strategies of differentiated teaching—constitutes the best approach to fully addressing the problem of learner diversity in SHL classes and mixed classes.

PROFESSIONAL DEVELOPMENT

Teacher training is a long-standing concern in the field of SHL. A review of the literature evidences both continuity and innovation in the proposals put forward over the years. In one of the earliest treatments of this topic, Melton (1997, 44) proposes that SHL teachers should have a basic understanding of language learning as both an individual and social act, and he outlines the following areas of knowledge for SHL teachers: (1) how one becomes bilingual; (2) the role of language in bilingual homes, schools, and communities; (3) the differences between the local and standard varieties; (4) the role of registers and language domains in teaching methodology; (5) the nature of code-switching; and (6) the significance of language maintenance. García-Moya (1981), another pioneer in the area of professional development, makes the case for training in dialectology, with a special emphasis on US varieties, SHL learner profiles (competencies, needs, motivations, etc.), the cultures and histories of US Latinos, and philosophies and theories of SHL teaching.

More recent proposals incorporate these components and offer additional ones. The AATSP volume *Spanish for Native Speakers* (2000, 88) proposes that SHL teachers should meet the requirements expected of all Spanish teachers, including a minimum of advanced language proficiency. In addition, it proposes training in areas outside the scope of foreign language methodology courses, such as pedagogical principles in language expansion and enrichment, language variation, the sociolinguistics of Spanish in the world and the United States, and theories of bilingualism. Webb and Miller (2000) support these competencies and add that HL teachers need to (1) understand the social and affective issues that go along with different levels of HL knowledge, (2) be aware of students' attitudes toward HL learning; (3) incorporate students' voices into instruction, and (4) function as advocates for HL learners and instruction. In addition, noting similarities between HL classes and English language arts classes, they suggest that HL teachers study the standards and practices that apply to language arts classes. This builds on the proposal by Valdés (1981) that SHL teaching, like language arts teaching, should focus on developing students' listening, speaking, reading, and writing skills and their ability to use Spanish effectively for both vocational and practical purposes.

Potowski and Carreira (2004) identify gaps in the National Foreign Language Standards as they apply to HL learners and argue that the standards put forth by the National Council of English Teachers align well with the needs of SHL learners, including not only those identified in the SHL research literature but also others, such as the need to deal with the impact of poverty, ethnic and cultural discrimination, family illiteracy, and sociopolitical disenfranchisement. To deal with learners' diversity, they call for training on placement testing, differentiated teaching, and action research (i.e., research conducted by teachers in their own classroom to solve particular problems they face (Burton 1998; Crookes 1993; Wallace 1998).

Focusing on the secondary level, Carreira (2007a) argues for expanding the role of SHL teaching to encompass one of the most critical issues facing the American educational system: the Latino academic gap. She notes that SHL teachers are uniquely positioned to bring about school conditions that are conducive to the success of Latino students, including a sense of shared trust and respect between Latino parents, teachers, and school staff; supportive relations between adults in school and Latino students; open communications between Latino children and parents; an institutional appreciation and understanding of home cultures, and the like. Accordingly, teacher training programs in Spanish should address the factors underlying the Latino academic gap and train teachers on strategies and activities that support the larger academic success of Latino students (García 2001; Pachon, Tornatzky, and Torres 2003).

Carreira and Kagan (2011) propose training teachers on the principles and practices of community-based instruction. This type of instruction, which is mainly understood as an approach to working with children with learning disabilities, can nevertheless help instructors design curricula that connect learners with local HL communities and teach skills that lead to their independent functioning within their HL community (Beakley, Yoder, and West 2003). Given the diversity of HL student profiles and the pervasiveness of mixed classes, they also prioritize training in differentiated teaching and action research.

Fairclough (2006) offers an in-depth look at a methodology course for SHL teachers taught at the University of Houston. The course's theoretical component focuses on the sociolinguistics of US Spanish, language ideology, and pedagogical theories, and many of the works cited in this chapter are on the reading list. Its practical component focuses on implementation issues such as content selection and the use of strategies and practices. The course also requires completion of a research project that involves interviewing and collecting writing samples from a US Spanish speaker, analyzing his or her language, and issuing pedagogical recommendations.

Potowski (2003) describes a model of in-service teacher training that targets the competencies identified in the AATSP volume *Spanish for Native Speakers* (2000). The program consists of (1) three graduate courses on teaching literature and culture, sociolinguistics, and SHL methods; (2) workshops on SHL topics; (3) classroom visits; and (4) various resources such as an SHL materials center, a newsletter, and assistance writing grants and conference proposals (see Potowski 2002 for a description of an orientation session for training teaching assistants; and see Webb and Miller (2000) for a non-language-specific HL methods course).

To date, SHL teachers and student teachers have only one textbook written expressly for them: Kim Potowski's *Fundamentos de la enseñanza del español a hispanohablantes en los EE.UU* (2005). There is also a non-language-specific online course for self-study by HL teachers created by the NHLRC (http://startalk.nhlrc.ucla.edu).

LIMITATIONS OF EXISTING RESEARCH AND CURRENT PRACTICES

In the eighty years since its inception, SHL teaching has made enormous strides. Yet there is still much work to be done. Notably, there is a pressing need for courses and materials for receptive bilinguals and Latinos who fit only the broad definition of the term "HL learner." The treatment of SHL learners in upper-division and graduate courses also merits attention. Recent, impressive advances in the area of HL learners' grammatical competence should be made accessible to nonlinguists who teach SHL and should be explicitly connected to the realities of the classroom through collaborations by researchers and practitioners. More classroom-based studies—such as those by Bowles (2011) and Potowski, Jegerski, and Morgan-Short (2009)—and longitudinal studies to evaluate different teaching methods and materials are also needed.

In the area of professional development, it is important to address the needs of practicing teachers. Online courses and summer workshops offered by a nationally recognized organization such as the NHLRC, the AATSP, the American Council on the Teaching of Foreign Languages, and the Center for Applied Linguistics would be very useful in this regard. An essay along the lines of Fillmore and Snow's (2000) *What Teachers Need to Know about Language* could also help meet the needs of practitioners. For program coordinators and program chairs, it would be useful to develop a database of model syllabi and activities for different instructional settings (e.g., specialized SHL classes, mixed L2 courses, content courses). These and other efforts in the area of professional development must be accompanied by a commitment on the part of teacher training programs to offer specialized courses on SHL pedagogy.

Finally, with 60 percent of programs lacking SHL courses, increasing the availability of such courses is a priority of the highest order. Where such courses are out of the realm of possibility, it is crucial to develop guidelines, methods, and materials for use in mixed classes so as to ensure that the needs of SHL learners are met.

CONCLUSION

Distilling good HL teaching to its essence: It is all about the learner. As this discussion has demonstrated, whether in specialized SHL classes or in mixed classes, effective HL teaching hinges on knowing the learner—his or her life experiences, level of academic preparedness, linguistic abilities, affective needs, and goals—and attending to all these factors with effective instructional tools and curricula.

NOTES

1. The curriculum can be found at http://nhlrc.ucla.edu/resources/index.asp.

2. A complete report on this study can be found at the website of the National Heritage Language Resource Center, www.international.ucla.edu/languages/nhlrc; also see Carreira and Kagan 2011. Two limitations of the study should be borne in mind: (1) Respondents were all drawn from language classes, and as such they are not representative

of all bilingual Latinos; and (2) the majority of respondents were from California, and as such they may not be representative of Spanish speakers in other geographical areas.

REFERENCES

AATSP (American Association of Teachers of Spanish and Portuguese). 2000. *Spanish for Native Speakers: AATSP Professional Development Series Handbook for Teachers K–12—A Handbook for Teachers*, vol. 1. Fort Worth: Harcourt College.

Aparicio, Frances. 1997. "La enseñanza del español para hispanohablantes y la pedagogía multicultural." In *La enseñanza del español a hispanohablantes: Praxis y teoría*, edited by Cecilia Colombi and Francisco X. Alarcón. Boston: Houghton Mifflin.

Au, Terry Kit-Fong, Leah Knightly, Sun-Ah Jun, and Janet Oh. 2002. "Overhearing a Language during Childhood." *Psychological Science* 13:238–43.

Beakley, Barbara, A., Sandy L. Yoder, and Linda L. West. 2003. *Community-Based Instruction: A Guidebook for Teachers*. Arlington, VA: Council for Exceptional Children.

Beaudrie, Sara. 2009. "Receptive Bilinguals' Language Development in the Classroom: The Differential Effects of Heritage Versus Foreign Language Curriculum." In *Español en Estados Unidos y otros contextos de contacto: Sociolingüística, ideología y pedagogía*, edited by Manel Lacorte and Jennifer Leeman. Madrid: Iberoamericana/Vervuert.

Beaudrie, Sara, and Cynthia Ducar. 2005. "Beginning Level University Heritage Programs: Creating a Space for All Heritage Language Learners." *Heritage Language Journal* 3. Available at www.heritagelanguages.org.

Berry, Eve, and Molly S. Williams. 1992. *Multilevel ESL Curriculum Guide*. Salem: Oregon State Department of Education.

Bowles, Melissa. 2011. "Exploring the Role of Modality: Second Language–Heritage Learner Interactions in the Spanish Language Classroom." *Heritage Language Journal* 8 (1). Available at www.heritagelanguages.org.

Burton, Jill. 1998. "A Cross-Case Analysis of Teacher Involvement in TESOL Research." *TESOL Quarterly* 32 (3): 419–46.

Carreira, Maria. 2003. "Profiles of SNS Students in the 21st Century: Pedagogical Implications of the Changing Demographics and Social Status of US Hispanics." In *Mi lengua: Spanish as a Heritage Language in the United States, Research and Practice*, edited by Ana Roca and Cecilia Colombi. Washington, DC: Georgetown University Press.

———. 2004. "Seeking Explanatory Adequacy: A Dual Approach to Understanding the Term Heritage Language Learner." *Heritage Language Journal* 2. Available at www.heritagelanguages.org.

———. 2007a. "Spanish for Native Speakers Matters: Narrowing the Latino Academic Gap through Spanish Language Instruction." *Heritage Language Journal* 5 (1). Available at www.heritagelanguages.org.

———. 2007b. "Teaching Spanish to Native Speakers in Mixed Ability Language Classrooms." In *Spanish in Contact: Policy, Social and Linguistic Inquiries*, edited by Kimberly Potowski and Richard Cameron. Washington, DC: Georgetown University Press.

———. 2011. "Heritage Language Teaching: Opportunities and Challenges for Community Colleges." Paper presented at the 126th Annual MLA Convention, Los Angeles, January 7.

Carreira, Maria, and Olga Kagan. 2011. "The Results of the National Heritage Language Survey: Implications for Teaching, Curriculum Design, and Professional Development." *Foreign Language Annals* 44 (1): 40–64.

Crookes, Graham. 1993. "Action Research for Second Language Teachers: Going Beyond Teacher Research." *Applied Linguistics* 14 (2): 130–44.

Fairclough, Marta. 2005. *Spanish and Heritage Language Education in the United States. Struggling with Hypotheticals.* Madrid: Iberoamericana.

———. 2006. "La enseñanza del español como lengua de herencia: Un curso de preparación para docentes." *Revista Iberoamericana de Lingüística* 1:31–50.

Fillmore, Lily Wong, and Catherine Snow. 2000. *What Teachers Need to Know about Language.* Special Report. Washington, DC: ERIC Clearinghouse on Languages and Linguistics. www.eric.ed.gov/ERICWebPortal/contentdelivery/servlet/ERICServlet?accno =ED44 4379.

García, Eugene. 2001. *Hispanic Education in the United States: Raíces y alas.* Lanham, MD: Rowman & Littlefield.

García-Moya, Rodolfo. 1981. "Teaching Spanish to Spanish Speakers: Some Considerations for the Preparation of Teachers." In *Teaching Spanish to the Hispanic Bilingual: Issues, Aims, and Methods,* edited by Guadalupe Valdés, Anthony Lozano, and Rodolfo García-Moya. New York: Teachers College Press.

Hess, Natalie. 2001. *Teaching Large Multilevel Classes.* New York: Cambridge University Press.

Hidalgo, Margarita. 1997. "Criterios normativos e ideología lingüística: Aceptación y rechazo del español de los Estados Unidos." In *La enseñanza del español a hispano-hablantes: Praxis y teoría,* edited by Cecilia Colombi and Francisco X. Alarcón. Boston: Houghton Mifflin.

Hornberger, Nancy H., and Sishun C. Wang. 2008. "Who Are Our Heritage Language Learners? Identity and Biliteracy in Heritage Language Education in the United States." In *Heritage Language Education: A New Field Emerging,* edited by Donna M. Brinton, Olga Kagan, and Susan Bauckus. New York: Routledge.

Kagan, Olga, and Maria Polinsky. 2008. "Heritage Languages: In the 'Wild' and in the Classroom." *Languages and Linguistics Compass* 1 (5): 368–95.

Kellough, Richard D., Noreen G. Kellough, and Eugene C. Kim. 1999. *Secondary School Teaching: A Guide to Methods and Resources; Planning for Competence.* Upper Saddle River, NJ: Prentice Hall.

Krashen, Stephen. 1998. "Language Shyness and Heritage Language Development." In *Heritage Language Development,* edited by Stephen Krashen, Lucy Tse, and Jeff McQuillan. Culver City, CA: Language Education Associates.

Leeman, Jennifer. 2005. "Engaging Critical Pedagogy: Spanish for Native Speakers." *Foreign Language Annals* 38 (1): 35–45.

Leeman, Jennifer, and Glenn Martínez. 2007. "From Identity to Commodity: Ideologies of Spanish in Heritage Language Textbooks." *Critical Inquiry in Language Studies* 4 (1): 35–65.

MacGregor-Mendoza, Patricia. 2000. "Aquí no se habla español: Stories of Linguistic Repression in Southwest Schools." *Bilingual Research Journal* 24 (4): 355–68.

Martínez, Glenn. 2003. "Classroom Based Dialect Awareness in Heritage Language Instruction: A Critical Applied Linguistic Approach." *Heritage Language Journal* 1 (1). Available at www.heritagelanguages.org.

Melton, Ronald. 1997. "Spanish for Native Speakers: Los Angeles Unified Schools—Suggested Syllabi along with Rationale, Bibliography, Etc." In *Spanish for the Spanish-Speaking: A Descriptive Bibliography of Materials*, edited by Guadalupe Valdés-Fallis and Richard V. Teschner. Austin: National Educational Laboratory.

Montrul, Silvina. 2002. "Incomplete Acquisition and Attrition of Spanish Tense/Aspect Distinctions in Adult Bilinguals." *Bilingualism: Language and Cognition* 5:39–68.

———. 2008. *Incomplete Acquisition in Bilingualism: Re-Examining the Age Factor*. Amsterdam: John Benjamins.

———. 2011. "Morphological Errors in Spanish Second Language Learners and Heritage Speakers." *Studies in Second Language Acquisition* 33 (2): 163–92.

Montrul, Silvina, and Melissa Bowles. 2010. "Is Grammar Instruction Beneficial for Heritage Language Learners: Dative Case Marking in Spanish." *Heritage Language Journal* 7 (1): 47–73. Available at www.heritagelanguages.org.

Montrul, Silvina, Rebecca Foote, and Silvia Perpiñán. 2008. "Gender Agreement in Adult Second Language Learners and Spanish Heritage Speakers: The Effects of Age and Context of Acquisition." *Language Learning* 58 (3): 503–53.

Montrul, Silvina, and Silvia Perpiñán. 2001. "Assessing Differences and Similarities between Instructed Second-Language Learners and Heritage Language Learners in Their Knowledge of Spanish Tense-Aspect and Mood (TAM) Morphology." *Heritage Language Journal* 8 (1). Available at www.heritagelanguages.org.

Montrul, Silvina, and Kim Potowski. 2007. "Command of Gender Agreement in School-Age Spanish Bilingual Children." *International Journal of Bilingualism* 11:301–28.

Mueller Gathercole, Virginia. 2002. "Grammatical Gender in Monolingual and Bilingual Acquisition: A Spanish Morphosyntactic Distinction." In *Language and Literacy in Bilingual Children*, edited by D. Kimbrough Oller and Rebecca Eilers. Clevedon, UK: Multilingual Matters.

Oh, Janet, and Terry Kit-Fong Au. 2005. "Learning Spanish as a Heritage Language: The Role of Sociocultural Background Variables." *Language, Culture, and Curriculum* 18 (3): 229–41.

Pachon, Harry P., Louis G. Tornatzky, and Celina Torres. 2003. "*Closing Achievement Gaps: Improving Educational Outcomes for Hispanic Children*." Los Angeles: Tomás Rivera Policy Institute, University of Southern California. www.trpi.org/update/education.html.

Pino, Cecilia R. 1997. "La reconceptualización del programa de español para hispanohablantes: Estrategías que reflejan la realidad sociolingüística de la clase." In *La enseñanza del español a hispanohablantes: Praxis y teoría*, edited by Cecilia Colombi and Francisco X. Alarcón. Boston: Houghton Mifflin.

Potowski, Kim. 2002. "Experiences of Spanish Heritage Speakers in University Foreign Language Courses and Implications for Teacher Training." *ADFL Bulletin* 33 (3): 35–42.

———. 2003. "Chicago's 'Heritage Language Teacher Corps': A Model for Improving Spanish Teacher Development." *Hispania* 86 (2): 302–11.

———. 2005. *Fundamentos de la enseñanza del español a los hablantes nativos en los Estados Unidos* (Foundations in teaching Spanish to native speakers in the United States). Madrid: Arco/Libros.

Potowski, Kim, and Maria Carreira. 2004. "Towards Teacher Development and National Standards for Spanish as a Heritage Language." *Foreign Language Annals* 37 (3): 421–31.

Potowski, Kim, Jill Jegerski, and Kara Morgan-Short. 2009. "The Effects of Instruction on Subjunctive Development among Spanish Heritage Language Speakers." *Language Learning* 59 (3): 537–79.

Reynolds, Rachel R., Kathryn M. Howard, and Julia Deák. 2009. "Heritage Language Learners in First-Year Foreign Language Courses: A Report of General Data across Learner Subtypes." *Foreign Language Annals* 42 (2): 250–69.

Roca, Ana, and Helena Alonso. 2006. "The Abuelos Project: A Multi-Disciplinary, Multi-Task Unit for Heritage and Advanced Second-Language Learners of Spanish." Paper presented at annual meeting of American Association of Teachers of Spanish, Salamanca, June 28–July 2.

Rodríguez-Pino, Cecilia. 1994. "Ethnographic Studies in the SNS Program." *Teaching Spanish to Native Speakers* 1:1–4.

Schreffler, Sandra. 2007. "Hispanic Heritage Language Speakers in the United States: Linguistic Exclusion in Education." *Critical Inquiry in Language Studies* 4 (1): 25–34.

Silva-Corvalán, Carmen. 2003. "Linguistic Consequences of Reduced Input in Bilingual First Language Acquisition." In *Linguistic Theory and Language Development in Hispanic Languages*, edited by Silvina Montrul and Francisco Ordoñez. Somerville, MA: Cascadilla.

Tomlinson, Carol Ann. 1999. *The Differentiated Classroom: Responding to the Needs of All Learners*. Alexandria, VA: Association for Supervision and Curriculum Development.

———. 2003. *Fulfilling the Promise of the Differentiated Classroom: Strategies and Tools for Responsive Teaching*. Alexandria, VA: Association for Supervision and Curriculum Development.

Valdés, Guadalupe. 1981. "Pedagogical Implications of Teaching Spanish to the Spanish-Speaking in the United States." In *Teaching Spanish to the Hispanic Bilingual: Issues, Aims, and Methods*, edited by Guadalupe Valdés, Anthony G. Lozano, and Rodolfo García-Moya. New York: Teachers College Press.

———. 1995. "The Teaching of Minority Languages as Academic Subjects: Pedagogical and Theoretical Challenges." *Modern Language Journal* 3:299–328.

———. 1997. "The Teaching of Spanish to Bilingual Spanish-Speaking Students: Outstanding Issues and Unanswered Questions." In *La enseñanza del español a hispanohablantes: Praxis y teoría*, edited by Cecilia Colombi and Francisco X. Alarcón. Boston: Houghton Mifflin.

———. 2001. "Heritage Language Students: Profiles and Possibilities." In *Heritage languages in America: Preserving a National Resource*, edited by Joy K. Peyton, Donald A. Ranard, and Scott McGinnis. Washington, DC: Center for Applied Linguistics.

Valdés, Guadalupe, Anthony G. Lozano, and Rodolfo García-Moya. 1981. *Teaching Spanish to the Hispanic Bilingual in the United States: Issues, Aims, and Methods*. New York: Teachers College Press.

Valdés, Guadalupe, Sonia González, Dania López García, and Patricio Márquez. 2003. "Language Ideology: The Case of Spanish in Departments of Foreign Languages." *Anthropology & Education Quarterly* 34 (1): 3–26.

Valdés-Fallis, Guadalupe. 1978. "A Comprehensive Approach to the Teaching of Spanish to Bilingual Spanish-Speaking Students." *Modern Language Journal* 62:102–10.

Valdés-Fallis, Guadalupe, and Richard V. Teschner. 1977. *Spanish for the Spanish-Speaking: Descriptive Bibliography of Materials*. Austin: National Educational Laboratory.

Valenzuela, Angela. 1999. *Subtractive Schooling: US-Mexican Youth and the Politics of Caring.* Albany: State University of New York Press.

Velez-Rendon, Gloria. 2005. "Las autobiografías lingüísticas: Una propuesta metodológica para el desarrollo de la lectoescritura de los alumnos hispanohablantes." *Hispania* 88 (3): 531–41.

Villa, Daniel. 1996. "Choosing a 'Standard' Variety of Spanish for the Instruction of Native Spanish Speakers in the US." *Foreign Language Annals* 29 (2): 191–200.

———. 2002. "The Sanitizing of US Spanish in Academia." *Foreign Language Annals* 35:222–30.

Wallace, Michael J. 1998. *Action Research for Language Teachers.* New York: Cambridge University Press.

Webb, John B., and Barbara L. Miller. 2000. *Teaching Heritage Language Learners: Voices from the Classroom.* Yonkers, NY: American Council on the Teaching of Foreign Languages.

CHAPTER 12

Advanced Biliteracy Development in Spanish as a Heritage Language

M. Cecilia Colombi and Joseph Harrington,
University of California, Davis

T HE FIELD OF HERITAGE LANGUAGE has expanded in both scope and depth in recent decades and thus has brought a new understanding of the nature of how heritage languages develop and are acquired, along with their use in various contexts. In educational institutions, specifically, there is heightened attention to how heritage language learners can develop biliteracy in their home language. However, research into the development of Spanish heritage language biliteracy—particularly at advanced levels—is only now becoming a topic of more active research in suggesting why and how these learners become biliterate. This chapter presents an overview of the research that is being done on the development of advanced biliteracy in Spanish as a heritage language in the university context.

CONTEXTUALIZING ACADEMIC SECOND-LANGUAGE LITERACY IN THE UNITED STATES

Indigenous, heritage, and immigrant languages have a problematic status in US society historically and contemporaneously. Stemming from strong monolingual ideologies, official and nonofficial policies have been at best indifferent toward the preservation and development of these languages locally and nationally and have often led to either their diminished presence in the public sphere or to linguistic extermination (Gal 1998; Ortega 1999; Ricento 2000).

241

This antagonism has more often than not resulted in restricting languages other than English primarily to the home and a limited number of public spaces, such as community religious observances. In short, the United States has not been a favorable environment for the maintenance of languages other than English.

These monolingual ideologies have also been strongly felt in educational institutions. Proposition 227 and Proposition 203, which, respectively, passed in California in 1998 and Arizona in 2000 (both states have a predominantly Latino population) aimed at eliminating both bilingual education in the schools and also academic opportunities that could facilitate the development of literacy in heritage languages.[1] In terms of literacy development, these propositions affected educational institutions in that they found themselves more focused on developing academic competence in English to the exclusion of advancing literacy in any other language. Consequently, these educational limitations severely denied opportunities for learners to both develop and acquire literacy in their home languages, in addition to English.

Moreover, the number of educational contexts that can support the academic literacy development of non-English languages is quite limited. Even where they do exist, their primary goals are more transitional than developmental. Although there are numerous bilingual education programs nationwide, they are distributed in an unbalanced manner toward the primary level, with scant offerings at the secondary and tertiary levels.[2] This is especially crucial because it is during secondary and later education courses that students develop the necessary advanced literacy practices to become full participants in the various academic and professional contexts. The near nonexistence of advanced bilingual education at an institutional level, therefore, severely circumscribes opportunities for learners to develop advanced literacy in their home language.

In addition to the limited number of contexts in which students can develop advanced literacy in a home language, the goals of most bilingual education programs that do exist often eventually favor transitional forms of bilingualism, with the resulting academic abilities in English far exceeding those in their home languages. For example, though learners may achieve incipient biliteracy through bilingual instruction, eventually these programs shift from balanced biliteracy instruction to teaching more advanced literacy skills in only one language, English, which becomes their primary academic and professional language for later schooling and higher education. As a result, "bilingual students rarely develop advanced biliteracy" (Colombi and Schleppegrell 2002, 4), due to bilingual pedagogy that does not provide opportunities for learning the academic registers for the duration of the students' education.[3] Therefore, many bilingual learners cannot gain access to any opportunities to develop advanced biliteracy until they gain entrance into higher levels of education.

HERITAGE LANGUAGE LEARNERS OF SPANISH
IN THE US EDUCATIONAL SYSTEM

Heritage speakers of Spanish in the United States constitute an important student population with unique linguistic and educational needs and challenges in learning both English and Spanish (for further discussion, see Valdés 2005). Spanish heritage speakers provide an example of a heterogeneous group of learners, both linguistically and culturally.

Heritage speakers' use of Spanish usually revolves around the home or community domains. As a result of having developed their linguistic registers in informal contexts, they have not used Spanish in situations where this particular type of language is utilized to construct knowledge or negotiate membership in an academic or professional community. In light of this fact, they are subsequently less prepared to meet the linguistic and literacy demands of these settings. To become legitimate participants, therefore, they not only need to expand their control over a range of oral and written academic registers but also, just as important, need to negotiate, construct, and index new identities as members of the academic community (Achugar and Colombi 2008). To be able to develop the academic and professional registers in Spanish as well as to negotiate these identities as proficient users of the language, it is important, first of all, to allow for the social and public contexts where the language is used and valued in society. Spanish, at the same time, is becoming the second-most-used language in the United States, and thus the need for proficient speakers of Spanish who can use both languages in a variety of registers is becoming more apparent in many public areas, such as the advertising, business, and health care professions (for further discussion, see Gorney 2007). With this burgeoning need and demand for bilingual workers at all levels, we hope that more institutional and economic opportunities and resources for developing biliteracy at advanced levels will follow, as well as more individual motivations for using the heritage language.

Up to this point, we have discussed the status of non-English languages in general and Spanish in particular in the United States and the lack of opportunities to develop advanced literacy within educational institutions. In this section we present the main contemporary theories about literacy and biliteracy development.

The Autonomous Model of Literacy

Historically, literacy was defined solely from a technical and structural perspective. Becoming literate, therefore, was seen as "technical acquisition" of the "mechanical processes" involved in reading and writing (Al-Kahtany 1996). This perspective implied that achieving literate competence merely consisted of the acquisition of determined discrete and quantifiable reading and writing skills. That skill- and competence-based perspective contributed to what Street (1993) has called the Autonomous Model of Literacy.[4] This model divorced literacy from any possible social, cultural, and functional relevance, and thus converted it into "purely a linguistic experience" (Al-Kahtany 1996, 549).

The Ideological Model of Literacy

In response to what he labeled as the Autonomous Model, Street (1993) proposed the Ideological Model of Literacy, which has been the cornerstone of what are known as the New Literacy Studies. This model rejects the skill-based and socially independent focus, finding it inadequate to explain the nature of literacy or how it develops. Instead, this perspective situates literacy directly within the social and cultural context; that is, the context and cultural (and ideological) power determine what is considered to be literacy in a given context and how literate activities are carried out, received, and interpreted.

When literacy is situated within a sociocultural frame, all "literacy practices are saturated with ideology" in one form or another (Street 1993, 9), "[reflecting] attitudes, values, and practices of particular social, cultural, and/or ethnic groups" (Devine 1994, 225). However, accepting "the social meaning of literacy" (Szwed 1981) and seeing it as "cultural activity" (Reder 1994), significantly opens up the definitional possibilities of what literacy is and exposes the multiple layers or forms of literate practices. Because these factors differ from culture to culture, and from community to community, this subsequently suggests that there can be multiple forms of literacy or even forms of literacies. In summing up the benefits of a sociocultural approach, (García, Bartlett, and Kleifgen 2007, 1) comment that this "[has] problematized the tendency to define literacy as a singular knowledge or developmentally ordered skill set; as unvarying across contexts and situations; and as primarily cognitive. Instead, they have demonstrated that literacy entails much more than the ability to read and write, that literacy practices are enmeshed within and influenced by social, cultural, political, and economic factors, and that literacy learning and use varies by situation and entails complex social interactions."

For heritage language speakers, this implies that the English literacy they learn in school will not be automatically compatible with Spanish literacy. Furthermore, the social, political, and cultural influences of the monolingual ideology (framed in anti-Latino immigrant campaigns) may have a strong impact on their development of Spanish literacy. In other words, if heritage students are not exposed to Spanish in the school context, they will hardly have the opportunity to use or develop literacy in Spanish in a context that will most likely favor and accept English as the language of use in public interactions.

BILITERACY

Up to this point, we have considered theories about literacy in general, which have shifted from a predominantly mental and skill-based perspective to an ideologically focused one. We now consider biliteracy, that is, how literacies in two languages might exist and interact.[5] This topic has long been of scholarly interest, even from early discussions about bilingualism (Goodman, Goodman, and Flores 1979; Fishman 1980; Williams and Snipper Capizzi 1990; Valdés 1981, 1997); however, despite early interest, biliteracy has not been researched in depth, and most research has focused on incipient development in primary grades. To facilitate this discussion, this section considers various definitions of biliteracy as well as Hornberger's Continua Model of Biliteracy.

Definitions of Biliteracy

Various definitions for biliteracy have been offered, of which the following are some of the better-articulated ones:

1. "Acquisition and learning of decoding and encoding of and around print using two linguistic and cultural systems in order to convey a message in a variety of contexts" (Pérez and Torres-Guzmán 1992, 54).
2. "Literate competencies in two languages, to whatever degree, developed either simultaneously or successively" (Dworin 2003, 171).
3. "Use of two or more languages in and around writing" (Hornberger 2003, xii).

The first definition underscores the underlying cognitive and mental processes of literacy employed for communicative purposes within a given context. This perspective is helpful because it unites both cognitive and social factors as complementary for language and literacy development, not just one or the other (Atkinson 2002; Van Dijk 2006). The second definition emphasizes the variability of two literacies, both linguistically and across time. Conscientious attention to variability is especially important for understanding heritage language biliteracy, especially the temporal aspect because, for heritage learners, frequently opportunities to develop literacy in their home language are delayed until much later in their schooling. And the third definition, which is perhaps the best known, brings into focus the context and the productive modality of biliterate language use. An interesting implication of this last definition is that the literacy event creates its own context. In summing up these definitions, biliteracy is thus a socioculturally aware use of two languages in the context of literate (reading and writing) activities.

Theorizing Biliteracy's Development: The Continua Model

In studies of biliteracy, Nancy Hornberger's (1989, 2003) Continua Model of Biliteracy has proved to be an important contribution for conceptualizing and evaluating some of the complexities associated with biliteracy's development. The creation of this ecological model stemmed from her research on how Puerto Rican youth learn English literacy in Philadelphia schools. Stemming from her initial and subsequent theorizations, the model has seen applications globally in diverse locations, language configurations, and contexts.[6]

Drawing from a wide range of sociocultural and linguistic theories, Hornberger proposes a multidimensional framework that conceptualizes biliteracy by examining factors that can contribute to or inhibit biliteracy development. These four continua are contexts, development, media, and content.[7] Within each of these interrelated spaces, she proposes a number of dimensions:

Contexts:
▶ micro–macro: range of contexts of language use
▶ oral–literate: interrelatedness of speech and literacy
▶ monolingual–bilingual: amount or frequency of switching between languages

Development:
▶ reception–production: interrelatedness of listening-reading and speaking-writing
▶ oral–written: interrelatedness of speech and written language
▶ L1–L2 transfer: interrelatedness of the language systems within the individual

Media:
▶ simultaneous–successive exposure: bilingual development temporally
▶ similar–dissimilar language structure: genetic distance between languages
▶ convergent–divergent scripts: difference in script types

Content:
▶ minority–majority: power and status relations in context
▶ vernacular–literary: localized and standardized literacy practices
▶ contextualized–decontextualized: embeddedness within the discourse context

By examining an individual's (or even a group's) position along these various dimensions, this person can be located within this multidimensional space and his or her development can be compared with that of others. This can also help uncover the "interrelationships" across all these features and disentangle the complex sociolinguistic web of biliteracy. It is also important to note that the polar endpoints "represent only theoretical endpoints on what is in reality a continuum of features" (Hornberger 1989, 273). Furthermore, given that this is a multidimensional space, Hornberger has emphasized that the four categories are themselves nestled within one another, with development at the core, then content, subsequently media, and finally contexts. This "nestledness" of the continua further emphasizes the multifaceted interactions that potentially can occur along and across these dimensions.

Linguistic Perspectives within Literacy and Biliteracy Studies

Up to this point, we have considered two models of literacy—the Autonomous Model, with its purely psycholinguistic definition, and have compared its deficiencies with the Ideological Model, with its grounding in the sociocultural context. One of the primary insights of this latter model has been its "re-evaluation of the importance of 'context' in linguistic analysis" (Street 1993, 13), in that in developing descriptions of literacy, one needs to start with the unique context where the studied literate practices are situated in order to understand them. Also, it is clear that the Continua Model of Biliteracy draws considerable strength from the ideological approach.

However, a "purely" ideological approach will not be enough to help support literacy development in one's first language, and it may prove to be even less helpful for heritage literacy development. The Continua Model explicitly recognizes this reality by including both social and linguistic continua as dimensions of biliterate development. Given the particular linguistic and contextual differences that an emergent heritage academic writer brings to his or her study, understanding the ideological structure and values of the context will be very relevant but not solely sufficient for literacy development. Thus it is crucial to carefully consider linguistic needs paired with a more complete understanding of how these distinct features are tied to and realized in a particular academic or professional context.

Systemic Functional Linguistics, which was established on the basis of the theories of Michael Halliday, has done much to theorize how language and context are related. In particular, genre and register theory (Byrnes 2006, 2009; Christie and Martin 1997; Chevalier 2004; Colombi 2009; Hyland 2002; Martin 2010; Paltridge 2001) was first developed by Jim Martin in Australia as a pedagogical model to develop literacy in students' first language in disadvantaged school contexts. This model has raised consciousness about the importance of focusing on language and culture as an inseparable unity. Language is a "meaning making resource" that is always embedded in culture, and "genre [is] a staged, goal-oriented, purposeful activity in which speakers engage as members of our culture" (Martin 1984, 25).

The research on academic writing in English as a second language as well as in Spanish as a heritage language in a bilingual context (Colombi 2000, 2002,

2006; Valdés and Geoffrion-Vinci 1998) has demonstrated how second-language writers of English and native speakers learning to write in academic Spanish often draw on informal, oral-like registers and the importance of the academic context for developing the academic and professional registers. Furthermore, these discourse and linguistic norms are often not consciously apparent, even to the full members of the community; yet the transgression of these conventions, especially when these breaches are linguistic, are often the justification for restricting or even denying participation within these communities. Thus, linguistics makes a valuable contribution in explaining heritage literacy because it helps identify features that are not readily apparent to the community. Moreover, as mentioned above, the school context is where we develop literacy (and biliteracy), so not to draw attention to the advantage that we may have in utilizing school resources in raising awareness of the different linguistic features used in different registers (and the social values attached to them) is to waste a unique opportunity for facilitating the development of literacy. In other words, (bi)literacy is learned primarily in a school context, where attention is explicitly given to the linguistic resources of writing and reading. Therefore, it is crucial for educators and language policymakers to maintain and create educational opportunities that will facilitate the development of biliteracy in heritage language learners.

SYSTEMIC FUNCTIONAL LINGUISTICS' CONTRIBUTIONS TO THEORIZING LITERACY

Systemic Functional Linguistics (SFL) takes a semantic perspective on writing and orality. From this perspective, grammar's meaning and form are not separated but stand in a dialectical relation to each other, and meaning is always construed in a social context. As such, meanings do not exist before the wordings that realize them. SFL further postulates that both speech and writing have distinct contextualized functions and that these account for the significant semiotic and lexicogrammatical features found in both. For example, Halliday (1994, 352) describes the "written language as more complex by being lexically dense: It packs a large number of lexical items into each clause [crystalline]; whereas spoken language becomes complex by being grammatically intricate: it builds up elaborate clause complexes out of parataxis and hypotaxis [choreographic]" (Halliday 1989, 86–87).

In other words, written and spoken languages are not just two different linguistic codes, but two different language resources to fulfill different functions in different social contexts. As such, the system constrains the possible choices and is changed by the choices speakers make. This means that the actual language that is used in a particular setting is therefore probabilistic; that is, in certain contexts users tend to make certain choices.

SFL models language and social context as semiotic systems in a relationship of realization with one another. According to this realization, language construes, is construed by, and (over time) reconstrues social context (Martin, Matthiessen, and Painter 1997, 4). As Schleppegrell and Colombi (2002, 10) state: "Writing is not only a different medium of expression than oral language but also a means of constructing a semiotic system which adds to the everyday language that we already have." Research related to this linguistic view of literacy development, and to writing in particular, has identified several key features of academic language that (could be and) are used in educational linguistics and school contexts (Colombi 2006; Schleppegrell 2004).

RESEARCH ON ADVANCED BILITERACY IN SPANISH AS A HERITAGE LANGUAGE

In this section we consider research that has explored the development of advanced biliteracy among Spanish heritage speakers and the implications of these investigations for curriculum development and (bi)literacy teaching in school contexts. To begin, since her early work, Colombi (1997) has focused on how Spanish heritage students move from the colloquial registers to the more formal ones within the oral–written continuum. In 1997 she studied Spanish heritage students at the university level who were learning to develop the academic registers. In this corpus analysis of students' essays in their first quarter of the program, Colombi showed how students use the conversational resources that they have developed in their heritage language, especially in interpersonal contexts, to write in the academic context, from the most obvious traces at the graphic/phonic level (the omission of orthographic "h"; the lack of written accents; no differentiation between "s," "c," or "z"; etc.) to the lexicogrammatical level (use of colloquialisms, repetitions, rhetorical questions, etc.) typical of the oral colloquial registers.[8]

Colombi pointed out that the development of biliteracy in Spanish in California was similar to that of Spanish as a first language in monolingual contexts in how school and explicit instruction can facilitate and accelerate the acquisition of advanced literacy. Schleppegrell and Colombi (1997) focused on bilingual writers whose prior formal academic writing instruction has only been in English and compared their essays written in English and Spanish. This analysis at the discourse-organizational level showed how students used the same strategies in both their essays in English and Spanish—one of them being more analytical and synthetic, and the other more hortatory and subjective. This study points out how students rely on their common underlying language proficiency (Cummins 1992a, 1992b) to develop their repertoire of styles and discourse strategies in both languages and how they transfer the academic strategies that they have developed in English while writing in the heritage language.

In a detailed rhetorical and discursive contrastive study of heritage learners' texts in English and Spanish, Spicer-Escalante (2005, 244) shows how the transfer of rhetorical strategies is bidirectional and global. Her findings indicate that heritage language writers "find their own pathway to expression, creating their own rhetorical space. [They] nourish their writing in both Spanish and English by using rhetorical strategies that correspond to both of these languages, reflecting the cultural borderland in which they live, where elements of North American and Latino cultures meld together into a unique syncretic composite." Furthermore, she stresses the need for instruction and programs in the heritage language to enable bilingual students to advance their literacy in Spanish.

Martínez (2007) also explores the area of literacy transfer from English into Spanish, by focusing on the variation between overt and null subject pronouns in heritage language writing. Thus he proposes a multidimensional model of transfer as a theoretical and methodological framework for the teaching of heritage language writing. He studied the distribution of null and overt subject pronouns in the writing of thirteen first-year heritage learners of Spanish in two different types of texts: a formal essay and a free writing sample, both based on the same topic. His findings show that students tent to use more overt subject pronouns in the formal writing, and thus he concludes that the genre of the text and context of the situation did have an effect on their writing. He argues in favor of a view of literacy/literacies that, from an "ideological" perspective (Street 1984; Collins and Blot 2003), is situated in a multiplicity of social practices that are bound up with ideologically driven schemes of signification. The view of transfer then becomes multidimensional. Such multidimensionality, moreover, opens up the potential transfer by including a multiplicity of contents and by drawing on practices developed within the context of the heritage language community. Finally, he proposes a multidimensional model of literacy transfer that can enhance and revalidate the literacy practices of the heritage language community.

Colombi's longitudinal studies of Spanish college heritage speakers detail the differences between oral and written language (Colombi 2000, 2002, 2006; Achugar and Colombi 2008). She charts writers' movement in the direction of incorporating more formal written register features into their texts and shows how students move from the interpersonal style characteristic of everyday speech to the abstraction and context reduction of academic registers. Her research suggests that an analysis of nominalization, together with clause-combining strategies, can provide a means of charting the development of academic writing skills in Spanish. She shows that as their writing develops toward more academic registers, its lexical density and nominal structure will grow while its grammatical intricacy decreases. She also demonstrates that nominalization and grammatical metaphors play an important role in the understanding of academic writing development (for a full treatment of linguistic features, see Colombi 2002, 2006).

Furthermore, these studies show how the development of biliteracy in the heritage language requires significant investments of time; that is, although there is significant variation within the heritage students because they may be at different points in their developmental stages, by and large the condensation of the information and the use of nominalizations and grammatical metaphor do not become part of their repertoire until the end of their first year of instruction. From a pedagogical point of view, an understanding of the functional meanings conveyed by different linguistic choices can provide teachers with a useful framework for effectively incorporating grammar into writing instruction, because it makes explicit how different grammatical choices help students produce the types of texts that are expected in academic contexts (Colombi 2009) as well as explaining how biliteracy develops.

Achugar's work investigates the relationship between identity in both languages and advanced or professional uses of Spanish by bilingual speakers. She looks at the role of language in academia and investigates how discourse practices help construct an academic identity whereby individuals and groups develop specialized ways of knowing and being. Achugar's first study of two participants' Spanish academic oral presentations showed the clear differences in the way they use language and "signaled their role as 'experts' in the field" (Achugar 2003). Her longitudinal, qualitative study of a bilingual creative writing program in El Paso seeks to explain how language indexes a professional identity and to identify particular cultural practices that contribute to the socialization and development of members in a community of practice (Achugar 2006, 2008; Achugar and Colombi 2008). This study offers a detailed description of the process and practices that play a role in the transformation and development of language and attitudes that shape a professional identity in a bilingual project and shows that there is an ongoing negotiation of what it means to be a bilingual professional writer. The exploration of participants' attitudes shows that there is a conflict in the community about how to evaluate the use of particular languages and their speakers. Although, in many cases, local varieties of Spanish tend to be considered less valuable or appropriate for use in academia (in contrast to standard varieties of Spanish), there is more acceptance and value for the use of code-switching or mixing codes. This is an interesting finding, given that previous studies have associated the use of code-switching to colloquial domains. Achugar's study is one of the few that explores the interconnection of identity and advanced levels of biliteracy at the tertiary level not only in written language but also in oral domains.

FUTURE DIRECTIONS

In the twenty-first century the value of speaking Spanish is transcending family circles and reaching mainstream businesses in the United States, and thus most of the marketing tools for the Latino population are now being done in Spanish or bilingually in Spanish/English (for more information on this topic, see AHAA 2010, which is its latest report). Therefore, there is a need to understand and document how advanced biliteracy in Spanish/English is developed in heritage speakers. However, as mentioned earlier in this chapter, although there are numerous biliteracy studies at the primary and secondary levels (especially of incipient biliteracy), there have been few studies of biliteracy in either university contexts or of biliterate learners at the advanced level in professional or academic contexts. We believe that the two theories presented here, Hornberger's Continua Model and SFL, can offer possibilities to inform instruction and research on how to track biliteracy's development in Spanish as a heritage language.

Additionally, literacy and biliteracy are fundamentally issues of development in an academic context. As such, it is imperative that scholars use longitudinal time frames to begin to see evidence of change. Unfortunately, there have been very few empirical and longitudinal studies of the development of advanced biliteracy in Spanish at the tertiary level. Furthermore, with few exceptions (Achugar 2003, 2008), most of them concentrate on writing and no attention has been given to the oral public registers.

The Continua Model offers a number of dimensions for describing and intervening in the biliteracy development of heritage speakers that deserve further investigation. The processes operating on each continuum, however, still need more detailed studies. As more work is done within this framework, additional processes will be identified. In this chapter we have considered linguistic and social processes from an SFL perspective, which could be interpreted as operating in the development and content–context continua, respectively. A more careful exposition of the interaction between SFL and the Continua Model would prove useful.

SFL's theories about register and genre have had broad application in literacy studies. They have also been used fruitfully in Colombi's work in heritage biliteracy development. How register and genre fit into the Continua Model, however, has not been explored and warrants investigation and theorization. Both are multidimensional frameworks starting most broadly with the context and have successively embedded levels with language at the core. What would be valuable to explore is how the different continua might relate to "the constellation of lexical and grammatical features that realizes a particular situational context" (Halliday and Hasan 1989, 39). Conversely, the notion of genre and register could expand scholars' understanding of the various continua proposed by Hornberger.

Finally, there is much to be gained by establishing connections between research in the field of L2 and heritage languages. The investigation of advanced biliteracy in Spanish as a heritage language could contribute in important ways to scholars' understanding of the multilingual reality of the United States; and, vice versa, studies in second-language development at advanced levels can prove beneficial for the field of heritage language development. Furthermore, research in both second- and heritage language development can help inform instruction and elucidate the effects of different types of instruction in developing heritage (and second) languages.

As was mentioned earlier in this chapter, although there have been numerous biliteracy studies at both the primary and secondary school levels, there have been few studies of either university contexts or biliterate learners. However, in the quest to develop to a more robust concept of what advanced biliteracy is and how it develops, higher education is crucial because it is nearly the only context where such development may occur and be studied. Therefore, university departments of foreign, modern, and second languages would be ideal sites for carrying out this type of research, because they increasingly offer either heritage language programs or have a high number of heritage language learners. In identifying universities as prime sites for heritage language research, it would be important to emphasize that these are also sites for advanced literacy development. Thus university departments should focus on biliteracy as a core focus and not one that is only ancillary to their mission.

CONCLUSION

In this chapter we have presented an overview of the sociocultural and linguistic perspectives on biliteracy's development in Spanish/English in the United States. We have outlined the most well-developed linguistic theoretical models in our understanding of biliteracy: the Continua Model and the Systemic Functional Grammar theoretical approach.

In a recent publication, Hornberger and Wang (2008) consider how the Continua Model can serve to discuss issues of biliteracy for heritage language speakers. They begin with an exposition and critique of the definitions of heritage language and heritage language speakers (Fishman 1991, 2001; Campbell and Peyton 1998; Webb and Miller 2000; Scalera 2000; Draper and Hicks 2000; Valdés 2001), and they conclude that these (1) pay insufficient attention to the sociocultural and psychological realities of heritage language populations; (2) fail to acknowledge the strong impeding language ideologies found in those contexts; and (3), crucially, do little to either describe or explain the nature of heritage languages and their speakers. Although not offering their own definition of heritage language or its learners to address these deficiencies, they do propose that the Continua Model, paired with contemporary theories about identity, can help scholars explore and explain some of the associated complexities of biliteracy for this group. Using a thematic approach, Hornberger and Wang consider each of the four continua for heritage language speakers. A parallel discussion along with each continuum is how they position themselves and are positioned within each continuum. This latter point is particularly vital for this group of learners who

experience the tension between their personal agency in defining their own biliterate (as well as nonliterate) identities while negotiating those other identities
that are being imposed through surrounding power structures.

Systemic Functional Linguistics identifies particular lexicogrammatical and
discourse-semantic resources that serve as indices of language development over
time (e.g., grammatical metaphor, grammatical intricacy, lexical density, modality, clause-combining resources). This linguistic approach toward (bi)literacy is
also anchored in the idea that language can never be isolated from its (social)
context. Given that functional perspectives of language understand language and
context as co-constituted, they enable scholars to consider language development
in the context of a particular culture. "Context" is understood on the level of
the context of the situation where language is produced and also on the level of
the larger cultural context that creates the conditions for what it is possible to
do with language within a particular group (i.e., register/genre theory). Biliteracy
development, from this perspective, is seen as the expansion of meaning-making
potential at the individual level as well as an evolving membership in a particular
social group, in this case in the public sphere at the professional level in bilingual
settings. Considering the limited opportunities available for the use of Spanish
in a professional context in the United States, and taking into account the reality
that literacy is mainly developed in academic contexts, these studies pointed to
the importance of explicit instruction that explains language use and expectations in an academic community.

NOTES

1. A similar initiative, Proposition 31, was rejected by the electorate in Colorado in
2002.

2. In the Southwest California's programs are primarily funded by the federal
government.

3. We refer to the term "register" as variation according to the use, versus a dialect
that would be a variation according to the users. Registers are language use in different
social contexts for different purposes, i.e., academic registers as opposed to colloquial
registers.

4. It is important to note that this so-called Autonomous Model is not in and of itself
an official theoretical model per se, but rather a prevailing "ideological framework"
(Street 1993) of literacy. It has been identified and critiqued by Street and others of the
New Literacy Studies. One of the theories especially criticized by this movement is Goody
and Watt's autonomous mode of communication (Goody 1968; Goody and Watt 1988)
and writing's which states unambiguity and autonomous representation of meaning
(Olson 1977).

5. We adhere to a definition of biliteracy as "a special form of literacy that must be
understood as distinct from that of monolinguals" (Dworin 2003, 173). In other words,
a biliterate individual does not have two separate literacies, but a common one (Cummins
1981).

6. For various applications of the model in cases worldwide, see Hornberger and Skilton-Sylvester (2000); Hornberger (2003).

7. This last continuum was added in a critical reassessment of the model and its relations to power (Hornberger and Skilton-Sylvester 2000).

8. In this respect Hornberger's and Halliday's oral–written continuum is similar.

REFERENCES

Achugar, Mariana. 2003. "Academic Registers in Spanish in the US: A Study of Oral Texts Produced by Bilingual Speakers in a University Graduate Program." In *Mi lengua: Spanish as a Heritage Language in the United States, Research and Practice*, edited by Ana Roca and María Cecilia Colombi. Washington, DC: Georgetown University Press.

———. 2006. "Writers on the Borderlands: Constructing a Bilingual Identity in Southwest Texas." *Journal of Language, Identity & Education* 5 (2): 97–122.

———. 2008. "Counter-Hegemonic Language Practices and Ideologies Creating a New Space and Value for Spanish in Southwest Texas." *Spanish in Context* 5:1–19.

Achugar, Mariana, and María Cecilia Colombi. 2008. "Systemic Functional Linguistic Explorations into the Longitudinal Study of the Advanced Capacities." In *The Longitudinal Study of Advanced L2 Capacities*, edited by Lourdes Ortega and Heidi Byrnes. New York: Routledge.

AHAA (Association of Hispanic Advertising Agencies). 2010. "Hispanic Ad Spend Trends Report 2010." http://ahaa.org/downloads/pdf/AHAA_TrendsReport.pdf.

Al-Kahtany, Abdallah Hady. 1996. "Literacy from a Linguistic and a Sociolinguistic Perspective." *International Review of Education/Internationale Zeitschrift für Erziehungswissenschaft/Revue Internationale de l'Education* 42 (6): 547–62.

Atkinson, Dwight. 2002. "Toward a Sociocognitive Approach to Second Language Acquisition." *Modern Language Journal* 86 (4): 525–45.

Byrnes, Heidi, ed. 2006. *Advanced Language Learning: The Contribution of Halliday and Vygotsky*. London: Continuum.

———. 2009. "Systemic-Functional Reflections on Instructed Foreign Language Acquisition as Meaning-Making: An Introduction." *Linguistics and Education* 20 (1): 1–9.

Campbell, Russel, and Joy K. Peyton. 1998. "Heritage Language Students: A Valuable Language Resource." *The ERIC Review: K–12 Foreign Language Education* 6 (1): 38–39.

Chevalier, Joan F. 2004. "Heritage Language Literacy: Theory and Practice." Center for World Languages, Heritage Language Literacy, Theory and Practice. www.internatio nal.ucla.edu/languages/article.asp?parentid = 16607.

Christie, Frances, and J. R. Martin, eds. 1997. *Genre and Institutions: Social Processes in the Workplace and School*. London: Cassell.

Collins, James, and Richard K. Blot. 2003. *Literacy and Literacies: Texts, Power, and Identity*. New York: Cambridge University Press.

Colombi, María Cecilia. 1997. "Perfil del discurso escrito: Teoría y práctica." In *La enseñanza del español a hispanohablantes: Praxis y teoría*, edited by María Cecilia Colombi and Francisco X Alarcón. Boston: Houghton Mifflin.

———. 2000. "En vías del desarrollo del lenguaje académico en español en hablantes nativos de español en los Estados Unidos." In *Research on Spanish in the United States: Linguistic Issues and Challenges*, edited by Ana Roca. Somerville, MA: Cascadilla Press.

―――. 2002. "Academic Language Development in Latino Students' Writing in Spanish." In *Developing Advanced Literacy in First and Second Languages: Meaning with Power*, edited by Mary Schleppegrell and María Cecilia Colombi. Mahwah, NJ: Lawrence Erlbaum Associates.

―――. 2006. "Grammatical Metaphor: Academic Language Development in Latino Student in Spanish." In *Advanced Language Learning: The Contribution of Halliday and Vygotsky*, edited by Heidi Byrnes. London: Continuum.

―――. 2009. "A Systemic Functional Approach to Teaching Spanish for Heritage Speakers in the United States." *Linguistics and Education: An International Research Journal* 20 (1): 39–49.

Colombi, María Cecilia, and Mary Schleppegrell. 2002. Theory and Practice in the Development of Advanced Literacy. In *Developing Advanced Literacy in First and Second Languages: Meaning with Power*. Mahwah, NJ: Lawrence Erlbaum Associates.

Cummins, Jim. 1981. "Four Misconceptions about Language Proficiency in Bilingual Education." *NABE: The Journal for the National Association for Bilingual Education* 5 (3): 31–45.

―――. 1992a. "Bilingualism and Second Language Learning." *Annual Review of Applied Linguistics* 13:50–70.

―――. 1992b. "Language Proficiency, Bilingualism and Academic Achievement." In *The Multicultural Classroom: Readings for Content-Area Teachers*, edited by Patricia A. Richard-Amato and Marguerite Ann Snow. White Plains, NY: Longman.

Devine, Joanne. 1994. "Literacy and Social Power." In *Literacy across Languages and Cultures*, edited by Bernardo M. Ferdman, Rose-Marie Weber, and Arnulfo G. Ramirez. Albany: State University of New York Press.

Draper, Jamie B., and June H. Hicks. 2000. "Where We've Been; What We've Learned." In *Teaching Heritage Language Learners: Voices from the Classroom*, edited by John Webb and Barbara Miller. Yonkers, NY: American Council on the Teaching of Foreign Languages.

Dworin, Joel. 2003. "Insights into Biliteracy Development: Toward a Bidirectional Theory of Bilingual Pedagogy." *Journal of Hispanic Higher Education* 2 (2): 171–86.

Fishman, Joshua. 1980. "Ethnocultural Dimensions in the Acquisition and Retention of Biliteracy." *Journal of Basic Writing* 3 (1): 48–61.

―――. 1991. *Reversing Language Shift: Theoretical and Empirical Foundations of Assistance to Threatened Languages*. Clevedon, UK: Multilingual Matters.

―――. 2001. "300-Plus Years of Heritage Language Education in the United States." In *Heritage Languages in America: Preserving a National Resource*, edited by Joy Kreeft Peyton, Donald A. Ranard, and Scott McGinnis. McHenry, IL: Center for Applied Linguistics.

Gal, Susan. 1998. "Multiplicity and Contention among Language Ideologies." In *Language Ideologies: Practice and Theory*, edited by Bambi B. Schieffelin, Kathryn Ann Woolard, and Paul V. Kroskrity. New York: Oxford University Press.

García, Ofelia, Lesley Bartlett, and Joanne A. Kleifgen. 2007. "From Biliteracy to Pluriliteracies." In *Handbook of Applied Linguistics on Multilingual Communication*. Mouton.

Goodman, Kenneth S., Yetta M Goodman, and Barbara Flores. 1979. *Reading in the Bilingual Classroom: Literacy and Biliteracy*. Rosslyn, VA: National Clearinghouse for Bilingual Education.

Goody, Jack, ed. 1968. *Literacy in Traditional Societies*. Cambridge: Cambridge University Press.

Goody, Jack, and Ian Watt. 1988. "The Consequences of Literacy." In *Perspectives on Literacy*, edited by Eugene R. Kintgen, Barry M. Kroll, and Mike Rose. Carbondale: Southern Illinois University Press.

Gorney, Cynthia. 2007. "How Do You Say 'Got Milk' en Español?" *New York Times*, September 23. www.nytimes.com/2007/09/23/magazine/23gallegos-t.html?_r = 1.

Halliday, M. A. K. 1989. *Spoken and Written Language*, 2nd ed. Oxford: Oxford University Press.

———. 1994. *An Introduction to Functional Grammar*, 2nd ed. London: Edward Arnold.

Halliday, M. A. K., and Ruqaiya Hasan. 1989. *Language, Context, and Text: Aspects of Language in a Social-Semiotic Perspective*, 2nd ed. Oxford: Oxford University Press.

Hornberger, Nancy H. 1989. "Continua of Biliteracy." *Review of Educational Research* 59 (3): 271–96.

———, ed. 2003. *Continua of Biliteracy: An Ecological Framework for Educational Policy, Research, and Practice in Multilingual Settings*. Clevedon, UK: Multilingual Matters.

Hornberger, Nancy H., and Ellen Skilton-Sylvester. 2000. "Revisiting the Continua of Biliteracy: International and Critical Perspectives." *Language and Education* 14 (2): 96–122.

Hornberger, Nancy H., and Shuhan C. Wang. 2008. "Who Are Our Heritage Language Learners? Identity and Biliteracy in Heritage Language Education in the United States." In *Heritage Language Education: A New Field Emerging*, edited by Donna Brinton, Olga Kagan, and Susan Bauckus. New York: Routledge.

Hyland, Ken. 2002. "Genre: Language, Context, and Literacy." *Annual Review of Applied Linguistics* 22:113–35.

Martin, James R. 1984. "Language, Register and Genre." In *Children Writing*, edited by Frances Christie. Geelong, Australia: Deakin University Press.

———. 2010. "Language, Register and Genre." In *Applied Linguistics Methods: A Reader: Systemic Functional Linguistics, Critical Discourse Analysis and Ethnography*, edited by Caroline Coffin, Theresa M Lillis, and Kieran O'Halloran. London: Routledge.

Martin, James R., Christian M. I. Matthiessen, and Clare Painter. 1997. *Working with Functional Grammar*. London: Edward Arnold.

Martínez, Glenn. 2007. "Writing Back and Forth: the Interplay of Form and Situation in Heritage Language Composition." *Language Teaching Research* 11 (1): 31–41.

Olson, David R. 1977. "From Utterance to Text: The Bias of Language in Speech and Writing." *Harvard Educational Review* 47 (3): 257–81.

Ortega, Lourdes. 1999. "Rethinking Foreign Language Education: Political Dimensions of the Profession." In *Foreign Language Teaching & Language Minority Education*, edited by Kathryn A. Davis. Honolulu: University of Hawaii Press.

Paltridge, Brian. 2001. *Genre and the Language Learning Classroom*. Ann Arbor: University of Michigan Press.

Pérez, Bertha, and Maria E. Torres-Guzmán. 1992. *Learning in Two Worlds: An Integrated Spanish/English Biliteracy Approach*. New York: Longman.

Reder, Stephen. 1994. "Practice-Engagement Theory: A Sociocultural Approach to Literacy Across Languages and Cultures." In *Literacy across Languages and Cultures*, edited by Bernardo M. Ferdman, Rose-Marie Weber, and Arnulfo G. Ramirez. State University of New York Press.

Ricento, Thomas, ed. 2000. *Ideology, Politics, and Language Policies: Focus on English.* Amsterdam: John Benjamins Pub.

Scalera, Diana. 2000. "Preparing Teachers to Work with Heritage Language Learners." In *Teaching Heritage Language Learners: Voices from the Classroom*, edited by John Webb and Barbara Miller. Yonkers, NY: American Council on the Teaching of Foreign Languages.

Schleppegrell, Mary J. 2004. *The Language of Schooling: A Functional Linguistics Perspective.* Mahwah, NJ: Lawrence Erlbaum Associates.

Schleppegrell, Mary J., and María Cecilia Colombi. 1997. "Text Organization by Bilingual Writers." *Written Communication* 14 (4): 481–503.

———, eds. 2002. *Developing Advanced Literacy in First and Second Languages: Meaning with Power.* Mahwah, NJ Lawrence Erlbaum Associates.

Spicer-Escalante, María. 2005. "Writing in Two Languages/Living in Two Worlds: A Rhetorical Analysis of Mexican-American Written Discourse." In *Latino Language and Literacy in Ethnolinguistic Chicago*, edited by Marcia Farr. Mahwah, NJ: Lawrence Erlbaum Associates.

Street, Brian V., ed. 1984. *Literacy in Theory and Practice.* Cambridge [Cambridgeshire]: Cambridge University Press.

———. 1993. "Introduction: The New Literacy Studies." In *Cross-Cultural Approaches to Literacy*, edited by Brian V. Street. Cambridge: Cambridge University Press.

Szwed, John. 1981. "The Ethnography of Literacy." In *Writing: The Nature, Development, and Teaching of Written Communication*, edited by Marcia Farr Whiteman, Carl H. Frederiksen, and Joseph F. Dominic. Hillsdale, NJ: Lawrence Erlbaum Associates.

Valdés, Guadalupe. 1981. "Pedagogical Implications of Teaching Spanish to the Spanish-Speaking in the United States." In *Teaching Spanish to the Hispanic Bilingual: Issues, Aims, and Methods*, edited by Guadalupe Valdés, Anthony G. Lozano, and Rodolfo García-Moya, 3–20. New York: Teachers College Press.

———. 1997. "The Teaching of Spanish to Bilingual Spanish-speaking Students: Outstanding Issues and Unanswered Questions." In *La enseñanza del español a hispanohablantes: Praxis y teoría*, edited by María Cecilia Colombi and Francisco X Alarcón. Boston: Houghton Mifflin.

———. 2001. "Heritage Language Students: Profiles and Possibilities." In *Heritage Languages in America: Preserving a National Resource*, edited by Joy Kreeft Peyton, Donald A Ranard, and Scott McGinnis. McHenry, IL: Center for Applied Linguistics.

———. 2005. "Bilingualism, Heritage Language Learners, and SLA Research: Opportunities Lost or Seized?" *Modern Language Journal* 89 (3): 410–26.

Valdés, Guadalupe, and M. Geoffrion-Vinci. 1998. "Chicano Spanish: The Problem of the 'Underdeveloped' Code in Bilingual Repertoires." *Modern Language Journal* 82 (4): 473–501.

Van Dijk, Teun A. 2006. "Discourse, Context and Cognition." *Discourse Studies* 8 (1): 159–77.

Webb, John, and Barbara Miller, eds. 2000. *Teaching Heritage Language Learners: Voices from the Classroom.* Yonkers, NY: American Council on the Teaching of Foreign Languages.

Williams, James D., and Snipper Capizzi, Grace. 1990. *Literacy and Bilingualism.* New York: Longman.

CHAPTER 13

Language Assessment

KEY THEORETICAL CONSIDERATIONS IN THE ACADEMIC PLACEMENT OF SPANISH HERITAGE LANGUAGE LEARNERS

Marta Fairclough, University of Houston

I N EDUCATION, assessment usually encompasses various procedures, ranging from informal observations and interviews to examinations or tests, that are designed to measure in some way the knowledge, abilities, attitudes, and so on, of an individual student, a group of learners, an institution, or a whole educational system. In contrast, tests "denote a particular type of formal, often carefully designed instruments" (Huhta 2008, 469). More specifically, language testing "is a process of gathering information about test-takers from observed performance under test conditions. This is done in order to draw inferences either about the likely quality of performance by the test-taker under non-test conditions, or about the test-taker's standing in relation to a relevant domain of knowledge and abilities" (McNamara 2004, 765).

In recent decades, the field of language assessment has significantly expanded, drawing on theoretical frameworks developed in language acquisition studies (e.g., Pienemann, Johnson, and Brindley 1988) and in models of language proficiency (Bachman 1990; Canale and Swain 1980). On a more practical level, "advances in the technology of test design and development, along with the availability and use of ever more sophisticated computer- and Web-based applications for test administration, scoring and analysis, have resulted in a greater range of test formats and assessment procedures than has ever been available" (Bachman 2000, 2).

Whereas assessment research on second-language (L2) learning, especially English, has constantly expanded in the last few decades, similar research in heritage language (HL) education has been limited. The number of HL learners enrolling in Spanish courses at US colleges and universities has increased steadily (see chapter 10 in this volume, by Beaudrie) and solid, well-researched measures of HL general proficiency are desperately needed at the postsecondary level to test incoming students. This chapter has two purposes: (1) to review some key issues in language assessment—including the purpose of testing, types of assessments, proficiency models, test qualities, and improvements in test design due to advances in technology; and (2) to summarize the research on language testing in HL education in the United States, focusing on the academic placement of Spanish heritage language (SHL) learners. By linking what the language assessment field has to offer to information about testing within HL education, this chapter presents key issues in language assessment and their implications for SHL, and suggests directions for future research.

LANGUAGE ASSESSMENT AND ITS IMPLICATIONS FOR HERITAGE LANGUAGE EDUCATION

A language test can be administered for educational, political, social, or economic reasons (e.g., immigration, employment) (McNamara 2004). There are three main educational purposes for testing: administrative (to place students into or exempt them from specific courses), instructional (to diagnose their language needs, determine if learning objectives are being met, and provide feedback on learning), or for research (to evaluate teaching methods or conduct experiments) (Cohen 1994). Although all uses of tests have value within the educational process, testing for administrative purposes has received special attention within HL education, mostly because placement exams are frequently the basis for language instruction or for other types of assessments.

Types of Assessments

The different types of language tests are usually presented as dichotomies or opposed models, based on the purpose of the test, its content, or its design.[1] Table 13.1 presents the more common types.

Purpura (2010) broadly classifies assessment tasks as receptive (e.g., multiple-choice items), limited production (e.g., cloze tests), and extended production (e.g., oral interview). Some activities commonly used to assess language skills include fill-in-the-blank grammar tests, cloze tasks, multiple-choice and open-ended comprehension questions, listening comprehension checklists, structured and open writing tasks, and planned or improvised oral interviews (Salaberry and Cohen 2007).

All these types of tasks can be applied with HL learners. The NEH Focus Group (2003) recommends that, for those students who are literate in the HL,

Table 13.1   Types of Language Tests

Norm-referenced
- Measure global abilities or proficiencies (e.g., overall academic reading ability in a certain language).
- Measure relative ability by interpreting a student's score relative to scores of all students taking the test (normal distribution).

Criterion-referenced
- Measure well-defined instructional objectives, often specific to a particular language course or program (e.g., narration skill in Spanish).
- Make an absolute decision about whether or not the student has mastered tested skills.

Proficiency
- Based on a general theory of language ability or proficiency.
- Used to predict language performance in some future activity.

Achievement
- Based on the content of a specific curriculum or course.
- Intended to determine how much language an individual has learned during the course of instruction.

Can be:
- Formative, administered while content is being taught and learned.
- Summative, administered following a learning unit to determine if what was taught was learned.

Direct
- Performance assessment (e.g., writing an essay).
- Authentic (incorporating the contexts, problems, and problem-solving strategies students would use in real life).

Indirect
- Assessment of underlying abilities in the language (e.g., since reading cannot be measured directly, we use questions to check comprehension).
- Extraction of knowledge and skills out of real-life contexts.

Internal
- Aimed at giving feedback to the classroom teacher, participating students, and perhaps parents.

External
- Meant to inform outsiders, e.g., the school district, the language program, an association, or government bodies.

Discrete-item
- Focus on specific aspects of language (e.g., fill in the blank with the correct verb conjugation).

Integrative/Global
- Bring several aspects of language competence together (e.g., write a personal narrative).

Formal
- Systematic, planned sampling techniques constructed to give an appraisal of student achievement.

Informal
- Usually embedded in classroom tasks designed to elicit performance without recording results.

proficiency testing should measure all four modalities of reading, writing, listening, and speaking. Students with few or no literacy skills in the HL should be tested for listening and speaking only. In addition to measuring students' literacy level in the HL, assessment procedures should also evaluate the range of functions they can successfully carry out and the different registers/language varieties present in their linguistic repertoire (Elder 2005; Li and Duff 2008; Valdés 2007).

Once what needs to be tested is determined, the next step is to design the assessment. Several studies (Kondo-Brown 2008; McGinnis 1996; Sohn and Shin 2003) recommend that receptive tests be supplemented with performance-based tests, because HL learners are generally very good at guessing the right answers based on what "feels" or "sounds" right. In 1981 Ziegler recommended composition as the best way to elicit a large amount of data efficiently. With reference to Russian as an HL, Kagan (2005) proposed a three-component assessment using an oral test based upon the American Council on the Teaching of Foreign Languages' (ACTFL's) *Oral Proficiency Interview,* a short essay (for learners literate in the HL), and a biographic questionnaire. Polinsky and Kagan (2007) evaluated two measures as predictors of HL proficiency: speech rate (words per minute in spontaneous speech) and lexical proficiency (based on the Swadesh 200-word basic vocabulary list), which appeared to correlate with grammatical knowledge. They concluded that a three-component placement procedure of a lexical test, an oral interview, and a biographic questionnaire is both practical and very reliable. Zentella (1997) suggests these strategies for eliciting language knowledge from SHLs: personal narratives, translation tasks focused on specific language features known to be problematic to SHLs, and student self-reports or self-ratings (although learners tend to underestimate their capabilities). In a working model of heritage language placement, Fairclough (2012) explains the rationale for content selection and the design of effective tasks in a language placement exam for incoming university students. In sum, many language tests consist mostly of discrete-type items, obviously due to their practicality; however, more holistic, open-ended approaches to language testing are more appropriate for HL learners because of the naturalistic fashion in which they usually acquire the HL. Overall, HL learners should be tested using a multifaceted approach that measures multiple abilities and types of tasks (Fairclough, Belpoliti, and Bermejo 2010; Ziegler 1981).

Heritage language researchers disagree about whether assessment procedures should focus on what students know and can do with the heritage language (Polinsky and Kagan 2007; Tucker 2005) or on problematic areas (Zentella 1997; Ziegler 1981). Ideally, a balance of both will produce the most complete picture: open-ended tasks (e.g., essay, oral interview) are useful measures of what students can do, whereas discrete items (e.g., fill-in-the-blanks) addressing specific aspects of the language can probe problematic areas, usually identified from sociolinguistic research. Several researchers (Elder 2005; Kagan 2005) argue that a brief biographical questionnaire is essential for understanding HL language profiles, whereas the NEH Focus Group (2003) adds that understanding students' motivations for learning the HL could also prove extremely useful.

The History and Theoretical Frameworks of Language Testing

Modern-day language testing started in about the 1960s (Bachman 2000; McNamara 2004). Spolsky (1978, 2008) views the history of language testing as a progression, with three distinct stages: the first, prescientific period was characterized by traditional exams consisting of written translations, composition, comprehension, and grammar. The psychometric-structuralist period focused on testing discrete elements of the language. Such tests primarily measured sounds, words, and structures in isolation, and they used classical test theory and item analysis to maximize test validity and reliability (Stansfield 2008). Finally, integrative-sociolinguistic assessment, first popularized in the 1970s, evaluated written and spoken language samples using scales (e.g., ACTFL, FSI) and for the first time assessed sociolinguistic aspects (as Cooper proposed in 1968). Challenging Chomsky's model of language knowledge, which was based on the underlying competence of an ideal native speaker, Hymes (1967, 1972) and others promoted more broadly based communicative competence models. In 1972, Savignon defined "communicative competence" as "the ability to function in a truly communicative setting—that is, in a dynamic exchange in which *linguistic competence* must adapt itself to the total informational input, both linguistic and paralinguistic, of one or more interlocutors (Savignon 1972, 8). In 1980 Canale and Swain published the first model of communicative competence, incorporating grammatical, sociolinguistic, and strategic competences. In 1988 Pienemann, Johnson, and Brindley challenged assessment experts to consider the language learner's developmental sequence when designing language tests. A few years later Bachman (1990) proposed a theoretical model of communicative language ability that built on Canale and Swain's work.

Bachman's model "provides a valuable framework for guiding the definition of constructs for any language testing development situation" (Bachman and Palmer 1996, 67). It divides language ability into two main components: language knowledge and strategic competence. The first component encompasses organizational knowledge (subdivided into grammatical and textual knowledge) and pragmatic knowledge (containing functional and sociolinguistic knowledge). Strategic competence includes a set of metacognitive strategies: goal setting, assessment, and planning (for detailed descriptions, see Bachman and Palmer 1996, 67–75). The authors argue that "it is not useful to think in terms of 'skills' [listening, reading, speaking, writing], but to think in terms of specific activities or tasks in which language is used purposefully" (p. 76).

Bachman and Palmer (1996, 19–36) expanded the original 1990 model to incorporate a series of test qualities that determine the usefulness of a test as a measure of language ability:

▶ practicality: the relationship between the resources needed and those available for the design, development, and use of the test
▶ reliability: the consistency of the measure across different testing situations
▶ construct validity: the extent to which a test score is an indicator of the measured abilities or constructs
▶ authenticity: the degree of correspondence between a given assessment task and functional linguistic use of that skill
▶ interactiveness: the extent and type of participation required to complete a test task
▶ impact: the impact of the test on the individual and on the society and educational systems in which s/he participates

Hughes (2003) suggested an additional quality: beneficial washback. "Washback" refers to how language testing affects the curriculum. Washback can be beneficial if it leads to positive changes in instruction, or it can have negative effects when the assessment does not match the objectives of the course that it is supposed to test (Salaberry and Cohen 2007).

Although most researchers agree that communicative language ability (CLA) is multicomponential, they disagree about what these components are (Purpura 2008), which has led to the development of several other theoretical models of language ability (Chapelle 1998; Douglas 2000; Purpura 2004). However, the goal of all these models is to "reflect the most scientifically credible ways in which learners represent L2 knowledge and the ability to use this knowledge for communication" and "provide a broad theoretical basis for the definition of CLA in creating and interpreting language tests in a variety of language use settings" (Purpura 2008, 53).

Models of language competence and research on test qualities have and will continue to inform HL education. Valdés (1995), for example, examined bilingual competence using Bachman's model. She argued that the language competence of bilingual speakers is spread across both languages, with varying linguistic strengths in each language and in the different linguistic components (e.g., a speaker may demonstrate more advanced grammatical competence in one language but greater sociolinguistic competence in the other). Several studies of SHL assessment have analyzed and reviewed existing assessment tools in light of the qualities of a truly useful test (i.e., validity: Fairclough 2006; MacGregor-Mendoza 2010; and practicality: Fairclough, Belpoliti, and Bermejo 2010; Fairclough 2011).

Recent years have also witnessed developments in other areas of language testing, which are expected to continue into the future, including:

1. testing social aspects of language use (culture and pragmatics) (McNamara and Roever 2006; Salaberry and Cohen 2007);

2. language testing for specific purposes (e.g., oral proficiency of international teaching assistants) (Douglas 2000);
3. identifying factors affecting student performance on language tests (e.g., strategies test takers use during exams, students' backgrounds) (Bachman 2000);
4. using portfolio assessment (Bachman 2000);
5. investigating the ethics of language testing and social fairness within the profession (e.g., avoiding bias in language testing, challenging the native speaker norm) (McNamara and Roever 2006; Shohamy 1997; Spolsky 1997);
6. professionalizing the language testing field (e.g., training of professionals, development of standards of practice and mechanisms for their implementation and enforcement) (Bachman 2000; Fulcher and Davidson 2007; Stansfield 1993); and
7. advancing computer-based assessment (see the next section).

Language Testing and Technology

Technological advances are gradually replacing traditional paper examinations with computerized language assessments; and real-world tasks requiring learners to produce open-ended responses (e.g., essays and oral discourse) are being added to discrete item types (e.g., multiple-choice and fill-in-the-blanks). Computer-based tests not only simplify test delivery but also offer multimedia capabilities, instant feedback, grading consistency, and analysis of results. Innovative test designs and item types are also making exams more efficient. Despite all these advances, certain challenges and limitations remain to be overcome (e.g., reliability and security issues), but as more computer-assisted language-learning materials are being developed and used in the classroom, teachers are using the same computerized media for testing, thus expanding the field of computer-assisted language testing (Winke and Fei 2008).

This expansion has been enabled by new software especially designed for language testing, the broader availability of computers and Internet access (which permits new test delivery methods), and scoring and feedback systems that facilitate the grading and analysis of test data. Some commercially available language testing and test-authoring software offers user-friendly templates for creating exams and tools for data analysis; other software can be used on the Web or integrated into classroom management software such as Blackboard or WebCT.[2]

In terms of feedback, whereas traditional closed-ended questions are easily scored by computer, open-ended items (e.g., essays and extended oral responses) present challenges for electronic scoring. Winke and Fei (2008) offer a comprehensive list of commercially available writing scoring tools; however, most are designed to assess English (see also Ericsson and Haswell 2006). Current speech recognition technology can extract and score several elements (fluency, pronunciation, vocabulary, and grammar) from extended discourse (Xi 2010). However, although the use of natural language processing technologies to evaluate students' spoken and written language is increasing, electronic scoring remains very controversial (see, e.g., Chapelle 2008) because even state-of-the-art automated scoring technologies are not yet sophisticated enough to rate organization, coherence, content, and meaning the way a trained human rater could (Xi 2010).

Technological advances in recent decades have generated new and better test designs and have enabled more complex statistical analyses of test data. Adaptive exams, developed in the 1980s (Barnwell 1996), made language testing much more efficient: "By evaluating examinees' responses immediately as they are entered, a computer-adaptive test avoids items that are either too easy or too difficult; such items waste time because they provide little information about the examinee's ability" (Chapelle 2008, 125).

Some innovative tests and test item types focus on specific features but are intended to predict more general aspects of language proficiency. Two such projects worthy of mention are the Versant speaking tests and the DIALANG project (see www.dialang.org). The Versant speaking tests (from Pearson, www.ordi nate.com), are offered in several languages, including Spanish. They use simple tasks that are scorable by computer, such as sentence repetition, reading sentences aloud, building sentences, and naming antonyms. As Xi (2010, 294) explains, the goal of the Versant tests is to "predict" language proficiency, but they do not "directly measure" communicative competence as defined by Bachman (1990) and Bachman and Palmer (1996). In a recent study the Versant Spanish test successfully distinguished different levels of oral proficiency among SHL students and first- and second-year L2 learners of Spanish (Blake et al. 2008).

Yes/no vocabulary tests—developed and used by Meara and colleagues (Meara 1996; Meara and Buxton 1987; Meara and Milton 2005)—are also claimed to correlate with other language abilities (e.g., grammar, reading). They follow a lexical decision format, in which test takers have to distinguish invented words from real words taken from a frequency dictionary vocabulary list. A short version of a similar lexical recognition test was incorporated into the DIALANG project as part of an online battery of learner self-assessments of language proficiency in fourteen European languages. Its purpose is to measure the test taker's global vocabulary size. The vocabulary test results are used to tailor the difficulty of the other portions of the exam (reading, listening, writing, grammar) to the test taker's level. Fairclough (2011) also used a lexical decision test to evaluate the abilities of 330 SHL and L2 students. The results suggest that the yes/no test (based on the 5,000 most frequent words in Spanish) is a practical and effective tool that correlates with other measures of language proficiency and distinguishes among proficiency levels.

Another advantage of computerized language exams is that computers can produce individually tailored reports of test results (Douglas and Hegelheimer 2007). Some current language testing software (e.g., QuestionMark) can generate comprehensive statistics, including item analysis and test analysis reports. Computers can also facilitate the analysis of test data, which can be instrumental in determining test validity and reliability. Not only can computers calculate basic statistical information (e.g., item facility and discrimination indexes) used in classical test theory, but by applying item response theory (IRT), they can now also make powerful generalizations about the test takers and the test items on the basis of samples (McNamara 2004, 772): "IRT has become the scoring method of choice for computer-based and computer-adaptive tests, where new items are selected according to difficulty on the basis of the current estimate of test taker ability" (Fulcher and Davidson 2007, 111).[3] IRT applies a probabilistic model to actual data to estimate test taker ability independent of the samples used to generate the estimate.

Although computerized tests are more efficient and overall more practical than paper exams, there is still much room for improvement. Major challenges include reliability issues (e.g., comparability with paper tests and human scoring; Chapelle 2008; Ericsson and Haswell 2006; Xi 2010), security problems and limitations in authoring tools (Chapelle and Douglas 2006), and the expense and learning curve needed to keep up with rapidly changing technology (Winke and Fei 2008).

Despite these challenges, language testing researchers are confident that computerized testing will flourish in the coming years. Chapelle and Douglas (2006) believe that multimedia and virtual reality hold great promise for language testing because of their ability to place test takers in virtual worlds where they must use language in realistic scenarios.

In sum, recent developments in computer technology have created innovative test designs and item types for second-language testing, especially for English. Computer-based tests can now automatically score not only discrete item types but also open-ended tasks such as essays and oral discourse. They offer multimedia capabilities, immediate scoring and feedback, and many options for test data analyses. Unfortunately, in comparison with these advances, heritage language assessment is still in its infancy. The next section turns to research in that area, with a focus on the academic placement of SHL learners in the United States.

HERITAGE LANGUAGE TESTING IN THE UNITED STATES

A growing number of US higher education institutions are offering specially designed programs for HL learners. One of the biggest challenges for such programs has been placing HL students into the right track (L2 versus HL) and at the right level. Having a clear assessment of the HL knowledge that a student brings to the classroom is essential for a successful learning experience; for that reason, research in HL education has increasingly focused on assessment issues. Overall, the recent literature regarding how to test learners' abilities in the HL has focused mainly on either (1) questioning traditional assessment tools or (2) presenting initiatives in placement test design and implementation.

Traditional Assessment Tools

Most foreign language programs in US universities have traditionally depended on standardized computerized exams to place incoming college students, whereas most HL programs have either used exams intended for L2 learners or have relied on self-placement, questionnaires, interviews, or locally designed paper exams (Fairclough 2006; Peyton 2008; Sohn and Shin 2007; Valdés et al. 2006).

A large number of tests are available for placing students in L2 courses. However, there is some concern about the applicability of those instruments to HL students (Barnwell 1996; McGinnis 1996; Polinsky and Kagan 2007; Tucker 2005; Valdés 1989; Ziegler 1981). As Valdés (1995, 322) argues, assessment measures for HL learners need to be grounded in theories of individual and societal bilingualism rather than second-language learning. Yet as Fairclough, Belpoliti, and Bermejo (2010) documented, many US institutions are using assessments designed for L2 students (e.g., Web S-CAPE, Spanish Computer Adaptive Placement Examination developed at Brigham Young University) as placement exams for SHL students.[4]

Most HL educators are aware of how different HL and L2 learners are. The learning behavior of L2 students is more predictable than that of HL learners, who are a very heterogeneous group. They learn the HL naturalistically in their homes and communities, with no clear single pattern of development, and they use a wide range of dialects depending on their country of origin, length of US residency, and sociolinguistic variables of their families and communities (González-Pino and Pino 2005). The heterogeneity of this student population and the different type of language knowledge they bring to the classroom render the contents of a test for L2 learners inappropriate. But the only commercially available test for college-age SHL students appears to be the one that Parisi and Teschner developed in the early 1980s at the University of Texas–El Paso. This 140-item blind multiple-choice test targets native speaker identifiers (Teschner 2000) to place all incoming students in either the heritage learners track or traditional foreign language courses. It was later converted to a computerized format and reduced to 100 items (Teschner 1990).

For lack of suitable placement exams, HL students are often placed in courses through time-consuming and subjective interviews, paper exams, or, in many cases, student self-placement. Valdés and colleagues (2006) surveyed thirty-five

California colleges and universities that have implemented SHL programs. Most responding institutions reported students self-select the heritage class (74 percent) or are placed by an adviser or counselor (77 percent); only four (11 percent) institutions were using a placement exam specifically designed for heritage learners. A survey of SHL programs in the US Southwest (Beaudrie 2011) also found that numerous universities (n = 18, or 47 percent) rely solely on student self-placement or self-identification to enroll in SHL courses.

Initiatives in Placement Test Design and Implementation

Following the sound recommendation of the Heritage Language Research Priorities Conference (UCLA 2001) that "current assessment instruments should be analyzed and reviewed or new instruments devised," several SHL programs have been evaluating existing assessment tools and/or creating new ones. For years, New Mexico State University has been administering the test designed at the University of Texas–El Paso to thousands of students every year. A thorough analysis revealed that the test failed to place students in the right track and level. There were problems with validity and reliability, scoring and cutoff points, the replacement of several items with unpiloted items, and reordering of items from order of difficulty to random order. At the time of this writing, New Mexico State was in the initial stages of designing a new test, which would be implemented in 2012. The new test (1) would be different from the one for L2 learners, although similar in length and level of difficulty; (2) would mirror SHL learners' abilities in the HL as well as the SHL program objectives; (3) would include multimedia and authentic materials; and (4) would place students in different levels according to their level of language proficiency (MacGregor-Mendoza 2010).

The SHL faculty at the University of Arizona also replaced their paper placement exam to improve test administration and increase test reliability and practicality (Beaudrie and Ducar 2007). After reviewing available exams, they designed and piloted a new test with specific questions targeting each level and with a cumulative scoring system. At the University of Illinois at Chicago, SHL students elect to take a heritage placement exam. L2 learners are placed in courses according to their previous studies in Spanish. These placement procedures have never been evaluated, so a new online test that separates L2 from HL learners and places them into courses using only linguistic criteria is being developed. The track decision will be based on metalinguistic knowledge (grammatical terminology), designed to identify L2 students, and on colloquial vocabulary, designed to identify HL learners. In addition, students will complete a demographic information questionnaire, a short essay, and several grammar sections: multiple-choice, error identification, and translation. The test is already piloted and will be implemented shortly (Potowski and Parada 2010). Faculty at the University of North Carolina, Wilmington (Mrak personal communication 2010), the University of

New Mexico (Vergara Wilson personal communication 2010), and Georgia State University (Moreno 2009) are also working to improve existing exams or create new ones.

Two publications describe in detail how to review an SHL placement exam (Fairclough 2006) and the challenges of designing and implementing a new test (Fairclough, Belpoliti, and Bermejo 2010). Fairclough (2006) analyzed placement tests taken by 459 SHL learners in the years 1996–98 at the University of Houston to develop recommendations for designing a new placement exam (originally a paper exam and later a computerized test). Through identifying SHL students' performance patterns on fill-in-the blank verb conjugation, a written paragraph, and a brief background questionnaire, the author reached the following main conclusions:

▶ Placement exams for SHL learners should distinguish between spelling accuracy and language use.
▶ Spanish compound tenses are good predictors of heritage learners' advanced language proficiency and should be included in placement exams.
▶ To capture HL students' knowledge, test items, especially fill-in-the-blank ones, must provide ample context. These students learned Spanish naturalistically, so may have difficulty completing single sentences with limited information.

Fairclough, Belpoliti, and Bermejo (2010) describe the new SHL Placement/Credit Exam developed at the University of Houston. All students entering the university's Spanish program with any previous knowledge of the language take a placement test to assign them to the L2 or HL track. The number of students taking this placement exam has been steadily increasing ($n = 174$ in 2000; $n = 391$ in 2010). The majority of students (about 60 percent) place at the intermediate level. Yet because the percentage of beginning-level students has doubled during the past decade (from 8.9 to 18.7 percent) a new intensive, first-year course exclusively for heritage language learners and tailored for receptive SHL was planned for the fall of 2011.

The SHL Placement/Credit Exam was implemented in 2009. As a curriculum-neutral, branched, online placement-and-proficiency test, it assesses academic knowledge of speaking, listening, reading, and writing. It contains discrete and integrative tasks:

1. background information (questionnaire)
2. receptive skills (lexical recognition task)
3. productive skills (dictation, partial translation, grammar, verbs)
4. creative skills (reading/writing, listening/speaking)

Sections 1 and 2 separate students into the L2 versus HL tracks. Students' scores on sections 2 and 3 (both computer-scored) determine whether they take section 4. Test takers who successfully complete all four sections can earn up to 12 college credit hours. Because the test is branched, only those students who reach the advanced level take the oral portion of the test and write a composition, minimizing the amount of hand grading needed. If students have a very limited vocabulary knowledge and make major errors in spelling, verb use, and so on, it makes little sense to ask them to write a 300-word argumentative essay.

HL placement tests must usually be individualized or adapted to particular institutions, to reflect the student population and program characteristics. It is extremely difficult to construct a placement test that is independent of the circumstances of local populations of speakers, students, and institutions, and of the curriculum objectives of a specific SHL program. Furthermore, language testing is closely related to the mission or ultimate goal of an HL program, whether that be, for example, to achieve grammatical accuracy by teaching the standard language or to connect students to local communities of speakers. Nonetheless, for many institutions it would be extremely practical to have the option of an effective commercially available computerized SHL placement exam that can be adapted to local needs.

LIMITATIONS OF EXISTING RESEARCH
AND A FUTURE AGENDA

Comparing the research done in the field of second-language testing to the preliminary steps taken in HL assessment reveals a plethora of test development opportunities and research prospects. Regarding placement procedures, more information is needed about

- ► the measures that programs in different locations and institutions are currently using to place incoming HL students, how effective those measures are, and what has been learned from past mistakes;
- ► the relationship between the design of placement tests and programmatic issues (e.g., how placement tests differ between a program with no HL track versus one with several courses, the ideal relationship between placement and curriculum design);
- ► criteria to measure sociolinguistic knowledge, such as dialects or registers, and how such knowledge should be measured in proficiency/ placement tests;
- ► alternatives to traditional test formats, along the lines of Polinsky and Kagan's (2007) speech rate and basic lexicon measurements, Fairclough's (2011) lexical recognition task, and the Versant for Spanish oral test (Blake et al. 2008);

▶ guidelines for both formative and summative classroom assessment, using L2 testing as a point of departure.

Moreover, certain current areas of concern in language testing are particularly relevant to the assessment of HL learners: social fairness within the profession, professionalization of the field, and technological advances. Regarding ethics of language testing and social fairness, there seems to be a double standard when assessing L2 versus HL students: "While the L2 learner's achievement, no matter how limited, is viewed favorably, to some instructors, the heritage learner's competence is always suspect, and both instructors and curriculum designers tend to take stock only of their deficiencies" (Polinsky and Kagan 2007, 374). Several studies corroborate disparities in proficiency between the two groups of students. McGinnis's (1996) evaluation of the Chinese Placement and Proficiency Test that he developed indicates that third- and fourth-year non-HL students achieved lower mean scores than first- and second-year HL students. Similar results emerge from a study comparing several levels of SHL and L2 students enrolled in university Spanish courses (Fairclough 2005). Finally, Blake and colleagues (2008) reported that SHL learners outperformed all non-HL students on the Versant for Spanish oral proficiency test, with first-year L2, second-year L2, and HL learners easily separable by score.

A second, unrelated issue is the professionalization of the field. HL education is in great need of professionals trained in language testing and statistical data analysis to design solid tests and prove their usefulness (Bachman and Palmer 1996). Finally, although HL education professionals try to keep up with the latest advances in technology, many of these are not yet available for Spanish. Even basics such as textbooks for HL courses and computerized ancillary materials are practically nonexistent. Software programs for testing still lag far behind the needs of language test designers, and most commercial scoring tools are available only for English.

CONCLUSION

Although L2 assessment research has been constantly developing during the last few decades, language testing in the field of SHL is still lagging behind. Within the field of education, L2 assessment has developed proficiency models and various types of language tests as well as an assortment of assessment tools and tasks to satisfy different needs. Test qualities are constantly being monitored to guarantee the best possible outcomes, and technological advances are allowing for more efficient and comprehensive tests. Conversely, language testing in the SHL field has focused mainly on academic placement issues. Overall, the themes that have seemed to recur in the literature published during the last decades have been mainly recommendations about what to assess and how to do it, a questioning of existing assessment tools, and, lately, initiatives in placement test design and implementation. However, even though language assessment for HL education is an emerging field, professionals are progressing steadily, guided by developments in language testing, and the future looks promising.

NOTES

1. For detailed explanations of these dichotomies, see Bachman (1990), Bachman and Purpura (2008), Brown (2003), Brown (2001), Liskin-Gasparro (1996, 171), and Salaberry and Cohen (2007).

2. Among the most popular commercially available language testing and authoring software at the time of this publication are QuestionMark/Perception (www.questionmark.com) and OWL (www.owlts.com).

3. For comprehensive explanations of classical test theory and IRT, see Baker and Kim (2004); Brown (1997), and Henning (1987).

4. For a list of tests for middle and high school SHL learners, see Otheguy and Toro (2000).

REFERENCES

Bachman, Lyle F. 1990. *Fundamental Considerations in Language Testing*. Oxford: Oxford University Press.

———. 2000. "Modern Language Testing at the Turn of the Century: Assuring That What We Count Counts." *Language Testing* 17 (1): 1–42.

Bachman, Lyle F., and Adrian S. Palmer. 1996. *Language Testing in Practice: Designing and Developing Useful Language Tests*. Oxford: Oxford University Press.

Bachman, Lyle F., and James E. Purpura. 2008. "Language Assessments: Gate-Keepers or Door-Openers?" In *Handbook of Educational Linguistics*, edited by Bernard Spolsky and Francis M. Hult. Malden, MA: Blackwell.

Baker, Frank B., and Kim Seock-Ho. 2004. *Item Response Theory: Parameter Estimation Techniques*, 2nd ed. New York: Marcel Dekker.

Barnwell, David. P. 1996. *A History of Foreign Language Testing in the United States: From Its Beginning to the Present*. Tempe: BRP.

Beaudrie, Sara. 2011. "Spanish Heritage Language Programs: A Snapshot of Current Programs in the Southwestern United States." *Foreign Language Annals* 44 (2): 321–37.

Beaudrie, Sara, and Cindy M. Ducar. 2007. "¡Dime cómo hablas y te diré en qué clase debes estar! Creating Your Own Spanish Heritage Language Placement Exam." Paper presented at Twenty-First Spanish in the United States/Sixth Spanish in Contact Conference, Arlington, VA, March 15–18.

Blake, Robert, Nicole Wilson, María Cetto, and Cristina Pardo Ballester. 2008. "Measuring Oral Proficiency in Distance, Face-to-Face and Blended Classrooms." *Language Learning and Technology* 12 (3): 114–27.

Brown, H. Douglas. 2003. *Language Assessment: Principles and Classroom Practices*. New York: Pearson.

Brown, James D. 1997. "Computers in Language Testing: Present Research and Some Future Directions." *Language Learning and Technology* 1 (1): 44–59.

———. 2001. "Developing and Revising Criterion-Referenced Achievement Tests for a Textbook Series." In *A Focus on Language Test Development: Expanding the Language Proficiency Construct across a Variety of Tests*, edited by Thom Hudson and James D. Brown. Honolulu: University of Hawaii Press.

Canale, Michael, and Merril Swain. 1980. "Theoretical Bases of Communicative Approaches to Second Language Teaching and Testing." *Applied Linguistics* 1:1–47.

Chapelle, Carol A. 1998. "Construct Definition and Validity Inquiry in SLA Research." In *Interfaces between Second-Language Acquisition and Language Testing Research*, edited by Lyle Bachman and Andrew Cohen. Cambridge: Cambridge University Press.

———. 2008. "Utilizing Technology in Language Assessment." In *Encyclopedia of Language and Education, Volume 7: Language Testing and Assessment*, 2nd ed., edited by Elana Shohamy and Nancy H. Hornberger. Heidelberg: Springer.

Chapelle, Carol A., and Dan Douglas. 2006. *Assessing Language through Computer Technology*. Cambridge: Cambridge University Press.

Cohen, Andrew D. 1994. *Assessing Language Ability in the Classroom*, 2nd ed. Boston: Heinle and Heinle.

Cooper, Robert L. 1968. "An Elaborated Language Testing Model." *Language Learning* 18:57–72.

Douglas, Dan. 2000. *Assessing Languages for Specific Purposes*. Cambridge: Cambridge University Press.

Douglas, Dan, and Volker Hegelheimer. 2007. "Assessing Language Using Computer Technology." *Annual Review of Applied Linguistics* 27:115–32.

Elder, Catherine. 2005. "Evaluating the Effectiveness of Heritage Language Education: What Role for Testing?" *International Journal of Bilingual Education and Bilingualism* 8 (2–3): 196–212.

Ericsson, Patrick F., and Richard Haswell, eds. 2006. *Machine Scoring of Student Essays: Truth and Consequences*. Logan: Utah State University Press.

Fairclough, Marta. 2005. *Spanish and Heritage Language Education in the United States: Struggling with Hypotheticals*. Madrid: Iberoamericana/Vervuert.

———. 2006. "Language Placement Exams for Heritage Speakers of Spanish: Learning from Students' Mistakes." *Foreign Language Annals* 39 (4): 595–604.

———. 2011. "Testing the Lexical Recognition Task with Spanish/English Bilinguals in the United States." *Language Testing* 28 (2): 273–97.

———. 2012. "A Working Model for Assessing Spanish Heritage Language Learners' Language Proficiency through a Placement Exam." *Heritage Language Journal* 9 (1): 121–38.

Fairclough, Marta, Flavia Belpoliti, and Encarna Bermejo. 2010. "Developing an Electronic Placement Examination for Heritage Learners of Spanish: Challenges and Payoffs." *Hispania* 93 (2): 270–89.

Fulcher, Glenn, and Fred Davidson. 2007. *Language Testing and Assessment*. Abingdon, UK: Routledge.

González-Pino, Barbara, and Frank Pino. 2005. "Issues in Articulation for Heritage Language Speakers." *Hispania* 88 (1):168–71.

Henning, Grant. 1987. *A Guide to Language Testing: Development, Evaluation, Research*. Cambridge, MA: Newbury House.

Hughes, Arthur. 2003. *Testing for Language Teachers*, 2nd ed. Cambridge: Cambridge University Press.

Huhta, Ari. 2008. Diagnostic and Formative Assessment. In *Handbook of Educational Linguistics*, edited by Bernard Spolsky and Francis M. Hult. Malden, MA: Blackwell.

Hymes, Dell. 1967. "Models of the Interaction of Language and Social Setting." *Journal of Social Issues* 23 (2): 8–38.

———. 1972. "On Communicative Competence." In *Sociolinguistics*, edited by J. B. Pride and Janet Holmes. London: Penguin.

Kagan, Olga. 2005. "In Support of a Proficiency-Based Definition of Heritage Language Learners: The Case of Russian." *International Journal of Bilingual Education & Bilingualism* 8 (2–3): 213–21.

Kondo-Brown, Kimi. 2008. "Issues and Future Agendas for Teaching Chinese, Japanese, and Korean Heritage Students." In *Teaching Chinese, Japanese, and Korean Heritage Language Students: Curriculum Needs, Materials, and Assessment*, edited by Kimi Kondo-Brown and James Dean Brown. Mahwah, NJ: Lawrence Erlbaum Associates.

Li, Duanduan, and Patricia A. Duff. 2008. "Issues in Chinese Heritage Language Education and Research at the Postsecondary Level." In *Chinese as a Heritage Language: Fostering Rooted World Citizenry*, edited by Agnes Weiyun He and Yun Xiao. Honolulu: National Foreign Language Resource Center, University of Hawaii.

Liskin-Gasparro, Judith. 1996. "Assessment: From Content Standards to Student Performance." In *National Standards: A Catalyst for Reform*, edited by Robert C. Lafayette. ACTFL Foreign Language Education Series. Lincolnwood, IL: National Textbook Co.

MacGregor-Mendoza, Patricia. 2010. "Heritage Language Assessment: Successes, Failures, and Lessons Learned." Paper presented at First International Conference on Heritage/Community Languages, University of California, Los Angeles, February 19–21.

McGinnis, Scott. 1996. "Teaching Chinese to the Chinese: The Development of an Assessment and Instructional Model." In *Patterns and Policies: The Changing Demographics of Foreign Language Instruction*, edited by Judith E. Liskin-Gasparro. Boston: Heinle and Heinle.

McNamara, Tim. 2004. "Language Testing." In *Handbook of Applied Linguistics*, edited by Alan Davies and Catherine Elder. Oxford: Blackwell.

McNamara, Tim, and Carsten Roever. 2006. *Language Testing: The Social Dimension*. Malden, MA: Blackwell.

Meara, Paul. 1996. "The Dimensions of Lexical Competence." In *Performance and Competence in Second-Language Acquisition*, edited by Gillian Brown, Kirsten Malmkjaer, and John Williams. Cambridge: Cambridge University Press.

Meara, Paul, and Bill Buxton. 1987. "An Alternative to Multiple Choice Vocabulary Tests." *Language Testing* 4:141–54.

Meara, Paul, and James L. Milton. 2005. *X_LEX: The Swansea Vocabulary Levels Test*, version 2.05. Swansea: Lognostics.

Moreno, Oscar. 2009. "Spanish and the Grammars of Heritage and Native Speakers in the Curriculum: The Crucial Role of Academic Placement." Paper presented at Twenty-Second Conference on Spanish in the United States/Seventh Spanish in Contact with Other Languages Conference, Miami, February 19–21.

NEH Focus Group Report. 2003. "Curriculum Guidelines for Heritage Language Classrooms at the University of California." Prepared at University of California, Los

Angeles, February 14–15. www.international.ucla.edu/article.asp?parentid = 24734#as
sessment.

Otheguy, Ricardo, and Jeannette Toro. 2000. "Tests for Spanish-for-Native-Speaker
Classes." In *Professional Development Series Handbook for Teachers K–16, Volume 1:
Spanish for Native Speakers*, edited by American Association of Teachers of Spanish
and Portuguese. Fort Worth: Harcourt College.

Parisi, Gino, and Teschner, Richard. 1983. *PASS: Parisi Assessment System for Spanish*. El
Paso: Vargas Printing Co.

Peyton, Joy. 2008. "Spanish for Native Speakers Education: The State of the Field." In
Heritage Language Education: A New Field Emerging, edited by Donna Brinton, Olga
Kagan, and Susan Bauckus. New York: Routledge.

Pienemann, Manfred, Malcolm Johnson, and Geoff Brindley. 1988. "Constructing an
Acquisition-Based Procedure for Language Assessment." *Studies in Second-Language
Acquisition* 10:217–43.

Polinsky, Maria, and Olga Kagan. 2007. "Heritage Languages: In the 'Wild' and in the
Classroom." *Language and Linguistics Compass* 1 (5): 368–95.

Potowski, Kim, and Mary Ann Parada. 2010. "An Online Placement Exam for Spanish
Heritage Speakers and L2 Students." Paper presented at First International Conference
on Heritage/Community Languages, University of California, Los Angeles, February
19–21.

Purpura, James E. 2004. *Assessing Grammar*. Cambridge: Cambridge University Press.

———. 2008. "Assessing Communicative Language Ability: Models and their Compo-
nents." In *Encyclopedia of Language and Education, Volume 7: Language Testing and
Assessment*, 2nd ed., edited by Elana Shohamy and Nancy H. Hornberger. Heidelberg:
Springer.

———. 2010. "The Socio-Cognitive Underpinnings of Learning-Oriented Classroom-
Based Assessment." Paper presented at East Coast Organization of Language Testers
Conference. Georgetown University, Washington, October 29–30.

Salaberry, Rafael, and Andrew D. Cohen. 2007. "Testing Spanish." In *The Art of Teaching
Spanish: Second-Language Acquisition from Research to Praxis*, edited by Rafael Salaberry and Barbara A. Lafford. Washington, DC: Georgetown University Press.

Savignon, Sandra J. 1972. *Communicative Competence: An Experiment in Foreign Language
Teaching*. Philadelphia: Center for Curriculum Development.

Shohamy, Elana. 1997. "Testing Methods, Testing Consequences: Are They Ethical?" *Language Testing* 14:340–49.

Sohn, Sung-Ock, and Sang-Keun Shin. 2003. "Assessment and Placement for Korean
Heritage Speakers." Paper presented at National Council of Organizations of Less
Commonly Taught Languages conference. Los Angeles, May 2–4.

———. 2007. "True Beginners, False Beginners, and Fake Beginners: Placement Strategies for Korean Heritage Speakers." *Foreign Language Annals* 40 (3): 407–18.

Spolsky, Bernard. 1978. "Linguistics and Language Testers." In *Papers in Applied Linguistics: Advances in Language Testing*, series 2B, edited by Bernard Spolsky. Arlington, VA:
Center for Applied Linguistics.

———. 1997. "The Ethics of Gatekeeping Tests: What Have We Learned in a Hundred
Years?" *Language Testing* 14:242–47.

———. 2008. "Language Assessment in Historical and Future Perspective." In *Encyclopedia of Language and Education, Volume 7: Language Testing and Assessment*, 2nd ed.,
edited by Elana Shohamy and Nancy H. Hornberger. Heidelberg: Springer.

Stansfield, Charles. W. 1993. "Ethics, Standards and Professionalism in Language Testing." *Issues in Applied Linguistics* 4 (2): 15–30.

———. 2008. "Where We Have Been and Where We Should Go." *Language Testing* 25 (3): 311–26.

Teschner, Richard. 1990. "Spanish Speakers Semi- and Residually Native: After the Placement Test Is Over." *Hispania* 73:816–22.

———. 2000. "Trade Secrets: Advising, Tracking, Placing, and Progressing through the College-Level Spanish-for-Native-Speakers Sequence." In *Professional Development Series Handbook for Teachers K–16, Volume 1: Spanish for Native Speakers*, edited by American Association of Teachers of Spanish and Portuguese. Fort Worth: Harcourt College.

Tucker, Richard G. 2005. "Innovative Language Education Programmes for Heritage Language Students: The Special Case of Puerto Ricans?" *International Journal of Bilingual Education and Bilingualism* 8 (2–3): 188–95.

UCLA (University of California, Los Angeles). 2001. *Heritage Language Research Priorities Conference Report*. Los Angeles: UCLA. www.cal.org/heritage/involved/hlpriorites conf00.pdf.

Valdés, Guadalupe. 1989. "Teaching Spanish to Hispanic Bilinguals: A Look at Oral Proficiency Testing and the Proficiency Movement." *Hispania* 72 (2): 392–401.

———. 1995. "The Teaching of Minority Languages as Academic Subjects: Pedagogical and Theoretical Challenges." *Modern Language Journal* 79(3): 299–328.

———. 2007. "Making Connections: Second-Language Acquisition Research and Heritage Language Teaching." In *The Art of Teaching Spanish: Second-Language Acquisition from Research to Praxis*, edited by Rafael Salaberry and Barbara A. Lafford. Washington, DC: Georgetown University Press.

Valdés, Guadalupe, Joshua A. Fishman, Rebecca Chávez, and William Pérez. 2006. *The Challenges of Maintaining Language Resources: The Case of Spanish in California*. Clevedon, UK: Multilingual Matters.

Winke, Paula, and Fei Fei. 2008. "Computer-Assisted Language Assessment." In *Encyclopedia of Language and Education, Volume 4: Second- and Foreign Language Education*, 2nd ed., edited by Nelleke Van Deusen-Scholl and Nancy H. Hornberger. Heidelberg: Springer.

Xi, Xiaoming. 2010. "Automated Scoring and Feedback Systems: Where Are We and Where Are We Heading?" *Language Testing* 27 (3): 291–300.

Zentella, Ana C. 1997. *Growing Up Bilingual: Puerto Rican Children in New York*. Malden, MA: Blackwell.

Ziegler, Janet D. 1981. "Guidelines for the Construction of a Spanish Placement Examination for the Spanish-Dominant Spanish-English Bilingual." In *Teaching Spanish to the Hispanic Bilingual: Issues, Aims, and Methods*, edited by Guadalupe Valdés, Anthony G. Lozano, and Rodolfo García Moya. New York: Teachers College Press.

Afterword

FUTURE DIRECTIONS FOR THE FIELD OF SPANISH AS A HERITAGE LANGUAGE

Guadalupe Valdés, Stanford University

A S THIS VOLUME MAKES PATENTLY CLEAR, research and writing focusing on heritage languages and heritage learners have increased enormously in the last two decades. This book provides an expert synthesis and a panoramic view of the various subareas and subfields that are contributing to scholars' and practitioners' understanding of the multiple theoretical, contextual, ideological, educational, and individual issues in what is now known as the field of Spanish as a heritage language (SHL). The book's editors have done an outstanding job in organizing the volume, in selecting knowledgeable researchers to probe and summarize the existing literature, and in asking each chapter's author to include an agenda for future research. It is an outstanding effort and will no doubt serve as a foundational text in the field of SHL itself as well as in the broader study of applied linguistics.

In the introduction, the editors point out that the volume is intended to contribute to "the field of SHL generally and to the field of Heritage Language (HL) education within applied linguistics more narrowly." For this reason, they adopt Fishman's (2001) broad definition of an HL learner or speaker "as an individual who has a personal or familial connection to a non-majority language." They note that this definition foregrounds both speakers' connection to the language as well as the status of the language in question vis-à-vis the dominant or majority language. It also avoids invoking the language proficiency requirement embedded in Valdés's (2001) definition of the same speakers. Nevertheless, the editors acknowledge that though the volume takes an interdisciplinary perspective on SHL research, they recognize "the central position of SHL education within the field."

From my perspective, this is an important distinction. The focus of the collection is clearly on what Cook (1992, 1996) terms "multicompetent" Latino speakers—that is, on speakers who use two languages in their everyday lives. Interest here is in the number of different dimensions that need to be considered in grouping or profiling this population, including the historical, educational, affective, and cultural factors that are central to its study. Additionally, the editors suggest that a thorough profiling of this population must of necessity provide details about the acquisition of varieties of both languages, the experience of language contact, and speakers' proficiency or perception of proficiency in each of the two languages. Given this positioning, Spanish language teaching and learning are conceptualized as only one important aspect of the complex lived experiences of Latinos in this country—rather than as the central dimension of the field of SHL.

The chapters in this book successfully build on the editors' conceptualization of the field of SHL and propose key directions for future work that are congruent with this perspective. Each chapter, moreover, directly addresses educational issues. Part I, which comprises chapters 1 through 4, gives an overview of the field. In chapter 1, Rivera-Mills raises important questions about Fishman's three-generational model of language shift and argues that the situation of US Spanish calls for a reworking of the classic intergenerational model. She argues for an alternative option that takes into account the notion of a reacquisition generation—that is, "one that takes into account the experience of the heritage speaker who seeks to develop or reacquire Spanish in formal courses." From her perspective, it will be important to consider the effect of this reacquisition experience on the shift process and on the dynamics of the speech community—which, she also maintains, must be more carefully defined. In closing, she reminds readers of the need to take into consideration the lines drawn between newly arrived and established residents of Latino communities, the ever-debated use of Spanglish, and the presence of stable contact varieties of Spanish present in many communities. She urges those working in the field of Spanish as a heritage language not to collude with dominant language ideologies that view the language of Latinos as inferior.

The subject of language ideologies is developed further in chapter 2, by Jennifer Leeman, which provides a synthesis of the literature on language ideologies and draws in particular from the work of Kroskrity (2004). Leeman illustrates how perspectives on, for example, European Spanish and code-switching are ideological and often remain unexamined by the very individuals who are negatively affected by these conceptions. In the case of Spanish as a heritage language, Leeman points out that educational systems reproduce the standard language ideology, with its notions of correctness and desirability, and at the same time invalidate varieties and practices associated with marginalized social groups. In looking toward the future, she emphasizes that decisions on what to teach, selections of teaching materials, and assessment practices are deeply ideological. She advocates additional research on the value of different languages and language learning in general and proposes ethnographic work that can examine how ideologies are embedded in instructional practice.

In chapter 3 Martínez examines language policy and planning efforts with regard to Spanish as a heritage language. Using the language-as-problem and the language-as-resource perspective proposed by Ruiz (1984), he examines efforts carried out on behalf of heritage language teaching and concludes that the language-as-resource perspective has much potential for contributing to Latino achievement. He also proposes that future efforts should focus on using SHL as a resource for the preparation of bilingual professionals (e.g., medical personnel, translators, and interpreters). Finally, he suggests that a strong network of former SHL students should be formed to play a role in advocating for future language policies that take into account the value of bilingualism.

In chapter 4 Lynch focuses on theoretical concerns as they have emerged in the field of Spanish as a heritage language. Lynch points out that notions of language loyalty, diglossia, proficiency, and educated or standard language were important in establishing early philosophical premises in the field. Appropriately problematizing these notions, he then examines them in current research and provides an extensive listing of studies that have concerned themselves with the question of proficiency, with assessment, and with the similarities between heritage students and intermediate and advanced second language (L2) learners. He then moves to other questions of concern, including conceptualizations of register, style, activity, task, function, agency, identity, community, and generation. This important list of key issues will require continued examination and debate as well as well-planned and well-focused research.

Part II of the volume, chapters 5 through 7, focuses on linguistic issues. In chapter 5 Montrul provides a very thorough synthesis of the sociolinguistic work on variation in Spanish in the United States, which she then contrasts with a summary of the work of formal linguistics and psycholinguistics. She carefully emphasizes these two perspectives' differences in methodological approaches as well as their views on the nature of language itself (i.e., a social versus an individual phenomenon). Proposals for future work include an integration of sociolinguistic and psycholinguistic perspectives that will illuminate how language is learned or fails to fully develop as well as longitudinal studies of bilingual children. She points out, however, that challenges to notions of proficiency, the context of acquisition (in the wild versus the classroom), and how heritage learners actually learn in classroom contexts must be considered by future researchers.

In chapter 6 Pinto addresses pragmatic/discourse issues related to the use of Spanish by heritage speakers in the United States and provides an excellent synopsis of existing work on speech acts (e.g., requests, complaints, expressions of gratitude, and compliment responses), pronoun usage, discourse markers (e.g., *entonces, so, tú sabes*), and other discourse-related issues. After critiquing the use of questionnaires and role-plays in pragmatic research, Pinto concludes with suggestions for future research, including linguistic (im)politeness, a wider range of speech acts, the explicit teaching of pragmatics in the classroom, the examination of the receptive/interpretive perspective, and pragmatic variations among native speakers' groups. He suggests, moreover, that it would be "productive to explore variation between heritage speaker groups that represent a variety of backgrounds and are in contact with dissimilar varieties of English."

In chapter 7 Carvalho focuses on the process of code-switching and takes into account both theoretical and pedagogical considerations. She provides a very thorough overview of the history of research on code-switching (CS) in general and English/Spanish code-switching in particular. She also discusses common evaluations of code-switching, many of which view its use as *ni uno ni otro*. She reminds readers that CS behavior originates from the simple fact of being bilingual and then reviews studies on both the linguistic and the functional aspects of CS. In looking toward the future, she makes the case that research on CS must begin by informing the goals and the practices of language education. A continuing research agenda, she maintains, must include detailed ethnographies of classrooms in order to investigate the effects of CS on learning, classroom behavior, the affective climate of the classroom, and the process of identity formation.

Part III, which focuses on learner perspectives, include very thorough and thought-provoking views on attitudes and motivation by Ducar in chapter 8, and on identity and heritage languages by Potowski in chapter 9. Ducar draws from the classic literature on motivation in L2 learning and raises important questions for future research including: Does participation in the HL community lead to an increase in both integrative and instrumental motivation? Are these two constructs useful in working with HL speakers? How do linguistic prejudices and negative attitudes toward Spanish in the United States in general interact with students' motivation for studying the language? She also points out that positive attitudes toward Spanish decline as a student's length of time in the United States increases and as Latinos become aware of how their varieties of the language are stigmatized. She argues for more qualitative and mixed methods approaches in the study of attitude and motivation that will examine the role of individual students' attitudes, the role of teachers' attitudes toward students' varieties of language, and the attitude of the members of the local Spanish-speaking community toward the specific dialect spoken.

Potowski begins by defining identity and includes perspectives on terms such as "performativity," "ambivalence," "hybridity," and "communities of practice." She emphasizes that there is no agreement among US Spanish-speaking communities on how to refer to themselves and points out that there is no macro-group identity, if a group cannot agree on a name. She also cites studies that argue that Latinos who use various different labels (e.g., Latino, Chicano, Puerto Rican, Hispanic) have more in common than they have divisions. Nevertheless, she emphasizes that individuals of higher socioeconomic status, documented legal status, knowledge of English, and lighter skin seek to distance themselves from Latinos that do not have these characteristics. Stressing that youth may have Spanish language inheritance but not have language expertise, Potowski argues that essentializations run the risk of homogenizing heritage speakers. She proposes that more classroom-based research is needed, as well as research that investigates how instructors' efforts can challenge students' conceptions about language. She maintains that instructors of heritage students must understand and examine negative stereotypes, intra-Latino hierarchies, and the relationship between language and culture.

Part V, chapters 10 through 13, addresses issues of teaching and learning more directly. In chapter 10 Beaudrie provides an excellent overview of survey research that has attempted to examine the nature and availability of SHL programs at the university level and on research on SHL students' perspectives on these language courses. She clearly describes the limitations of foreign language classrooms for SHL students and argues that, most important, instruction must meet the needs of the students. With respect to future research, she argues for a wider range of methodologies, both qualitative and quantitative, that might allow researchers to gain more comprehensive insights about SHL teaching and learning. She calls attention to the fact that scholars need to understand the optimal program sequences for learners at different points on the bilingual continuum as well as the number of courses that might be required for learners at different proficiencies to reach desired levels. She includes in her research agenda program evaluations, investigations of teacher development, and the study of the competencies and knowledge that teachers need in order to manage mixed classes.

In chapter 11 Carreira evaluates historical developments in SHL teaching, offers a synthesis of best practices, and identifies pressing classroom, curricular, and programmatic views. She begins by discussing the socioaffective needs of learners and offers examples of innovative approaches (e.g., Roca and Alonso 2005) that use ethnographic research to move students to more demanding writing assignments. She then discusses the teaching implications of research on grammatical competence and explains that "research on SHL learners' grammatical competence points to areas in need of particular instructional attention by virtue of their susceptibility to attrition and or incomplete acquisition." Drawing from several sources (Montrul 2002; Montrul, Foote, and Perpiñan 2008; Montrul and Bowles 2010), she lists features such as "a personal," copulas, articles, tense/aspect, and mood as benefiting from form-focused instruction. She also cites Fairclough (2005), however, who raises questions about the effectiveness of form-focused instruction for teaching a second variant. Carreira attends to the reality of mixed classes, to learner diversity, and to low-proficiency and non-Spanish-speaking Latinos. She offers suggestions for dealing with such diversity and emphasizes the importance of teacher preparation. She concludes by suggesting that advances in the study of SHL students' grammatical competence should be made available to teachers, and she proposes collaborations between researchers and practitioners.

In chapter 12 Colombi and Harrington focus on advanced literacy development in Spanish as a heritage language. They begin by conceptualizing literacy and discuss both the autonomous and the ideological models of literacy as well as biliteracy broadly conceived. They then examine the Continua Model developed by Hornberger (1990, 2000, 2003), as well as the contributions of Systemic Functional Linguistics to theorizing literacy. After reviewing research on biliteracy in SHL, they call for future work to document how advanced biliteracy develops in these learners and suggest that much can be gained by establishing connections between research in the field of heritage languages and L2 teaching and learning.

Finally, in chapter 13 Fairclough focuses on language assessment. She first discusses key background issues and concepts that will be of enormous use to readers who are unfamiliar with the particular subfield. Then she skillfully introduces the field of assessment and testing and discusses language testing and technology. She describes a number of assessments available for placement purposes in Spanish departments and notes their suitability or lack thereof for SHL students. And she explains how and why placement examinations are needed for SHL students and describes several promising initiatives and directions. She concludes by calling for research on placement procedures that attend to the relationship between measures used and curriculum, the ethics of language testing, and the professionalization of SHL researchers and practitioners in the area of measurement.

Overall, the entire volume is a sophisticated, state-of-the-art view of SHL that suggests how attention can be given to areas of particular interest and concern. The interest in educational issues is clearly present, and it is evident that the chapter authors recognize that language ideologies shape students', researchers', and instructors' views of "normal" language acquisition. They thus problematize "balanced" bilingualism along with traditional expectations of accuracy, monolingual-like performance, and "good" Spanish. The questions identified by the authors as needing attention are well grounded in the literature and will guide current researchers and doctoral students for many years to come.

FUTURE DIRECTIONS FOR THE FIELD

In the last several years the new, emerging field of heritage language education (HLE) has grown in important ways. The work of the Alliance for the Advancement of Heritage Languages and of the National Heritage Languages Resource Center has been definitive. The alliance's mission is to advance language development for heritage language speakers in the United States as part of a larger effort to educate members of society so they can function professionally in both English and other languages. The center's mission is to develop effective pedagogical approaches to teaching heritage language learners, first by creating a research base and then by pursuing curriculum design, materials development, and teacher education. Scholars' knowledge of heritage language programs around the country is clearly increasing, as evidenced by the number of publications focusing on heritage languages that appear regularly in a variety of journals. Moreover, languages that are truly uncommonly taught (Gambhir 2001) are being added to the existing menu of languages that are commonly taught in schools, colleges, and universities; and important basic research is being carried out on the characteristics of the varieties of heritage languages spoken in American minority language communities, as well as on such communities and speakers around the world.

Given the context of the rapidly growing HLE field, in imagining the future of SHL, I want to focus on one particular tension of which researchers must be mindful as they continue to work primarily in Spanish, only one of the languages on which the larger HLE initiative focused. Briefly stated, the tension involves commonality of purpose versus particularity and specificity of language and language circumstances. The first tension is clearly obvious in the concern that has been expressed about the term to be used in describing the field itself. Much attention has been given by various individuals to discussions about the appropriate term to be used to refer to the languages of nondominant groups in different settings, and a variety of terms have been proposed and problematized, including "minority languages," "indigenous languages," "nondominant languages," "community languages," "immigrant languages," "languages other than _____," and "heritage languages." I maintain that none of these terms are entirely satisfactory to the many researchers and scholars engaged in this work because we are focusing on various different aspects of issues that affect the lives of individuals who do not speak a societal language. I suggest that these terms are not satisfactory—even if we simply narrow the discussion to a focus on education—because scholars engaged in work with nonmajority languages are attending not only to different populations (e.g., indigenous minorities vs. immigrant minorities) but also to different groups within those populations (e.g., adults engaged in language revitalization vs. young students seeking to develop an acquired nonsocietal language that is widely used). Educational solutions aimed at these different populations and groups have related but dissimilar goals, and these goals are pursued in programs that are established at different academic levels, in diverse settings, and in various types of institutions within a variety of programs. They do not do the same kind of work. They do not make the same assumptions about students; and they function within different professional communities that are constrained by different regulations, traditions, requirements, and expectations. There is an enormous difference between individuals who work in educational contexts such as community schools to revitalize indigenous languages and those who focus on bilingual education programs of various types (transitional, maintenance, two-way immersion). The first group may work with entire families and involve elders who are speakers of the HL in traditional cultural activities with both young adults and their children. The second group, by comparison, carries out work that is constrained by regulations and requirements governing elementary education and must address the development of the societal language at the same time that it teaches school subjects in the minority language. Similarly, the work of researchers and practitioners involved in secondary and university "foreign" language-teaching programs is constrained by traditions in the language-teaching field, by the presence of L2 learners in the same program, and by expectations about the outcomes of classroom language instruction.

Even when focusing exclusively on the United States, the settings in which we as heritage language educators work, the problems on which we focus, and the challenges that we face are dissimilar in important ways. The constraints and challenges we face are different for the various levels and programs in which the heritage language activity takes place. Individuals working in HLs in bilingual education programs, for example, are faced with requirements having to do with state and national testing and other accountability expectations. Much energy might be devoted, for example, by particular groups (e.g., ethnic Koreans) merely to establish dual language programs in public schools. By comparison, foreign language educators at both the secondary and postsecondary levels work within traditions in which languages are part of the established curricula, and the challenge when addressing the needs of particular groups can be remedied by simply adding to the menu of non–commonly taught languages. In addressing the needs of HL learners, these educators need simply to adapt or modify long-standing established professional routines and teaching traditions for meeting the needs of these students.

Finally, the various levels of activity in HLE are informed by different areas of knowledge. Educators working with HLs at the elementary level in bilingual education programs, for example, must be prepared to develop their students' acquisition of English at the same time they are required to teach beginning reading and writing, mathematics, science, and history in the minority language. They therefore need to draw on areas of knowledge that can support their understanding of child development, of the acquisition of basic skills and knowledge, and of established methods for developing children's proficiency in English. By comparison, foreign language educators teaching heritage languages may be informed by research carried out in linguistics and in sociolinguistics about the features of the varieties spoken by their students as well as by the literature on second-language acquisition and second-language pedagogy.

My point, as will be obvious, is that the HLE profession is multifaceted, even when it is examined exclusively in the United States. SHL researchers and practitioners therefore must take into account the existing commonality of purpose that is part of the HL field, but they must also understand, appreciate, and problematize important differences. Singular definitions in some instances will be useful to the SHL subfield, but in other instances they may obstruct important work that needs to be carried out on the particularity and singularity of Spanish, not only in the United States but also in the world.

In looking toward the future of HLE, then, and to the future of the role of SHL education within the larger entity, it is important to be clear about the areas and settings in which scholars and practitioners are working and about how research on Spanish can and cannot inform the teaching, learning, and maintenance of other heritage languages. What this volume does particularly well is to clearly delineate the areas of interest that are its focus, which are important and legitimate for those who work with the Spanish-speaking population in this country. Moreover, much of what is examined here and proposed for future study can also well inform the teaching other HLs in those contexts (secondary and postsecondary) that are parallel to the ones described here. Other language groups must attend to the sociolinguistic study of their languages in American communities, to policies about the use of these languages, and to the linguistic characteristics of HL speakers as first and second language users. They must also be concerned about the attitudes and motivations of these students if they are to study their languages in foreign language classes, as well as design of programs that can support their instructional needs and their development of biliteracy. Additionally, they must attend to testing and to assessment as proposed here.

What the work on the SHL subfield surveyed here may not do is inform researchers working with very small languages, or with languages that are not part of the menu of foreign language offerings currently available in schools. It may also not have much to say to HL educators working in languages whose presence is this country is fundamentally different. As the contributors in this volume make evident, Spanish is spoken in the United States by 50 million people. Moreover, according to some researchers, Spanish is currently emerging as a global language in ways that require examination and are not parallel to the current situations of other European and non-European languages. For example, Mar-Molinero and Paffey (2011, 752) speak of Spanish's process of globalization in terms of linguistic imperialism and argue that Spanish as a product or commodity is being promoted and enhanced by global media and communications. Attributing this promotion in part to Spain's pan-Hispanic policy, they contend that "the spread of Spanish means that the global 'interdependence' of Spanish-speaking communities to one another and to other parts of the world system has a significant impact on the language itself." The policy imagines that Spain is the custodian of *castellano* and responsible for safeguarding a "unified" Spanish modeled on the central peninsular variety, "because of its supposed purity from the effects of language contact and borrowings" (p. 757).

Needless to say, attention to the particularity of Spanish by SHL researchers will require the examination of such policies as well as the study of the influence of their ideological positioning on Spanish language educators around the world. Mar-Molinero and Paffey (2011, 761) would probably caution SHL researchers that "it may well be that eventually a 'Spanish as a lingua franca,' linguistic community (or, more likely, communities) may emerge, but it would only ever be one among many other Spanish-speaking communities—all of which will have to compete against the power, symbolic and actual, of the original home of the Spanish empire."

The implication of these tendencies for the field of SHL will be obvious to readers of this volume. As will also be obvious, these challenges are not necessarily shared with other heritage languages. It is important, therefore, that in conceptualizing a future research agenda for the field of Spanish as a heritage language, SHL researchers attend to the unique issues that characterize Spanish and maintain a healthy balance between what is particular and singular and what is common to the entire field of heritage language education.

REFERENCES

Cook, Vivian. 1992. "Evidence for Multi-Competence." *Language Learning* 42 (4): 557–91.

———. 1996. "Competence and Multi-Competence." In *Performance and Competence in Second Language Acquisition*, edited by Gillian Brown, Kirsten Malmkjaer, and John Williams. Cambridge: Cambridge University Press.

Fairclough, Marta. 2005. *Spanish and Heritage Language Education in the United States: Struggling with Hypotheticals.* Madrid: Iberoamericana.

Fishman, Joshua. 2001. "300-Plus Years of Heritage Language Education in the United States." In *Heritage Languages in America: Preserving a National Resource*, edited by Joy K. Peyton, Donald A. Ranard, and Scott McGinnis. McHenry, IL: Center for Applied Linguistics and Delta Systems.

Gambhir, S. 2001. "Truly Less Commonly Taught Languages and Heritage Language Learners in the United States." In *Heritage languages in America: Preserving a National Resource*, edited by J. K. Peyton, D. A. Ranard, and S. McGinnis. McHenry, IL: Center for Applied Linguistics and Delta Systems.

Hornberger, Nancy. H. 1990. "Creating Successful Learning Contexts for Bilingual Literacy." *Teachers College Record* 92 (2): 212–29.

———. 2000. "Multilingual Literacies, Literacy Practices, and the Continua of Biliteracy." In *Multilingual Literacies: Reading and Writing Different Worlds*, edited by Marilyn Martin-Jones and Kathryn Jones. Amsterdam: John Benjamins.

———. 2003. "Continua of Biliteracy." In *Continua of Biliteracy: An Ecological Framework for Educational Policy, Research, and Practice in Multilingual Settings.* Clevedon, UK: Multilingual Matters.

Kroskrity, Paul. 2004. "Language Ideologies." In *A Companion to Linguistic Anthropology*, edited by Alessandro Duranti. Malden, MA: Blackwell.

Mar-Molinero, Clare, and Darren Paffey. 2011. "Linguistic Imperialism: Who Owns Spanish?" In *Handbook of Hispanic Sociolinguistics*, edited by Manuel Diaz-Campos. Malden, MA: Wiley-Blackwell.

Montrul, Silvina. 2002. "Incomplete Acquisition and Attrition of Spanish Tense/Aspect Distinctions in Adult Bilinguals." *Bilingualism: Language and Cognition* 5:39–68.

Montrul, Silvina, and Melissa Bowles. 2010. "Is Grammar Instruction Beneficial for Heritage Language Learners: Dative Case Marking in Spanish." *Heritage Language Journal* 7 (1): 47–73.

Montrul, Silvina, R. Foote, and S. Perpiñán. 2008. "Gender Agreement in Adult Second-Language Learners and Spanish Heritage Speakers: The Effects of Age and Context of Acquisition." *Language Learning* 58 (3): 503–53.

Roca, Ana, and Helena Alonso. 2005. *Nuevos mundos: Lectura, cultura y comunicación—Curso de español para bilingües*, 2nd ed. Hoboken, NJ: John Wiley & Sons.

Ruiz, Richard. 1984. "Orientations in Language Planning." *NABE Journal* 8:15–34.

Valdés, Guadalupe. 2001. "Heritage Language Students: Profiles and Possibilities." In *Heritage Languages in America: Preserving a National Resource*, edited by Joy Peyton, Donald Ranard, and Scott McGinnis. McHenry, IL: Center for Applied Linguistics and Delta Systems.

Contributors

Sara M. Beaudrie is an assistant professor in the Spanish and Portuguese Department at the University of Arizona. She also directs the program on Spanish for heritage learners. She has published articles in leading academic journals such as the *Heritage Language Journal, Spanish in Context, Hispania, Linguistics and Education,* and *Foreign Language Annals.* She has also presented papers at regional and national conferences on heritage language pedagogy and development and heritage language program and curriculum development. Her current research focuses on the acquisition of orthography by heritage language learners and heritage language pedagogical issues. She received a PhD in second-language acquisition and teaching from the University of Arizona.

Maria M. Carreira is a professor of Spanish in the Department of Romance, German, and Russian Languages and Literatures at California State University, Long Beach, and codirector of the National Heritage Language Resource Center at the University of California, Los Angeles. Her research focuses on heritage languages in the United States, particularly Spanish; heritage language pedagogy; and Spanish as a world language. She is the author of four college-level Spanish textbooks for heritage language learners, including *Sí se puede* (Cengage, 2008).

Ana M. Carvalho is an associate professor at the University of Arizona, where she also directs the Portuguese Language Program. She is a sociolinguist who is interested in language variation and change in situations where languages are in contact. Her recent publications include a coedited volume, *Romance Linguistics* (John Benjamins, 2010); and an edited volume, *Português em Contato* (Iberoamericana, 2009). In addition, she has published articles in journals such as *Language Variation and Change, Hispania, Spanish in Context,* and *Southwest Journal of Linguistics,* and chapters in *Linguistic Theory and Language Development in Hispanic Languages, Language Diversity in the United States,* and *Portugués del Uruguay y Educación Bilingüe.* She is also the associate editor of *Studies in Hispanic and Lusophone Linguistics.*

M. Cecilia Colombi is a professor and chair of the Department of Spanish and Portuguese at the University of California, Davis. She is a Fulbright Specialist for Applied Linguistics/TESOL-Second-Language Education (2011–16). Her research areas include Spanish linguistics, educational linguistics, sociolinguistics, Spanish in the United States, second-language acquisition, writing development, and Spanish systemic functional grammar. She is currently working on a pedagogical introduction to systemic functional grammar of Spanish. Her recent publications include the book *Palabra abierta*, coauthored with Jill Pellettieri and Mabel Rodríguez; the chapter "Multilingual California: Spanish in the Market," in *Multimodal Texts from Around the World: Cultural and Linguistic Insights*, (Palgrave, 2012); and "A Systemic Functional Approach to Teaching Spanish for Heritage Speakers in the United States," in the journal *Linguistics and Education* (2009).

Cynthia M. Ducar is associate professor of Hispanic linguistics at Bowling Green State University. Her research interests include attitudes and motivations of Spanish heritage language learners, US varieties of Spanish, and textbook presentations of Spanish, as well as the intersection of language politics and ideologies of language in the United States. Her recent publications have appeared in *Language, Culture & Curriculum*, *Foreign Language Annals*, and *Heritage Language Journal*, as well as in several edited volumes.

Marta Fairclough is associate professor of Spanish linguistics and director of heritage language education in the Department of Hispanic Studies at the University of Houston. She previously served as department chair and director of undergraduate studies. Her research focuses on heritage language education, language acquisition, and sociolinguistics, with an emphasis on US Spanish. She has published *Spanish and Heritage Language Education in the United States: Struggling with Hypotheticals* (Iberoamericana, 2005), and numerous book chapters and articles in journals. Some of her recent publications appeared in *Language Testing*, *Hispania*, and *Foreign Language Annals*. She received her PhD from the University of Houston.

Joseph Harrington is currently finishing his doctorate in Spanish linguistics at the University of California, Davis. His primary research focus is literacy in Spanish as a second language, particularly the longitudinal development of academic writing. His other research interests include functional linguistics, discourse analysis, lexical development, corpus linguistics, sociocultural theory, and technology-supported pedagogy.

Jennifer Leeman is associate professor of Spanish at George Mason University and research sociolinguist at the US Census Bureau. Her research focuses on ideologies and discourses of language, race, ethnicity, and nation; Spanish in the

United States; and critical approaches to Spanish language education. Her recent articles have appeared in *Critical Inquiry in Language Studies, Heritage Language Journal, Journal of Sociolinguistics,* and *Modern Language Journal.* Her recent book chapters in edited volumes include "Selling the City: Language, Ethnicity and Commodified Space" (with Galey Modan), in *Linguistic Landscape in the City* (Multilingual Matters, 2010) and "Illegal Accents: Qualifications, Discrimination and Distraction in Arizona's Monitoring of Teachers," in *Arizona Firestorm* (Rowman & Littlefield, 2012).

Andrew Lynch is associate professor of Spanish linguistics and Latin American studies at the University of Miami, where he also directs the Spanish Heritage Language Program. He is coauthor of *El español en contacto con otras lenguas* (Georgetown University Press, 2009) and has published numerous articles and essays on sociolinguistic aspects of Spanish in the United States and heritage language acquisition and use. He was a contributor to the *Enciclopedia del español en los Estados Unidos* (Instituto Cervantes, 2009). He teaches courses on topics of sociolinguistics, language and culture, and translation, and has worked as a translator and forensic linguist. He currently forms part of the Miami Observatory on communication and creative industries.

Glenn Martínez is a professor of Spanish linguistics and director of the medical Spanish for heritage learners program at the University of Texas–Pan American. He has published two books on Spanish in the US Southwest and dozens of articles in journals such as *Spanish in Context, Language Policy, Journal of Sociolinguistics,* and *Language Problems and Language Planning.* His most current line of research focuses on the analysis language policies for providing quality health care to Spanish speakers in the United States and on novel approaches in the language development of current and future health care workers. He received his PhD from the University of Massachusetts–Amherst.

Silvina Montrul is head of the Department of Spanish, Italian, and Portuguese and professor of linguistics at the University of Illinois at Urbana-Champaign. She is author of *The Acquisition of Spanish* (Benjamins, 2004) and *Incomplete Acquisition in Bingualis: Re-Examining the Age Factor* (Benjamins, 2008), as well as numerous articles in journals. She is coeditor of the journal *Second Language Research.* Her research focuses on linguistic and psycholinguistic approaches to adult second-language acquisition and bilingualism, in particular syntax, semantics, and morphology. She also has expertise in language loss and retention in minority-language-speaking bilinguals, or heritage speakers.

Derrin Pinto is associate professor of Spanish linguistics at the University of Saint Thomas in Minnesota. He has published studies involving different areas of pragmatics, discourse analysis, and second-language acquisition. His articles

have appeared in journals such as *Hispania, Spanish in Context, Multilingua, Journal of Politeness Research,* and *Interlanguage Pragmatics.* One of his latest projects is the coedited book *En (re)construcción: Discurso, identidad y nación en los manuales escolares de historia y de ciencias sociales* (Under (re)construction: Discourse, identity and nation in history and social science textbooks). He received his PhD from the University of California, Davis.

Kim Potowski is associate professor of Hispanic linguistics at the University of Illinois at Chicago. Her research focuses on Spanish in the United States, including *Language and Identity in a Dual Immersion School* (Multilingual Matters, 2007) and studies on discourse markers, Spanish use in *quinceañera* celebrations, and "MexiRican" ethnolinguistic identity. She is executive editor of the journal *Spanish in Context* and coeditor of the *Heritage Language Journal.* Her recent edited volumes include *Language Diversity in the USA* (Cambridge University Press, 2010) and *Bilingual Youth: Spanish in English-Speaking Societies* (coedited; John Benjamins, 2011).

Susana V. Rivera-Mills is associate dean and professor of Spanish linguistics and diversity advancement at Oregon State University. She has published several books and numerous articles on the topics of Spanish in the United States, issues in sociolinguistics, second-language acquisition, and Spanish for heritage speakers. She is a sought-after speaker at national and international conferences, where she shares her expertise on the topics of Spanish language teaching and learning, Spanish-speaking communities in contact with English, and issues of ethnic identity. She received a BA and an MA from the University of Iowa and a PhD from the University of New Mexico.

Guadalupe Valdés is the Bonnie Katz Tenenbaum Professor of Education at Stanford University. She specializes in language pedagogy and applied linguistics, and she has carried out extensive work on bilingualism and education and in maintaining and preserving heritage languages among minority populations since the 1970s. She is coauthor of *Developing Minority Language Resources: The Case of Spanish in California* (Multilingual Matters, 2006), which examines Spanish language maintenance and instruction in both secondary and postsecondary institutions. Her most recent book, *Latino Children Learning English: Steps in the Journey* (Teachers College Press, 2010), examines the interactional language development of K–2 children over a three-year period.

Index

Numbers in italic indicate a figure or a table.

Aaron, Jessi Elana, 128–29
AATSP (American Association of Teachers of Spanish and Portuguese), 68, 223–24, 233, 234, 235
Achugar, Mariana, 34, 85, 131, 251
ACTFL (American Council on the Teaching of Foreign Languages), 68, 69, 83, 235, 262
advanced biliteracy development, 14–15, 241–54
  context for, 241–42
  Continua Model of Biliteracy, 246–47, 252, 253–54
  defining biliteracy, 245, 254n5
  future directions in, 251–53
  historical and current research on, 249–51
  L2 learners and speakers and, 246, 252–53
  language ideologies and, 241–42
  linguistic perspectives on, 247–48
  literacy, theoretical models for, 243–44, 247, 254n4
  oral academic discourse analysis, 130–31
  population of SHL speakers in U.S. and, 243
  Systemic Functional Linguistics (SFL) and, 247, 248–49, 252, 254
African Americans and SHL speakers, 189–90
age and language acquisition, 89–90, 228
agency, concept of, 80, 86–89
agendas, as teaching tool, 231
Akst, Geoffrey, 216
Al-Kahtany, Abdallah Hady, 243–44
Alarcón, Irma, 29, 170, 171

Alba, Richard, 187, 194n10
Alliance for the Advancement of Heritage Languages, Center for Applied Linguistics, 69, 203, 218n2, 235, 284
Alonso, Helena, 225
Alvarez, Celia, 148
American Association of Teachers of Spanish and Portuguese (AATSP), 68, 223–24, 233, 234, 235
The American Bilingual Tradition (Kloss, 1977), 64–65
American Council on the Teaching of Foreign Languages (ACTFL), 68, 69, 83, 235, 262
Anderson, Raquel, 108, 114
Anderson, Tyler Kimball, 143
anxiety and learners' attitudes and motivations, 163, 168–70, 172
anxiety and motivations of learners, 163, 172
Anzaldúa, Gloria, 190
Arellano, Silvia, 124, 125
Arizona, Proposition 203, 242
Armengol, Regla, 70–71
Asian heritage language speakers and learners
  assessment of, 272
  attitude and motivation studies of, 164–65, 170
  identity studies of, 184–85
assessment, 15, 259–73
  defining, 259
  formative assessment, 232
  future directions in, 271–72
  grammatical competency, 114
  historical background, 263–65

assessment (*continued*)
  L2 learners and speakers, 259, 264, 266, 267–72
  language ideologies and, 54–55
  limitations of current research, 271–72
  Oral Proficiency Interview (ACTFL), 69, 83, 262
  placement exams, 210–12, 268–71
  proficiency, concept of, 83
  purposes of, 260
  special programs for HL learners, 267–71
  technology and, 265–67
  theoretical models for, 263–65
  types of, 260–63, *261*
  university-based SHL programs, 216
Attinasi, John, 26, 188
attitudes and motivations of learners, 12–13, 161–74, 282
  anxiety and, 163, 168–70, 172
  change over time, 165, 169–70
  definitions, 162
  employment opportunities and, 165, 170
  future directions in, 173–74
  general HL research on, 161, 164–67
  heritage language, significance of specific attitude toward, 169–70
  identity and, 170–72
  integrative and instrumental motivation, 162, 165, 166–67, 170–71, 173–74
  intrinsic and extrinsic motivation, 163
  of L2 versus SHL ad HL learners, 162, 165–69, 171–72
  language attitude research, 43
  language ideologies affecting, 167–68, 172
  limitations of current research, 172–73
  qualitative versus quantitative approaches, 162–63, 173
  SHL research on, 167–72
  SLA research on, 161–65, 172
  sociocultural perspective, need for, 163–64, 173
  socioeducational model of, 162–64
  teacher handling of, 229–30
attitudes toward language. *See* language ideologies
Au, Terry Kit-Fong, 174
Auer, Peter, 148
Austin, John, 122

Autonomous Model of Literacy, 243–44, 247, 254n4

Bachman, Lyle F., 259, 263–64, 266
Bailey, Benjamin, 48, 189
Baker, Pauline, 66, 140
Barnwell, David, 82
Bartlett, Lesley, 29, 244
basic interpersonal communication skills (BICS), 84
Bayley, Robert, 89
Beaudrie, Sara M.
  on assessment, 260
  on attitudes and motivations, 168, 169, 170, 171
  biographical information, 291
  on code-switching, 150
  on identity, 193
  on language ideologies, 53
  on maintenance of SHL, 29
  on Spanish as heritage language in US, 1
  on teachers and teacher development, 230
  on theoretical models, 83
  on university-based SHL programs, 14, 203, 204, 206–12, 213–14, 218n1, 218n3, 283
Bell-Corales, Maritza, 169
Belpoliti, Flavia, 268, 270
Beltramo, Anthony, 23
beneficial washback, 264
Benmamoun, Elabbas, 102
Benson, Erica, 140
Bermejo, Encarna, 268, 270
Bernstein, Basil, 84, 92n3
BICS (basic interpersonal communication skills), 84
bilingualism and biliteracy. *See also* advanced biliteracy development; code-switching
  agency, concept of, 88
  biculturalism and, 187
  Continua Model of Biliteracy, 246–47, 252, 253–54, 284
  defining biliteracy, 245, 254n5
  diglossia and, 80–81
  employment and value of, 71–72, 165, 170
  grammatical competence and, 107, 109
  language ideologies affecting, 51–52
  maintenance patterns and, 23–24
  proficiency concerns, 82–84

register, concept of, 84–85
social change and, 91
Bills, Garland D., 23–24, 25, 30, 167
Birdsong, David, 90
Blackboard, 265
Blackledge, Adrian, 180, 182–83
Blake, Robert, 272
Block, David, 180, 181, 182
Blom, Jan-Petter, 146
Blondeau, Hélène, 90
Blum-Kulka, Shoshana, 122, 133
Boswell, Thomas D., 27
Bourdieu, Pierre, 183
Bowles, Melissa, 109–10, 112, 113, 193, 226, 227, 235
Brigham Young University, 268
Brindley, Geoff, 263
Brinton, Laurel J., 123
Brown, Dolores, 126–27
Brown, James, 215
Brown, Penelope, 122
Brown, Roger W., 123
Bucholtz, Mary, 180
Bullock, Barbara E., 142
Butler, Judith, 180

Caldas, Steven, 183–84
California, Proposition 227, 242
CALP (cognitive academic language proficiency), 84
Canada, heritage languages in, 5, 89, 163, 203
Canale, Michael, 263
Caron-Caldas, Suzanne, 183–84
Carrasco, Roberto, 192
Carreira, Maria M.
on attitudes and motivations, 165, 171
biographical information, 291
on language ideologies, 50
on policy and planning issues, 69–71
on teachers and teacher development, 14, 223, 230, 231, 233–34, 283
on university-based SHL programs, 204, 215
Carvalho, Ana M., 12, 139, 282, 291
Cashman, Holly R., 131, 147, 148
Castellanos, Isabel, 25
centers, as teaching tool, 231–32
Chapelle, Carol A., 266, 267
Chicano Discourse (Sánchez, 1983), 23, 87–88

Chicano Movement, 23, 50, 67
Chicano Sociolinguistics (Peñalosa, 1980), 23
children's discourse analysis, 131
Cho, Grace, 165, 169
Chomsky, Noam, 263
civil rights movement and SHL, 6, 10, 32, 50, 64, 66–67, 79, 224
CLA (communicative language ability), 264
Clachar, Arlene, 187
Clark, M. Carolyn, 168–69
classroom-oriented studies
of code-switching, 148–50
of grammatical competence, 111–13, 115
Cleary, T. Anne, 205
code-switching (CS), 12, 139–51, 282
classroom-oriented studies of, 148–50
conversation analysis, 141, 148
defined, 139
functions and rules of, 145–48
future directions in, 151
historical overview of research on, 140–42
identity and, 190
language ideologies and, 139, 140, 142–44, 148–50
lexical borrowing and, 142
as ni uno ni otro, 143, 144, 282
oral academic discourse analysis and, 130–31
psycholinguistic studies, 141
sociolinguistic studies, 141, 146–47, 150–51
standard language ideology and, 143, 148–50
structural accounts of, 142
syntax studies, 141–42
cognitive academic language proficiency (CALP), 84
Cohen, Andrew, 23
Colombi, M. Cecilia
on advanced biliteracy development, 14–15, 241, 242, 249, 250–51, 252, 284
biographical information, 292
on maintenance of SHL, 29
on theoretical models, 85
Colomer, Soria, 70
Colón, Manuel, 150
communicative language ability (CLA), 264
communities of practice and identity formation, 182

community languages, as Australian and British term, 5
Comprehensive Approach to teaching SHL, 224
computerized assessments, 265–67
Continua Model of Biliteracy, 246–47, 252, 253–54, 284
conversation analysis and CS, 141, 148
Cook, Vivian, 84, 280
Cooper, Robert L., 64, 263
Coryell, Joellen, 168–69
Crawford, James, 34
creolization, 83
Critical Approach to teaching SHL, 225
Critical Discourse Analysis, 123
Cross-Cultural Pragmatics: Requests and Apologies (Blum-Kulka, House, and Kasper, 1989), 122
CS. See code-switching
Cuban communities, study of, 25, 27
Cumming, Alister, 216
Cummins, Jim, 6, 84, 92n5

Dame Edna (Barry Humphries), 62, 74
Davidson, Fred, 267
Dávila, Alberto, 28
Deák, Julia, 165–66, 230
Deci, Edward, 163
Delgado, Rocio, 148
Denersesian, Chabram, 67
Departments of Spanish, language ideologies in, 52
Devine, Joanne, 244
DIALANG project, 266
dialect variety
    identity and, 189–90
    internal and intraethnic discrimination and racism regarding, 33–34, 167, 186
Diccionario pan-hispánico de dudas (Pan-Hispanic dictionary of doubts, Real Academia Española), 45
differentiated teaching, 231–32
diglossia, concept of, 79–82, 85, 91
discourse analysis. See pragmatics and discourse analysis
discourse markers, 123, 128–30
discourse strategies, 130
discrimination and racism
    attitudes and motivations of learners affected by, 167–68, 172

identity and, 186, 189–90, 192–93
    internal and intraethnic, 33–34, 167, 186
    language ideologies and, 48, 61–62
    standard language ideology and, 49
Dörnyei, Zoltan, 174
Douglas, Dan, 267
Draper, Joan, 68
Ducar, Cynthia M.
    on attitudes and motivations, 12–13, 161, 168, 170, 171, 193, 282
    biographical information, 292
    on language ideologies, 54
    on maintenance of SHL, 29
    on university-based SHL programs, 213, 214
Dumitrescu, Domnita, 125
Dworin, Joel, 245, 254n5

Echeverría, Begoña, 47
Eckert, Penelope, 182
Edmonston, Barry, 31
Edstrom, Anne, 192
educational perspectives on SHL. See pedagogical perspectives on SHL
Elýás-Olivares, Lucia, 130
Ely, Christopher, 166–67, 175n4
employment advantages of bilingualism, 71–72, 165, 170
English as a second language (ESL) research, 247–48
English interference/influence
    on identity, 190–91
    in pragmatics and discourse analysis, 133–34
English-only laws, 167, 242, 254n1
erasure, 47
ESL (English as a second language) research, 247–48
Español para los hispanos (Baker, 1966), 66
Espinosa, Aurelio, 22, 23, 140
essentialization and identity, 180
ethnic discrimination. See discrimination and racism
ethnicity, language, and identity, 182–84, 184
ethnographic interviews, as instructional technique, 225
evaluation. See assessment
exit cards, 232

Expression and Meaning (Searle, 1979), 122
extrinsic motivation, 163

Fairclough, Marta
  on assessment, 15, 259, 262, 268, 270, 271,
    284
  biographical information, 292
  on Spanish as heritage language in US, 1
  on teachers and teacher development, 226,
    234, 283
  on theoretical models, 86
  on university-based SHL programs, 204,
    206
Farr, Marcia, 187
Fei, Fei, 265
Felix, Angela, 212
Ferguson, Charles, 11, 80
Fernández, Rosa, 143
Figueroa, Richard, 82
Fillmore, Lilly Wong, 235
first language speakers. *See* L1 speakers
Firth, Alan, 82
Fishman, Joshua
  definitions of, 6–7, 10, 11, 279
  on diglossia, 11, 80–81
  on intergenerational language shift, 10,
    24–25, 30, 31–32, 34, 280
  on policy and planning issues, 63
Fitts, Shanan, 149
Flores-Ferrán, Nidia, 106
Foote, Rebecca, 226
foreign study by SHL speakers, 192
formal linguistic studies of grammatical
    competence, 107–11
formative assessment, 232
fractal recursivity, 47
Fulcher, Glenn, 267
Fuller, Janet M., 149
*Fundamentos de la enseñanza del español a
    hispanohablantes en los EE.UU*
    (Potowski, 2005), 234
future directions in SHL, 15, 284–88
  advanced biliteracy development, 251–53
  assessment, 271–72
  attitudes and motivations of learners,
    173–74
  on code-switching, 151
  grammatical competence studies, 114–15

heritage language education (HLE) field
  generally and, 284–87
  identity, 193–94
  language ideologies, 55–56
  maintenance issues, 34–35
  policy and planning issues, 72–74
  pragmatics and discourse analysis, 132–33
  teachers and teacher development, 235
  theoretical models, 91
  university-based SHL programs, 215–17

Gal, Susan, 46–47
Garafanga, Joseph, 148
García, Carmen, 123
García, MaryEllen, 126, 128
García, Ofelia
  on advanced biliteracy development, 244
  definitions of, 5–6
  on identity, 45, 190, 244
  on language ideologies, 45
  on maintenance of SHL, 25, 26, 27, 28, 29,
    32
García-Bedolla, Lisa, 184, 186
García Delgado, José Luis, 21
García-Moya, Rodolfo, 224, 233
García Pastor, Maria D., 124, 126
Gardner, Robert, 13, 162–64, 171
generation
  age-of-immigration criterion, 80, 89–90
  identity and, 188, 189
  intergenerational model of language shift,
    23–27, 30–31
  maintenance effects of continuing influx of
    native Spanish speakers, 28
genre and register theory, 247
Geoffrion-Vinci, Michelle, 83–85, 92n3,
    130–31, 132, 191
Georgia State University, 270
Gervasi, Kareen, 128
Gibson, Ferguson, 149, 151
Gilman, Albert, 123
Gingrich, Newt, 48
globalization and SHL, 51, 54, 70, 91, 182–83,
    224, 287
Goody, Jack, 254n4
Gorman, Lillian, 192
government relations theory, 141–42
Graham, Clayton, 187

grammatical competence of SHL speakers, 11–12, 101–16, 281
  classroom-oriented studies, 111–13, 115
  current research on, 102–4
  defining heritage language speakers and, 101–2
  formal linguistic and psycholinguistic studies of, 107–11, 113
  future directions in, 114–15
  L2 learners and speakers compared, 106, 108–13
  limitations of current research on, 113–15
  proficiency, assessing, 114
  sociolinguistic studies of, 104–7, 113, 115, 281
  teacher development and instructional strategies, 225–26, 235
  variability and anomalous usage explained in terms of, 82
Grosjean, François, 142, 149
Guitiérrez-Rivas, Carolina, 126
Gumperz, John L., 146–47

Hakuta, Kenji, 89
Hall, Kira, 180
Halliday, M. A. K., 85, 247, 248, 252, 255n8
Harklau, Linda, 53
Harrington, Joseph, 14–15, 241, 284, 292
Harris, Roxy, 193
Hasan, Ruqaiya, 252
Haugen, Einar, 92n2, 140
He, Agnes, 184–85, 191, 193
Hecht, Miriam, 216
Heller, Monica, 91, 149
Hélot, Christine, 151
heritage language (HL), Spanish as. See Spanish as a heritage language
heritage language education (HLE) field and SHL, 284–87
Heritage Language Journal, 203
Heritage Language Research Priorities Conference (UCLA 2001), 269
Herman, Deborah, 53–54
Hernández-Chávez, Eduardo, 23, 25, 30, 67
heterogeneous SHL communities, 26, 27–28, 33
Hicks, June, 68
Hidalgo, Margarita, 31, 67

higher education, SHL programs in. See university-based SHL programs
Hispanic/Latino/Spanish, as identity terms, 185–86, 194n1
HL (heritage language), Spanish as. See Spanish as a heritage language
HLE (heritage language education) field and SHL, 284–87
Hornberger, Nancy
  on advanced biliteracy development and Continua Model, 245, 246–47, 252, 253–54, 255n8, 284
  on identity, 191
  on teachers and teacher development, 230
House, Juliane, 122
How to Do Things with Words (Austin, 1962), 122
Howard, Kathryn, 165–66, 230
Hudson, Alan, 25, 30
Huebner, Thom, 69
Hughes, Arthur, 264
Huhta, Ari, 259
Humphries, Barry (as Dame Edna), 62, 74
Hutchison, Ray, 33
hybrid identities and hyphenated Americans, 181–82, 185, 190–91, 229
Hymes, Dell, 263

iconization, 46–47
identity, 13, 179–94, 282–83
  agency, concept of, 87
  ambivalence regarding, 181
  attitudes and motivations of learners and, 170–72
  as classroom issue, 192, 229–30
  code-switching and, 190
  common contemporary dimensions of, 180, 181
  communities of practice and, 182
  concentration levels and, 187
  dialect variety and, 189–90
  discrimination and racism affecting, 186, 189–90, 192–93
  English interference/influence, 190–91
  essentialization and, 180
  ethnicity, language, and identity, 182–84, 184
  future directions in studying, 193–94

hybrid identities and hyphenated
   Americans, 181–82, 185, 190–91, 229
importance of language in, 179, 180,
   182–84, 193
L2 learners and speakers and, 191, 193
language ideologies and, 47–48, 183
Latino identity and ability to speak
   Spanish, 184–91
maintenance of SHL and, 22–23, 28, 31,
   32, 34
performativity and, 180, 182, 190
proficiency and, 187–89
stereotyping and, 186
in transnational communities, 187
ideological issues. *See* language ideologies
Ideological Model of Literacy, 244, 247
immigration, generation of. *See* generation
indexical expressions, 123
Ingold, Catherine W., 205
Instituto Cervantes, 45
instructional approaches. *See* teachers and
   teacher development
integrative and instrumental motivation, 162,
   165, 166–67, 170–71, 173–74
interdisciplinary approach to SHL, 8, 10,
   279–80
intergenerational model of language shift,
   23–27, 30–31
Interlanguage Pragmatics (Kasper and Blum-
   Kulka, 1993), 122
internal and intraethnic prejudices, 33–34,
   167, 186
interpreters and interpretation, 70, 71, 73
intrinsic motivation, 163
Ionin, Tania, 110–11
Irvine, Judith, 44, 46–47
item response theory (IRT), 267

Jaramillo, June, 127
Jegerski, Jill, 83, 110, 112–13, 235
Jensen, Anne, 69
John Jay College of Criminal Justice, New
   York City, 73
Johnson, Jacqueline, 90
Johnson, Malcolm, 263

Kagan, Olga, 115, 165, 171, 230, 234, 262,
   271, 272
Kasper, Gabriele, 122

Keating, Gregory D., 110
King, Kendall, 74
Kiser, Samuel, 61–62
Klee, Carol, 193
Kleifgen, Joanne A., 244
Kloss, Heinz, 10, 64
Kohnert, Kathryn, 114
Koike, Dale, 148, 187
Kondo/Kondo-Brown, Kimi, 164–65, 170,
   183, 215
Krashen, Stephen, 169
Kroskrity, Paul, 10, 44, 45, 46, 47, 51, 280

L1 (first or native language) speakers
   advanced biliteracy development, 246
   grammatical competence and, 105, 107,
      108
   pragmatics and discourse analysis, 124,
      125, 132
   theoretical models and, 82–84, 87, 90, 92n5
L2 learners and speakers
   advanced biliteracy development and, 246,
      252–53
   age and, 90
   agency, concept of, 87
   assessment, 259, 264, 266, 267–72
   attitudes and motivations, 162, 165–69,
      171–72
   grammatical competency and, 106, 108–13
   identity issues, 191, 193
   language ideologies and, 45–47, 51–56
   mixed HL and L2 classes, 226–27
   policy and planning issues, 66, 69, 72
   pragmatics and discourse analysis, 122,
      124, 125, 132
   proficiency of, 82–84
   SLA (second-language acquisition), 79,
      82–84, 91, 161, 162–65, 172
   teaching SHL and, 226–27, 230–32, 235
Labov, William, 84, 89, 174
Lambert, Wallace, 162
language anxiety, 163, 168–70, 172
language assessment. *See* assessment
language attitude research, 43
language ideologies, 10, 43–56, 280–81. *See*
   also standard language ideology
   advanced biliteracy development and,
      241–42
   agency, concept of, 87

language ideologies, (*continued*)
  attitudes and motivations of learners
    affected by, 167–68, 172
  code-switching and, 139, 140, 142–44,
    148–50
  conscious awareness of, 46
  defined, 43–44
  in discrimination and racism, 48, 61–62
  future directions in study of, 55–56
  identity and, 47–48, 183
  L2 learners and speakers and, 45–47, 51–56
  maintenance or shift and, 48
  as mediators between social structures and
    forms of talk, 46–47
  multiplicity and variability of, 45
  policies, practices, and products affected
    by, 50–55, 61–62
  socioaffective needs of SHL learners and,
    224–25
  specific social, political, or economic
    interests, links to, 44–45, 46
  of teachers and staff, 55, 224–25
  theoretical framework for, 44–48
language "loyalty," 91–92n1
language policy. *See* policy and planning
  issues
Languages in Contact (Weinreich, 1953), 140
Latino/Hispanic/Spanish, as identity terms,
    185–86, 194n1
Laureano, Marta, 61–62, 74
law enforcement and Spanish language, 73
learners of SHL, 12–13, 282–83. *See also* atti-
    tudes and motivations of learners;
    identity; pedagogical perspectives on
    SHL
  defining, 5–6, 101–2, 230, 279
  socioaffective needs of, 224–25
  teacher management of learner variables,
    228–32
  university-based SHL programs, learner
    perspectives on, 212–14
Lee, Sharon M., 31
Leeman, Jennifer
  biographical information, 292–93
  on grammatical competency, 103
  on language ideologies, 10, 43, 54, 280–81
  on maintenance of SHL, 29
  on policy and planning issues, 65
  on teachers and teacher development, 224

Lemke, Jay, 89
*El Lenguaje de los Chicanos: Regional and
  Social Characteristics Used by Mexican
  Americans* (Hernández-Chávez, Cohen,
  and Beltramo, 1975), 23
Lenneberg, Eric, 89
Leung, Constant, 193
Levinson, Steven, 122
lexical borrowing and code-switching, 142
lexical recognition tests, 266, 270, 271
linguistic autobiographies, as instructional
  technique, 225
"linguistic market," concept of, 183
linguistic perspectives on SHL, 11–12,
    281–82. *See also* code-switching; gram-
    matical competence of SHL speakers;
    pragmatics and discourse analysis
  advanced biliteracy development, 247–48
  proficiency, concept of, 82–83
Lippi-Green, Rosina, 149–50
Lipski, John M., 28, 83, 104, 105–6, 108, 111
literacy. *See also* advanced biliteracy devel-
    opment; bilingualism and biliteracy
  SHL learner diversity regarding, 229
  theoretical models for, 243–44, 247, 254n4
Livert, David, 88, 89, 104, 106, 113
longitudinal studies
  in advanced biliteracy development, 250,
    251, 252
  on attitudes and motivation, 165, 170, 174
  of code-switching, 141
  of grammatical competence, 108, 114, 281
  of teachers and teacher development, 235
  theoretical models and, 90
  of university-based SHL programs, 215
Lope Blanch, Juan M., 49
Lopez, George, 186
López, Luís, 47
Lozano, Anthony, 224
LPLP (language policy and language
    planning). *See* policy and planning issues
Lynch, Andrew
  on attitudes and motivations, 173
  biographical information, 293
  on grammatical competency, 108–9
  on maintenance of SHL, 27, 29
  on theoretical models, 11, 79, 83, 281

MacIntyre, Peter, 168
MacSwan, Jeff, 86, 92n5

maintenance of SHL, 9–10, 21–35, 280
current research in, 27–29
future directions in, 34–35
historical background to research in, 22–26
identity and, 22–23, 28, 31, 32, 34
immigration of native Spanish speakers, community effects of, 28
intergenerational model of language shift, 23–27, 30–31
language ideologies and, 48
limitations of current research into, 29–34
pedagogical integration of research results, 29–30
percentage, distribution, and demo-graphics of Hispanics and SHL speakers and, 21–22
reacquisition generation, 31
speech communities, concepts of, 31–33
transitional studies of, 26–27
Maldonado, Wendy, 62
Maloof, Valerie, 183
Mar-Molinero, Clare, 287–88
Márquez Reiter, Rosina, 121
marriage, exogamous/interlinguistic, 31, 188, 194n10
Martin, Jim, 247
Martin-Jones, Marilyn, 149
Martínez, Glenn
on advanced biliteracy development, 250
biographical information, 293
on grammatical competency, 103
on language ideologies, 52, 54
on policy and planning issues, 10–11, 61, 281
on teachers and teacher development, 224
Matrix Language Frame Model, 142, 146
Matts, Jeanine, 188
McConnell-Ginet, Sally, 182
McGinnis, Scott, 272
McGroarty, Mary, 71
McNamara, Tim, 259
Meara, Paul, 266
medical Spanish programs, 72–73
Meechan, Marjory, 142
Melton, Ronald, 232–33
Mendieta, Eva, 26
Merino, Barbara, 108, 114
"MexiRicans," 129, 190

Miami, distinctive features of Spanish-speaking communities in, 23, 25, 27, 88, 126, 187
Mikulski, Ariana, 169, 170
Miller, Ann Neville, 183
Miller, Barbara L., 233, 234
Mills, Susana V., 28
Milroy, Lesley, 147
minimalist approach, 141
Missing Surface Inflection Hypothesis, 109
mixed HL and L2 classes, 226–27
"mock Spanish," 48
Molina, Isabel, 26
Molis, Michelle, 90
Montes-Alcalá, Cecilia, 143
Montrul, Silvina
biographical information, 293
on grammatical competency, 11–12, 101, 102, 107–12, 114, 281
on teachers and teacher development, 226, 229
on theoretical models, 83, 90
Mora, Marie T., 28
Morales, Dan, 61
Morales, Ed, 186
Morgan-Short, Kara, 83, 112–13, 235
Morin, J. L., 26
motivations of SHL learners. See attitudes and motivations of learners
Mougeon, Raymond, 89
Moyer, Melissa, 148
Mueller-Gathercole, Virginia, 114
Muysken, Pieter, 145
Myers-Scotton, Carol, 145

Nadasdi, Terry, 89
National Association of Hispanic Journalists, 62
National Council for La Raza, 62
National Council of English Teachers, 233
National Foreign Language Standards, 233
National Heritage Language Resource Center (NHLRC), University of California, Los Angeles, 203, 225, 228, 234, 235, 284–85
native speakers. See L1 speakers
NEH Focus Group, 260–62, 263
New Mexico State University, 269
Newport, Melissa, 90

NHLRC (National Heritage Language Resource Center), University of California, Los Angeles, 203, 225, 228, 234, 235, 284–85
ni uno ni otro, 143, 144, 282
Nichols, Patricia C., 150
Noels, Kimberly, 166, 175n5
norma culta, 49–50

Occupational Outlook Handbook (US Bureau of Labor Statistics 2009), 170
Oh, Janet, 174
oral academic discourse, 130–31
oral discourse. *See* pragmatics and discourse analysis
Oral Proficiency Interview (ACTFL), 69, 83, 262
"Orientations in Language Planning" (Ruiz, *NABE Journal,* 1984), 64–65
Otheguy, Ricardo
  on grammatical competency, 104, 106, 113
  on identity, 190
  on maintenance of SHL, 25, 27, 28
  on theoretical models, 88, 89
OWL, 273n2

Paffey, Darren, 287–88
Palmer, Adrian S., 263–64, 266
pan-Hispanic norms, 45, 287
Parisi, Gino, 268
Pavlenko, Aneta, 180, 182–83
Pease-Álvarez, Lucinda, 89, 188–89
pedagogical perspectives on SHL, 14–15, 283–84. *See also* advanced biliteracy development; assessment; learners of SHL; teachers and teacher development; textbooks; university-based SHL programs
  code-switching , classroom-oriented studies of, 148–50
  Departments of Spanish, 52
  grammatical competence, classroom-oriented studies of, 111–13, 115
  identity in the heritage speaker classroom, 191–93
  language ideologies and, 50–55
  study abroad by SHL speakers, 192
Peñalosa, Fernando, 23
Pérez, Bertha, 245

Pérez, Gina, 187
performativity and identity, 180, 182, 190
Perpiñán, Silvia, 226, 229
personal pronouns, use of, 123, 126–28
Pessoa, Silvia, 34
Petrón, María, 172, 213
Pew Hispanic Center, 2, 185
Pfaff, Carol W., 140
Phinney, Jean, 183, 188
pidginization, 83
Pienemann, Manfred, 263
Pino, Cecilia, 125, 126
Pinto, Derrin, 12, 83, 124–25, 133, 281–82, 293–94
placement exams, 210–12, 268–72
Placencia, María Elena, 121, 123
policy and planning issues, 10–11, 61–74, 281
  defining, 63–64
  development of research on, 63–65
  future directions in, 72–74
  L2 learners and speakers, 66, 69, 72
  language ideologies affecting, 50–55, 61–62
  problem, language viewed as, 65–66
  resource, language viewed as, 68–72
  right, language viewed as, 66–67
Polinsky, Maria, 102, 115, 230, 262, 271, 272
Pomerantz, Anita, 125
Poplack, Shana, 140, 142, 144, 146, 147
postsecondary SHL programs. *See* university-based SHL programs
Potowski, Kim
  on attitudes and motivations, 165, 171
  biographical information, 294
  on code-switching, 129
  on grammatical competency, 103, 112–13, 114
  on identity, 13, 179, 188, 190, 192, 282–83
  on language ideologies, 48
  on teachers and teacher development, 233, 234, 235
  on theoretical models, 83
  on university-level SHL programs, 212
pragmatics and discourse analysis, 12, 121–34, 281
  children's discourse, 131
  defined, 123
  discourse markers, 123, 128–30
  discourse strategies, 130
  English interference, role of, 133–34

future directions in, 132–33
goals of, 134
indexical expressions, 123
L2 learners and speakers, 122, 124, 125, 132
limitations of current research in, 131–32
limited exposure to monolingual Spanish,
    effects of, 134
oral academic discourse, 130–31
personal pronouns, use of, 123, 126–28
productive versus receptive/interpretive
    perspective, 132
qualitative versus quantitative approaches,
    132
speech acts, 122–23, 124–26
variations between groups, 132, 133
prejudice. *See* discrimination and racism
problem, language viewed as, 65–66
professional development for SHL teachers,
    232–34
proficiency. *See also* assessment
concept of, 79–80, 82–84
grammatical competence and, 114
identity and, 187–89
of L2 learners and speakers, 82–84
teacher handling of low-proficiency and
    non-Spanish-speaking students, 230–31
pronouns, use of, 123, 126–28
Proposition 31 (Colorado), 254n1
Proposition 203 (Arizona), 242
Proposition 227 (California), 242
psycholinguistic studies, 107–11, 113, 141
Puerto Rican communities, study of, 25, 26
Purpura, James F., 260

qualitative and quantitative approaches, 132,
    162–63, 173, 194, 215, 217–18
QuestionMark, 267, 273n2
Quintana-Sarellana, Rosalinda, 69

racism. *See* discrimination and racism
Rampton, Ben, 193
Raschio, Richard, 124–25, 133
La Raza, 62, 79
reacquisition generation, 31
Real Academia Española, 45
Reder, Stephen, 244
register, concept of, 80, 83, 84–86, 91, 247,
    254n3
Relaño-Pastor, Ana, 193, 214

Resnick, Melvyn C., 27
resource, language viewed as, 68–72
Reversing Language Shift (Fishman, 2001),
    31–32
Reynolds, Rachel, 165–66, 230
Ricento, Tom, 69
Riegelhaupt, Florencia, 149, 192
right, language viewed as, 66–67
Rivera, K., 26
Rivera-Mills, Susana
    on attitudes and motivations, 188
    biographical information, 294
    on language ideologies, 48
    on maintenance of SHL, 9–10, 21, 27–28,
        31, 280
    on theoretical models, 89, 91
Roca, Ana, 27, 29, 225
Romaine, Suzanne, 31, 187
Rubin, Donald, 183
Ruiz, Richard, 10, 64, 281
Ryan, Richard, 163

Sacks, Harvey, 123
Said-Mohand, Aixa, 129
Sánchez, Rosaura, 23, 87–88, 91–92n1
Sánchez-Muñoz, Ana, 130, 133
Sankoff, Gillian, 90
Santiago, Bill, 190
Savignon, Sandra J., 263
Sayer, Peter, 150
Schegloff, Emanuel, 123
Schiffrin, Deborah, 123
Schleppegrell, Mary J., 242, 249
Schreffler, Sandra B., 127
Schwartz, Adam, 54
Schwarzer, David, 172, 213
Searle, John, 122
second-language acquisition (SLA), 79,
    82–84, 91, 161–65, 172
second-language learners and speakers. *See* L2
    learners and speakers
Selinker, Larry, 83
SFL (Systemic Functional Linguistics), 247,
    248–49, 252, 254
Shannon, Sheila, 149
Sheffer, Hadass, 133
Shenk, Scott, 87, 88
Shin, Fay, 169
SHL. *See* Spanish as a heritage language

SHL Placement/Credit Exam, University of
Houston, 270–71
Shohamy, Elana, 63
Showstack, Rachel, 191
Sigüenza-Ortiz, Consuelo, 127–28, 133
Silva-Corvalán, Carmen
on code-switching, 141, 144
on grammatical competency, 104–6, 108,
113, 114
on pragmatics and discourse analysis, 133
on theoretical models, 81, 83, 85, 89
SL. *See* L2 learners and speakers
SLA (second-language acquisition), 79,
82–84, 91, 161–65, 172
Smith, Robert Courtney, 187
Snow, Catherine, 235
social network studies of CS, 147
socioaffective needs of SHL learners, 224–25
sociolinguistic studies
of code-switching, 141, 146–47, 150–51
of grammatical competence, 104–7, 113,
115, 281
Solé, Carlos, 25, 27
"Spanglish," 32, 143, 151n1, 170, 190,
195n12, 280. *See also* code-switching
Spanish as a heritage language (SHL), 1–15
conceptualization of field, 279–80
defining, 5–7, *8*, 101–2, 279
future directions in, 15, 284–88. *See also*
future directions in SHL
globalization and, 51, 54, 70, 91, 182–83,
224, 287
heritage language education (HLE) field
generally and, 284–87
historical background, 1–2, 3–5, 22–26,
203–5
ideological issues, 10, 43–56, 280–81. *See
also* language ideologies
interdisciplinary approach to, 8, 10,
279–80
language policy and planning, 10–11,
61–74, 281. *See also* policy and planning
issues
learner perspectives, 12–13, 282–83. *See
also* learners of SHL
linguistic perspectives on, 11–12, 281–82.
See also linguistic perspectives on SHL
maintenance of, 9–10, 21–35, 280. *See also*
maintenance of SHL

pedagogical perspectives on, 14–15,
283–84. *See also* pedagogical perspectives on SHL
percentage, distribution, and demographics of Hispanics and SHL speakers
in US, 2, 3–5, 21–22, 204
terminology of, 5–6
theoretical models for, 11, 79–91, 281. *See
also* theoretical models
Spanish Departments, language ideologies in,
52
Spanish for Native Speakers (AATSP, 2000),
233, 234
Spanish/Hispanic/Latino, as identity terms,
185–86, 194n1
Spanish in Context (journal), 121
Spanish language input and exposure, 228
Spanish language schooling of SHL learners,
229
speech acts, 122–23, 124–26
Speech Acts (Searle, 1969), 122
speech communities, concepts of, 31–33
Spicer-Escalante, María, 250
Spolsky, Bernard, 63
standard language ideology
code-switching and, 143, 148–50
concept of, 48–50
of teachers in university-based SHL
programs, 217
theoretical models and, 79–80, 84
Standards for Foreign Language Learning
(ACTFL, 1996 and 2006), 47, 68
Starks, Donna, 151
Street, Brian V., 244, 247, 254n4
structural accounts of code-switching, 142
study abroad by SHL speakers, 192
Swain, Merril, 263
syntax studies of code-switching, 141–42
Systemic Functional Linguistics (SFL), 247,
248–49, 252, 254
Szwed, John, 244

Tallon, Michael, 168
teachers and teacher development, 14,
223–35, 283
Comprehensive Approach, 224
Critical Approach, 225
differentiated teaching, 231–32
future directions in, 235

grammatical competence and, 225–26, 235
historical background, 223–24
identity in the heritage language classroom
and, 192, 229–30
L2 learners and speakers, 226–27, 230–32,
235
language ideologies and, 55, 224–25
learner variables, managing, 228–32
limitations of current research, 234–35
low-proficiency and non-Spanish-speaking
students, 230–31
for mixed HL and L2 classes, 226–27
professional development, 232–34, 235
socioaffective needs of SHL learners and,
224–25
in university-based SHL programs, 217
technology and assessment, 265–67
Teschner, Richard, 268
testing. *See* assessment
textbooks
historical evolution of, 224
identity and, 192–93
language ideologies and, 53–54
theoretical models, 11, 79–91, 281
agency, 80, 86–89
for assessment, 263–65
of biliteracy, 246–47
diglossia, 79–82, 85, 91
future directions in, 91
generation and age group, concepts of, 80,
89–90
of literacy, 243–44, 247, 254n4
proficiency, 79–80, 82–84
register, 80, 83, 84–86, 91, 247, 254n3
standard or educated language, 79–80, 84
Systemic Functional Linguistics (SFL), 247,
248–49
Threshold Hypothesis, 84, 92n5
Timm, Eleonora, 140
Tollefson, James, 63
Toribio, Almeida Jacqueline, 32, 48, 143,
189–90
Torras, Maria-Carme, 148
Torres, Lourdes, 26, 128, 129
Torres-Guzmán, Maria E., 245
translation and translators, 73
transnational communities, 187

university-based SHL programs, 14, 203–18,
283

advanced biliteracy development and, 253
assessment issues, 216
curriculum design and implementation,
215
defined, 218n1
design of, 215–16
future directions in researching, 215–17
historical and current research on, 205–12
learner perspectives on, 212–14
limitations of current research, 214–15
number of programs in US, 207, *208,* 217
placement exams, use of, 210–12, 268–72
plans for new or extended programs, 210
regional distribution of programs in US,
210, *211,* 217
size of Hispanic student population and
availability of, 207–10, *209*
teacher development, 217
University of Arizona, 73, 269
University of Houston, 234, 270
University of Illinois at Chicago, 269
University of New Mexico, 269–70
University of North Carolina, Wilmington,
269–70
University of Texas–El Paso, 268, 269
University of Texas–Pan American, 72–73
Urciuoli, Bonnie, 52, 86, 87, 88, 189, 190
Urzúa, Alfredo, 71
US Census, 2, 185, 188
US intelligence community, language deficit
in, 68–69

Val, Adriana, 183, 188
Valdés, Guadalupe
on assessment, 264, 268–69
biographical information, 294
on code-switching, 141
definition of SHL, 6, 101–2, 279
on future directions in SHL, 15, 279
on identity, 189, 191
on language ideologies, 52–53, 55
on policy and planning issues, 66, 68, 71
on pragmatics and discourse analysis, 124,
125, 126, 130–31, 132
on teaching SHL, 224, 227, 233
on theoretical models, 79, 80, 82–85, 92n3
on university-based SHL programs, 204,
205–6
Vanity Fair, 62

VanPatten, Bill, 110
Velez-Rendon, Gloria, 192
Versant speaking tests, 266, 271
Vilar Sánchez, Karin, 86–87
Villa, Daniel J., 28, 31, 45, 71–72, 89, 91, 224–25
Villa, Jennifer, 71–72
Vinogradova, Polina, 183, 188

Wagner, Johannes, 82
Wang, S. C., 191, 230, 253–54
washback, beneficial, 264
Watt, Ian, 254n4
Web S-CAPE, 268
Webb, John B., 233, 234
WebCT, 265
Wei, Li, 147
Weinreich, Uriel, 140
Wen, Xiaohong, 165
Wenger, Ettiene, 31
What Teachers Need to Know about Language (Fillmore and Snow, 2000), 235
Wherritt, Irene, 205

Wiley, Terrence, 6, 64, 74
Winke, Paula, 265
Wright, Wayne, 71

X-bar theory, 141
Xi, Xiaoming, 266

Yáñez, Rosa H., 125
Yang, Jean, 165
Yanguas, Áñigo, 171–72

Zentella, Ana Celia
    on assessment, 262
    on attitude and motivation, 167
    on code-switching, 141, 144, 145, 146, 148, 151, 190
    on grammatical competence, 104, 106, 113, 114
    on identity, 189, 190
    on maintenance of SHL, 25, 34
    on theoretical models, 88, 89
Zhou, Min, 182, 185
Ziegler, Janet D., 262